Literacy Development in the Early Years

Helping Children Read and Write

Lesley Mandel Morrow

PEARSON

Boston ■ New York ■ San Francisco
Mexico City ■ Montreal ■ Toronto ■ London ■ Madrid ■ Munich ■ Paris
Hong Kong ■ Singapore ■ Tokyo ■ Cape Town ■ Sydney

Senior Series Editor: Aurora Martínez Ramos
Series Editorial Assistant: Erin Beatty
Senior Editorial-Production Administrator: Beth Houston
Editorial-Production Service: P. M. Gordon Associates
Composition and Prepress Buyer: Linda Cox
Manufacturing Buyer: Andrew Turso
Cover Administrator: Linda Knowles
Interior Design and Electronic Composition: Omegatype Typography, Inc.

Library of Congress Cataloging-in-Publication Data

Morrow, Lesley Mandel.
    Literacy development in the early years : helping children read and write / Lesley Mandel Morrow.—5th ed.
      p.   cm.
    Includes bibliographical references (p.   ) and index.
    ISBN 0-205-39256-3
    1. Language arts (Preschool)—United States.   2. Reading (Preschool)—United States.   3. Children—Books and reading—United States.   I. Title.

LB1140.5.L3 M66   2005
372.6'0973—dc22   2004045371

Printed in the United States of America

10 9 8 7 6 5 4 3 2 1   08 07 06 05 04

Photographs: Lenore Arone, Susan Arone, Kate Brach, Douglas Bushnell, Joyce Caponigro, Lynn Cohen, Cheryl Devine, Tami-Lynne Eisen, Michelle Grote, Deborah Hanna, Lori Harrje, Katherine Heiss, Pam Kelliher, Danielle Lynch, Mary Jane Kurabinski, Milton E. Mandel, Howard Manson, Franklin A. Morrow, Lesley Mandel Morrow, Dana Pilla, Amy Sass, Andrea Shane, Kristen Valvanis

To Mary, Milton, Frank, Stephanie, Douglas, and Sweet Baby James,
my very special parents,
my very special husband,
and my very special daughter, son-in-law, and grandson

Contents

chapter 6 *Developing Comprehension of Text and Concepts about Books*   *157*

chapter 7 *Writing, Spelling, and Literacy Development*   *203*

chapter 8 *Motivating Reading and Writing*   *245*

chapter 9

Organizing and Managing the Literacy Program   289

chapter 10

Family Literacy Partnerships: Home and School Working Together   333

Foreword

Dramatic changes in our understanding of early literacy development have occurred during the past two decades. We once thought that children learned to speak and listen during their early years and later learned to read and write at five or six years. We now know that they begin to develop early forms of language and literacy ability concurrently and from the day they are born.

We also have discovered that the conditions that promote first language learning are the same conditions that promote total literacy development. These conditions, created in the social context surrounding a child, involve immersion, explicit instruction, opportunity to practice, modeling by teachers, and feedback.

Lesley Mandel Morrow demonstrates the value of involving children in many types of language and literacy experiences. She provides numerous examples of children's approximations of writing and reading as she establishes the necessity of giving them unlimited opportunities to practice. Further, she illustrates the ways adults provide models, direct instruction, and feedback for young learners as they attempt to read and write. Dr. Morrow takes a comprehensive perspective toward literacy instruction by selecting the best techniques from learning theory, such as a constructivist model or problem-solving approach to more explicit instruction.

Children's literature plays an important role in Morrow's literacy environment. Literature serves as a model for language learning and provides strong motivation for learning to read and write. It is a springboard for many literacy-related activities. Most important, literature is a way of knowing. It is shaped around story—a primary act of human minds. Morrow is also aware that in early literacy development materials designed for instructional purposes are necessary for skill development and to accomplish national, state, and local standards for literacy learning.

Dr. Morrow recognizes the importance of parents, siblings, grandparents, and other caregivers reading to children and enjoying the wealth of books. She shows how reading to babies influences their grasp of language and story patterns that serve them well as they learn to read and write. She illustrates how children learn concepts about print, book handling, and conventions of stories as they interact with books. Morrow establishes that adults teach by example as they enjoy shared reading and shared writing with children. She shows the impact of having a literacy center in a classroom and the effects of storybook reading aloud by a teacher. She shows that when children know authors and illustrators as real people, they want to read their works and write in a manner similar to them. Morrow states that storytelling is similar to reading aloud in its impact on children. She also recognizes the necessity of skills that involve learning concepts about print and books. For example, children need to develop phonemic awareness, alphabetic principles, and phonics for reading success. They also must learn to construct meaning from text by learning strategies for comprehension. Speaking from her own experiences as a teacher, researcher, parent, and grandparent, Morrow charts a path that leads to successful literacy learning.

Lesley Mandel Morrow has taken a long view of literacy development in the early years, showing its historical roots. She also knows and draws on the research of today's leaders because she is a member of that research community. She succinctly summarizes language theories and relates current research to shape sound practices. She has conducted much of the original research herself, testimony to the fact that she can bridge the gap among theory, research, and practice. Her examples are anchored in real classroom experiences—her own and those of other teachers with whom she works collaboratively. The examples are authentic and add credibility to her argument.

Dr. Morrow's treatment of literacy development is on the cutting edge of current knowledge. She is well informed about her subject and makes connections among all aspects of literacy learning. She is a sensitive observer and writer as she lets children and teachers speak for themselves through their work.

Dr. Morrow states that few children learn to love books by themselves. Someone must lure them into the joys of the printed word and the wonderful world of stories. She shows us how to do that and enriches our lives and the lives of children through her work. Her contribution to the literacy development of young children is a lasting one.

D. Ray Reutzel

D. Ray Reutzel
EEJ Professor
Utah State University

Preface

Literacy Development in the Early Years, Fifth Edition, is for teachers, reading specialists, administrators, students in teacher education programs, and parents. It is appropriate for graduate, undergraduate, and professional development courses in early literacy, and it complements texts on teaching reading in the elementary school, child development, the early childhood curriculum, and teaching language arts in the elementary school.

I wrote the book because of my special interest in literacy development in early childhood. I taught in preschools, kindergartens, and in the primary grades; I was a reading specialist; and then I taught early childhood curriculum and literacy courses at the university level. My research has focused on instructional strategies in early literacy. Over the years research in early literacy has generated new theory and given new strength to certain older theories of learning. It has implications for new instructional strategies and reinforces older practices that had little or no research to establish their validity. The book describes a program that nurtures literacy development from birth to third grade.

The ideas in the book are based on research. They have been tried and they have worked, but not all are appropriate for all teachers or all children. The good teacher functions most effectively with strategies he or she feels most comfortable with. The teacher needs to be a decision maker who thinks critically about the design of his or her literacy program and the selection of materials. Children come to school with diverse cultural backgrounds, experiences, exposures to literacy, and abilities. Instructional programs can differ in different parts of the country, in different localities, and for different children in the same classroom.

Underlying this book is the merging of the art and the science of teaching. The science involves theories based on research findings that have generated instructional strategies. This book contains descriptions of strategies and steps for carrying them out. But the scientific research does not necessarily take into account individual differences among teachers and children. The art of teaching concentrates on those human variables. This book provides a *balanced approach* to early literacy instruction. It discusses research that tested successful instructional strategies based on several learning theories. A blend of constructivist ideas that involve problem-solving techniques with some explicit direct instruction approaches are presented so that teachers can decide what works best for the children they teach.

Chapter 1 provides a framework of theory and research, past and current, that has influenced strategies for developing early literacy.

Chapter 2 covers the important issues of assessment and provides the reader with concepts for authentic assessment, portfolio assessment, and standardized assessment. This chapter introduces the concept that instruction and assessment are linked. Because that is the philosophy of the author, strategies for assessment are integrated into all chapters.

Chapter 3 is about diversity, including children from diverse cultural backgrounds as well as children with special learning needs. This chapter provides an overview of diversity and some important teaching strategies. However, meeting the needs of individuals is focused on throughout the book.

Chapters 4 through 8 deal with areas of oral language and vocabulary development, word analysis, comprehension, and writing to enhance reading. These chapters discuss theory and research—specifically, developmental trends, instructional strategies, and methods for assessment. The book views the development of literacy skills (reading, writing, and oral language) as concurrent and interrelated: The development of one enhances the development of the others. Furthermore, the theories, stages, acquisition, and strategies associated with each are similar, and it is difficult to separate them entirely. To make the volume more readable, however, I have treated the different areas of literacy in different chapters.

Chapter 9 discusses the preparation and management of the components presented in the book that are organized to create a successful program. This chapter emphasizes the interrelatedness of the areas of literacy and describes how they can be integrated into the entire school day within content areas.

Chapter 10 discusses the strong influence of the home on the development of literacy, especially in a child's earliest years. It discusses broad perspectives concerning family literacy, such as integrated home/school programs, intergenerational programs, and sensitivity to cultural differences to provide programs that are not intrusive but build on the strengths of the families being served.

Each chapter begins with questions to focus on while reading the text. This is followed by a vignette for the classroom, theory and research, and then practice and assessment. Each chapter ends with suggested activities, questions, and ideas for the classroom written by classroom teachers. The second idea for the classroom is always especially for English Language Learners. The appendixes list materials that teachers use in carrying out a successful program to develop early literacy. Appendix D offers the instructor ideas for carrying out activities in his or her classroom. Key words dealing with early literacy development are defined in the glossary at the end of the book.

New Features of the Fifth Edition

New features of the fifth edition include:

- A new separate chapter on assessment
- A new separate chapter on diversity

- New marginal icons drawing the reader's attention to strategies that are particularly beneficial to English Language Learners
- A new emphasis on the use of expository texts in the classroom
- A new emphasis on the lastest theories and research on early literacy development, including findings from the National Reading Panel, Preventing Reading Difficulties, Reading First, The Rand Report, and the implications of the No Child Left Behind legislation
- New ideas for the classroom, with one in each chapter especially for English Language Learners
- New photographs
- Enhanced methods chapters, with more strategies and skills for literacy development related to language and vocabulary development, phonological and phonemic awareness, phonics, comprehension, motivation, writing, and spelling development
- Updated appendixes for children's literature, children's television shows with associated books, and early literacy software and web sites
- An emphasis on early literacy, beginning in preschool, with chapters on language development and family literacy and an emphasis on integraton of the language arts into content area teaching and literacy and play
- An appendix giving activities for the classroom

Acknowledgments

I want to thank many individuals who helped in the preparation of the first, second, third, fourth and fifth editions of this book. Thank you to Julie Anastasi, Lara Heyer, and Kristen Valvanis, who helped update the appendixes and references, obtain permissions, and edit the revised chapters.

Students who helped in the past are Patricia Addonizio, Mary Belchik, Susan Burks, Kathleen Cunningham, Katie Farrell, Donna Fino Nagi, Mary Ann Gavin, Laura Babarca, Tricia Lyons, Melody Murray Olsen, Michele Preole, Mary Joyce Santoloci, Sari Schnipper, and Karen Szabo. Students who helped with this edition include Patricia DeWitt, Erica Erlanger, Michael Gravois, Katherine Heiss, Pamela Kelliher, Lisa Lozak, Stacey Rog, Monica Saraiya, Amy Sass, and Connie Zauderer.

Thank you to the teachers and administrators who helped with past editions and this present edition: Stephanie Adams, Ellen Abere, Bonita Bartholomew, Maxine Bell, Karen Buda, Pat Burton, Barbara Callister, Jennifer Castio, Mehzga Colucci, Tom DelCasale, Judy DeVincenzo, Fran Diamente, Tami-Lyn Eisen, Arlene Hall, David Harris, Lori Harrje, Catherine Hickey, Adriann Jean-Denis, Noreen Johnson, Tracy Kahn, Linda Keefe, Sheryl King, Penelope Lattimer, Gail Martinez, Nancy Mason, Joyce McGee, Carna Meechem, Dennis Monaghan, Stephanie Moretti, Joyce Ng, Susan Nitto, Ellen O'Connor, Catherine Ogletree, Lucy Oman, Barbara Oxfeld, Mary Payton, Tammye Pelovitz, Cynthia Peters, John Quintaglie, Robert Rosado, Sonia Satterwhite, Joyce Schenkman, Linda Schifflette, Christine Temple, Patty Thaxton, and Margaret Youssef.

Thank you to Andrea Shane, Milton Mandel, Howard Manson, Cheryl Devine, Kate Brach, Tami-Lyn Eisen, Danielle Lynch, Lynn Cohen, and Amy Sass for many of the photographs, and to Pamela Cromey and Michael Gravois for many of the illustrations.

Thank you to Aurora Martínez Ramos, Editor at Allyn and Bacon, for supporting the concept of a fifth edition of this book, and for the guidance she offered during the revision process.

Thank you, in particular, to the children I have taught, my college students, and the excellent teachers I have observed and from whom I've learned so much. Thank you to the researchers in early literacy who have provided exciting information in the field. I consider this book a cooperative effort as a result of the contributions of so many in both direct and indirect ways.

Thank you to those who reviewed the fifth edition of the book and offered suggestions for what to cover. These include Vikki Boatman, Stephen F. Austin State University; Maria Elena Marguelles, University of Miami; Carol J. Nelson, Lewis-Clark State College; Edith Norris, West Texas A&M University; Becky Oekerman, The University of Texas at the Permian Basin; and Irma C. Woods, Del Mar College. Thank you to the college professors, college students, teachers, and parents who purchased the book and demonstrated their support for the publication. The fifth edition was made possible by you.

Thank you to my parents, Mary and Milton Mandel, who provided a rich literacy environment for me. Thank you to my family, specifically Stephanie Morrow and Doug Bushell, and my grandson, Sweet Baby James, for demonstrating the validity of many of the concepts expressed in the book.

L.M.M.

Foundations of Early

Literacy Development

Surveying the Past
to the Present

What a dangerous activity reading is: teaching is. All this plastering of foreign stuff. Why plaster on at all when there's so much inside already? So much locked in? If only I could draw it out and use it as working material. . . . If I had a light enough touch, it would just come out under its own volcanic power.

—Sylvia Ashton-Warner
Spinster (1959)

Focus Questions

▪ Several theorists, philosophers, and psychologists are mentioned in the chapter. Name and describe each one's unique contribution to early childhood education.

▪ Describe the major thrust in different approaches to early literacy instruction from the early 1900s to the present.

▪ The emergent literacy and whole language philosophies are considered constructivist approaches to literacy instruction. Describe the characteristics of these constructivist perspectives.

▪ What does integrating the language arts using thematic instruction mean?

▪ Describe the characteristics of the explicit, direct skill instruction that is associated with behaviorist learning theory.

▪ What do we mean when we speak of a balanced perspective on literacy instruction?

▪ What implications does the "No Child Left Behind" legislation have for early literacy instruction?

Four-year-old James and his mother were driving in the car to do some errands. As they approached the mall, James said, "Look Mommy, I can read those letters. M . . . A . . . C . . . Y . . . S. Those letters spell Sears." James's mother smiled and praised him. "That was great, James. You got every letter right. Now I'll read the sign for you; it says Macy's. This is another department store like Sears. You did some good thinking when you tried to read that word."

Not too long ago we would have chuckled at James's remarks as cute but incorrect. Today, we realize that he is demonstrating a great deal of literacy knowledge that needs to be recognized. First, he knows what letters are, and he can identify the ones in the sign. Next, he knows that letters spell words. He knows that words are read and have meaning. Although he did not read the word correctly, he made an informed guess. James was aware that this building was a department store, but even though he had never been to this one, he called it by a store name he knew. He was trying out some of his literacy knowledge on an adult who he knew was interested and willing to interact positively with him. His mother offered positive reinforcement for what he did know and support by modeling the correct response when he needed some help.

Babies begin to acquire information about literacy from the moment they are born. They continue to build on their knowledge of oral language, reading, and writing as they go through early childhood and beyond. A great deal of attention is now being focused on literacy development in early childhood, an area somewhat neglected in the past. Teachers, parents, and administrators did not perceive preschoolers as readers or writers. Their emphasis was on oral language development and preparation for reading. Because of increased research, thinking about early literacy has changed: Very young children are now viewed as individuals with literacy skills. Although the literacy skills of preschoolers and kindergartners are not the same as older children or adults, they must be acknowledged because they have implications for instructional practice.

Like a child's first words and first steps, learning to read and write should be an exciting, fulfilling, and rewarding experience. This book draws on current research and blends it with theory and practice that have proved successful in developing literacy. It presents a program for developing literacy in children from birth to eight years. It takes into account the joint position statement of the International Reading Association and the National Association for the Education of Young Children entitled *Learning to Read and Write: Developmentally Appropriate Practices for Young Children* (1998). It also takes into account the National Reading Panel Report (2000) and *Put Reading First* (2001), published by the U.S. Department of Education, as well as other work that will be documented throughout. The book is based on the following rationale:

1. Literacy learning begins in infancy.
2. Families need to provide a literacy-rich environment and literacy experiences at home to help children acquire skills. Families need to be actively involved in their children's literacy learning when they enter school.
3. School personnel must be aware that children come to school with prior knowledge about reading and writing and that this knowledge is different from one child to the next.
4. Children need to continue to develop reading and writing skills through experiences at school that build on their existing knowledge.
5. Literacy learning requires a supportive environment that builds positive feelings about self and literacy activities.

6. Learning requires a rich literacy environment with accessible materials and varied experiences.

7. Adults must serve as models for literacy behavior by scaffolding and demonstrating strategies to be learned.

8. During their literacy experiences children should interact within a social context to share information. Such interactions help motivate them to learn from one another.

9. Early reading and writing experiences should be meaningful and concrete and should actively engage children.

10. Early reading and writing experiences need to provide systematic and explicit instruction on skills.

11. A literacy development program should focus on experiences that include reading, writing, listening, speaking, and viewing.

12. Diversity in cultural and language backgrounds must be acknowledged and addressed in early literacy development.

13. Differences in literacy development will vary and must be addressed with small-group instruction. Struggling readers, for example, must be provided for in early intervention programs or inclusion-based classroom programs.

14. Assessment of achievement should be frequent, match instructional strategies, and use multiple formats for evaluating student behavior.

15. Standards for early literacy grade-level benchmarks should be tied to instruction and assessment and used as a means for reaching goals for all children to read fluently by third grade.

16. Programs should be designed that are appropriate for the development of children being taught, with high, yet achievable, expectations.

17. Programs should be research based. For example, from the results of the National Reading Panel Report (2000) we know some of the components in reading instruction to ensure student success. These components of instruction include phonemic awareness, phonics, vocabulary development, comprehension, and fluency. We also have preschool literacy variables determined by the National Early Literacy Panel to predict later achievement in decoding and reading comprehension (2004).

This book incorporates the work of philosophers, educators, psychologists, and researchers who have described how young children learn and what they need to be taught. The book emphasizes that literacy development occurs in prepared literacy-rich environments where planned experiences facilitate development in language, reading, writing, listening, viewing, and speaking, in coordination with content-area subjects. Though some chapters concentrate on language, reading, or writing, an important concern at all times is the integration of all these literacy dimensions.

Literacy development early in life must focus on both learning and teaching. The teacher prepares an environment rich in literacy materials and activities. She includes some explicit direct instruction, and children are encouraged to be actively involved in learning with other children, with materials, and with the teacher. Another major focus of the book is how to provide an environment that will encourage children to take an interest in reading, to associate it with pleasure, and ultimately to read by choice.

Learning Theories, Research, and Philosophies That Have Shaped Practices

Several important philosophers, theorists, psychologists, and educators have addressed learning in early childhood, including the issue of appropriate educational practice. These ideas represent varying responses to the question of whether learning is primarily a matter of the nature or the nurture of the child. All have strong implications for planning early literacy instruction.

Theory and Philosophy from the 1700s and 1800s

ROUSSEAU. Jean-Jacques Rousseau (1762) strongly suggested that a child's early education be natural. That is, children should only be asked to learn things for which they are developmentally ready. Rousseau advocated abandoning contrived instruction and instead allow children to grow and learn with the freedom to be themselves. He believed that education follows the child's own development and readiness for learning. According to Rousseau, children learn through curiosity. He believed that children have individual ways of learning and that formal instruction can interfere with development. Rousseau's philosophy suggests that the role of the educator is to use strategies that mesh with the child's readiness to learn and that require as little intervention by an adult as possible.

PESTALOZZI. Johann Heinrich Pestalozzi (Rusk & Scotland, 1979) was influenced by Rousseau's emphasis on natural learning, but he added a dimension to it. He started his own school and developed principles for learning that combined natural elements with informal instruction. He found it unrealistic to expect children to learn totally on their own initiative. Although Pestalozzi felt that children may be able to teach themselves to read, for example, he also felt that it was necessary for teachers or parents to create the conditions in which the reading process grows. The natural potential of a child develops, he believed, through sensory manipulative experiences, so he designed lessons that involved manipulating objects he called gifts. Children learned about them through touch, smell, language, size, and shape.

FROEBEL. Friedrich Froebel's (1974) approach was similar in some ways to his predecessors. Like Rousseau, he believed in the natural unfolding of a child. He also followed Pestalozzi's ideas and provided plans for instructing young children. But he is best known for emphasizing the importance of play in learning. He specified that the benefits of playing-to-learn require adult guidance and direction and a planned environment. Froebel saw the teacher as a designer of activities and experiences that facilitate learning. On this premise he designed a systematic curriculum for young children involving objects and materials that he called gifts and occupations. In handling and playing with these objects and materials, children not only use psychomotor skills but also learn about shape, color, size, measurement, and comparison. It was Froebel who coined the word *kindergarten*, which means "children's garden." The phrase illustrates his basic philosophy that children, like plants, will grow only if they are tended to and cared for. He often referred to the child as the seed being cared for by the gardener, or teacher.

Froebel was the first educator to design an organized curriculum for young children, and many of his strategies are evident in preschools and kindergartens today. Significant among his strategies were his emphasis on guided play for learning, the learning of certain concepts through manipulative materials that use the senses. He also created circle time—an opportunity to sing songs and learn new ideas through discussion.

Moving into the Twentieth Century

DEWEY. John Dewey's (1966) views in the twentieth century were not unlike Froebel's. His philosophy of early childhood education led to the concept of the child-centered curriculum, or progressive education as it was often called. Dewey believed that the curriculum should be built around the interests of children. He agreed with Froebel that children learn best through play and in real-life settings. He maintained that social interactions encourage learning and that interests are the vehicles for learning information and skills. Dewey rejected the idea of teaching skills as ends unto themselves. He also believed that learning is maximized through integrating content areas.

Froebel and Dewey significantly influenced programs in American preschools and kindergartens throughout the twentieth century, especially from the 1920s through the 1950s. During those decades, preschools and kindergartens typically had different areas for different activities. Shelves in a "block corner" held various sizes and shapes of blocks, small cars, trucks, and wooden figures of people. An art area contained easels with watercolors, crayons, paper, paste, scissors, construction paper, clay, and scraps of interesting materials such as fabric, plastic foam, and pipe cleaners for making collages. The dramatic-play corner was set up like a kitchen, with sink, oven, refrigerator, empty food boxes, table and chairs, telephone, mirror, dolls, and some clothing for dressing up. Still another area held manipulative toys that taught concepts about color, shape, and size.

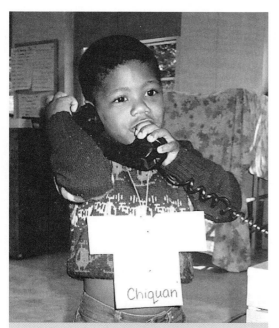

According to Pestalozzi, Froebel, Dewey, and other philosophers and theorists, learning in early childhood occurs when youngsters have the opportunity to explore, experiment, and play at real-life experiences.

A science area revealed a water-play table, shells, interesting rocks, plants, a class animal, magnets, and magnifying glasses. The music area usually had a piano, rhythm instruments, and a record player. Sometimes there was a rug for children to sit on when they came to sing by the piano. One corner of the room had a shelf of children's literature and, depending on the teacher, soft pillows to lie on when looking at books.

The daily routine was similar in most of these settings. As children entered the classroom, they played with quiet toys. The teacher then called them to circle time to talk about the weather and the calendar. Conversation soon focused on a topic in social studies or science—animals or community helpers, for instance—with perhaps a song in keeping with the theme. Circle time was commonly followed by a long period called free play in which children could use the materials in the different areas of the room. There was minimal guidance during free play; children could explore and experiment with the materials. A snack, sometimes followed by a rest period, was an integral part of the daily routine. The day might also include a special lesson in art, social studies, or science appropriate to the unit being studied. Outdoor play allowed children to run, climb, play in sandboxes, and use riding toys. The teacher read a story daily, probably at the end of the day, often relating it to the topic being studied.

Reading and mathematics were not taught formally or as isolated skills. Instead, the teacher might ask a child to count out enough cookies for all the children in the class, to name the date on the calendar, or to compare the sizes of different children. There were no workbooks or commercial reading materials. Teachers led some informal activities that could eventually lead to reading, but they did not attempt to teach children to read. The letters of the alphabet might be found strung across the wall, the days of the week pointed out on a calendar, children's names written on their cubbies, and some other items in the room labeled with words. The general atmosphere was relaxed. The goal was to accustom children to school routines and make them comfortable in the school environment. The focus was on social, emotional, and physical development. There was no place in these programs for formal reading and writing instruction.

SKINNER AND BEHAVIORISM. According to behaviorists, the outcome of learning is a relatively permanent change in behavior that is caused by an individual's response to an experience or stimulus (Slavin, 1997). Behaviorists suggest that we learn through imitation and association, and through conditioning, or a series of steps that are repeated so the response becomes automatic. Skinner (1954) realized that human learning is not all automatic and unintentional. People operate on their environment to produce learning themselves. These purposeful actions are called operants. The individual learns to behave in certain ways as he or she interacts with the environment. Skinner also discovered in his research that positive reinforcement for a desired behavior increased the frequency of use of that behavior. From a behavioristic point of view, skills are acquired in a series of steps, small enough to avoid failure and frustration, with rewards at each level. Learning with a behavioristic perspective includes an organized program presented in a systematic and direct manner. Learning requires time on task, structure, routines, and practice. Behaviorist programs are skills based with little time or concern for social, emotional, or physical development. The main concern is the acquisition of cognitive skills. The materials in behaviorist programs can be rated according to difficulty, can include programmed sequential lessons, and can have scripted guides for the teacher. In these programs, guides for teachers give the objective for learning for a specific page and then provide a script for the teacher similar to the following:

> *Teacher: ch, ch, ch: What sound is this?*
> *Wait for Response: ch, ch, ch. Good*
> *Teacher: ch, ch, ch,: Tell me ch,*
> *Wait for Response: Yes ch, ch, Good*
> *(From S. Englemann and E. C. Bruner, Distar Reading I, An Instructional System. Copyright 1969 by Science Research Associates. Reprinted with permission of McGraw-Hill Education.)*
>
> *Reading programs that use some behavioristic methods are DISTAR: Direct Instruction System for Teaching Arithmetic and Reading (Engleman & Bruner, 1968), Sullivan Programmed Readers (Sullivan & Buchanan, 1963), and Success for All (Slavin, 1998).*

MONTESSORI. Maria Montessori (1965) created a method of instruction that departed from the educators and philosophers mentioned thus far. Although she believed in the use of the senses to promote learning, her emphasis on the senses was not based on the natural unfolding of the child, the child's interests, or play. She believed that children needed early, orderly, systematic training in mastering one skill after another, so she supplied her teaching environment with materials for learning specific concepts in order to meet specific objectives and ways of using them. The use of the materials is modeled by the teacher and then provides the source of learning for the child. Children educated themselves by using these manipulatives, and because the materials were self-correcting, the children could determine their own errors and make corrections independently. All materials in the classroom were stored in their own containers, on a particular shelf and in order of difficulty. According to Montessori, it is the role of the teacher and parent to watch for the child's sensitive periods for learning and take advantage of them by preparing the environment with appropriate materials and experiences for learning. In short, according to Montessori, the teacher is a guide who prepares an environment for learning. But unlike the educators already discussed, Montessori carefully designed learning materials to teach specific skills. These materials are attractive and sturdy, and have influenced the creation of manipulatives we use for learning today. In Montessori's curriculum, children work with **practical life** materials first, which include activities such as buttoning clothes, pouring water, and scrubbing tables. There are precise steps to complete each task correctly. The second area of learning is called **sensorial.** Through the senses of touch, taste, smell, hearing, and sight, children learn about size, color, shape, and the like by manipulating materials designed to teach these skills. Finally the early childhood curriculum includes the learning of **reading** and **math,** which are taught using manipulative materials as much as possible. In math education, Montessori is well known for her colored beads that teach counting, addition, subtraction, multiplication, and division. Early reading instruction includes learning the sounds of letters with the help of beaded letter cards that are traced by the child as they make the sound. Sight words are taught using real objects and pictures. In the Montessori curriculum, which is drawn from a behavioristic theory, children's natural curiosity and exploration are of less concern than their ability to work with specific materials to achieve a particular goal. Play is not as important as work because it might waste precious opportunities for goal achievement during sensitive periods for learning. Montessori promotes independent learning and respect for the child. She insists on a systematic organization of the school day.

PIAGET. Jean Piaget's theory (Piaget & Inhelder, 1969) of cognitive development describes the intellectual capabilities of children at their different stages of cognitive development. The cognitive stages of development he describes include the following:

1. Sensorimotor period (0–2 years): Thinking is determined by a baby's sensory explorations related to what he hears, sees, tastes, and feels.
2. Preoperational period (2–7): A child's language develops and she begins to organize her world. The child's thinking is concrete.
3. Concrete operational period (7–11): The child begins his thought processes in the concrete. With the use of concrete objects, the child is able to move from there into some abstract ideas.
4. Formal operations period (11–adult): In this highest level of thinking, the person uses language to deal with abstract thoughts.

Trying to involve children in abstract thinking experiences during the preoperational stages would be considered inappropriate. Piaget believed that a child acquires knowledge by interacting with the world. Educators who have applied his theories involve children in natural problem-solving situations where they learn through assimilation and accommodation. **Assimilation** means that the child incorporates new information into already existing schemes. That is, she interprets new information in terms of other information she has from the past. For example, when Michael saw a cat for the first time he said, "Look at the dog, Mommy." Michael used what he knew about four-legged animals from his past experience with dogs and applied it to the cat, an animal he had never seen before. **Accommodation** requires changing existing schemes to incorporate new information. A child accommodates when a new situation is unfamiliar. In this situation the child has to create a totally new response. For example, consider Michael, whose structure of meaning with respect to the class concept of dog is limited to what dogs do and look like, such as bark and have four legs. When he perceived a cat, to be a dog, he had assimilated the new experience with reference to his present comprehension level. The complementary process of accommodation may be engaged when the child finds that the object is not a dog, rather a cat, and that the cat meows and doesn't bark. His conceptual understanding of cat must be refined to handle this apparent incongruity; he accommodates his reference system to fit the external reality more accurately.

According to Piaget, children need to be active participants in their own learning, constantly changing and reorganizing their own knowledge.

Piaget stressed that learning occurs when children interact with peers and adults in a social setting as they act upon the environment. Educators who have incorporated Piaget's theories in curricula for early childhood education have designed constructivist-type programs that look very much like what Pestalozzi or Froebel might have created: a setting with many real-life materials, including the opportunities to play, explore, experiment, and use language. In addition, a Piagetian preschool curriculum emphasizes decision making, problem solving, using self-discipline, goal setting, planning one's own activities, and cooperating with teachers and peers to evaluate learning. Unlike Dewey's approach, Piaget's theories interpreted into classroom practice do not stress the creation of content-area centers such as math, science, and social studies. The Piaget curriculum stresses the use of centers that involve children in the following cognitive activities:

1. Language development: Talking, listening to stories, describing, etc.
2. Classifying: Children describe attributes of objects, notice sameness and differences, sort, match, etc.
3. Seriating: Children arrange objects by color, size, shape, etc.
4. Representing in different modalities: Learning about something in many different ways; for example, to learn about an apple we can eat it, make it into applesauce, draw an apple, write and read the word *apple,* sing a song about apples, etc.
5. Spatial relations: Children are asked to put things together, take things apart, rearrange things, reshape things, see things from a different point of view, describe direction, distance, etc.

Piaget agreed that young children should use their curiosity, inquisitiveness, and spontaneity to help themselves learn.

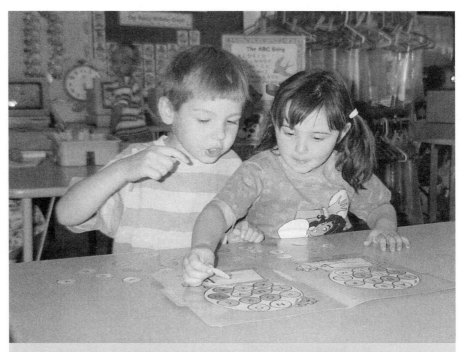

Piaget stressed that learning occurs when children interact with peers and adults in a social setting as they act upon the environment.

VYGOTSKY. Lev S. Vygotsky's (1981) general theory of intellectual development, like Piaget's, suggests that learning occurs as children acquire new concepts or schemas. A schema is a mental structure in which we store information we know. We store information about concepts or schemas and call that to mind to make predictions, generalizations, inferences.

According to Vygotsky, all types of mental functions are acquired through social relationships. To extend or build a new concept, children must interact with others who provide feedback for their thoughts or help them to complete a task they could not do on their own. Children need to talk about new ideas in order to understand them. Parents and teachers provide the language children need to help them solve a problem. Children learn by internalizing the activities and language of others into their world. Vygotsky speaks of the "zone of proximal development," the period of time when a child can do some parts of a task, but not all. This is a sensitive time for learning and growth. The child needs the help of a more knowledgeable person to *scaffold* the new ideas. Adults scaffold by showing children how to complete a task or modeling what a particular behavior looks like. Scaffolding talk gives information about finishing a task, gives advice, and directs a child's attention to what she needs to know. When the help a child receives is internalized, she then becomes capable of performing the new task alone. It is important at this time for the teacher, parent, or more knowledgeable person to step back and allow the child to perform and practice the new skill independently.

The learning theories of the individuals discussed have contributed to the way we look at literacy development in early childhood education. Their ideas are the basis for early literacy instruction as it is described in this book. Particularly applicable among their concepts are the following:

1. Concern for a child's level of development—physical, social, emotional, and intellectual

2. Concern for prepared environments in which learning can take place

3. Emphasis on learning and on teaching

4. Emphasis on social interaction with supportive adults

5. Focus on learning through real experiences in meaningful and natural settings as well as in settings for explicit teaching

6. Focus on actively engaging students in their own learning and the use of manipulative materials and experiences that are functional and interesting

7. Practicing and repeating skills learned.

Practices in the Past: Early 1900s to the End of the 1950s

READING READINESS. Judging from the professional literature of the early 1900s, little attention was paid to a child's literacy development before he entered school. It was generally assumed that literacy began with formal instruction in first grade. A strong influence on reading instruction came from developmental psychologists like Gesell (1925) who advocated maturation as the most important factor in learning to read. Reading instruction was not given until the child was ready to read. Preschool and kindergarten teachers generally ignored or avoided reading instruction. But they did follow some of the teachings of Pestalozzi and Froebel. Typically, they read to children; encouraged play, exploration, and problem solving; and led songs and discussions in circle times based on unit themes. Methods were child centered with great concern for social, emotional, and physical development. The perspectives presented were based on a constructivist learning theory.

This child needs a more knowledgeable person to model and help with new tasks.

Influenced by the climate of the times, Morphett and Washburne (1931) supported the postponement of reading instruction until a child was developmentally "old enough." Their study concluded that children with a mental age of six years six months made better progress on a test of reading achievement than younger children. But although many educators believed that natural maturation was the precursor to literacy, others grew uncomfortable with simply waiting for children to become ready to read. They did not advocate formal reading instruction in early childhood, but they did begin to provide experiences that they believed would help children become ready for reading.

The growing popularity of testing during the 1930s and 1940s helped educators in this effort and affected the next several decades of early childhood reading instruction. Generally, the standardized tests served the prevailing concept of maturation by indicating whether a child had reached the maturity she needed to be able to learn to read. The tests usually included sections on specific skills. Unfortunately, those skills came to be seen as elements on which to base experiences that would help children become ready to read. The term **reading readiness** came into popular use during these decades. Instead of waiting for a child's natural maturation to unfold, educators focused on nurturing that maturation through instruction in a set of skills identified as prerequisites for reading. The concept gained strength when publishers of basal readers (reading instructional materials prepared for children) capitalized on the idea of readiness skills and began to prepare materials for preschool and kindergarten that would make children ready to read. Skills associated with reading readiness include (a) **auditory discrimination:** the ability to identify and differentiate familiar sounds, similar sounds, rhyming words, and the sounds of letters; (b) **visual discrimination:** including color recognition, shape, and letter identification; (c) **visual motor skills:** such as left-to-right eye progression, cutting on a line with scissors, and coloring within the lines of a picture; and (d) **large motor skills:** such as skipping, hopping, and walking on a line.

Early childhood literacy instruction based on the reading readiness model implies that one prepares for literacy by acquiring a set of prescribed skills. These skills are taught systematically on the assumption that all children are at a fairly similar level of development when they come to preschool or kindergarten. The system does not consider experiences or information that a child may already have about literacy, and it focuses on a set of skills perceived as those needed for learning to read.

Early Literacy Research and Practice from the 1960s to the Present

In the 1960s, '70s, and '80s researchers investigating early childhood literacy development brought about many changes in practice. Investigators looked at cognitive development of the child using varied research methodologies for data collection. There were experimental studies with treatment and control groups, correlational research, interviews, observations, videotapes, and case studies. The research was done in diverse cultural, racial, and socioeconomic settings. The research was field based, taking place in classrooms and homes rather than in laboratories as in the past. Research in the areas of oral language development, family literacy, early reading, and early writing had a strong impact on our understanding of how children learn and consequently how we should teach reading and writing. This research is reviewed in the appropriate chapters.

The findings of the research from the 1960s through the 1980s enabled us to understand more of the processes involved in becoming literate. Certain levels of maturity are required for a child to reach specific levels of ability. To acquire skill in oral language, writing, and reading, children need models to emulate and the freedom to create their own forms of reading, writing, and speaking. The work that was done brought about the emergent literacy perspective in early literacy instruction.

Emergent Literacy

Research concerning early readers and what they learn about books, print, and writing before going to school has changed attitudes and ideas about early childhood strategies for literacy development. Although some of the skills

Children need to be exposed to books and writing early in life. Early attempts at literacy should be encouraged and rewarded.

associated with reading readiness are important to literacy learning, new concepts have broadened approaches to early literacy development. One such concept is **emergent literacy,** a phrase first used by Marie Clay (1966). Emergent literacy assumes that the child acquires some knowledge about language, reading, and writing before coming to school. Literacy development begins early in life and is ongoing. There is a dynamic relationship among the communication skills (reading, writing, oral language, and listening) because each influences the other in the course of development. Development occurs in everyday contexts of the home, community, and school through meaningful and functional experiences that require the use of literacy in natural settings. The settings for the acquisition of literacy are often social, with adults and children interacting through collaboration and tutoring. Literacy activities occur and are embedded purposefully within content areas such as art, music, play, social studies, and science, to ensure that there is meaning involved. For example, in art, children should have a recipe to read in order to be able to make play dough.

Children at every age possess certain literacy skills, although these skills are not fully developed or conventional as we recognize mature reading and writing to be (Teale, 1986). Emergent literacy acknowledges a child's scribble marks on a page as rudimentary writing, even if not one letter is discernible. The child who knows the difference between such scribbles and drawings has some sense of the difference between writing and illustration. Similarly, when children narrate familiar storybooks while looking at the pictures and print, and give the impression of reading, we acknowledge the activity as legitimate literacy behavior, even though it cannot be called reading in the conventional sense. Literacy development approached in this manner accepts children at any level of literacy at which they are functioning and provides a program for instruction based on individual needs. The emergent literacy perspective exposes children to books early; it is a child-centered approach with more emphasis on problem solving than on direct instruction of skills.

Definitions of Whole Language

Whole language is similar to the emergent literacy perspective but considers all children at all ages. Advocates of whole language support the constructivist and natural approaches to learning fostered by many of the early philosophers, psychologists, and theorists already discussed. From a content analysis of 64 professional articles related to whole language, Bergeron (1990) composed this definition:

> Whole language is a concept that embodies both a philosophy of language development as well as the instructional approaches embedded within, and supportive of, that philosophy. This concept includes the use of real literature and writing in the context of meaningful, functional, and cooperative experiences in order to develop in students motivation and interest in the process of learning. (p. 319)

From my perspective, whole language is a philosophy about how children learn, from which educators derive strategies for teaching. In a whole language approach literacy learning is child centered because it is designed to be meaningful and functional for children. The purpose and significance are drawn from the child's life experiences at home or those created in school. For example, if a beehive is discovered at school and removed by an exterminator, children may be interested in discussing, reading, or writing about bees. Although learning about bees is not built into the prescribed curriculum, the teacher allows children to pursue this spontaneous interest.

Literacy activities are purposefully integrated into the learning of content-area subjects such as art, music, social studies, science, math, and play. The use of social studies and science themes, such as the study of ecology, links content areas and literacy experiences. Equal emphasis is placed on teaching reading, writing, listening, and oral language because all help create a literate individual. In the past, this program has been referred to as an integrated language arts approach. Varied genres of children's literature are the main source of reading material for instruction. This method is called literature-based instruction. Classrooms must be rich with literacy materials for reading and writing throughout the room and also housed in special literacy centers. This design is often called the rich literacy environment.

In a classroom that uses holistic strategies, teachers place more emphasis on learning than on teaching. Learning is self-regulated and individualized, with self-selection and choices of literacy activities. Rather than only teaching lessons in literacy, teachers are more likely to provide models of literacy activities for children to emulate. There is adult and peer interaction as children observe one another and adults engaged in literacy acts. There is opportunity for peer tutoring and collaboration with each other in active literacy experiences. Children also can learn through practice by engaging in long periods of independent reading and writing and sharing what is learned—by reading to others and presenting written pieces to an audience. A major objective for literacy instruction is the development of a desire to read and write.

In classrooms that use holistic approaches, skills are taught when they are relevant and meaningful—for example, when studying a theme such as dinosaurs, the teacher may focus on some letters and sounds in the initial consonants found in the names of dinosaurs. In early implementation of whole language programs, some thought that skills were not to be taught in any systematic way, and that children would acquire those that they needed by being immersed in experiences with reading children's literature and writing. Certainly skills are assimilated through this immersion, but specific skills such as how to use decoding strategies to figure out unknown words, require some explicit instruction by the teacher.

In a whole language approach, assessment is continuous and takes many forms: Teachers collect daily performance samples of work; they observe and record children's behavior; they audio- and videotape them in different situations; and they build a portfolio filled with information about each youngster. The evaluation process is for both teacher and child, and conferences are held to discuss progress.

In a whole language orientation, teachers along with children are the decision makers about instructional strategies, the organization of instruction, and instructional materials used. Commercial materials do not dictate the instructional program, although they may be used if desired. Literacy learning is consciously embedded throughout the curriculum in the whole school day. Large blocks of time are needed for projects. Children are able to read and write independently for long periods of time.

Integrating the Language Arts with Thematic Instruction

With whole language based strongly on authentic, relevant learning, the integrated language arts concept combined with thematic instruction became important to the literacy curriculum. In classrooms that use an integrated language arts approach, literacy is taught not as a subject, but as a mechanism for learning in general. Literacy learning becomes meaningful when it is consciously embedded into the study of themes and content-area subjects.

Thematic units vary, but the main goal is to teach content information and literacy skills in an interesting way. One type of thematic unit involves selecting a topic that usually has a science or social studies thrust, such as the farm, and identifying several relevant pieces of children's literature that vary in genre as the source of reading instruction. All writing activities revolve around the topic and are driven by the children's literature. For example, if the theme was the farm and one of the stories used in the unit was *The Little Red Hen,* some related activities might be to role-play the story or write another version of the story. One problem with using literature to drive the unit is that one piece may be overused for general activities and skill development. This practice could ruin the pleasure that can be received from the book.

Another type of thematic unit is one that uses a science or social studies topic and consciously integrates literacy into all content-area lessons, including music, art, play, math, social studies, and science. Many selections of children's literature are used as a major part of the unit; however, the literature does not drive the unit—the topic of the unit is the main focus. In this type of unit, the classroom centers are filled with materials that relate to the topic, including literacy materials to encourage reading and writing. In all science and social studies

Thematic units often use a science or social studies topic, and teachers integrate literacy activities into content-area lessons.

lessons, reading and writing are purposefully incorporated. Skills are taught when they seem appropriate—for example, in the unit on the farm, when the class hatches baby chicks in an incubator, journals may be kept on the progress of the chicks, and the digraph *ch* could be emphasized. Topics may be predetermined by the teacher, selected by the children and teacher, or spontaneously based on something of interest that occurs in the school, in someone's home, or in the world. Chapter 9 elaborates on the use of thematic units. A description of how units are implemented throughout the school day is also included. Appendix A provides a list of popular early childhood unit topics with related selections of children's literature to use when studying those topics.

Explicit Instruction and Constructivist Approaches: Phonics and Whole Language

Some problems evolved with the "whole language" movement. Schools did not provide adequate staff development, materials, and in-class support for the ambitious changes proposed in classrooms. Many misunderstood the philosophy when interpreting it to develop strategies. Many thought that "whole language" meant teaching children only in whole groups. Thus, teachers stopped meeting with small groups of children for instruction to meet individual needs. Many thought that "whole language" meant that one could not teach phonics. This was not the case at all. The manner in which phonics was to be taught involved immersion into literature and print, together with spontaneous and contextual teaching of skills. As a result of the misinterpretations, many children received little or no instruction in phonics. Many schools did not follow a scope or sequence of skills or did not monitor skill development. Because of misinformation, misinterpretation, and incorrect implementation, many children did not develop skills they needed to become fluent, independent readers.

Many placed the blame for these problems on the whole language philosophy. Researchers quoted from meaning-based whole language studies and phonics-based investigations to make a case for their point of view. Those advocating whole language suggested that rich literacy environments with immersion in literature not only helped children construct the meaning in the text but also developed positive attitudes toward reading that would lead them to become lifelong voluntary readers (Anderson, Hiebert, Scott, & Wilkinson, 1985).

On the other side of the debate were those who favored an approach to early literacy development with more explicit use of phonics, and they cited many studies to substantiate their claims. According to Juel (1989), as children first begin to experiment with reading and writing, they need to focus on the sounds that make up words. Knowing that words are made up of individual sounds and having the ability to segment those sounds out of the words and blend them together is called phonemic awareness. According to research, phonemic awareness instruction in preschool, kindergarten, and first grade strengthens reading achievement. Phonemic awareness is also thought to be a precursor to phonics instruction (Byrne & Fielding-Barnsley, 1993, 1995; Stanovich, 1986). With phonemic awareness, children can learn principles of phonics including (1) alphabetic understanding (knowing that words are composed of letters) and (2) cryptoanalytic intent or sound–symbol relationships (knowing that there is a relationship between printed letters and spoken sound). Research also suggests that knowledge of sound–symbol relationships, or phonics, is necessary for success at learning to read and write (Adams, 1990; Juel, 1994).

Over the years those who propose a behaviorist or explicit-skills approach for literacy instruction have argued for a strong phonics program in early literacy. The materials for instruction are systematic and provide direct instruction of skills with scripted manuals for teachers to use. On the other side of the debate are the constructivists, who propose more natural settings for literacy instruction based on function and meaning and the integration of skill development. The constructivists prefer children's literature as the source for literacy instruction.

Politics, the U.S. economy, and the statistics about how children are doing in reading determine the type of reading instruction that is adopted. The First Grade Studies (Bond & Dykstra, 1967a, 1967b) tried to answer the question as to which method was the best for early literacy instruction. This exemplary piece of work found that no one method was more effective than another. It seems certain to me that this debate will continue.

Balanced Literacy Instruction

A position statement by the International Reading Association, entitled *Using Multiple Methods of Beginning Reading Instruction* (1999), suggests that there is no single method or single combination of methods that can successfully teach all children to read. "Therefore, teachers must have a strong knowledge of multiple methods for teaching reading and a strong knowledge of the children in their care so they can create the appropriate balance of methods needed for the children they teach."

This perspective on literacy instruction, which emerged as a result of the whole language versus phonics discussion, is a balanced approach. A balanced perspective includes careful selection of the best theories available and use of learning strategies based on those theories to match the learning styles of individual children to help them learn to read (Figure 1.1). More skill-based explicit instruction or some holistic and constructivist ideas, which include problem-solving strategies, might be used (Morrow & Tracey, 1997). According to Pressley (1998), explicit teaching of skills is a good start for constructivist problem-solving activities, and constructivist activities permit consolidation and elaboration of skills. One method does not preclude or exclude the other.

A balanced perspective is not simply a random combination of strategies. A teacher may select strategies from different learning theories to provide balance. One child, for example, may be a visual learner and not benefit much from instruction in phonics; and another child, whose strength may be auditory learning, will learn best from phonics instruction. The balanced approach is a thoughtful and mature approach. It focuses more on what is important for individual children than on what the latest fad in literacy instruction is.

Balanced instruction is grounded in a rich model of literacy learning that encompasses both the elegance and the complexity of the reading and language arts processes. Such a model acknowledges the importance of both form (phonics, mechanics, etc.) and function (comprehension, purpose, meaning) of the literacy processes and recognizes that learning occurs most effectively in a whole-part-whole context. This type of instruction is characterized by meaningful literacy activities that provide children with both the skill and desire to become

| Figure 1.1 | *Strategies and Structures in a Comprehensive, Balanced Literacy Program* |

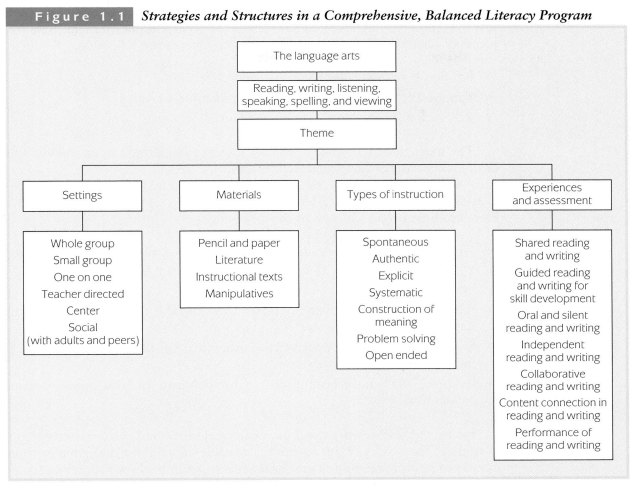

Source: Adapted from L. M. Morrow, D. S. Strickland, & D. G. Woo, *Literacy Instruction in Half- and Whole-Day Kindergarten: Research to Practice* (Fig. 2, p. 76). Newark, DE: International Reading Association. Copyright © 1998 by the International Reading Association.

proficient and lifelong literacy learners. A balanced program includes the components in Figure 1.1.

Reading First and Scientifically Based Reading Research

In January 2002 the No Child Left Behind Act was passed. This act proposes that every child in the United States has the right to become a fluent reader by grade three. The legislation was designed to help close the gap in literacy development between the rich and the poor and help prevent problems before they occur. Grants from the federal government called Reading First are intended to help accomplish the goal. The funding is for kindergarten through grade-three children from "at risk" school districts. To qualify for grants, states and school districts must identify the reading assessments and programs they will use and demonstrate that the programs are reliable and valid.

For the assessment and programs to be considered reliable and valid, scientifically based reading research has to have been carried out on them. Requirements of scientifically based reading research include the following:

- Randomly chosen subjects in the experiment
- Experimental designs with treatment and control groups
- Research published in a peer review journal

The states that are funded must base their reading programs on the findings of the National Reading Panel Report (2000).

A broader definition of research has been offered by those in the field of education. It is called evidence-based research as opposed to scientifically based. Evidence-based research is all of the following:

- Objective—data would be identified and interpreted similarly by any evaluator
- Valid—data adequately represent the tasks that children need to perform to be successful readers
- Reliable—data will remain essentially unchanged if collected on a different day or by a different person
- Systematic—data were collected according to a rigorous design of either experimentation or observation
- Refereed—data have been approved for publications by a panel of independent reviewers

Evidence-based research will use both qualitative and quantitative designs in studies. The results of this research is considered valid for designing instructional programs in reading as long as the investigations follow the definition described above (International Reading Association, 2001).

National Reading Panel Report (2000)

The National Reading Panel Report (2000) presents findings about the most effective strategies for teaching children to read. The panel reviewed more than 100,000 studies to come up with their results. They admit, however, that some areas that may be important to literacy instruction, such as writing development and motivation for reading, were not studied because of a lack of adequate numbers of high-quality investigations to analyze. In addition, only experimental studies with treatment and control groups were selected for analysis. Other research designs, such as qualitative or case study and correlational research, for example, were not included.

The results of the report indicate that teaching the following elements is crucial to reading success in early literacy:

- Phonemic awareness
- Phonics
- Vocabulary
- Comprehension
- Fluency

Schools where children do not score well on testing measures will be identified as in need of help. For teachers to be successful, the report recommends that they provide the following:

- More time on task
- More structure and routines
- More background knowledge
- Lots of practice
- Feedback

The research, theory, philosophies, and methods through the years have helped us to understand that children learn in situations that are significant and purposeful. They develop literacy in social and cultural contexts and through interaction with adults and other children. The instruction they receive should reflect on their background knowledge and be sensitive to a child's stage of development socially, emotionally, physically, and intellectually. We have also learned that organized, systematic presentation of skills is necessary to literacy development as well.

National Early Literacy Panel Report (2004)

The National Early Literacy Panel of the National Center for Family Literacy studied existing scientifically based research to identify the skills and abilities of young children from birth through age five that predict later achievement in reading, such as the ability to decode and comprehend. After identifying the variables, it was the panel's task to determine environments, settings, programs, and interventions that contribute to or inhibit the skills that are linked to later outcomes in reading. The variables the panel has identified thus far include the following:

- Oral language development: expressive and receptive vocabulary
- Alphabetic code: alphabet knowledge, phonological/phonemic awareness, invented spelling
- Print knowledge: environmental print, concepts about print
- Other skills: rapid naming of letters and numbers, visual memory, and visual perceptual abilities

It appears that involving children in appropriate activities that will help them develop these areas is an important recommendation.

Throughout the years there has been a great deal of interest in early literacy. Trends in thinking about early literacy development change often. In the mid-1990s a change was occurring that moved away from incidental teaching of skills to more systematic teaching of skills in early literacy. Taking a balanced perspective, the International Reading Association along with the National Association for the Education of Young Children worked on a document called *Learning to Read and Write: Developmentally Appropriate Practice.* Box 1.1 is a section of the document that lays out goals for preschool through grade-three instruction, with roles for children, teachers, and parents described.

B o x   1 . 1

Continuum of Children's Development in Early Reading and Writing

Note: *This list intended to be illustrative, not exhaustive. Children at any grade level will function at a variety of phases along the reading/writing continuum.*

Phase 1: Awareness and exploration (goals for preschool)

Children explore their environment and build the foundations for learning to read and write.

Children can
- enjoy listening to and discussing storybooks
- understand that print carries a message
- engage in reading and writing attempts
- identify labels and signs in their environment
- participate in rhyming games
- identify some letters and make some letter-sound matches
- use known letters or approximations of letters to represent written language (especially meaningful words like their name and phrases such as "I love you")

What teachers do
- share books with children, including Big Books, and model reading behaviors
- talk about letters by name and sounds
- establish a literacy-rich environment
- reread favorite stories
- engage children in language games
- promote literacy-related play activities
- encourage children to experiment with writing

What parents and family members can do
- talk with children, engage them in conversation, give names of things, show interest in what a child says
- read and reread stories with predictable texts to children
- encourage children to recount experiences and describe ideas and events that are important to them
- visit the library regularly
- provide opportunities for children to draw and print, using markers, crayons, and pencils

Phase 2: Experimental reading and writing (goals for kindergarten)

Children develop basic concepts of print and begin to engage in and experiment with reading and writing.

Kindergartners can
- enjoy being read to and themselves retell simple narrative stories or informational texts
- use descriptive language to explain and explore
- recognize letters and letter-sound matches
- show familiarity with rhyming and beginning sounds
- understand left-to-right and top-to-bottom orientation and familiar concepts of print
- match spoken words with written ones
- begin to write letters of the alphabet and some high-frequency words

What teachers do
- encourage children to talk about reading and writing experiences
- provide many opportunities for children to explore and identify sound–symbol relationships in meaningful contexts

- help children to segment spoken words into individual sounds and blend the sounds into whole words (for example, by slowly writing a word and saying its sound)
- frequently read interesting and conceptually rich stories to children
- provide daily opportunities for children to write
- help children build a sight vocabulary
- create a literacy-rich environment for children to engage independently in reading and writing

What parents and family members can do
- daily read and reread narrative and informational stories to children
- encourage children's attempts at reading and writing
- allow children to participate in activities that involve writing and reading (for example, cooking, making grocery lists)
- play games that involve specific directions (such as "Simon Says")
- have conversations with children during mealtimes and throughout the day

Phase 3: Early reading and writing (goals for first grade)
Children begin to read simple stories and can write about a topic that is meaningful to them.

First graders can
- read and retell familiar stories
- use strategies (rereading, predicting, questioning, contextualizing) when comprehension breaks down
- use reading and writing for various purposes on their own initiative
- orally read with reasonable fluency
- use letter-sound associations, word parts, and context to identify new words
- identify an increasing number of words by sight
- sound out and represent all substantial sounds in spelling a word
- write about topics that are personally meaningful
- attempt to use some punctuation and capitalization

What teachers do
- support the development of vocabulary by reading daily to the children, transcribing their language, and selecting materials that expand children's knowledge and language development
- model strategies and provide practice for identifying unknown words
- give children opportunities for independent reading and writing practice
- read, write, and discuss a range of different text types (poems, informational books)
- introduce new words and teach strategies for learning to spell new words
- demonstrate and model strategies to use when comprehension breaks down
- help children build lists of commonly used words from their writing

What parents and family members can do
- talk about favorite storybooks
- read to children and encourage them to read to you
- suggest that children write to friends and relatives
- bring to a parent–teacher conference evidence of what your child can do in writing and reading
- encourage children to share what they have learned about their writing and reading

(continued on next page)

Phase 4: Transitional reading and writing (goals for second grade)

Children begin to read more fluently and write various text forms using simple and more complex sentences.

Second graders can

- read with greater fluency
- use strategies more efficiently (rereading, questioning, and so on) when comprehension breaks down
- use word identification strategies with greater facility to unlock unknown words
- identify an increasing number of words by sight
- write about a range of topics to suit different audiences
- use common letter patterns and critical features to spell words
- punctuate simple sentences correctly and proofread their own work
- spend time reading daily and use reading to research topics

What teachers do

- create a climate that fosters analytic, evaluative, and reflective thinking
- teach children to write in multiple forms (stories, information, poems)
- ensure that children read a range of text for a variety of purposes
- teach revising, editing, and proofreading skills
- teach strategies for spelling new and difficult words
- model enjoyment of reading

What parents and family members can do

- continue to read to children and encourage them to read to you
- engage children in activities that require reading and writing
- become involved in school activities
- show children your interest in their learning by displaying their written work
- visit the library regularly
- support your child's specific hobby or interest with reading materials and references

Phase 5: Independent and productive reading and writing (goals for third grade)

Children continue to extend and refine their reading and writing to suit varying purposes and audiences.

Third graders can

- read fluently and enjoy reading
- use a range of strategies when drawing meaning from the text
- use word identification strategies appropriately and automatically when encountering unknown words
- recognize and discuss elements of different text structures
- make critical connections between texts
- write expressively in many different forms (stories, poems, reports)
- use a rich variety of vocabulary and sentences appropriate to text forms
- revise and edit their own writing during and after composing
- spell words correctly in final writing drafts

What teachers do

- provide opportunities daily for children to read, examine, and critically evaluate narrative and expository texts
- continue to create a climate that fosters critical reading and personal response
- teach children to examine ideas in texts
- encourage children to use writing as a tool for thinking and learning

- extend children's knowledge of the correct use of writing conventions
- emphasize the importance of correct spelling in finished written products
- create a climate that engages all children as a community of literacy learners

What parents and family members can do
- continue to support children's learning and interest by visiting the library and bookstores with them
- find ways to highlight children's progress in reading and writing
- stay in regular contact with your child's teachers about activities and progress in reading and writing
- encourage children to use and enjoy print for many purposes (such as recipes, directions, games, and sports)
- build a love of language in all its forms and engage children in conversation

Source: From *Learning to Read and Write: Developmentally Appropriate Practices for Young Children.* Copyright © 1998 by the International Reading Association and National Association for the Education of Young Children. All rights reserved.

An Idea for the Classroom from the Classroom

The following experiences were created by early childhood teachers for the children in their classrooms. The ideas reflect theories discussed in this chapter. You may find them useful for your teaching.

■ I Can Read on My Own!: An Independent Reading Activity

In this activity for my first grade class, the children have the opportunity to practice the skill of sequencing. I incorporated Montessori theory in this activity to help them learn; consequently, the materials are manipulative and self-correcting. During center time, children have the opportunity to engage in independent reading of books they are familiar with, since they have read them previously in guided reading groups. Children select books from those in reading bins that are categorized by level. After reading the book the children carry out an activity I provide. The activity is on a sheet of paper that has the book title and the author's name as well as about six key sentences from the story that are not in sequential order. After children read the book on their own, they cut the activity sheet into sentence strips and put them in the right order. The teacher should be sure to model how to cut the sentence strips and tape them onto a sheet of paper. After the children have finished, they can self-check their work in two ways. First, they can look through the book and compare their answers with the order of events in the books. To be extra sure that they have the correct order, the children can then look on the back of the sentence strips, which are numbered.

Joanne R. Coppola, Kindergarten Teacher

■ Preschoolers Go Restaurant Hopping

As part of a unit dealing with nutrition, I have individual conferences with my preschoolers to help them create their own restaurant menus to be used during dramatic play. This activity is great for diverse learners because it celebrates cultural differences, engages the universal theme of food, and is hands-on and tailored to individual ability levels. The children can write their menus themselves (any form of early writing will be accepted—from drawing a picture, to scribble writing, to random letters), or they can dictate their menus and I will write them down. Their menus contain such savory items as fried chicken on the bone; apple juice; pink ice cream with sprinkles, whipped cream, and chocolate sauce; and cherry tacos. The children decorate covers for their menus and choose a name for their restaurant. The children have the opportunity to discuss and share their menus with the class during our "Morning Message" time.

The next step is to transform our housekeeping area into a restaurant. The play food and utensils are already there. We add items such as a tablecloth, serving trays, and small writing pads and pencils for taking orders. I've made large signs with every child's restaurant name on it. I rotate the names so that each child has a chance for his or her restaurant to be the restaurant of the day. When the children come to school, the first thing they do is rush over to the play area to see whose restaurant sign is posted.

During a typical playtime, a great deal of literacy behavior occurs. Children read menus and take orders. They discuss the specials of the day and how the food tastes, and they pay the check. This science unit on good nutrition is conducive to providing meaningful literacy experiences for young readers and writers.

Meeting with each child individually in a conference allows me to identify and deal with his or her needs. The needs span from finding strategies for early reading and writing that suit a child's learning style to realizing that each one can share his or her diverse background. For example, in addition to traditional hamburger and pizza places, we had a Japanese restaurant, one that featured Hispanic delicacies, and a Jewish deli.

Marcia Wesalo, Nursery School Teacher

1. Answer the focus questions at the beginning of the chapter.

2. Select from the National Reading Panel's list to develop such skills as phonemic awareness, phonics, vocabulary, comprehension, or fluency. Create an experience for an early childhood classroom that reflects the doctrines of Piaget and Vygotsky combined when teaching your selected skill. Create three addi-

tional experiences using the same skill with the doctrines of Montessori, Dewey, and Skinner. In other words, teach the same lesson four different ways based on four different approaches.

3. Observe an early childhood classroom (preschool through second grade). Decide which theoretical influences have determined the type of practices carried out. Document your findings with specific anecdotes illustrating the theory.

Assessing Early Literacy Development in Order to Design Instruction

On the test there was a picture of Sally and Tom. Sally was giving Tom something. It looked like a baloney sandwich. Underneath it said:

Sally is taller than Tom. __

Tom is taller than Sally. __

Jim wondered what being tall had to do with getting a baloney sandwich. And was it really a baloney sandwich? It might be tomato . . . Jim took a long time on that one. (Cohen, 1980, pp. 9–10)

Focus Questions

- Define authentic assessment and identify some measures.
- Describe the nature of standardized tests and standardized testing.
- What is meant by high-stakes assessment?
- What are the pros and cons of authentic assessment and standardized measurement?
- What do we mean when we speak about standards for early literacy development?
- How can we tie standards for instruction and assessment together?

When the teacher passed out the standardized test booklets, Rosa was confused and frightened. She had limited English skills and had been in her present second grade for just four months. She had been learning English, but her ability was limited. She could read Spanish quite well and was capable of decoding printed English, but with little comprehension. As she looked at the test, she knew that she could not understand the questions or answers. She decided the only thing to do was to fill in the answers by marking an X in a box for each of the questions. She appeared busy at work filling in all the boxes without reading one question or answer. She felt better about doing this than letting the teacher know that she could not read the test.

In her book *First Grade Takes a Test,* Miriam Cohen describes the experience of a first-grade class taking a standardized test, as well as the consequences of the test results for the dynamics of the interpersonal relationships within the class. In one section of the account she writes:

> George looked at the test. It said: Rabbits eat
>
> ☐ lettuce   ☐ dog food   ☐ sandwiches
>
> He raised his hand. "Rabbits have to eat carrots or their teeth will get too long and stick into them," he said. The teacher nodded and smiled, but she put her finger to her lips. George carefully drew in a carrot so the test people would know. (1980, pp. 5–6)

In both incidents, children answered questions incorrectly on the standardized tests given to them but for different reasons. Rosa could not read the test in English. Although she was reading at grade level in Spanish, she was jeopardized because of her cultural background. George, relating his own experience to the question at hand, actually had a more sophisticated answer than those provided. His answer was marked incorrect because his background experience with rabbits was different from that of the person who wrote the test. In addition, George may not have understood how to take the test, that is, to fill in the box beside the best answer provided. In both incidents, children answered incorrectly, but not because they did not know the answer.

This chapter deals with critical issues facing early childhood educators today: achieving standards by assessing the needs of children. Assessment must be sensitive to children's different backgrounds and abilities. Only when we recognize individual differences based on our assessment of special needs can appropriate instructional strategies be planned and standards be achieved.

In this chapter, I will introduce the topic of assessment. Some basic assessment instruments will be described. The practical applications for assessment of children's performance will be discussed in the chapters that deal with the various skills and instructional strategies.

Theory and Research on Assessing Early Literacy Development

Early literacy educators, with their concern for children's interests, learning styles, and individual levels of ability, have made us begin to take a closer look at our methods for assessing performance. It is apparent that standardized group paper-and-pencil tests are not always sensitive to strategies drawn from early literacy constructs. In addition, it has become clear that one measure cannot be the main source for evaluating a child's progress. Rather than testing children, we need to assess their performance for growth in many areas and under many conditions. Assessment should help the teacher, child, and parent determine a child's strengths and weaknesses and plan appropriate instructional strategies. Assessment should match educational goals and practices. To meet the needs of the different populations in our schools, assessment measures need to be diverse because there are children who perform better in some situations than in others.

The International Reading Association (IRA) and the National Association for the Education of Young Children's (NAEYC) joint position statement on learning to read and write (1998) makes the following recommendations: "Use evaluative procedures that are developmentally and culturally appropriate for the children being assessed. The selection of evaluative measures should be based on the objectives of the instructional program and should consider each child's total development and its effect on reading performance." Quality assessment should be drawn from real-life writing and reading tasks and should continuously follow a range of literacy activities.

The type of assessment referred to is often called **authentic assessment.** There are many definitions for the term, but one that seems to capture its essence is assessment activities that represent and reflect the actual learning and instructional activities of the classroom and out-of-school world. Several principles emerge from an authentic assessment perspective as outlined by Ruddell and Ruddell (1995):

Objectives for Assessment

1. Assessment should be based primarily on observations of children engaged in authentic classroom reading and writing tasks.
2. Assessment should focus on children's learning and the instructional goal of the curriculum.
3. Assessment should be continuous, based on observations over a substantial period.
4. Assessment should take into account the diversity of students' cultural, language, and special needs.
5. Assessment should be collaborative and include the active participation of children, parents, and teachers.
6. Assessment should recognize the importance of using a variety of observations rather than relying on one assessment approach.
7. Assessment must be knowledge based and reflect our most current understanding of reading and writing processes.

To accomplish these goals, assessment must be frequent and include many types. The main goal is to observe and record actual behavior that provides the broadest possible picture of a particular child. Every chapter in this book that deals with a specific area of literacy development contains a section with suggestions for collecting material related to assessment for that particular skill. A list of authentic assessment measures that will help paint a comprehensive picture of a child is provided in this chapter.

Authentic Assessment: Measures and Strategies

Anecdotal Observation Forms. Prepared forms or teacher-created forms may be used for observing and recording children's behavior. Observation forms usually have broad categories with large spaces for notes about children's activities. Goals for observing should be planned and forms designed to meet the goals. Teachers can write down interesting, humorous, and general comments about the child's behavior in the classroom. Observations should focus on one particular aspect of the child's performance, such as oral reading, silent reading, behavior while listening to stories, or writing. Within the descriptions of behavior, dialogue is often recorded. Figure 2.1 presents a sample observation form that can be used for several different types of observations.

Daily Performance Samples. Daily performance samples are samples of the child's work in all content areas that is done on a daily basis. Various types of samples should be collected periodically. Samples of writing, artwork, and

---

Figure 2.1

Sample Observation Form

Teacher's Name: _____

Date: _____

Time: _____

Location: _____

Classroom or Setting: _____

Purpose of Observing: _____

Prediction or Expectation during Observation: _____

Significant Events during Observation:

Reflective Analysis of Significant Event (this reflection should include what you have learned):

List at least three ways you can use or apply what you observed to your future teaching:

Source: Morrison, George S., *Fundamentals of Early Childhood Education,* 3rd Edition, © 2003, by permission of Pearson Education, Inc., Upper Saddle River, NJ.

Figure 2.2

*A Daily
Performance
Sample of
Nicole's Writing
at the End of Her
Kindergarten Year*

science and social studies reports can be collected throughout the school year (Figure 2.2).

Audiotapes. Audiotapes are another form of assessment that can be used to determine language development, to assess comprehension of story through recorded retellings, to analyze progress in the fluency of oral reading, and so on. They can also be used in discussion sessions related to responses to literature to help understand how youngsters function in a group and the types of responses they offer. Children can listen to their own audiotapes to evaluate their story retellings, and fluency as well. In Chapter 6 there is an evaluation of story retelling which requires an audiotape for evaluation of the student's performance.

Videotapes. Videotapes relate information similar to that in audiotapes with the additional data that can be gained by seeing the child in action. Videotapes can be used for many different purposes. Therefore, they should be done with a purpose in mind and evaluated with a checklist or observation form. Videotapes of the teacher can be used for assessing their own performance.

Surveys and Interviews. Surveys can be prepared by teachers to assess children's attitudes about how they think they are learning or what they like or dislike in school. Surveys can be in the form of questionnaires or interviews with written or oral answers. Chapter 8 provides a **motivation survey** to be administered to children. It is a multiple-choice questionnaire that also asks for open-ended responses from the child.

Teacher-Prepared Pencil-and-Paper Tests. These tests will probably match instruction better than measures designed by commercial companies; therefore, teachers need to provide this type of experience for children.

Student Evaluation Forms. Authentic assessment must involve the child. Forms are prepared for children to evaluate their own performance (see Figure 2.3). Children should regularly evaluate their performance by collecting samples of their work and discussing them with the teacher and other children. Children are an integral part of the assessment process.

Parent Assessment Forms. Authentic assessment also involves parents as evaluators of their children. Parents may be asked to collect work samples from home and to write anecdotes about behavior. It is good to provide parents with forms for observing and recording behavior. Children should talk about their work with their parents. The parent is an important resource for providing more information about the child from the home perspective. (See Figure 10.3 for a parent assessment form entitled **Observing My Child's Literacy Growth.**)

Figure 2.3

Children's Self-Evaluation Form

Name _____ Date _____

1. I know all the letters of the alphabet.   yes ☐   no ☐

2. I can write the letters.   yes ☐   no ☐
   Here is a sample of some letters I can write:

3. I know letter sounds.   yes ☐   no ☐
   Here are some letter sounds I know:

4. Things I need help with letters are:

- -

1. I like to read: yes ☐   no ☐   Why?

2. Things I like to read are:

3. The things I do well in reading are:

4. The things I need to learn how to do better in reading are:

- -

1. I like to write: yes ☐   no ☐   Why?

2. Things I like to write are:

3. The things I do well in writing are:

4. The things I need to learn how to do better in writing are:

Conferences. Conferences allow the teacher to meet with a child on a one-to-one basis to assess skills such as reading aloud, to discuss a child's progress, to talk about steps to improve, to instruct, and to prescribe activities. Children should take an active role in evaluating their progress and are equal partners in the assessment process. Parents also are involved in conferencing with teachers about their child's progress. They meet with teachers alone and with their child. They bring materials they have collected at home to add to the packet of information.

Checklists. Inventories including lists of developmental behaviors or skills for children to accomplish are a common form of authentic assessment. The list is prepared based on objectives a teacher may have for instruction. Therefore the inventory is designed to determine whether goals set forth have been accomplished. Box 2.1 entitled **Developmental Characteristics of Children** at the end of this chapter can be used as a checklist to determine how children are developing socially, emotionally, physically, and cognitively based on their age. In several chapters in the book checklists for skills are presented.

Running Records and Informal Inventories

Marie Clay (1993a) created **running records** for closely observing and recording children's oral reading behavior and for planning instruction. In the analysis, what a child can do and the types of errors the child makes when reading are recorded. Running records also determine the appropriate material for instructional purposes and for independent reading. In addition, a student's frustration level will be identified. Determining the level of material for instruction and the types of strategies for instruction based on errors made is crucial for productive guidance in reading to occur. Running records spend more time indicating the types of errors students make in oral reading than evaluating their ability to comprehend text.

In taking a running record the child is asked to read a short passage of 100 to 200 words. Younger children have shorter passages, and older children have longer ones. The teacher has a copy of the passage, and as the child reads the teacher uses the prescribed coding system to indicate on a running record form whether words are read correctly and what type of errors are made. The types of errors recorded are insertion of a word, omission, deletion, repetition, substitution, reversal, refusal to pronounce a word, and an appeal for help. Self-corrections are recorded but aren't considered errors. As the child reads, the teacher records that the reading is accurate with a check over each word, or the type of error (see Figure 2.4).

If a child reads 95 to 100 percent of the words correctly, the material is at his or her independent level; if 90 to 95 percent of the words are correct, the material is at the instructional level; less than 90 percent of the words read correctly suggests the child's frustration level. Calculations for running records for percent of accuracy rate follow:

1. Record the number of words in a testing passage (for example, 70).
2. Count the number of errors made by the child and subtract that from the total number of passage words (for example, 5 errors subtracted from 70 equals 65).
3. Divide that number (65) by the total words in the passage (70).
4. Multiply that by 100; the result equals the percent of accuracy for the passage read (about 93 percent in this example).

Figure 2.4	*Running Record Coding System*

Type of error or miscue	Code	Description
Accurate reading	√√√√	For each word read correctly a check or dash is placed above the word. Some prefer no marking to mean accurate reading.
Self-correction (not counted as an error)	his | sc her |	Child reads the word incorrectly, pauses, and then corrects the error.
Substitution (counted as an error)	boat barge	The student substitutes a real word that is incorrect.
Refusal to pronounce Told word (counted as an error)	— | table | T	The student neither pronounces the word nor attempts to do so. The teacher pronounces the word so that testing can continue.
Insertion (counted as an error)	at —	The student inserts a word or a series of words that do not appear in the text.
Omission (counted as an error)	— rat	The student omits a word or a continuous sequence of words in the text, but continues to read.
Repetition (not counted as an error)	◄ The horse ran away �	The student repeats one or more words that have been read. Groups of adjacent words that are repeated count as one repetition.
Reversal	he\said w\as	The student reverses the order of words or letters.
Appeal for help (counted as an error)	--- | App | house | T	Child asks for help with a word he or she cannot read.

Source: Adapted from A. P. Shearer & S. P. Homan, *Linking Reading Assessment to Instruction.* Mahwah, NJ: Erlbaum, 1994.

An important part of a running record is to analyze further why errors are being made. This is done by classifying them one step further as M for meaning, S for structure, or V for visual. To determine the type of error, go back to the text and look at the error and predict what it might be. Here are some examples:

1. A child makes a meaning error when the word read is incorrect but the meaning of the text is intact and makes sense. For example, if a child reads, "This is my house," instead of "This is my home," although the word is not correct the meaning is intact. That error should be marked with an M.

2. A child makes a structure error when the word in the sentence sounds correct in the sentence, but was not read correctly. For example, if a child reads, "I went to the zoo," instead of "I ran to the zoo," the English grammar or syntax is correct, but the word is not. Therefore the error is marked S for structure.

3. The last type of error is visual. Here the child might say "spilt" for "spill," because the words look similar and he or she is not looking carefully enough.

For kindergarten and first-grade children the running record can start with a letter-recognition test. This test simply has the letters of the alphabet printed

Figure 2.5

*Running
Record Form*

Name _____   Date _____

Book _____   Book level_____

Words: Error rate: Accuracy rate:

Errors:

Self-correction rate:

Cues used

E	SC	Text	E—errors			SC—self-correction		
			M	S	V	M	S	V

M—meaning, S—structure, V—visual, E—error, SC—self- correction

Reading level

Independent: 95 to 100% accuracy

Instructional: 90 to 95% accuracy

Difficult (or Frustration):   89% or less accuracy

Reading proficiency: fluent _____ word by word _____ choppy _____

Retelling

Setting: characters _____ time _____ place _____

Theme: problem or goal _____

Events: number included _____

Resolution: solved problem _____ achieved goal _____ ending _____

Source: Adapted from M. Clay, *Running Records for Classroom Teachers.* Portsmouth, NH: Heinemann, 2000.

out of order in upper and lower case. Children are asked to read the letter names one row at a time. The teacher records letters correct and incorrect. The test can go one step further to determine whether students know sound–symbol correspondence by asking children if they know the sound that particular letters make and a word that begins with each letter or sound, and recording their responses. In addition, high-frequency word recognition assessment can be done. In Figure 5.3, a high-frequency word list is presented. The list can be divided by grade level according to which words are considered most difficult. The teacher asks children to read words from the list beginning with what are considered to be the easiest first. If they are successful, the next group of words for the next grade level are tried.

Running records document children's oral reading behavior and help teachers to plan instruction.

Running records should be done about once a month for all early childhood students. The teachers should talk to children about the types of errors they make in a running record to give them strategies such as listening to the meaning of a sentence and looking at the letters in the word to figure out a word.

There is place on the running record form to indicate if the child's reading was fluent, word by word, or choppy. Teachers can ask children to retell stories read to determine comprehension of text (Harp, 2000).

Informal reading inventories (IRI) similar to running records are tests to determine a child's instructional level. IRIs consist of paragraphs of graded reading materials for children to read silently. After reading, the students answer comprehension questions. IRIs can be carried out when students read aloud. Errors are counted and an accuracy percentage calculated, which indicates if the child reads at the independent, instructional, or frustration level. Errors typically are not analyzed for type, for example, to determine whether a child has a decoding problem or one that involves the use of context or meaning from text. IRIs do reveal the material that is suitable for a child's instructional level. IRIs can also include graded word lists for students to read (Gunning, 2003).

Another quick way to determine reading level is as follows: 0 to 3 errors in the passage is considered independent level; 4 to 10 errors instructional; 11 or more errors frustration. If a child is at the frustration level with the first book he or she tries, for kindergarten to first grade, stop testing. If the child is at the frustration level for grade 2–3 material, use K–1 material to test.

Portfolio Assessment

A portfolio provides a way for teachers, children, and parents to collect representative samples of children's work. The portfolio can include work in progress and completed samples. It provides a story of where children have been, and what they are capable of doing now, to determine where they should go from this point forth. The teacher's portfolio should include work selected by the child, teacher, and parent. It should represent the best work that children can produce and illustrate difficulties they may be experiencing. It should include many different types of work samples, and represent what the child has been learning.

The physical portfolio is often an accordion-type folder with several pockets to hold work. The folder can be personalized with a drawing by the child, a picture of the child, and his or her name. Because portfolios often are passed on to the next grade, the pieces collected need to be carefully selected to limit the size of the folder. The portfolio should include different samples representing different areas of literacy and the best work the child has to offer. Included, for example, should be the following:

- Daily work performance samples
- Anecdotes about behavior
- Audiotapes of oral reading
- Language samples
- Story retellings
- Checklists recording skill development
- Interviews
- Standardized test results
- Child's self-assessment form
- Journals
- Expository and narrative writing samples
- Artwork

Some schools have formal schedules for collecting portfolios and administering tests (see Figure 2.6). A portfolio also should be prepared by the child with the teacher that he or she can keep and take home at the end of a school year (Gunning, 2003).

Throughout the chapters of this book, assessment will be discussed at the end of sections that deal with specific skill development. Multiple measures will be offered to include a portfolio of assessment materials for children. These materials should help teachers create appropriate instructional strategies, help parents understand their child's development, and make children aware of their strengths and weaknesses and how they can improve.

Standardized Tests

Standardized tests measure what students have learned. Standardized tests are prepared by publishers and are norm referenced; that is, they are administered to large numbers of students in order to develop norms. Norms are the average performance of students who are tested at a particular grade and age level. When selecting a standardized test, it is important to check its validity for your students. That is, does the test evaluate what it says it tests for, and does it match the goals you have for your students? The reliability of the test is important as well. That is, are scores accurate and dependable?

Other features of standardized tests are as follows:

1. *Grade equivalent scores* are raw scores converted into grade level scores. For example, if a child is in first grade and receives a grade equivalent score of 2.3, his performance would be considered above grade level.

2. *Percentile ranks* are raw scores converted into a percentile rank. They tell where the child ranked as compared to all children who took the test at the same grade and age level. Therefore, if a youngster received a percentile rank of 80, it would mean that this student scored better than or equal to 80 percent of students taking the test at the same grade and age level, and that 20 percent of the children taking the test scored better.

| Figure 2.6 | *Schedule for Collecting Portfolio Samples and Tests* |

Student _____ Grade _____

School _____ Teacher _____

Tests are given in September, January, and May. Record the test when given in the space provided.

Grade	Sept. Pre-K	Jan. Pre-K	May Pre-K	Sept. K	Jan. K	May K	Sept. 1	Jan. 1	May 1	Sept. 2	Jan. 2	May 2
1. Child interview												
2. Parent interview												
3. Self-portrait												
4. Concepts about print test												
5. Story retelling/ reenactment												
6. Written retelling*												
7. Free writing												
8. Letter recognition												
9. Running record*												
10. High-frequency sight words												
11. Observation comments												

*Not applicable for Pre-K.
Source: Adapted from South Brunswick, New Jersey, public schools portfolio.

Although many criticisms are associated with standardized measures, they do present another source of information about a child's performance. Parents like receiving the information from the test because it is concrete information regarding where their child ranks among others in the same grade. It must be realized, though, that it is just one type of information that is no more important than all of the other measures discussed earlier. Taking a standardized test does expose children to another type of literacy situation that they are likely to encounter in later years both in and out of school. Many question, however, whether it is necessary to use standardized tests with very young children.

Concerns Associated with Standardized Testing

There are a number of problems associated with standardized tests. We must recognize that they represent only one form of assessment; their use must be coordinated with that of other assessment measures. Some standardized tests for early literacy evaluate children on skills such as auditory memory, rhyme, letter recognition, visual matching, school language, and listening. By contrast, practices that nurture early literacy that may not be included in the test emphasize children's prior knowledge, book concepts, attitudes about reading, association of meaning with print, and characteristics of printed materials. One child might pass all portions of a standardized test yet not be able to begin to read, whereas a second child might not pass any portion of the test but may already be reading.

Some standardized tests do not match the instructional practices suggested by the latest research and theory on early literacy. Because school districts are often evaluated on how well children perform on the standardized tests, teachers may feel pressured to teach for the test. This situation is often referred to as **high-stakes assessment** because major decisions are being made from the results of one test score. Teachers who succumb to this temptation could use inappropriate strategies for teaching young children. In addition, such teachers spend a great deal of time preparing children for standardized tests by drilling them on sample tests similar to the real ones. The sample tests are graded, and instruction is geared to remedy student weaknesses indicated. If teachers do not prepare children for the test with practice sessions, and do not teach to the test, their children may not score well. Aside from the content of the test, the knowledge of how to take the test is crucial for success. Thus, teachers may feel they are jeopardizing their own jobs if they refuse to teach to standardized tests. It is a difficult dilemma.

Another high-stakes issue with standardized tests is that the results of such tests are commonly used in placing children in specific classrooms and reading groups. Once placed, a child may never be moved to a different group. Yet, the standardized tests on which placement decisions are based can yield inaccurate information. Figure 2.7 illustrates hypothetical subscores and overall percentile ranks of three kindergarten children on a typical standardized test.

Child A scored well in auditory and visual skills, and poorly in language skills. The child's overall score is at the 50th percentile. Child B has good auditory skills, poor visual skills, and good language skills and also scored overall at the 50th percentile. Child C scored fairly consistently across visual, auditory, and language skills and likewise scored overall at the 50th percentile. All three children will go to the first grade and could be placed in the same reading group, even though Child A has a possible language deficit and is missing one of the most important ingredients for reading success—a strong language base. These three children are quite different in ability yet have scored at the same overall percentile on a standardized test. It is very unlikely that the three will achieve similar success in reading, although they might be expected to on the basis of their test scores.

Another concern with standardized tests is bias. For example, standardized test scores are less reliable with younger children than with older children. Furthermore, some standardized tests are still biased in favor of white, middle-class children despite genuine attempts to alleviate the problem. Their use tends to place rural, African American, and bilingual youngsters at a disadvantage. Prior knowledge plays a large role in how well children will do on the test. Children from white, middle-class homes tend to have experiences that lead to better achievement on the tests. In addition, following test directions such as "Put your finger on the star" or "Circle the goat that is behind the tree" is often a problem for the young child. Children who have never seen a goat may not circle anything because the animal on the page might look like a dog to them.

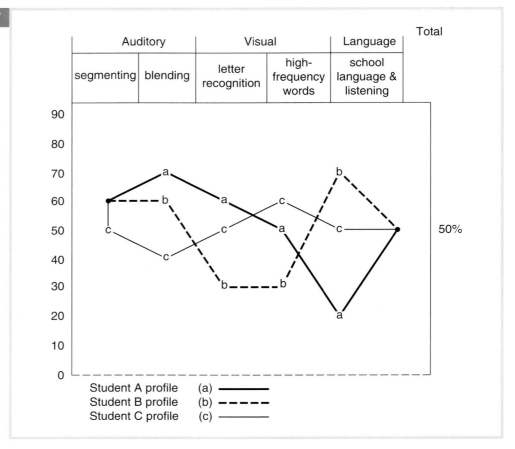

Figure 2.7

Hypothetical Subtest Profiles on Three Kindergarten Children Achieving about the Same Test Performance Rating

The joint IRA/NAEYC position statement *Learning to Read and Write: Developmentally Appropriate Practices for Young Children* (1998) suggests that evaluative procedures used with young children be developmentally and culturally appropriate and that the selection of evaluative measures be based on the objectives of an instructional program and consider each child's total development and its effect on reading performance. Various steps can be taken to remedy the abuse of standardized testing in early childhood education. Administrators and teachers must understand the shortcomings of standardized tests and that the use of multiple assessment tools given frequently throughout the school year would tend to prevent undue emphasis on standardized test results.

Standardized tests are a source of concern with young children; however, if they are used, teachers need to help youngsters learn about them. Children need to learn how to follow the directions and how to fill in the answers. Children must have the advantage of knowing what the test is like before they are faced with taking it.

Finding suitable tests is a difficult task. However, some test makers are becoming aware of the discrepancies between new instructional strategies and the design of the present tests. There are tools for assessing many aspects of early literacy that acknowledge and reflect the instructional strategies we evaluate today, specifically Clay's (1979) *Concepts about Print Test*. This test evaluates what the child knows about print and how it is used in books. In addition to any standardized test, authentic assessment measures such as interviews, anecdotal records, collection of work samples, and others described throughout the book should be used frequently.

According to recommendations by the International Reading Association (1999) concerning high-stakes assessment in reading, it is recommended that teachers

- construct rigorous classroom assessments to help outside observers gain confidence in teacher techniques.
- educate parents, community members, and policy makers about classroom-based assessment.

Standards and Standardized Tests for Reading and Writing

With the call for all children in the United States to be fluent readers by the end of third grade, professional literacy organizations and many states are outlining standards for achievement. **Standards** define what students should know about reading and writing and be able to do with reading and writing. The purpose of standards is to articulate what students need to learn at each grade level in the English language arts—reading, writing, listening, speaking, viewing, and visually representing.

Tests to determine whether children have become fluent readers are now being given at the fourth-grade level. These standardized tests could represent high-stakes assessment for school districts and children because the scores might influence promotion decisions and ratings of districts, and could put jobs at risk for principals and teachers. One test should never be the determining factor for important decisions such as these. Nonetheless, to be successful in these tests, and more importantly, to help students become fluent readers, schools must begin with a set of standards for children to achieve from kindergarten to the third grade. In reality the test is not a fourth-grade test, but rather an accumulation of specific behaviors learned from the beginning of a child's school experiences. The creation of standards helps develop fluent readers who will accomplish the goals.

The *Standards for the English Language Arts,* a project of the International Reading Association (IRA) and National Council of Teachers of English (NCTE, 1996), suggests that standards are needed to do the following:

1. Prepare students for literacy now and in the future with specific concerns about how technology will change the manner in which we deal with literacy in the future.
2. Ensure that students attain the vision of parents, teachers, and researchers about expectations for their achievement in the language arts.
3. Promote high expectations for literacy achievement among children and bridge inequities that exist in educational opportunities for all.

General standards were articulated by IRA and NCTE, and since this first endeavor, many states have adopted their own standards for the English language arts. These state standards and others being generated by various groups are extremely specific. They list expectations for reading and writing for every grade level. In addition, standards, instruction, and assessment are being linked to ensure accountability for achieving the goals that have been set forth.

The National Center on Education and the Economy (NCEE) and the University of Pittsburgh Learning Research and Development Center (LRDC) developed a document entitled *Reading and Writing Grade by Grade: Primary Literacy Standards for Kindergarten through Third Grade* (1999). There are a set of general standards for all grade levels followed by specifics outlined for each level. For early literacy the standards are linked to instruction and assessment. In kindergarten, for example, one of the standards is the acquisition of phonemic awareness, more specifically the ability to segment and blend sounds. The standard is even more detailed and suggests that it is expected that by the end of kindergarten children be able to do the following in the area of phonemic awareness:

> produce rhyming words and recognize pairs of rhyming words;
> isolate initial consonants in single-syllable words (for example, /t/ is the first sound in *top*);
> when a single-syllable word is pronounced (for example, *cat*), identify the **onset** (/c/) and the **rime** (-at) and begin to segment, or separate, the sounds (/c/-/a/-/t/) by saying each sound aloud; and
> **blend** onsets (/c/) and rimes (-at) to form words (*cat*) and begin to blend separately spoken phonemes to make a meaningful one-syllable word (for example, when the teacher says a word slowly, stretching it out as "mmm–ahhh–mmm," children can say that the word being stretched out is *mom*). (p. 54)

Instructional activities are being presented with standards to help teachers achieve these goals with children. In addition, a means for assessing the standard is provided. Standards may differ somewhat from one state to the other. However, there are a great many similarities among them as they are adopted throughout the country. The *Primary Literacy Standards* (NCEE/LRDC, 1999) mentioned suggest the areas for the development of literacy in grades K through 3. For the different areas specific expertise for each grade level is suggested. The following is the general outline for reading and writing:

Reading Standards

Print—Sound Code

Knowledge of letters and their sounds.

Phonemic awareness: The ability to hear the different sound segments at the beginning, middle, and end of words and say, or blend, separate phonemes to make meaningful utterances.

Reading words: The ability to figure out words from knowledge of the alphabetic principles and the ability to read words learned by sight.

Getting the Meaning

Accuracy and fluency when reading: Accuracy is the ability to recognize words correctly. Fluency is the ability to read aloud with appropriate intonations and pauses indicating that students understand the meaning.

Self-monitoring and self-correcting strategies.

Comprehension.

Reading Habits

Reads a lot.

Discusses books.

Has a large vocabulary.

Writing Standards

Habits and Processes

Writing Purposes and Resulting Genres

Sharing events, telling stories: narrative writing.

Informing others: report or informational writing.

Getting things done: functional writing.

Producing and responding to literature.

Language Use and Conventions

Style and syntax.

Vocabulary and word choice.

Spelling.

Punctuation, capitalization, and other conventions.

In each of the chapters dealing with reading and writing, objectives for instruction that match standards will be listed.

Prekindergarten standards are being written for literacy development of three- and four-year-olds. We are recognizing that children this young are capable of learning many literacy skills and enjoy learning them if engaged in activities in an appropriate manner. Following are representative of some prekindergarten literacy objectives being created by different groups.

Listening Comprehension

Listens with increased attention.

Listens for different purposes.

Understands simple oral directions.

Listens to and engages in conversation.

Listens to tapes and responds to directions on the tapes.

Speech Production and Discrimination

Identifies differences between similar sounding words (e.g., tree and three).

Produces speech sounds with increased ease and accuracy.

Experiments with language.

Vocabulary

Shows an increase in listening and speaking vocabulary.

Uses new vocabulary in daily communication.

Refines understanding of words.

Increases listening vocabulary.

Verbal Expression

Uses language for a variety of purposes.

Uses sentences of increasing length and grammatical complexity.

Uses language to express routines.

Tells a simple personal narrative.

Asks questions.

Begins to retell stories in sequence.

Phonological Awareness

Begins to identify rhymes.

Begins to attend to beginning sounds.

Begins to break words into syllables or claps along with each syllable.

Begins to create words by substituting one sound for another.

Print and Book Awareness

Understands that reading and writing are ways to obtain information and knowledge, and communicate thoughts and ideas.

Understands that illustrations carry meaning but cannot be read.

Understands that letters are different from numbers.

Understands that a book has a title and an author.

Understands that print runs from left to right and top to bottom.

Begins to understand basic print conventions (e.g., letters are grouped to form words, words are separated by spaces).

Letter Knowledge and Early Word Recognition

Begins to associate letter names with their shapes.

Identifies ten or more printed letters.

Begins to notice beginning letters in familiar words.

Begins to make some letter–sound matches.

Begins to identify some high-frequency words.

Motivation to Read

Demonstrates an interest in books and reading.

Enjoys listening to and discussing books.

Requests being read to and rereads the same story.

Attempts to read and write.

Knowledge of Literary Forms

Predicts what will happen next in a story.

Imitates special language in a book.

Asks questions about the information or events in a book.

Connects information and events in books to real life.

Written Expression

Attempts to write messages.

Uses letters to represent written language.

Attempts to connect the sounds in a word with its letter forms.

Begins to dictate words and phrases to an adult who records it on paper.

Stages of Child Development

Early childhood education has always been concerned about the physical, social, emotional, and cognitive development of the child. The curriculum, therefore, should emphasize all four areas. One cannot discuss early literacy without being concerned with the total child. This information is needed when preparing instructional environments and activities. This knowledge will also help determine whether children have special needs related to learning disabilities, giftedness, or communication disorders, for example. Considering the total development of the child and not just the cognitive has been and always should be a hallmark in early childhood education and must influence early literacy development as well. Box 2.1 describes the developmental characteristics of children from birth through eight years (Seefeldt & Barbour, 1986, pp. 63–69). It can be used as a reference throughout this volume, in teaching and assessing child development. The chart can be used as a checklist for evaluating child development.

Box 2.1	Birth through Twelve Months

Developmental Characteristics of Children during Stages of Development

Birth through Twelve Months

Physical
Develops rapidly.
Changes from waking because of hunger and distress to sleeping through the night with two naps during the day.
Changes eating patterns from every three hours to regular meals three times a day.
Develops control of muscles that hold up the head. By four months enjoys holding up head.
Focuses eyes and begins to explore the environment visually.
Begins to grasp objects at about sixteen weeks. Can grasp and let go by six months.
Rolls over intentionally (four to six months).
Holds own bottle (six to eight months).
Shows first tooth at about six months. Has about twelve teeth by age one.
Sits well alone, can turn and recover balance (six to eight months).
Raises body at nine months. May even pull self up to a standing position.
Starts to crawl at six months and to creep at nine or ten months.
May begin walking by age one.

Social
Begins to smile socially (four or five months).
Enjoys frolicking and being jostled.
Recognizes mother or other significant adult.
Notices hands and feet and plays with them.
By six months likes playing, alone or with company.
Begins to be wary of strangers.
Cooperates in games such as peekaboo and pat-a-cake.
Imitates actions of others.

Emotional
Differentiates crying according to specific discomforts, such as being hungry, cold, or wet.
Shows emotions by overall body movements such as kicking, arm waving, and facial expressions.
Begins to show pleasure when needs are being met.
By six months shows affection by kissing and hugging.
Shows signs of fearfulness.
Pushes away things not liked.

(continued on next page)

(continued from previous page)

Cognitive

First discriminates mother from others; later, discriminates familiar faces from those of strangers.

Explores world through looking, mouthing, grasping.

Inspects things for long periods.

As a first sign of awareness, protests disappearance of objects.

Discovers how to make things happen and delights in doing so by repeating an action several times.

Between six and twelve months becomes aware of object permanency by recognizing that an object has been taken away and by looking for a hidden object.

Begins intentional actions by pulling at an object or removing an obstacle to get at an object.

Becomes increasingly curious about surroundings.

One and Two Years Old

Physical

Begins to develop many motor skills.

Continues teething till about 18 months; develops all 20 teeth by age 2.

Develops large muscles. Crawls well, stands alone (at about a year), and pushes chair around.

Starts to walk at about a year to fifteen months.

Places ball in and out of box.

Releases ball with thrust.

Creeps down stairs backward.

Develops fine motor skills. Stacks two blocks, picks up a bean, and puts objects into a container. Starts to use spoon. Puts on simple things—for instance, an apron over the head.

By end of eighteen months, scribbles with a crayon in vertical or horizontal lines.

Turns pages of book.

During second year, walks without assistance.

Runs but often bumps into things.

Jumps up and down.

Walks up and down stairs with one foot forward.

Holds glass with one hand.

Stacks at least six blocks and strings beads.

Opens doors and cupboards.

Scribbles spirals, loops, and rough circles.

Starts to prefer one hand to the other.

Starts day control of elimination.

Social

At age one, differentiates meagerly between self and other.

Approaches mirror image socially.

By eighteen months, distinguishes between terms *you* and *me*.

Plays spontaneously; is self-absorbed but notices newcomers.

Imitates behavior more elaborately.

Identifies body parts.

Responds to music.

Develops socialization by age two. Is less interested in playing with parent and more interested in playing with a peer.

Begins parallel play, playing side by side, but without interaction.
By age two learns to distinguish strongly between self and others.
Is ambivalent about moving out and exploring.
Becomes aware of owning things and may become very possessive.

Emotional

At age one is amiable.
At eighteen months is resistant to change. Often suddenly—won't let mother out
     of sight.
Tends to rebel, resist, fight, run, hide.
Perceives emotions of others.
At age one, shows no sense of guilt. By age two, begins to experience guilt and
     shows beginnings of conscience.
Says no emphatically. Shows willfulness and negativism.
Laughs and jumps exuberantly.

Cognitive

Shows mental imagery: looks for things that are hidden, recalls and anticipates events,
     moves beyond here and now, begins temporal and spatial orientation.
Develops deductive reasoning: searches for things in more than one place.
Reveals memory: shows deferred imitation by seeing an event and imitating it later.
     Remembers names of objects.
Completes awareness of object permanence.
By age two or three distinguishes between black and white and may use names
     of colors.
Distinguishes one from many.
Says "one, two, three" in rote counting, but not often in rational counting.
Acts out utterances and talks about actions while carrying them out.
Takes things apart and tries to put them back together.
Shows sense of time by remembering events. Knows terms today and tomorrow,
     but mixes them up.

Three to Four Years Old

Physical

Expands physical skills.
Rides a tricycle.
Pushes a wagon.
Runs smoothly and stops easily.
Climbs jungle gym ladder.
Walks stairs with alternating feet forward.
Jumps with two feet.
Shows high energy level.
By four can do a running broad jump.
Begins to skip, pushing one foot ahead of the other.
Can balance on one foot.
Keeps relatively good time in response to music.
Expands fine motor skills, can do zippers and dress oneself.
Controls elimination at night.

Social

Becomes more social.
Moves from parallel play to early associative play. Joins others in activities.

(continued on next page)

(continued from previous page)

Becomes aware of racial and sexual differences.
Begins independence.
By four shows growing sense of initiative and self-reliance.
Becomes aware of basic sex identity.
Not uncommonly develops imaginary playmates (a trait that may appear as early as two and a half).

Emotional
Begins enjoying humor. Laughs when adults laugh.
Develops inner control over behavior.
Shows less negativism.
Develops phobias and fears, which may continue until age five.
At four may begin intentional lying but is outraged by parents' white lies.

Cognitive
Begins problem-solving skills. Stacks blocks and may kick them down to see what happens.
Learns to use listening skills as a means of learning about the world.
Still draws in scribbles at age three, but in one direction and less repetitively.
At age four, drawings represent what child knows and thinks is important.
Is perceptually bound to one attribute and characteristic. "Why" questions abound.
Believes everything in the world has a reason, but the reason must accord with the child's own knowledge.
Persists in egocentric thinking.
Begins to sort out fantasy from reality.

Five and Six Years Old
Physical
Well controlled and constantly in motion.
Often rides a bicycle as well as a tricycle.
Can skip with alternating feet and hop.
Can control fine motor skills. Begins to use tools such as toothbrush, saw, scissors, pencil, hammer, needle for sewing.
Has established handedness well. Identifies hand used for writing or drawing.
Can dress self but may still have trouble tying shoelaces.
At age six begins to lose teeth.

Social
Becomes very social. Visits with friends independently.
Becomes very self-sufficient.
Persists longer at a task. Can plan and carry out activities and return to projects next day.
Plays with two or three friends, often for just a short time only, then switches play groups.
Begins to conform. Is very helpful.
By age six becomes very assertive, often bossy, dominating situations and ready with advice.
Needs to be first. Has difficulty listening.
Is possessive and boastful.
Craves affection. Often has a love–hate relationship with parents.
Refines sex roles. Has tendency to type by sex.
Becomes clothes-conscious.

Emotional

Continues to develop sense of humor.

Learns right from wrong.

At age five begins to control emotions and is able to express them in socially approved ways.

Quarrels frequently, but quarrels are of short duration.

At age six shifts emotions often and seems to be in emotional ferment.

New tensions appear as a result of attendance at school all day. Temper tantrums appear.

Giggles over bathroom words.

At age five develops a conscience, but sees actions as all good or all bad.

At age six accepts rules and often develops rigid insistence that they be obeyed.

May become a tattletale.

Cognitive

Begins to recognize conservation of amount and length.

Becomes interested in letters and numbers. May begin printing or copying letters and numbers. Counts.

Knows most colors.

Recognizes that one can get meaning from printed words.

Has a sense of time, but mainly personal time. Knows when events take place in the child's own day or week.

Recognizes own space and can move about independently in familiar territory.

Seven and Eight Years Old

Physical

Great variation in height and weight, but rate of growth slows.

Masters physical skills for game playing and enjoys team sports.

Is willing to repeat a skill over and over to mastery.

Increases in fine-motor performance—can draw a diamond correctly and form letters well.

Has sudden spurts of energy.

Loss of baby teeth continues and permanent teeth appear.

Physique begins to change. Body more proportionately developed and facial structure changes.

Social

Beginning to prefer own sex—has less boy/girl interaction.

Peer groups begin to form.

Security in sex identification.

Self-absorption.

Begins to work and play independently.

Can be argumentative.

Seven still not a good loser and often a tattle teller.

By eight plays games better and not as intent on winning.

Conscientious—can take responsibility for routine chores.

Less selfish. Able to share. Wants to please.

Still enjoys and engages in fantasy play.

Emotional

Difficulty in starting things but will persist to end.

Worries that school might be too hard.

Beginning of empathy—sees other's viewpoint.

Sense of humor expressed in riddles, practical jokes, and nonsense words.

Discriminates between good and bad, but still immature.

Is sensitive and gets hurt easily.

Has sense of possession and takes care of possessions (makes collections).

(continued on next page)

Box 2.1	*(continued from previous page)*

Cognitive

Attention span is quite long.

Can plan and stay with a task or project over a long period.

Interested in conclusions and logical ends.

Aware of community and the world.

Expanding knowledge and interest.

Some sevens read well and by eight really enjoy reading.

Can tell time—aware of passage of time in months and years.

Interested in other time periods.

Conscious of other's work and their own. May comment, "I'm good at art, but Sue is better at reading."

Differences in abilities widening.

Source: Early Childhood Education: An Introduction, 4th ed., by C. Seefeldt and N. Barbour, pp. 63–69. © 1997. Reprinted by permission of Pearson Education, Inc., Upper Saddle River, NJ.

An Idea for the Classroom from the Classroom

■ Today I Learned

I like my second-grade students to reflect and evaluate what they have learned on a daily basis, so I created a way for them to maintain an ongoing record that chronicles knowledge they have constructed over time. I created a chart that hangs on the wall with one pocket for each student on the chart. There is a stack of index cards in a pocket for that purpose. At the end of each day I allow ten minutes for the children to complete the evaluation task. They are to take an index card and for two to three minutes review the learning activities that took place that day. Then they are to take two to three minutes to write down key concepts learned. Students should write down only three to five concepts. After they write these concepts, they "pair and share" with a partner. Each one reads what he or she wrote. When the children leave the class to go home, they put the index card into their pocket on the chart. On occasion I have the students review the cards. I also review the cards; reviewing gives me insight into what concepts the children have understood and recalled correctly.

Cards are sent home at the end of a week so parents may be kept up to date about what their child is learning. Encourage children and parents to discuss the contents of the cards and to extend the learning at home. For young children, draw pictures to represent learning for the last few days and have them circle what they have learned.

Christine Zehnder, Graduate Student at Rutgers Graduate School of Education

An Idea for the Classroom for Diverse Learners

■ You Write, I Write: Using Interactive Writing as a Means of Authentic Assessment

During journal time, I pull aside one student or a small group of students to conduct an interactive writing activity in my first-grade class. This activity is beneficial to ELL students because it is collaborative and provides excellent teacher support for individualized instruction. Have the students bring their journals and materials for drawing and writing. Give the students two to three minutes to select what they want to write about from three topics you present. Some will start by drawing a picture. Others will begin writing. Interact with the children as they write. Ask them to tell you about what they are writing and prompt them at their point of need. For example, "What sound do you hear at the beginning of that word? What letter makes that sound? Can you hear any sounds at the end of the word? How about in the middle?" For more fluent writers, encourage them to elaborate upon their ideas. For example, "If you added some describing words I would be able to clearly see that picture in my mind."

Encourage the children to do as much of the problem solving and writing as possible. They may refer to word walls, charts, and other print sources in the classroom. When a child needs more support, write what the child could not write using a felt-tip pen. For example, a child may be able to record beginning and ending sounds in words but is developing hearing middle sounds. A word in their journal may look like the following: he**a**rt (bold print is the teacher's writing). You may note other areas in the journal entry where strong teacher support was required by marking a dot at the beginning of the passage and a dot at the end, indicating where you helped the child. Make sure to use lots of specific, positive praise in your interactions. For example, "Placing the exclamation point at the end of that sentence was perfect. I could tell you really were surprised when you found what the tooth fairy left for you."

By looking over the children's journals, you can see progress over time as well as the children's areas of need. You may, for example, see the need to teach certain sight words, punctuation usage, or prefixes and suffixes. These can be addressed in whole-group shared reading and writing lessons or in a one-on-one context. As the year progresses, it is rewarding to both the children and the teacher to see the student's participation in the interactive writing increase while the teacher's decreases.

Susan Yoder, Kindergarten Teacher

Activities and Questions

1. Answer the focus questions at the beginning of the chapter.

2. Begin a portfolio for yourself that will reflect the work you do in this course. Place in the portfolio pieces of work that you and your instructor would like to have there. Occasionally look over the materials, and at the end of the semester review them to help you remember things you have learned and to assess your own accomplishments.

3. Parents in your district are not pleased with the authentic measures for assessment being used. They want to know if their children are doing as well as others. Based on a test, they want to know if their child is above, below, or at grade level. You are convinced that authentic assessment is the right way to evaluate children. What can you do to help parents understand and accept the authentic assessment strategies?

4. Plan a parent workshop to inform them about standards and how you link your instruction and assessment to them.

Literacy and Diversity

Meeting Needs of Children with Special Concerns

Thomas Jefferson articulated three fundamental beliefs about literacy and education that have become part of our national ethos: (1) the ability of every citizen to read is necessary to the practice of democracy, (2) it is therefore the duty of the general public to support the teaching of reading for all youngsters, and (3) reading should be taught during the earliest years of schooling. Among the reasons he cited, "none is more important, none more legitimate, than of rendering the people safe, as they are the ultimate guardians of their own liberty."

—Thomas Jefferson
The Life and Selected Writings of Thomas Jefferson

Focus Questions

- How do we plan for early literacy instruction with children from diverse cultural backgrounds in our classrooms?
- What do we need to plan for children who are English language learners?
- How do we deal with children who have physical impairments in the regular classroom?
- Describe the multiple-intelligence theory and how it relates to literacy instruction.
- What is meant by early intervention programs?
- What is meant by inclusion?

Quality literacy instruction is appropriate for all children. Small group settings are particularly good for children with diverse needs. Small group settings encourage communication and meaningful, natural conversation. ELL students will pick up much of their English from informal conversations and interactions with their peers. More capable children will help struggling readers to learn in small groups, as we see in the following examples.

> *Mrs. Nash had a literacy center time in her classroom where small groups of children had the opportunity to work together and be independent of the teacher. She had modeled the materials for the children so they would know how to use them.*
>
> *It became apparent when speaking with Mrs. Nash that children with special needs gained a lot from the independent work during literacy center time. Mrs. Nash described an incident involving a struggling reader in her classroom who was well below grade level in her work. According to Mrs. Nash, Charlene never read aloud. One day Mrs. Nash noticed her reading aloud to a rag doll while another child was listening. Mrs. Nash offered positive reinforcement to Charlene very quietly, and the reading aloud continued daily during literacy center time.*
>
> *Mr. Abere, a second-grade teacher in the same school, described another situation with an English language learner. This child would not speak in class at all. One day during literacy center time, Mr. Abere observed Tasha acting as a teacher with a group of children she had organized. She had the group of three sitting in a circle. Each had a copy of the same book. Tasha called their names and asked each one to take a turn reading.*
>
> *Marcel was a gifted child in Mrs. Rosen's classroom with mostly low achievers. He worked alone most of the time. About two months after literacy center time was initiated in his classroom, he was able to participate with other children in literacy activities. The first time I observed him with others, he was reading the newspaper and checking out the weather in other parts of the country. Patrick asked Marcel if he could look too. Marcel was pleased, and then David joined them. Together they read and discussed how hot and cold it was in Florida, Colorado, and so on.*

Numerous anecdotes from literacy center time described how children were able to find a way to participate in spite of special problems. One teacher commented, "There seems to be something that every child can find to do during literacy center time."

Theory and Research about Literacy and Diversity: Addressing Children's Individual Needs

Many of the theoretical and philosophical perspectives presented in Chapter 1 and throughout the book discuss the necessity for meeting the individual needs of children. Early childhood education has always been child centered and concerned about the social, emotional, physical, and intellectual needs of children.

In early childhood, every youngster is seen as a unique individual; however, there is greater diversity than ever in classrooms today, and there are more and more individual needs to meet.

Identifying special needs is the first step in dealing with diversity. Identification makes us more aware that differences exist and then helps us determine the educational implications for instructional programs.

I had a difficult time deciding whether to have a separate chapter about diversity or to integrate strategies for teaching diverse students throughout the book. My first inclination was to integrate concerns about diversity throughout the book. Our classrooms, however, are so diverse and teachers are so concerned about meeting the needs of these children that I decided to do both. This chapter begins the discussion and introduces readers to the types of diversity they might find in their classrooms. Some strategies are discussed here. In addition, throughout the book, strategies are discussed that are designed to meet individual needs. Since issues of diversity such as teaching English language learners and students at risk are of particular interest, from Chapter 4 to the end of the book I have provided icons that suggest when particular strategies are especially good for the students discussed in this chapter. There are many different types of diversity represented in our schools today. It has been found that good instructional techniques for all children will be appropriate with some modifications for those with special needs (Delpit, 1995).

Addressing the Literacy Needs of a Diverse Multicultural Society

The demographics of the United States population are becoming more racially and ethnically diverse. Current statistics show that one in every three children is from a different ethnic or racial minority group, and one in every seven children speaks English as a second language (Miramontes, Nadeau, & Commins, 1997).

Much of the research on the academic achievement in U.S. schools demonstrates that if English is not a child's first language, the child is less likely to be successful (Rossi & Stringfield, 1995). Some reasons for this problem are the lack of support for the home culture provided by schools, the complex nature of learning a second language, and the low socioeconomic status of many of the families who do not speak English as a first language (Banks & Banks, 1993; Connell, 1994; Garcia & McLaughlin, 1995).

In the past diversity was disregarded in the United States, and children were expected to ignore their cultural backgrounds and language differences and learn the English language and American customs. If we are to live in harmony in a pluralistic society, it is imperative that educational leaders accept the charge to provide a culturally relevant education for all students. We must be sensitive toward cultural and language differences and recognize that children can and should maintain their cultural heritage, and that they can still be considered American and learn English without abandoning their native language (Templeton, 1991).

Cultural Diversity

Multiculturalism is a complicated issue. Multiculturalism refers not only to race and ethnicity, but also to class, religion, sex, and age. The multiracial, multiethnic, multicultural, and multilingual nature of our dynamic society mandates that we teach tolerance and understanding of differences as an ongoing process involving self-reflection, self-awareness, increasing knowledge, and developing relevant skills (Schickedanz, York, Stewart, & White, 1990). We need to welcome diversity in our schools. It adds a rich dimension to the classroom and to topics of study. By recognizing students' diverse backgrounds, we will enhance their self-image. Differences should be the norm rather than the exception. Differences in cultural backgrounds often provide explanations of why children behave as they do. Behaviors that are acceptable in one culture might be thought of as disrespectful in another. Goals for classrooms in our multicultural society need to be as follows:

1. An improved understanding of cultural differences, and their effect on lifestyle, values, world view, and individual differences.
2. An increased awareness of how to develop strategies to enhance learning in a multicultural environment.
3. A framework for conceptualizing ways to create a climate conducive to learning and development.

The goals we need to pursue for children in ethnically diverse classrooms and for children whose language is other than English are as follows:

1. Children need to learn to accept and be comfortable with their ethnic identities.
2. Children need to learn to function in other cultures, particularly in the dominant culture.
3. Children need to relate positively with individuals from varied ethnic backgrounds.
4. Children who do not speak English or standard English need to retain and value their first languages but learn English as well.

Teachers need to develop their own understanding of the multiethnic groups they serve. They must recognize that the children they deal with are multiethnic. They must respect the ethnic identities, heritages, and traditions of others. Teachers must be aware of their own ethnic heritages, traditions, and beliefs (Barone, 1998; Schickedanz, York, Stewart, & White, 1990; Tabors, 1998).

Helping English Language Learners in Your Classroom

A major instructional concern in early childhood literacy programs is the varied language backgrounds of the children who come to day-care centers, preschools, kindergartens, and first, second, and third grades. Any given group may contain children using words, syntax, and language patterns quite different from those of standard English. Particularly in the United States, there are many different forms of English usage. There are, for example, distinct grammars in rural New England, Appalachia, and some African American communities. There are children whose families have immigrated from Latin America, the Middle East, or Asia. Foster (1982, p. 14) compiled the following six categories that represent the diverse language abilities of young children:

Diverse Language Abilities of Children

1. Children who are recent immigrants with little or no English.

2. Children who come from homes in which the language is something other than English but who speak some English because of their experiences with television and their contacts outside the home.

3. Children who speak both English and another language fluently. Such children are usually easily assimilated into the majority group. Often English becomes the major language with which they communicate. They then risk losing the advantages that bilingualism gives them.

4. Children who speak mainly English but who have poor skills in their parents' or family's language. Often these children speak English at home, but their parents speak to them in another language.

5. Children who speak nonstandard English because the English spoken at home is not fluent or is a dialect. Although they need to learn a more standard English at school, they must not be made to feel that their home language is inferior.

6. Children who are monolingual in English.

All six categories represent major concerns because a firm base in oral language is strongly linked to literacy development. In addition to skill development, we need to think about emotional concerns. Unfortunately, we have often looked down on children with language differences and classified them as students with potential learning problems. We have come to realize, however, that differences do *not* mean deficits. Linguists have found, for example, that black English is a systematic, rule-governed dialect that can express all levels of thought.

Diversity in language and heritage should be shared in classrooms to enrich the classroom experience.

Teachers must be sensitive to the differences in language among youngsters in their classrooms. Children must not be embarrassed or made to feel inferior because they do not speak standard English. Teachers need to respect language differences and help children take pride in their backgrounds. Diversity in language and heritage should be shared in classrooms to enrich the classroom experience (Neuman & Roskos, 1994).

Children's Responses to Language Differences

Children tend to choose playmates who speak the same language, presumably because it is easier to communicate. They usually do not reject those who speak a different language, however, and will use gestures and other means of communication when interacting with them. Bilingual children will often act as interpreters for their parents and friends who are less skilled in the language of the classroom. Although children are curious about differences in speech and will often "correct" one another, they have not developed the biases that adults have toward nonstandard usage.

Preschool and kindergarten children will acquire the language easily when immersed in language-rich classrooms where there are good models of English and sensitive teachers.

How Many English Language Learners Are in Our Classrooms?

According to the Census Bureau, about 329 languages are spoken in the United States (Gollnick & Chinn, 2002). The number of students who are English language learners grew from 1.6 million in 1986 to 9.9 million in 1999 and continues to rise at a rate two and a half times faster than the population of native English speakers (International Reading Association, 2001). Teachers today must face the reality of having students in their classroom whose primary language is not English. Right now a disparity exists between the student and teacher populations because 86.5 percent of teachers are white (Gollnick & Chinn, 2002) and most feel they are not prepared to instruct ELL students (Gunning, 2003). Most good strategies for teaching early literacy development for native English speakers, however, are also good strategies to use with ELL.

Respecting Family and Cultural Heritage

It is crucial that teachers show that they respect the cultural heritage and value the native language of their students from the moment the students walk into their classrooms. Imagine how scary it is for a young child to come into a place where everyone speaks a different language. Teachers should show interest in their students' native languages and try to learn at least a few key phrases in each of the languages represented in their classrooms (Xu, 2003). It is helpful to talk with parents about their child's level of familiarity with English. Teachers can invite parents to bring a translator to their initial conference or can provide one if the parents wish. Whenever possible, schools should consider the parents' preference for their child's literacy instruction in order to determine whether the child should be taught with English-only instruction or in the family's primary language (International Reading Association, 2001). Parents should be encouraged to participate in the classroom as much as possible and to share their culture and language with their child's class.

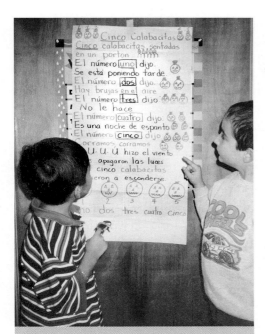

If teachers become familiar with their students' cultures, the teachers are more likely to respond effectively to the students' needs.

The classroom should have plenty of texts in the native languages of the ELL students. These include translations of favorite books, as well as newspapers, menus, and other everyday texts that a student might encounter at home. Teachers should do everything they can to create a connection between each child's home and school literacy experiences. This is especially challenging because different cultures and communities embrace different approaches to literacy (Xu, 2003; Espinosa & Burns, 2003). Again, communication with parents about their children's home literacy practices will help teachers to improve instruction with ELL students. A teacher can also ask parents to introduce new concepts from the classroom in the child's native language, further enhancing the connection between home and school. If teachers become familiar with their students' cultures, the teachers are more likely to respond effectively to the students' needs.

Methods of Instruction for English Language Learners

There are three well-known types of instruction for English language learners: (1) English immersion, (2) bilingual education, and (3) primary language programs. English immersion, or English-only instruction, may work for younger students who are able to acquire new languages more easily. Students may learn English through interaction in their regular classrooms or be pulled out for **English as a second language** (ESL) program, in which they are taught English. English immersion instruction does not help maintain or further develop a child's native language (Espinosa & Burns, 2003).

There are several approaches to bilingual education. The *transitional approach* promotes subtractive bilingualism, in which English eventually replaces the student's native language. The goal of the *maintenance approach* is additive bilingualism, which means that students learn English while maintaining their first language. The two languages have equal value. The *two-way bilingual approach* can be used in classrooms with a mix of English speakers and non–English speakers (Espinosa & Burns, 2003; Gollnick & Chinn, 2002). Roughly half of the curriculum is taught in English, and half is taught in the other language. This approach benefits ELL students, who acquire English, and English speakers, who learn a second language.

Primary language instruction for ELL students develops literacy in the primary language first, before shifting to bilingual or English-only instruction. Children are taught concepts, knowledge, and skills in their primary language as English skills are gradually incorporated into instruction (Gollnick & Chinn, 2002). Research shows that programs that provide initial literacy instruction in a child's primary language and promote long-term primary language development have proved the most effective with English language learners (Espinosa & Burns, 2003; International Reading Association, 2001). The Committee on the Prevention of Reading Difficulties in Young Children recommends that children learn to read in their first language while learning to speak English over time (Snow, Burns, & Griffin, 1998). Two-way bilingual instruction, for example a mix of English and Spanish, has also been successful.

People naturally learn spoken language before they learn to read and write. Therefore, it is beneficial if students become proficient with oral skills in English before they have formal English instruction for reading and writing (Espinosa & Burns, 2003; Gunning, 2003). Because there are many factors at play in each ELL student's educational development, there is no one perfect method of instruction for all ELL students. Teachers need to decide with other professionals and parents what is best for different children.

Good Strategies for Teaching Reading to English Language Learners

Teachers who have ELL students in their classrooms must find as many creative ways as possible to encourage their students' language and literacy development. There are numerous strategies for attending to English language learners in the classroom. Many of these strategies for promoting English language development are strategies for all students, not just second-language learners. Good literacy practice is good practice for all.

ELL students may be very timid and nervous when they first enter an English-speaking classroom, so it is crucial that teachers foster a sense of belonging immediately for these students. Teachers may want to have someone who speaks the child's language record a welcoming greeting to be played on the first day of class. The classroom library should contain a variety of texts in the primary languages of all of the students. It is quite helpful to assign a classmate (ideally a bilingual student) as a buddy of each ELL student. This buddy should be friendly, knowledgeable, respectful, and eager to show the ELL student around and assist the student when necessary. English language learners can have non-verbal class jobs, like passing out folders or watering the plants, in the beginning of the school year so that they can contribute to the classroom despite the language barrier. A teacher can help her students develop empathy for the ELL students by having someone come in to the class and teach a lesson in an unfamiliar language (Shore, 2001). This experience will help the students to better understand how an ELL student feels in an English-only classroom. The teacher should also establish a predictable, comfortable routine for the class in order for ELL students, and all students, to feel safe and confident in their environment. Finally, teachers must make a point of teaching school-related vocabulary to the ELL students so that the students can navigate their way through the classroom and school. Children can collect this new vocabulary in their Very Own Words container. It is helpful if the Very Own Words index cards have the word in both English and the child's primary language and have an accompanying picture.

Teachers may want to use a technique called **sheltered English** to assist their students in English language development. Sheltered English, which involves using simple language, slow and repeated phrases, gestures, and visual references (Shore, 2001), is actually appropriate for literacy instruction of all young children. Teachers should avoid using idioms if possible, as well as other culturally specific expressions. Teachers can also help their students follow instruction by previewing all reading selections for vocabulary, syntax, semantics, cultural references, or background knowledge that may be challenging for ELL students (Gunning, 2003). After a thorough preview, teachers will be able to preteach new vocabulary and go over any possible difficulties with a text ahead of time. Texts with a universal knowledge base, like informational or concept books, are especially beneficial to ELL students because they are not culturally specific (Xu, 2003).

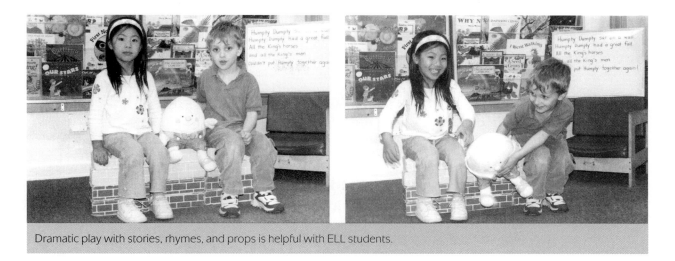

Dramatic play with stories, rhymes, and props is helpful with ELL students.

High-interest picture books and books with predictable patterns are also particularly useful for the literacy instruction of ELL students. Teachers should give children as many language clues as possible through visuals, gestures and expressions, and repetitive phrases. Repetition should be encouraged, through predictable books as well as fun songs and rhyming games. Dramatic play with stories, rhymes, and props is helpful with ELL students.

A strategy that is particularly effective with ELL students involves children in creating their own texts about subject matter that is familiar to them. Original text is not bogged down by unfamiliar vocabulary, syntax, or cultural references, so it is easier for ELL students to embrace and to attempt to read (Xu, 2003; Gunning, 2003). Children can also build on the language and ideas of their classmates as they create a text together. Younger children will dictate their

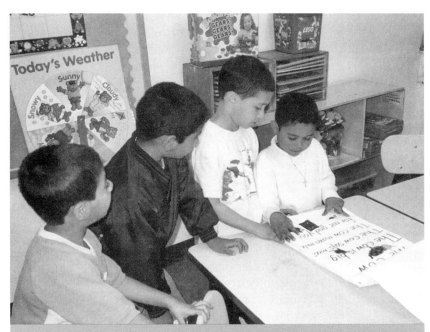

Because original text is not bogged down by unfamiliar vocabulary, syntax, or cultural references, it is easier for ELL students to embrace and try to read.

sentences for the teacher to record. English language learners may naturally dictate their stories using words in both English and their native language. This tendency should be allowed and might help their English language development (Gunning, 2003). Throughout the book at the end of each chapter one or more ideas have been provided that are especially appropriate or helpful with English language learners. Most strategies that are good for native English speakers, as mentioned earlier, will also be good for students learning English.

Gifted Children, Learning Disability, and Attention Deficit Hyperactivity Disorder

Gifted youngsters are often identified as having an intelligence quotient (IQ) of approximately 130. Those who develop other skills in addition to academic skills, such as playing a musical instrument, at an ability level far above that expected of a same-age child are also considered gifted. Gifted children are often leaders. These special talents need to be encouraged, but not at the expense of recognizing the social, emotional, and physical needs of the child. Differentiating assignments to make them more challenging for the ability levels of these children will accommodate their special talents.

Learning disabled youngsters are those who perform at a level below what is expected for their age or grade. Children are learning disabled for a variety of reasons. Children who are learning disabled are usually of normal intelligence but performing below their level of ability. Learning disabled children cannot process language properly. That is, they have trouble speaking, writing, or understanding language. Some conditions associated with learning disabilities are perceptual problems, dyslexia, or some type of brain injury causing minimal brain dysfunction. Children with these conditions are often easily distracted and have short attention spans.

Attention deficit hyperactivity disorder (ADHD) is a condition affecting children who have trouble focusing, paying attention, sitting still, and staying on task. The problem is usually due to a chemical imbalance and causes learning problems.

Programs for the learning disabled and children with ADHD need to be highly structured, with short periods of direct instruction. In addition, programs must provide students with programs that will be of interest to them. Many of the strategies throughout the book will be good for learning disabled children.

Students Who Are at Risk

Children considered at risk are affected by several factors that have been identified. The areas under discussion in this chapter often put students at risk. Such students may come from diverse backgrounds, speak a language other than English, have physical difficulties, or live in poor, disadvantaged homes. Poverty does not mean that children can never be successful in school; however, research about literacy achievement illustrates that about 55% of children below the poverty level read below grade level (Donahue, Doane, & Grigg).

If children who are at risk and already behind at age three and four attend preschool, their chances for success in school are significantly improved.

According to the report *Preventing Reading Difficulties in Young Children* (Snow, Burns, & Griffin, 1998) good strategies are good for all children. Good strategies usually consist of a **balanced approach to literacy** with some **explicit instruction** that follows a systematic sequence of skill development, allowing time for problem solving and providing real-life materials and **experiences.** We have learned from brain research and from research dealing with the fact that children who attend preschool are more successful in school that we need to start early. Many at-risk children are already behind at three and four years of age. Teachers need to select activities in which children can experience success. When you are successful, you want to try more. If you are not successful, you often want to quit.

At-risk children lack **background experiences,** and this limitation affects their vocabulary and language development, which in turn affects their literacy learning. Many have no books or printed matter in their homes. Providing experiences that cause talk are helpful in building vocabulary. Having access to books in your classroom is crucial.

Multiple Intelligences and Literacy Development

Howard Gardner (1993) has discussed the concept of multiple intelligences. His theory suggests that some people have all seven types of intelligences that he outlines and others have fewer. I have placed this topic in this chapter because it has to do with diverse learning styles. Gardner believes that most people can acquire a type of intelligence in which they may not be strong. Therefore, we need different learning experiences—some that foster our strengths and some that help us develop skills in other areas. Gardner's list of intelligences follows, along with types of activities that are appropriate for each of the intelligences (Armstrong, 1994).

Linguistic: lectures, discussions, word games, storytelling, choral reading, journal writing

Logical mathematical: brain teasers, problem solving, science experiments, mental calculations, number games, critical thinking

Spatial: visual presentations, art activities, imagination games, mind mapping, metaphor, visualization

Bodily kinesthetic: hands-on learning, drama, dance, sports that teach, tactile activities, relaxation exercises

Musical: rapping, songs that teach

Interpersonal: cooperative learning, peer tutoring, community involvement, social gatherings, simulations

Intrapersonal: individualized instruction, independent study, options in course of study, self-esteem building

When we teach children to read, we need to remember that not all children learn in the same way. We should, therefore, think about the different intelligences and provide many experiences to meet individual needs.

Children with Physical Impairments

Physical impairments include visual or hearing impairments, communication disorders, and orthopedic impairments. **Inclusion** is a term that suggests that children with impairments become a part of the regular classroom, even if they have severe problems, with necessary assistance provided. Children with *visual impairments* are legally blind, have no useful vision, or have very limited sight. For these children, strategies that include auditory and tactile experiences are important. There are learning materials available in large print for low-vision children. Children with no vision must learn to read through the use of braille, a system of reading for the blind consisting of characters represented by raised dots on paper. These materials are available in basal readers from the American Printing House for the Blind (Ward & McCormick, 1981). For the most part, only children with minimal visual problems will be present in the regular classroom.

Hearing-impaired children are completely deaf or have some useful limited hearing. Some hearing-impaired youngsters can be helped through the use of a hearing aid, which amplifies sounds for them. Hearing-impaired children who are likely to be included in regular classrooms will be those with some hearing ability. Visual and tactile methods for learning are encouraged with these students. Those who are deaf or have very limited hearing may use sign language to communicate. Some knowledge of signing would be helpful for classroom teachers.

Mobility impairment in this context refers to handicaps that are often congenital or acquired during childhood through such diseases as cerebral palsy, muscular dystrophy, spina bifida, and rheumatoid arthritis. Children who suffer from these problems to a severe degree are not usually in regular classrooms; however, those with mild cases may be included in the classroom. Children with these problems may have normal intelligence but often need help with mobility. Learning strategies will be similar to those used with all children. If the ability to use fine motor control is compromised, alternative methods for writing need to be found, such as using a computer or having a teacher or peer take dictation. Youngsters with diseases that cause mobility problems may need more time to complete assignments, not necessarily because of their intellectual ability, but because of motor coordination problems. Because their disability is more obvious than others, an important goal with these youngsters is helping non–special needs children feel more positively toward them so that all are comfortable in one another's presence. Discussing the problems, how they occurred, and how everyone feels about them will often help.

Children with *communication disorders* are likely to be a part of the regular classroom. These are children who have speech or language difficulties. Speech impairments include problems in articulation, voice disorders (abnormal loudness, pitch, or voice quality), and fluency disorders such as stuttering.

Children with *language disorders* have difficulty acquiring and using language. Delayed-language children are significantly behind their peers in both the production and comprehension aspects of language development. These children will go to special classes for help with their problems. For the most part, strategies that are appropriate for all children will be appropriate for these youngsters in the regular classroom. Chapter 4, which deals with language development, discusses instructional contexts appropriate for children with minimal language problems.

Techniques for instruction need to be concrete and include active involvement. Helping these youngsters stay on task is an important goal. Activities that will grasp their attention are those that are most likely to be successful. Working with them on an individual basis is crucial to finding out the best ways for these children to learn. As with the gifted child, differentiating regular classroom activities to meet their ability levels will accommodate their needs.

When trying to meet the special needs of children, focusing on the instructional goal rather than activities is important. A team of school personnel needs to be involved in preparing plans for disabled youngsters. This team needs to figure out how to help these children compensate for their disability and therefore be able to carry out activities successfully. For example, a child who has an attention deficit disorder and moves too quickly during independent center work from one task to the next can be paired with a peer who is known to be able to stay focused. This peer can read directions for the student who has the disability, thus providing explicit instruction about the activity.

Parents can be an excellent resource for informing the teacher about a child's strengths, weaknesses, and interests. The collective guidance of other children, special education consultants, and aides also can help support the engagement of children with special needs.

All those involved in dealing with children with special needs must have tolerance for differences. Thinking of children with differences as less fortunate is not conducive to learning. The attitude must be, How do we help children compensate for their disabilities, so they can learn to function independently (Erickson & Koppenhaver, 1995)?

Following are some instructional guidelines that can prove helpful when dealing with children who have physical impairments or developmental learning differences, whether they are learning disabled or gifted (Ruddell & Ruddell, 1995).

1. Observe students on a regular basis for indications that they may have some physical impairment or developmental learning differences. For example, a child who seems to have difficulty seeing the chalkboard, who copies things

incorrectly, and who squints to see things may have a visual problem that needs attention.

2. Seek help from your district's support services with children you find are experiencing problems. Be sure you have suspected problems identified and appropriate assistance given to children in need.

3. When you find out the nature of the problem a child may be experiencing, become informed about it by discussing it with special education teachers and other staff members.

4. Use learning principles that are successful with all youngsters, such as encouragement, praise, and positive feedback.

5. Adapt instruction to meet special needs. Good strategies are often good for all children, with some adaptations to meet their individual differences.

6. Involve parents with children who have special needs. Discuss the help the school is providing, inform them of additional help they might seek outside the school environment, and enlist their help with activities they can do with their youngsters at home.

Early Intervention

Meeting individual needs is a major concern for teachers of children with language differences and children who are considered "at risk." Others may struggle with acquiring skills in kindergarten and first grade. Many programs have been used throughout the years to help these youngsters, and it has become apparent that meeting individual needs requires time with a teacher and child working together. Early intervention programs are based on the premise that more can be done and needs to be done in school to support young children's literacy learning. Many children from at-risk populations could be successful if early intervention were available (Hiebert & Taylor, 1994).

The term **early intervention** refers to programs in the primary grades that encourage instruction that is developmentally appropriate as far as reading and writing experiences are concerned. The purpose is to improve and enhance the literacy development of children entering school who have not achieved early literacy abilities similar to their peers. In programs that have been implemented, it has been found that children can be prevented from falling behind their peers and from experiencing failure (Slavin & Madden, 1989; Stanovich, 1986).

Educators have questioned whether it is more appropriate for early intervention to occur in the classroom with the support of special teachers who work with the classroom teacher, or whether **pull-out programs** are more successful, in which youngsters go to a special teacher to work on skill improvement. The ultimate goal of such programs is to provide supplemental instruction to accelerate literacy development with the use of quality instruction in reading and writing. There is a movement toward integrating the intervention into the regular classroom rather than taking children out of class. The rationale for this trend toward **inclusion** is to limit the movement of children in and out of the classroom during the school day, and for the special instruction to be an integral part of the regular classroom instruction. In this way, children do not miss what is going on in the regular classroom. The instruction is coordinated with their classroom instruction. The stigma of being taken out for special help is eliminated, and the classroom teacher and special teacher work together toward helping children.

A well-known early intervention pull-out program is **Reading Recovery,** developed in New Zealand (Clay, 1987) and studied extensively at Ohio State University (Pinnell, Freid, & Estice, 1990). Reading Recovery is a program for young readers who are having problems in their first year of reading instruction. Children receive daily 30-minute one-to-one instructional sessions in addition to their regular classroom reading instruction. Reading Recovery lessons are tailored to the special needs of children and contain authentic literacy experiences that are collaborative and active between teacher and child, and also use specific skill instruction. Some Reading Recovery strategies within a lesson include the following:

1. The child reads a familiar story to enhance fluency and experience success.
2. The teacher introduces a new book, and the teacher and the student walk through the book together, looking at the pictures predicting what the book is about.
3. The child reads the new book without assistance from the teacher.
4. The teacher takes a running record to check the child for types of errors made and comprehension through a retelling.
5. The teacher carries out a lesson that helps the child with word-analysis strategies looking at onsets of words and letter chunks or rimes at the end of words.

To make the experience more concrete, the teacher engages the child in the use of manipulating letters and chunks that are magnetic on a magnetic board. The child is asked to use words learned by writing them on a slate within a sentence. Also, sentences from the book are written on sentence strips for children to put into sequence, and sentences are cut into words for children to identify out of context and to sequence into context. These familiar activities are repeated in different lessons.

Teachers who participate in Reading Recovery receive special training to help develop their ability to observe and describe the behavior of children when they are engaged in literacy acts. Reading Recovery teacher training emphasizes how to respond to children with appropriate modeling and scaffolding to help them progress. Another feature of the program is the use of authentic literacy experiences balanced with skill development. Reading Recovery has demonstrated increased performance by at-risk children. In addition, Reading Recovery strategies have been adapted for small-group guided reading instruction within the classroom.

Many schools are creating their own early intervention programs with high-quality instructional strategies used to work with children who are not performing well. It is quite likely that if a teacher works with a student on a one-to-one basis using good strategies, the child should improve because of the extra and personal help received. A brief description of two intervention programs designed for at-risk children by school districts follows.

The *Early Intervention in Reading* program was designed for first-grade children in diverse communities. The purpose was to supplement instruction for groups of low-achieving students provided by their teachers. Teachers took 20 minutes a day to provide supplemental reading instruction to a group of five to seven children. Children in the program demonstrated improved literacy skills (Taylor, Strait, & Medo, 1994).

An early intervention program entitled *A Storybook Reading Program* was incorporated into a regular class for kindergarten children identified as at risk.

In addition to traditional instruction with a skills-based program, the following were added to their literacy program: (1) directed listening and thinking activities when reading to children, (2) retelling of stories read to the children, (3) repeated readings of storybooks so that children could engage in attempted readings of these stories from hearing them frequently, (4) active discussions to construct meaning from stories read to the children, (5) provision for classroom reading and writing centers containing materials that encourage literacy activity, and (6) time for children to engage in periods of independent reading and writing to practice skills learned (Morrow & O'Connor, 1995). Work took place in whole-class, small-group, and one-to-one settings when teachers worked with children to discover their strengths and weaknesses. Basic skills teachers worked along with the classroom teachers in the room during the small-group and one-to-one periods to help with instruction. Students in this program made significant improvement over children also identified as at risk who did not have the advantage of the intervention described.

When deciding to implement intervention programs, consider the children involved, the resources you have, and how best to use the talent within your own school. Recognizing that special needs exist and what they are is the most important step for a teacher. Next is to respect and accept differences that exist in the children whom you teach.

In a speech given at a National Reading Conference meeting, Lisa Delpit (1995) spoke about teaching "Other People's Children." She discussed general characteristics for a successful literacy program in urban school settings with children from diverse backgrounds and disadvantaged backgrounds. Some of the main points in her presentation were as follows:

1. Learn and respect the child's home culture.
2. Do not teach less content to children from disadvantaged backgrounds. They can learn as all other children learn. Teachers, parents, children, and the community should recognize children's ability and teach them accordingly.
3. Whatever instructional program or methodology is used, critical thinking should be a goal. Children achieve because of teachers who believe in them and have a vision for them. Poor children practice the use of critical skills on a regular basis because they have had to be independent and have many responsibilities at home.
4. All children must gain access to basic skills, the conventions and strategies that are essential to succeed in American education and life. Adults need to help children learn the skills they need to succeed outside of school.
5. Help children view themselves as competent and worthy.
6. Use familiar metaphors and experiences from children's lives to connect what they already know to school knowledge. If you cannot justify what you are teaching, you should not be teaching it.
7. Create a sense of family and caring in your classroom. Make the children your own while you have them. Tell them they are the smartest children in the world, and expect them to be. Then they will learn for the teacher, not just from the teacher.
8. Monitor and assess needs and then address them with a wealth of diverse strategies.
9. Recognize and build on strengths that children and families already have.

10. Foster a connection between the child and the community so there is something greater than themselves to use for inspiration. Help them understand that they go to school for their community and predecessors. If they fail, they fail not only for themselves but for their community as well; if they succeed they succeed for everyone including themselves.

Put Yourself in the Place of the Child

It is difficult for us as adults to understand and appreciate the various processes involved in learning to read and write because as adults we have been reading and writing for many years. Reading is a complex process and to the novice is overwhelming. For children who have additional problems such as visual impairments or those who are English language learners, think how difficult it will be. To understand better the nature of learning to read or write, put yourself in the place of the learner. With a contrived alphabet called the Confusabet, I have taken college students and parents back to when they were five and six and first taught to read and write (Figure 3.1). Whole words are introduced in the unfamiliar alphabet, accompanied by picture clues and context clues. They are reinforced with worksheets. After being introduced to about 25 words, the students are given a book containing pictures and stories that use these words. They are called on to read just as they were in a reading group in an early childhood classroom. They are also asked to write one sentence about what they read in the Confusabet alphabet.

After the lesson we discuss how they have just learned to read and write with the Confusabet. Students consistently report similar strategies: They try to relate information they already know about writing and reading to the situation. They realize quickly that Confusabet words have the same number of letters as words written in our regular alphabet, and their knowledge of words in general helps them make sense of Confusabet words. Certain similarities in letter forms help them figure out words. They use context and picture clues as much as possible. Their knowledge of syntax (language structures) and the meanings of words surrounding an unknown word helps them determine words they cannot otherwise identify. They skip around within a sentence looking for words they might know. Some rely on the first letter of a word to identify it. Many try to memorize words by the look–say method. Most agree that words with unusual shapes or lengths are easy to identify. They acknowledge that to learn they have to involve themselves actively in the reading process. In short, they guess, make mistakes, and correct themselves.

In addition to the strategies just described, my observations of the students' behavior during this class experience revealed another powerful strategy—the natural tendency to collaborate and cooperate with one another during learning. The students discussed successes and failures with those around them. They

Figure 3.1

Illustration of the Confusabet

Look at the red automobile

wanted to talk about the words they had figured out and share that excitement with others. They spontaneously expressed frustration when they experienced difficulty, and they sought help of those nearby. Some said that they were experiencing such difficulty that they wanted to stop trying and just quit. The room was noisy at times because of the social interaction of the literacy-learning experience. At times, two or three of them disagreed about a particular word, finally arriving at consensus. Sometimes problems were solved through peer tutoring, with one student helping another who was having trouble. They demonstrated a natural curiosity as they flipped eagerly through new materials.

All the students agreed that working together gave them a sense of security, provided easily accessible sources of information, and made the task more fun. They were almost unaware of their socially cooperative behavior until I pointed it out to them. Most commented that seeking and relying on social interaction when trying to learn to read with the Confusabet seemed to be a natural inclination.

In their descriptions of how they learned to read and write with the Confusabet, the students used problem solving and some behavioristic-type strategies. In all cases they sought meaning. They approached a printed message looking for visual clues and auditory cues, and they looked at the total piece trying to draw on past experience as well as the help of one another. They guessed, predicted, and invented to construct meaning. They also used strategies such as trying to decode words by focusing on the first letter, using context clues, and using the sight-word approach. The many different approaches that were used by the college students to try and learn to read indicated the diversity among them. Regardless of the difficulties a child may have, each is entitled to instruction that suits his or her individual needs. (The Confusabet lesson can be found in Appendix D.)

Ideas for Diverse Classrooms

■ Where in the World Are You From?

At the beginning of the school year, I send a notice home with my first graders with the heading "Where in the World Are You From?" The parents are asked to fill in information about their heritage and the heritage of their child. They are to do this with their child. The responses have been more than I anticipated. Parents have been happy to cite the countries of origin and to offer information about these lands. This exercise has helped me begin my year with a clear view of the cultural diversity within my class.

From the information returned, I found that one of my students was related to Daniel Boone, and another had a grandfather who was one of the first African American pilots in the U.S. Air Force. One child, who was adopted from Peru, had an American father, his mother was German, and his brother, who was also adopted, was from Colombia. I had several children from Hispanic backgrounds and from many different countries. There were some Asian children as well. I received photographs and artifacts from the various countries. With this information, I was able to use books and activities that represented the diversity within my class. I also had parents come to school to share information about their heritage.

We began a class book about the countries represented by the heritage of the children and called it *The Passport*. I met with all children on a one-to-one basis about their page in the book for which they could write things about their backgrounds. In addition, I featured one child a week on a small bulletin board where I placed a photograph of the child with information about his or her heritage. I tried to include things that are interesting to children such as food, stories, songs, dances, and clothing pertaining to the featured child's heritage. A map showing the country of origin was also included. Parents were invited to share their backgrounds.

This project gave me an immediate wealth of knowledge about my class and a glimpse into each child's background. It was a wonderful way to celebrate diversity, involve parents, read, write, and be involved with social studies within a meaningful context.

Katherine Heiss, First-Grade Teacher

A Multicultural Bakery in the Dramatic-Play Area

In coordination with a unit on Community Helpers, we set up a bakery in the dramatic-play area. Materials included a baker's hat and apron, cookie cutter, rolling pin, mixing bowls, measuring spoons, and trays and boxes with labels for baked goods, such as donuts, cookies, cakes, and pies. Some classroom recipes that had already been made were hung in the area, and pens and pencils and books with recipes for baking were also placed in the area. A disk for the computer in the bakery has recipes recorded. The Internet is consulted if a new recipe is needed. Children were encouraged to bring recipes from home and especially recipes from their cultural background such as strudel from Germany, biscotti from Italy, or a Jewish challah bread.

For buying and selling baked goods, which were actually made, there were an ordering pad, a cash register, receipts for purchases, number tickets for standing in line, and name tags for the baker and salesperson.

To guide the children in their play, on different days, I modeled the behavior for a salesperson, a customer, and the baker. This was a popular play area in which a great deal of literacy behavior occurred. For example, the salesperson took orders on the phone and in person and wrote them down; the bakers followed recipes in the cookbook and on the wall; and the customers counted out money and read the labels naming the baked goods. Children participated in behaviors that I modeled and generated their own ideas when participating in play in the bakery.

Joyce C. Ng, First-Grade Teacher

Activities and Questions

1. Answer the focus questions at the beginning of the chapter.

2. In this chapter the term *diversity* applies to children who are English language learners (those who are non–English speaking or have limited English proficiency); children with learning differences (gifted, learning disabled, ADHD); children who are at risk; children with physical impairments (visual, hearing, mobility, communication disorders); and children from different cultural backgrounds. Select one of these areas of diversity and describe a theory that you feel has implications for instructional strategies appropriate for a child with that special need. Outline the strategies for learning.

3. Throughout the book, strategies will be presented for teaching literacy learning in classrooms. At all times have the interest of children with special needs in mind, and decide the strategies appropriate for these youngsters.

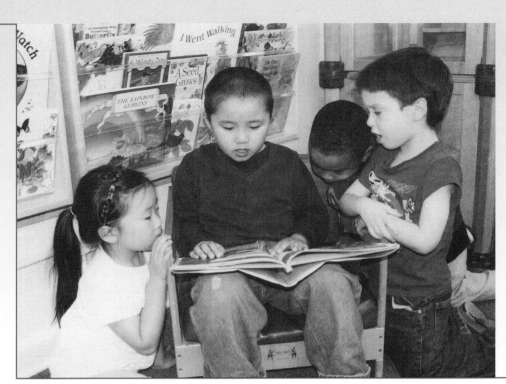

Language and

Vocabulary

Development

"The time has come," the Walrus said,
"To talk of many things:
Of shoes and ships and sealing-wax,
Of cabbages and kings"

—Lewis Carroll
"The Walrus and the Carpenter"

Focus Questions

- According to the theorists described in this chapter, how is language acquired?
- What is important to know about how the brain develops and how it relates to language and literacy development?
- How does language develop and progress from birth to age eight?
- What do we mean when we speak of children with language differences?
- What are some practical activities that demonstrate how we respect different cultural backgrounds in our classrooms?
- What classroom practices are particularly good for helping children learn English?
- What are the objectives for language development in early childhood?
- What strategies can teachers and parents carry out to encourage language development from birth to age two?
- What strategies can teachers and parents carry out to encourage language development from preschool through third grade?
- Describe specific strategies for building vocabulary and word meaning for second and third grade.
- What techniques can be used for a portfolio of materials that assesses children's language development?

From the moment of birth, the infant is surrounded by oral language. The development of language is one of the child's first steps toward becoming literate; it helps make reading and writing possible. Using research methods that involve close observation of children, investigators have been able to describe the strategies by which youngsters learn and use language. Among the many things these researchers have observed is that children are active participants in their learning of language. To learn, children involve themselves in problem solving, first creating hypotheses based on background information that they already have, and then interacting with those individuals around them who are generating language. These strategies have implications for initial instruction in early literacy.

A parent of a child in one of my kindergarten classes related a conversation she had had with her daughter Melody. Mrs. Tracey said they were outside looking at the sky one evening, and she noticed that the moon was full. She said to her daughter, "Look, Melody, the moon is full tonight." Melody looked up at the moon with a slightly confused expression on her face and said, "Why is it full, Mommy, did the moon eat too much for dinner?" Melody used her background language information to help her understand her mother. Until this time the word *full* meant filled up with food, and Melody made sense of the discussion with what she knew. Her mother explained what she meant by a full moon and that different words can have different meanings depending on the situation in which they are used.

Children do not learn language passively; they actually construct—or reconstruct—language as they learn. In another of my kindergarten classes, we were talking about what the children wanted to be when they grew up. It was Michael's turn. He started by telling us that his dad is a doctor and recently he had taken him to see the operating room where he works. Michael said, "I liked the people and all the machines that my daddy uses and so when I grow up, I want to be an *operator,* just like my daddy." Michael selected a word for the situation that made wonderful sense under the circumstances.

Although language acquisition is based somewhat on developmental maturity, research has found that children play an active role in their acquisition of language by constructing language. They imitate the language of adults and create their own when they do not have the conventional words they need to communicate their thoughts. Their first words are usually functional words, and they are motivated to continue generating language when their attempts are positively reinforced. Children who are constantly exposed to an environment rich in language and who interact with adults using language in a social context develop more facility with oral language than children lacking these opportunities (Gaskins, 2003).

Findings from research on language acquisition motivated investigators to carry out similar studies of how reading and writing were acquired. Because reading and writing involve the use of language, many believed that the acquisition of oral language, reading, and writing might share some similarities.

Language Development and Reading

Now that language processes are commonly recognized as the basis for learning to read, *language learning* is considered an important part of *learning to read.* Ruddell and Ruddell (1995) define reading as the use of one's language ability to decode and comprehend text. Reading is the interaction between the reader and the written language. It is the attempt by a reader to reconstruct the author's message. The graphic sequences and patterns that appear as print represent the

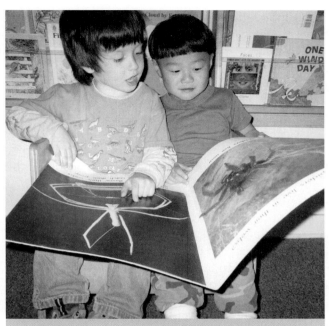

Book language takes children beyond their own language patterns.

oral sequences of language. In the process of reading, we look and listen for recognizable grammatical sequences and patterns that trigger appropriate phrasing. Using what we already know of language structure, we then test how each word fits into the context of what we are reading. As readers, we use syntactic and semantic cues that enable us to predict what comes next. Our skill in processing semantics (meaning) and syntax (language structure) makes us more adept readers. The reader who encounters unfamiliar language structures and unfamiliar concepts in material to be read has difficulty understanding it. Familiarity with both syntax and semantics enables even very young readers to anticipate the format and content of sentences in print. Past theory held that it was our accumulation of letters and words that led to competent reading. Now we realize that our ability to understand what we are reading is based on our *reconstruction* of the meaning behind a printed word. Such reconstruction is based on our previous experience with the topic, our familiarity with its main concepts, and our general knowledge of how language works.

The relationship between reading and language is evident in studies of children who are early readers. It has been found, for instance, that early readers score higher on language screening tests than children who were not reading early. Early readers come from homes where rich language and a great deal of oral language are used (Dickinson & Tabors, 2001). When interviewed, parents of early readers revealed that their children tended to use very descriptive language and sophisticated language structures. The youngsters invented words, used humor, and talked a lot. The mother of a four-year-old early reader reported that while watching the first snowfall of the year, her youngster said, "The snow is swirling down and looks like fluffy marshmallows on the ground." One spring day a few months later, the same child noted, "Look, Mommy, the butterflies are fluttering around. They look like they are dancing with the flowers."

Halliday (1975) notes that, among other functions, language helps children learn how to ascertain meaning from the world around them. Early readers demonstrate an awareness of story language. They can retell stories using such literary conventions as "Once upon a time" and "They lived happily ever after." When telling stories they tend to use delivery and intonation like those of an adult reading aloud. This "book language" takes children beyond their own language patterns and is distinctively characteristic of early readers (Burns, Griffin, & Snow, 1999; Dickinson & Tabors, 2001).

Theory and Research on How Children Acquire Language

Although we do not have all the answers about language acquisition, there are many theories that help explain how babies learn to speak. Knowing how language is acquired has strong implications for providing environments that promote language development. It also implies how reading and writing skills develop.

The Behaviorist Theory

The **behaviorists** have influenced our thinking about how language is acquired. Although behaviorism does not present the total picture, it still offers ideas about language acquisition that should be considered for instruction. Skinner (1957) defined language as the observed and produced speech that occurs in the interaction of speaker and listener. Thinking, he said, is the internal process of language; both language and thought are initiated through interactions in the environment—interactions such as those between a parent and a child, for instance. According to behaviorists, adults provide a language model that children learn through imitation. The child's acquisition of language is enhanced and encouraged by the positive reinforcement of an adult (Cox, 2002).

Early attempts at language are often rewarded, and this reinforcement leads to additional responses by children. These attempts are also *interactive;* that is, the language is mediated by adults through interactions designed to elaborate and extend meaning (Hart & Risley, 1999). When newborns coo or make other verbal sounds, most parents are delighted and respond with gentle words of encouragement. The infant, in turn, responds to the positive reinforcement by repeating the cooing sounds. As babies become able to formulate consonant and vowel sounds, they try them out. It is not uncommon to hear a ten-month-old playing with sounds such as *ba, ba, ba,* or *ma, ma, ma.* The responsive interactive parent perceives such sounds as the child's first words and assumes that the child's *ma-ma* means *mommy.* The delighted adult says more warm and loving things to the baby and adds hugs and kisses. The parent might say, "Come on, now say it again, *ma, ma, ma.*" The baby is pleased with the warm reception and tries to repeat the sounds to receive additional interaction and positive reinforcement.

Unfortunately, the converse is also true. If a baby's babbling is considered annoying, if the parent is aggravated by the sound and responds with negative reinforcement by telling the baby in harsh tones, "Be quiet and stop making so much noise," the child is less likely to continue to explore the use of language.

It is evident that children imitate adult models and are motivated to continue using language because of positive reinforcement. Children surrounded by rich language begin to use the language they hear, even though imitation sometimes occurs with erroneous comprehension or no comprehension at all. A child can imitate the sounds of the "words" of a familiar song, for instance, with no concern for meaning. A three-year-old girl sang "My country 'tis of thee" as "My country tis a bee." A four-year-old sang "Torn between two lovers" as "Torn between two mothers." Both children were imitating what they heard and were thus acquiring language. But when they heard unfamiliar words in context, both substituted similar-sounding words that had meaning for them from their own experiences.

The Nativist Theory

Chomsky (1965), Lennenberg (1967), and McNeil (1970) have described the **nativist** theory of language acquisition. They contend that language develops innately. Children figure out how language works by internalizing the rules of grammar, which enable them to produce an infinite number of sentences. They do so even without the practice, reinforcement, and modeling offered by adult language, which are considered necessary by the behaviorists. The ability to learn language must be innate to humans, the nativists believe, because almost all children develop and use language in the first few years of their lives. Language growth depends on maturation: As children mature, their language grows. Children learn new patterns of language and unconsciously generate new rules for new elements of language. The child's rule system increases in complexity as he or she generates more complex language. Lennenberg (1967), an extreme nativist, finds nothing in the child's environment to account for language development. Rather, language acquisition is motivated *inside* children; learning language is a natural ability (Pinker, 1994). Although maturation does play a role in language development, and it is innate to humans, newer theories offered by Piaget and Vygotsky have come to be the more accepted ideas concerning language acquisition.

Piagetian and Vygotskian Theories

Piaget's theory of *cognitive development* is built on the principle that children develop through their activities. Children's realization of the world is tied to their actions or their sensory experiences in the environment. According to this theory, children's first words are egocentric, or centered in their own actions. Children talk about themselves and what they do. Their early language and their general development relate to actions, objects, and events they have experienced through touching, hearing, seeing, tasting, and smelling (Piaget & Inhelder, 1969).

Vygotsky's theory of *basic learning* also has implications for language development. According to Vygotsky, children learn higher mental functions by internalizing social relationships. Adults initially provide children with names of things, for instance; they direct youngsters and make suggestions. Then, as children become more competent, the adults around them gradually withdraw the amount of help they need to give. Vygotsky (1978) describes a **zone of proximal development,** a range of social interaction between an adult and child. Theoretically, the child can perform within that range, but only with adult assistance. Proximal development ends when the child can function independently.

The implications for language instruction are clear: To promote language development, adults need to interact with children by encouraging, motivating, and supporting them (Sulzby, 1986a).

As a child builds an oral vocabulary, he or she tries words more frequently. Children will point to a toy and name it. While playing with a ball, a child may say the word *ball* over and over again. The attentive parent now interacts with the child by expanding and extending the original language (Burns, Griffin, & Snow, 1999). After the child says *ball,* the parent may say, "Yes, that is a nice, big, round, red ball." Through such *expansion* and reinforcement of words by the adult, the child acquires new language. The adult often *extends* upon the baby's words by asking questions, for instance, "Now what can you do with that nice red ball?" Such extension requires the child to think,

Children learn language from social interaction with an adult who provides a language model and positive reinforcement for the child's early language attempts.

understand, and act. Positive interactions encourage practice, which helps continue language development (Dickinson & Tabors, 2001).

The Constructivist Theory

The more contemporary perspective of language acquisition is the **constructivist** theory emerging from the work of Piaget and Vygotsky and described and supported by those who have studied language development (Brown, Cazden, & Bellugi-Klima, 1968; Halliday, 1975). Constructivists describe children as the creators of language on the basis of an innate set of rules or underlying concepts. They describe language as an active and social process. The child constructs language, often making errors. But making errors is a necessary part of learning how language works. We need to accept language errors in a child's first years.

The implications of the constructivist theory are important for early literacy development. Even though language development charts show when to expect certain stages of development on average, we do not discipline babies who have not uttered their first words at eight months or their first complete sentences by two and a half years. Sometimes we find their errors cute. We seem to respect their individuality and their right to grow at their own pace. Yet when children enter school, we neglect to recognize developmental differences; we prescribe tasks based on a curriculum, not on the child.

The process of acquiring language is continuous and interactive; it takes place in the social context of the child's interacting with others (Hart & Risley, 1999). Children also learn by playing with language themselves. They try out new words, involve themselves in monologues, and practice what they have learned. The acquisition of language varies from child to child, depending on each child's social and cultural background (Au, 1998). Children's remarks illustrate that they do not *simply* imitate adult language. It is as if children need to express themselves but do not have sufficient conventional language to draw upon, so they create their own based on their backgrounds and their awareness of semantics and syntax.

A three-year-old girl saw a freckled youngster for the first time and said, "Look, Mommy, that little girl has *sprinkles* on her nose." A four-year-old boy observed an elderly man with deep wrinkles and said, "I wonder why that man has *paths* all over his face." A father and his three-year-old daughter were toasting marshmallows; the little girl said, "Mmmm, I can smell the taste of them." After a quick summer rain, a three-year-old boy observed the sun returning to the sky and the water evaporating all around him. "The sun came out and ate up all the rain," he observed. Toward the end of the winter as the snow was melting, a four-year-old girl noted, "See how the grass is peeking out from underneath the snow."

Halliday's Theory of Language Development

Halliday (1975, p. 7) describes language development as a process by which children gradually "learn how to mean." According to his theory of developmental language, what a child can do during interactions with others has meaning and meaning can be turned into speech. In other words, children's initial language development is based on *function:* What can be said reflects what can be done. Language is learned when it is relevant and functional. The seven functions evident in the language of young children that Halliday (1975, pp. 19–21) identifies are found in the following chart, with examples.

Halliday's Functions of Language

1. *Instrumental:* Children use language to satisfy a personal need and to get things done.

    Example: Cookie Mommy.

2. *Regulatory:* Children use language to control the behavior of others.

    Example: No sleep now.

3. *Interactional:* Children use language to get along with others.

    Example: You want to play?

4. *Personal:* Children use language to tell about themselves.

    Example: I'm running now.

5. *Heuristic:* Children use language to find out about things, to learn things.

    Example: What are cows for?

6. *Imaginative:* Children use language to pretend, to make believe.

    Example: Let's play space.

7. *Informative:* Children use language to communicate something for the information of others.

    Example: I'll tell you how this game works.

The theories just discussed explain how language is acquired. Each has something to offer, but none by itself presents a complete picture. We *do* know, however, that children's language grows according to their need to use it, their interests, and the meaning it has for them. Children's language is acquired through exploration and invention and is controlled by their own maturity, the structure of the language, and its conventions. Language acquisition is fostered by positive interactions regarding language between the child and an adult.

Brain Development and Language and Literacy Development from Birth to Three

The study of brain research has made it very apparent that what happens to a child from birth to age three can effect his or her language and literacy development. Babies are programmed to learn. Every minute, they search to learn about the environment they are in and to connect with the experiences it has to offer.

When a child is born it has about 100 billion neurons. This is all of the neurons or brain cells it will ever have. For learning to take place, neurons must make brain connections. Brain connections that are repeated and used become permanent; when brain connections are not used, they disintegrate and vanish. This is referred to as **neural shearing** or loss of brain cells (Shaywitz, 2003). At birth, the baby's billions of neurons or brain cells have already formed 50 trillion connections, or synapses. By one month of age, they have formed 1,000 trillion brain cell connections. The connecting of the brain cells is called **synapto-genesis,** or the rapid development of neural connections. The brain connections form as a result of experiences the baby has and become permanent when those experiences are repeated. The permanent connections mean that learning has occurred (Newberger, 1997). The right experiences must occur to help with language and literacy development, and those experiences need to begin at birth.

Different parts of the brain are responsible for different kinds of development: The motor cortex is responsible for the control of movement; the cerebellum for the development of motor skills; the temporal lobe for auditory processes of hearing including learning, memory, and emotion; Wernicke's area for language understanding; Broca's area for speech production; the frontal lobe for planning, reasoning, and emotional expression; the somatosensory cortex for body sensations, touch, and temperature; the parietal lobe for perceptions and special processing; and the occipital lobe for visual processing. There are specific periods of time when the different areas in the brain are most sensitive for development. For example, the first year of life is the most critical time for language to be learned. During this time, the auditory channels for language develop. At birth, the child has neurons waiting to be connected for every language in the world. Neuron shearing occurs as early as six months of age, when the baby can no longer recognize sounds of languages it has not heard. By one year, babies are programmed to listen to and learn the language they have heard and are no longer programmed to hear those they haven't been exposed to. Those neurons no longer remain (Kuhl, 1994).

What does this mean for families and child care providers who are engaged with children from birth to age three? What experiences do they need to provide to create a strong base for language and literacy development so that neurons for language and literacy connect and remain permanent? From the time the child is born through age three, family members and child care providers need to do the following:

> Provide love, food, and clothing.
> Talk to them.
> Use sophisticated vocabulary.
> Use complex sentences.
> Respond to cries, smiles, and so on.
> Be playful with language, such as using rhymes.
> Play with different toys.
> Sing songs.
> Read books.
> Play many different types of music.

Stages in Language Development

Children acquire language by moving through predictable stages. In doing so, they discover the rules that govern the structure of language—specifically, those of phonology (sound), syntax (grammar), and semantics (meaning).

There are 44 separate sounds, or **phonemes,** in English. With them we produce oral language. Children who grow up in a language-rich environment can learn these sounds quite easily. They learn appropriate articulation, pronunciation, and intonation. *Intonation* involves pitch, stress, and juncture. *Pitch* refers to how high or low a voice is when producing a sound, *stress* to how loud or soft it is, and *juncture* to the pauses or connections between words, phrases, and sentences (Berk, 1997).

Syntax refers to the rules that govern how words work together in phrases, clauses, and sentences. Internalizing the syntactic rules of language helps children understand what they hear and what they read. Syntax includes rules for forming basic sentence patterns, rules for transforming those patterns in order to generate new sentences, and rules for embedding, expanding, and combining sentences to make them more complex. Brief examples follow:

1. Some Basic Sentence Patterns
   a. Subject—verb: *The girl ran.*
   b. Subject—verb—object: *The girl ran the team.*
   c. Subject—verb—indirect object—direct object: *Susan gave Lynn a dime.*
   d. Subject—to be—noun or adjective or adverb complement: *Tom was the captain. He was happy. He was there.*
   e. Subject—linking verb—adjective: *Jane is tall.*

2. Some Basic Sentence Transformations
   a. Question
      (1) kernel: *Jim went to the store.*
      (2) transformation: *Did Jim go to the store?*
   b. Negative
      (1) kernel: *Jane is a cheerleader.*
      (2) transformation: *Jane is not a cheerleader.*
   c. Passive
      (1) kernel: *Jennifer gave Lisa some bubble gum.*
      (2) transformation: *Some bubble gum was given to Lisa by Jennifer.*

3. Some Embeddings (sentence expansion and combination)
   a. Adding modifiers (adjectives, adverbs, adverbial and adjective phrases)
      (1) kernel: *The boy played with friends.*
      (2) transformation: *The boy in the red pants played with three friends.*
   b. Compounding (combining words, phrases, or independent clauses to form compound subjects, verbs, etc.)
      (1) kernel: *Jane ran. Jane played. Jack ran. Jack played.*
      (2) transformation: *Jane and Jack ran and played.* (Morrow, 1978)

Semantics deals with the meaning that language communicates, both through content words and through function words. It largely governs vocabulary development. *Content words* carry meaning in themselves. *Function words* have no easily definable meanings in isolation, but they indicate relationships between other words in a sentence. Function words include prepositions, conjunctions, and determiners (Pflaum, 1986).

Although we have identified stages of language growth, the pace of development may differ from child to child. An individual child's language development also tends to progress and then regress, so that the stages of growth are not always easy to recognize. However, language development has been studied to the extent that it can be described generally.

From Birth to One Year

In the first few months of infancy, oral language consists of a child's experimenting or playing with sounds. Infants cry when they are uncomfortable and babble, gurgle, or coo when they are happy. Parents are able to distinguish cries. One cry is for hunger and another is for pain, for instance. Infants learn to communicate specific needs by producing different cries. They communicate nonverbally as well as by moving their arms and legs to express pleasure or pain.

When babies are about eight to ten months old, their babbling becomes more sophisticated. They are usually capable of combining a variety of consonant sounds with vowel sounds. They tend to repeat these combinations over and over. As mentioned, it is at this stage that parents sometimes think they are hearing their child's first words. The repeated consonant and vowel sounds, such as *da, da, da,* or *ma, ma, ma,* do sound like real words. Most parents reinforce the child's behavior positively at this stage. Repetition of specific sounds and continued reinforcement lead the child to associate the physical mechanics of making a particular sound with the meaning of the word the sound represents.

From eight to twelve months, children increase their comprehension of language dramatically; their understanding of language far exceeds their ability to produce it. They do, however, tend to speak their first words, usually those most familiar and meaningful to them in their daily lives: *Mommy, Daddy, bye-bye, hi, baby, cookie, milk, juice,* and *no,* for instance. As they become experienced with their first words, children use holophrases—one-word utterances that express an entire sentence (Hart & Risley, 1999). For example, a baby might say "cookie," but mean "I want a cookie," "My cookie is on the floor," or "I'm done with this cookie."

From One to Two

A child's oral language grows a great deal between the ages of one and two. Along with one-word utterances, the child utters many sounds with adult intonation as if speaking in sentences. These utterances are not understandable to adults, however. Children begin to use telegraphic speech from 12 months on—the first evidence of their knowledge of syntax. Telegraphic speech uses content words, such as nouns and verbs, but omits function words, such as conjunctions and articles. In spite of the omissions, words are delivered in correct order, or syntax: "Daddy home" for "Daddy is coming home soon," or "Toy fall" for "My toy fell off the table."

Language grows tremendously once the child begins to combine words. By 18 months most children can pronounce four-fifths of the English phonemes and use 9 to 20 words (Bloom, 1990).

From Two to Three

The year between ages two and three is probably the most dramatic in terms of language development. Typically, a child's oral vocabulary grows from 300 words to 1000. The child can comprehend, but cannot yet use, 2000 to 3000 additional words. Telegraphic sentences of two or three words continue to be most frequent, but syntactic complexity continues to develop, and the child occasionally uses such functional words as pronouns, conjunctions, prepositions, articles, and possessives. As their language ability grows, children gain confidence. They actively play with language by repeating new words and phrases and making up nonsense words. They enjoy rhyme, patterns of language, and repetition (Bloom, 1990). Consider the following transcription of Jennifer's dialogue with her dog. Jennifer was two years ten months at the time. "Nice doggie, my doggie, white doggie, whitey, nicey doggie. Good doggie, my doggie, boggie, poggie. Kiss doggie, kiss me, doggie, good doggie." Jennifer's language is repetitive, playful, silly, and creative, demonstrating some of the characteristics of language production typical for a child her age.

From Three to Four

A child's vocabulary and knowledge of sentence structure continue to develop rapidly during the fourth year. Syntactic structures added to the child's repertoire include plurals and regular verbs. Indeed, children of this age are prone to overgeneralization in using these two structures, mainly because both plural formation and verb inflection are highly irregular in the English language (Jewell & Zintz, 1986). Four-year-old Jesse illustrated both problems when he had an accident in class and came running over very upset. He said, "Mrs. Morrow, hurry over, I knocked over the fishbowl and it broked and all the fishes are swimming on the floor." Jesse knew how to form the past tense of a verb by adding *ed,* but he did not know about irregular verbs such as *broke.* He also knew about adding an *s* to form a plural but again was unaware of irregular plural forms such as *fish.*

As they approach age four, children *seem* to have acquired all the elements of adult language. They can generate language and apply the basic rules that govern it. However, although their ability with language has grown enormously and they sound almost as if they are using adult speech, children have acquired only the basic foundations. Language continues to grow throughout our lives as we gain new experiences, acquire new vocabulary, and find new ways of putting words together to form sentences. At the age of three to four, children talk about what they do as they are doing it. They often talk to themselves or by themselves as they play. It seems as if they are trying to articulate their actions (Seefeldt & Barbour, 1986). While painting at an easel, four-year-old Christopher said to himself, "I'm making a nice picture. I'm making colors all over. I'm painting, pit, pat, pit, pat. I'm going back and forth and up and down. Now I'm jumping as I paint." As he talked and painted, he did exactly what he said, words and actions coinciding.

From Five to Six

Five- and six-year-olds sound very much like adults when they speak. Their vocabularies are always increasing, and so is the syntactic complexity of their language. They have vocabularies of approximately 2500 words, and they are extremely articulate. Many, however, still have difficulty pronouncing some sounds, especially *l, r,* and *sh* at the ends of words. They become aware that a word can have more than one meaning. When they are embarrassed or frustrated at misunderstanding things, they say something silly or try to be humorous. They also tend to be creative in using language. When they do not have a word for a particular situation, they supply their own. Adults often find the language used by children of this age to be amusing as well as delightful and interesting (Seefeldt & Barbour, 1986):

> Benjamin ran into school very excited one morning. "Mrs. Morrow," he said, "you'll never believe it. My dog grew puppies last night!"

> My husband and I were going to a formal dance one evening. My five-year-old daughter had never seen us dressed up like this before. When I walked into the room wearing a long gown and asked Stephanie how I looked, she

said, "Mommy, you look soooo pretty. What is Daddy's costume going to be like?"

Escorted by her mother, Allison was on her way to her first day of kindergarten. She seemed a little nervous. When her mother asked her if she was okay, Allison replied, "Oh, I'm fine, Mommy. It's just that my stomach is very worried."

There are other characteristics of kindergarteners' language. Kindergartners have discovered bathroom talk and curse words, and they enjoy shocking others by using them. They talk a lot and begin to use language to control situations. Their language reflects their movement from a world of fantasy to that of reality.

From Seven to Eight

By the time children are seven years of age, they have developed a grammar that is almost equivalent to that of adults. Of course they do not use the extensive numbers of grammatical transformations found in adult language, nor do they have the extent of vocabulary found in adult speech. Seven- and eight-year-olds are good conversationalists who talk a lot about what they do.

Helping English Language Learners in Your Classroom

The number of English language learners (ELL) with different languages and different language proficiency in American classrooms is increasing rapidly. There are children who do not speak any English; these children come from homes where English is not spoken at all. And there are children with very limited English proficiency; the English proficiency of this group of youngsters varies. Many of them are more proficient in the home language than in English. The goal is for them to become truly bilingual—that is, equally proficient in English and the home language.

Children also come to school speaking different dialects. A *dialect* is an alternative form of one particular language used in a different cultural, regional, or social group (Leu & Kinzer, 1991). Such differences can be so significant that an individual from a region with one English dialect may have difficulty understanding someone from another region because the pronunciation of letter sounds is so different. Dialects are not inherently superior to one another; however, one dialect typically emerges as the standard for a given language and is used by the more advantaged individuals of a society. Teachers must be aware of different dialects and help youngsters with the comprehension of standard dialects. Children are not to be degraded or viewed as less intelligent for speaking different dialects. Although it is important for children to achieve a level of standard English to help them succeed in society, emphasizing the need to become a standard English speaker before learning literacy in their first language is inappropriate and likely to create difficulties for the children by slowing their literacy development.

There are general strategies that will support the first language of students in regular classrooms. It is helpful when there is someone in the school who speaks the English language learner's first language. It could be a child or adult in the school who can speak the home language of ELL children to provide translation. The following strategies expose children in the class to other languages, thus creating an interest and appreciation for different backgrounds:

- Include print in the classroom that is from children's first language.
- Suggest that ELL students create books in their first language and share their stories.
- Be sure that children from different language backgrounds have the opportunity to read and write with others who speak their language, such as parents, aides, and other children in the school (Freeman & Freeman, 1993).

Along with the support of children's first language, it is also important to support the learning of English. Assign an English-speaking child as a buddy for the English language learner to help with that child's English. A few strategies that are helpful with young ELL students are included in the **language experience approach.** The following types of activities are used in this method.

- Allow children to talk.
- Have routine story times.
- Provide thematic instruction that elicits talk, reading, and writing, and heightens interests in exciting topics.
- Write charts based on talk about children's home life and experiences in school.
- Encourage children to copy experience charts, have them dictate their ideas for you to write, and encourage them to write themselves (Lindfors, 1989; Miramontes, Nadeau, & Commins, 1997).

Assign an English-speaking child as a buddy to help with the English language learner's English.

In the discussion of diversity in Chapter 3, the topic of English language learners is dealt with in depth. Throughout the book icons indicate when a strategy is especially good for ELL children.

Strategies for Language Development

The review of theory and research suggests how we can help children acquire and develop language pleasantly, productively, and appropriately. Children acquire language by emulating adult models, interacting with others when using language, and experiencing positive reinforcement for their efforts. If language is innate, it can develop naturally as individuals pass through common stages of development at certain times in their lives. As children mature, they become capable of generating ever more complex language structures. They learn language by doing, by acting on and within familiar environments. Their first spoken words are those that are meaningful for them within their own experiences. Their earliest language is an expression of needs. They learn language through social interaction with individuals more literate than they, whether adults or older children. Children also create their own language, play with it, and engage in monologues.

Using what we know of language acquisition and developmental stages as guidelines, we can begin to create appropriate materials, activities, and experiences in a suitable atmosphere to nurture children's language development. The following objectives are formulated for a program fostering language development in children from birth to age eight.

Objectives for Receptive Language Development

1. Provide children with an atmosphere in which they will hear varied language frequently.
2. Allow children the opportunity to associate the language that they hear with pleasure and enjoyment.
3. Give children the opportunity to discriminate and classify sounds they hear.
4. Expose children to a rich source of new vocabulary on a regular basis.
5. Offer children the opportunity to listen to others and demonstrate that they understand what is said.
6. Provide children with opportunities for following directions.
7. Provide children with good models of standard English, and allow them to hear their home language in school.

Objectives for Expressive Language Development

1. Encourage children to pronounce words correctly.
2. Help children increase their speaking vocabularies.
3. Encourage children to speak in complete sentences at appropriate stages in their development.
4. Give children opportunities to expand their use of various syntactic structures, such as adjectives, adverbs, prepositional phrases, dependent clauses, plurals, past tense, and possessives.
5. Encourage children to communicate with others so that they can be understood.

6. Give children the opportunity to use language socially and psychologically by interpreting feelings, points of view, and motivation and by solving problems through generating hypotheses, summarizing events, and predicting outcomes.

7. Give children opportunities to develop language that involve mathematical and logical relations, such as describing size and amount, making comparisons, defining sets and classes, and reasoning deductively.

8. Provide children with the opportunity to talk in many different settings: in the whole group with the teacher leading the discussion, in teacher-led small groups, in child-directed groups for learning, or in conversation in social settings.

9. Give opportunities for children to use their own language freely at any stage of development. This could be a different dialect or mixtures of English and Spanish. Their desire to communicate should be encouraged, accepted, and respected.

Language is best learned when it is integrated with other communication skills and embedded within topics or content areas that have meaning and function for children. Children are constructive learners; they are active meaning makers who are continuously interpreting and making sense of their world based on what they already know.

Language is the major system by which meanings are communicated and expressed in our world. Language is best understood when it is related to some meaningful context. Language is learned through use, as part of our daily social activities. In addition to being aware of all these things, we need to accept language differences and help youngsters with special needs acquire skills and develop, enhance, and practice language. (Au, 1998).

Strategies for Language Development from Birth to Two

Providing children with rich sources of new words in storybook reading, for example, will develop receptive language and vocabulary.

"Hi, James. How's my great big boy today? Let's change your diaper now, Upsy-daisy. My goodness, you're getting heavy. Now I'll put you down right here on your dressing table and get a nice new diaper for you. Here, want this rubber ducky to hold while I change you? That's a good boy. You really like him. You're really yucky; let's clean you up now. This is the way we clean up James, clean up James, clean up James. This is the way we clean up James, so he'll feel so much better. You like that singing, don't you. I can tell. You're just smiling away, and cooing. Want to do that again? This is the way we clean up James, clean up James, clean up James. This is the way we clean up James, so he'll feel so much better. Wow, you were singing with me that time. That's right, ahhh-ahhh-ahh, now do it again. Mmmmm, doesn't that smell good? The baby lotion is so nice and smooth."

DEVELOPING LANGUAGE IN THE CHILD'S FIRST YEAR. My grandbaby, James, was four months old when I had that conversation with him. In print, it reads like a monologue; in reality, James was a very active participant in the conversation. He stared intently at me. He cooed, he waved his arms, he smiled, and he became serious. I was providing a rich language environment for him. I encouraged his participation in the dialogue and acknowledged his responsiveness in a positive way. I provided him with the environmental stimuli necessary for his language to flourish. I engaged him in this type of conversation during feedings and while changing, bathing, and dressing him. I talked to him even when he was in his crib and I was in another room, or while in the same room but involved in other things. The baby knew that communication was occurring because he responded to the talk with body movements, coos, babbles, and smiles. When he responded, I responded in turn.

Surround Infants with Sounds. Infants need to be surrounded by the sounds of happy language. Whether from mother, father, or caregiver at home, or a teacher or aide in a child-care center, sounds and interaction should accompany all activities. Adults responsible for babies from birth through the first year need to know nursery rhymes, chants, finger plays, and songs. It is important for children to hear the *sounds* of language as well as the meanings. Thus, adults can make up their own chants to suit an occasion, as I did when I spontaneously adapted "Here We Go Round the Mulberry Bush" while changing my grandson's diaper. Such experiences make the baby conscious of the sounds of language. Children learn that they can have control over language and that oral language can be a powerful tool as well as fun.

In addition to the conversation of nearby adults, infants should experience other sounds and other voices, such as lots of different kinds of music, including classical, jazz, popular, and so on. Babies need to hear the sounds of "book language," which differs in intonation, pitch, stress, juncture, and even syntax from normal conversation. They need familiarity with language in all its variety so they can learn to differentiate among its various conventions and patterns. Speaking to infants, singing to them, reading to them, and letting them hear the radio and television provide sources of language that help their own language grow. In addition, there are sounds in the immediate environment that need no preparation and are not the sounds of language but that provide practice in auditory discrimination—the doorbell ringing, the teapot hissing, the clock chiming, the vacuum cleaner humming, a dog barking, a bird singing, a car screeching, and so on. Bring them to the baby's attention, give them names, and heighten the child's sensitivity to them.

Surround Infants with Sensory Objects. In addition to hearing a variety of sounds, babies need objects to see, touch, smell, hear, and taste. Objects should be placed in the baby's immediate environment—the crib or playpen. They will stimulate the baby's activity and curiosity and become the meaningful things within the environment from which language evolves. Some of the objects should make sounds or music when pushed or touched. They can have different textures and smells. They should be easy to grab, push, kick, or pull. They can be placed so they are visible and within the child's reach, and at least one item should be suspended overhead: stuffed animals, rubber toys, music boxes made of soft material, mobiles that can be kicked or grasped, mobiles that hang from the ceiling and rotate by themselves, and cardboard or cloth books with smooth edges. Books can be propped open against the side of the crib or playpen when the baby is lying on its back, or against the headboard when the baby is on its stomach.

Certain familiar objects should always remain, and new objects frequently should be made available. In addition to allowing the child to play independently with these objects, the adults in charge need to talk about them, name them, occasionally join the child in playing with them, and discuss their characteristics.

From 3 to 6 to 12 months, the baby gurgles, coos, begins to laugh, and babbles. Adults or caregivers should recognize an infant's sounds as the beginning of language and reinforce the infant positively with responses aimed at encouraging the sounds. When the baby begins to put consonants and vowels together, again adults should reinforce the behavior, imitating what the baby has uttered and urging repetition. When the babies become aware of the ability to repeat sounds and control language output, they will do these things. Babies also will begin to understand adult language, so it is important to name objects, carry on conversations, and give the baby directions. At the end of its first year, assuming he or she has experienced appropriate sounds of language as well as encouragement and pleasant interaction, the baby will be on the verge of extensive language growth during its second year.

LANGUAGE DEVELOPMENT AT AGES ONE AND TWO. Through the second year of a child's life, the adults in charge need to continue the same kinds of stimulation suggested for developing oral language during the first year. However, because the baby is likely to develop a vocabulary of up to 150 words and to produce two- and possibly three-word sentences during the second year, additional techniques can be used to enhance language growth. As described earlier, one- and two-word utterances by children at this age usually represent sentences. When a 12-month-old points to a teddy bear and says "bear," the child probably means "I want my bear." Parents and caregivers at home or in child-care centers can begin to expand and extend the child's language by helping increase the number of words the child is able to use in a sentence or by increasing the syntactic complexity of their own utterances.

Scaffolding to Help Language Develop. One method for helping a child develop language ability is a kind of modeling called **scaffolding** (Applebee & Langer, 1983). In scaffolding, an adult provides a verbal response for a baby who is not yet capable of making the response itself. In other words, the adult provides a language model. When the baby says "bear," for instance, the adult responds, "Do you want your teddy bear?" or "Here is your nice, soft, brown teddy bear." In addition to expanding on the child's language, the adult can extend it by asking the youngster to do something that demonstrates understanding and extends his or her thinking. For example, "Here is your nice, soft, brown teddy bear. Can you hug the teddy? Let me see you hug him." In addition to questions that require action, the adult can ask questions that require answers. Questions that require answers of more than one word are preferable—for example, "Tell me about the clothes your teddy is wearing." *How, why,* and *tell me* questions encourage the child to give more than a yes/no answer and more than a one-word response. *What, who, when,* and *where* questions, however, tend to elicit only one-word replies. As the child's language ability develops, the adult provides fewer and fewer such "scaffolds"; the child learns to build utterances along similar models.

New Experiences Help Develop Language. Adults should select songs, rhymes, and books for one- to two-year-olds that use language they can understand. They are capable of understanding a great deal of language by now, and the selections should help expand and extend their language. Both vocabulary and conceptual understanding are enhanced by experiences. For the one- to two-year-old, frequent outings such as visits to the post office, supermarket, dry cleaners, and park provide experiences to talk about and new concepts to explore. Household tasks taken for granted by adults are new experiences that enrich children's language. Adults should involve toddlers in activities. For example, an 18-month-old can put a piece of laundry into the washing machine or give one stir to the bowl of food being prepared. During such daily routines, adults should surround the activity with language, identifying new objects for the baby and asking for responses related to each activity (Hart & Risley, 1999).

Overgeneralizations and Language Development.   As children become more verbal, adults sometimes want to correct their mispronunciations or overgeneralization of grammatical rules. The child who says, "Me feeded fishes," for instance, has simply overgeneralized the rules for the following:

> Forming most past tenses (*feeded* for *fed*)
> Using pronouns (objective *me* for subjective *I*)
> Forming most plurals (*fishes* for *fish*)

Children also can overgeneralize concepts. A child who has learned to associate a bird with the word *bird* might see a butterfly for the first time and call it a bird, thinking that anything that flies is a bird. Correcting such an overgeneralization is best done positively rather than negatively. Instead of saying, "No, that's not a bird," it is better to refer to the butterfly as a *butterfly,* commenting on its beauty, perhaps, and thus expanding the child's verbal repertoire. Eventually, with positive reinforcement and proper role models in language, the child will differentiate between birds and butterflies as well as between regular and irregular grammatical conventions and forms.

Correcting overgeneralizations negatively as absolute error, alternatively, is not likely to help young children understand the error or use proper tense and plural forms. Rather, it is likely to inhibit the child from trying to use language. In learning, children need to take risks and make mistakes. Hearing good adult models will eventually enable them to internalize the rules of language and to correct their errors themselves. At least until age five, children should be allowed to experiment and play with language without direct concern for 100 percent correctness in syntax and pronunciation. The English language is extremely complex and irregular in many of its rules; in time, children will master these rules in all their complexity, if they have good adult models and plenty of verbal interaction. At the same time, encouraging "baby talk" simply because it is cute, for instance, is likely to inhibit growth because children will use whatever language they believe will please the adults around them.

Materials for Language Development at One and Two.   Materials for the one- to two-year-old should be varied and more sophisticated than those in the first year. Now that the baby is mobile in the home or child-care center, books need to be easily accessible to the child. Toys should still include items of various textures, such as furry, stuffed animals and rubber balls. Other toys should require simple eye—hand coordination. Three-to-five—piece puzzles, trucks that can be pushed and pulled, dolls, a child-size set of table and chairs, crayons and large paper, and puppets are examples. Choose objects that require activity, for activity encourages exploration, use of the imagination, creation, and the need to communicate. The number of books in a child's library should be increasing. Those they are allowed to handle and use alone should still be made of cloth or cardboard.

Strategies for Language Development in Early Childhood Classrooms

From ages three to eight a great deal of language development occurs. Children should continue to hear good models of language. They need constant opportunities to use language in social situations with adults and other children. Their oral language production must be reinforced positively. They must be actively involved in meaningful experiences that will expand their knowledge and interest in the world around them. Language should be purposeful and its development integrated with other subjects rather than taught separately.

To accomplish these continuing goals, early childhood teachers provide an environment in which language will flourish. They organize centers of learning, one for each content area, that include materials for encouraging language use. A science center, for instance, can include class pets such as a pair of gerbils. Gerbils are active, loving animals that are fun to watch and handle. Children surround the cage often and generate talk just from watching the animals. Gerbils reproduce in 28-day cycles. When litters arrive, the birth process can be observed. The new babies cause much excitement and generate questions, comments, and unlimited conversation.

In my own classroom, our parent gerbils reproduced a second litter 28 days after the first and before the first babies had been weaned. The mother looked tired and thin from feeding and caring for 10 baby gerbils. One morning one of the children noticed that the mother was not in the cage. We could not imagine what had happened to her. A few days later, we found her hiding behind the refrigerator in the teachers' room. We never figured out how she got out of the cage, but we hypothesized all kinds of possibilities, and there was lots of discussion about why she left. No teacher alone could provide a lesson in which language flourished and grew the way it did during that incident, simply because gerbils were part of the classroom.

 CENTER MATERIALS FOR LANGUAGE DEVELOPMENT. Here are some examples of learning centers and appropriate materials in early childhood classrooms that will help generate language:

Science: aquarium, terrarium, plants, magnifying glass, class pet, magnets, thermometer, compass, prism, shells, rock collections, stethoscope, kaleidoscope, microscope, informational books and children's literature reflecting topics being studied, and blank journals for recording observations of experiments and scientific projects.

Social Studies: maps, a globe, flags, community figures, traffic signs, current events, artifacts from other countries, informational books and children's literature reflecting topics being studied, and writing materials to make class books or your own books about topics being studied.

Art: easels, watercolors, brushes, colored pencils, crayons, felt-tip markers, various kinds of paper, scissors, paste, pipe cleaners, scrap materials (bits of various fabrics, wool, string, and so forth), clay, play dough, food and detergent boxes for sculptures, books about famous artists, and books with directions for crafts.

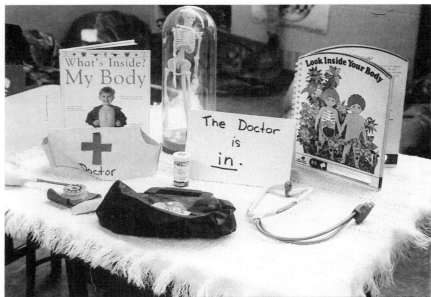

Experiences with science themes lead to new discoveries, new vocabulary, and reasons to talk and discuss.

Music: piano, guitar, or other real instruments, CD and or tape players, and tapes and CDs of all types of music, rhythm instruments, songbooks, and photocopies of sheet music for songs sung in class.

Mathematics: scales, rulers, measuring cups, movable clocks, stopwatch, calendar, play money, cash register, calculator, dominoes, abacus, number line, height chart, hourglass, numbers (felt, wood, and magnetic), fraction puzzles, geometric shapes, math workbooks, children's literature about numbers and mathematics, writing materials for creating stories, and books related to mathematics.

Literacy: multiple genres of children's literature, CD players or tape recorders, headsets and stories on tape or CDs, pencils, writing paper, stapler, construction paper, three-by-five cards for recording words, hole punch, letter stencils, computer, puppets, storytelling devices such as felt-board and roll movies, stationery with envelopes, letters (felt, wood, and magnetic) and letter chunks for building words, sets of pictures for different units (seasons, animals, space exploration, and so on), rhyme games, color games, cards for associating sounds and symbols, alphabet cards, and pictures and words representing out-of-school environmental print. (The literacy center also includes a library corner, a writing center, oral language materials, and language arts manipulatives, all of which are described in later chapters.)

Dramatic Play: dolls, dress-ups, telephone, stuffed animals, mirror, food cartons, plates, silverware, newspapers, magazines, books, telephone book, class telephone book, cookbook, notepads, cameras and photo album, table and chairs, broom, dustpan, child-size kitchen furniture such as refrigerator, sink, ironing board, and storage shelves. (The dramatic-play area can be changed from a kitchen to a grocery store, beauty shop, gas station, business office, restaurant, and the like, with the addition of materials for appropriate themes when they are studied.) Include appropriate materials for reading and writing related to the theme of the dramatic-play area.

Block Area: blocks of many different sizes, shapes, and textures, figures of people, animals, toy cars, trucks, items related to themes being studied, paper and pencils to prepare signs and notes, and reading materials related to themes.

Workbench: wood, corrugated cardboard, hammer, scissors, screwdriver, saw, pliers, nails, glue, tape, and work table.

Outdoor Play: sand, water, pails, shovels, rakes, gardening area and gardening tools, climbing equipment, riding toys, crates, playhouse, balls, tires, and ropes.

Children need opportunities to use such areas for interacting with one another and the teacher. They should be given enough time to touch, smell, taste, listen, and talk about what they are doing. Exploring and experimenting with the materials in the centers are creative, imaginative, problem-solving, decision-making experiences in which children use language. The opportunity to *use* language is one of the key elements in language development.

Some materials remain permanently in the centers; others are replaced or supplemented occasionally so that new items of interest become available. Materials added to the centers are often coordinated with thematic units of instruction. For example, if a unit on Native Americans is introduced, Native American dolls and artifacts are added to the social studies center, and books about Native Americans to the literacy center. The different content-area centers provide sources for language use and development; the literacy center is devoted *primarily* to language development. Thematic units of instruction that integrate all areas make learning more meaningful and expand concepts. (Interdisciplinary instruction is described more fully in Chapter 9.)

 DEVELOPING LANGUAGE WITH STRATEGIES USED IN THEMATIC UNITS. Each new unit of instruction offers specific language experiences that expand vocabulary and develop syntax, pronunciation, and the ability to understand others and be understood. Again, these experiences should incorporate all content areas and make use of the senses (Tompkins & Koskisson, 1995). The suggestions that follow can be used each time a new theme is initiated. They reflect or describe activities designed to aid language growth in early childhood classrooms. For purposes of illustration, assume that the topic throughout these suggestions is *winter*.

Discussion: Hold discussions about the unit topic. What is the weather like in winter? What kind of clothing do children need to wear in winter? What fun things can they do in winter that they can not do at other times of the year? What problems does winter bring? What is winter like in different parts of the country, for example, New York, Florida, and California?

Word Lists: Ask the children to name words that makes them think of winter. Your list might include

snow, ice, cold, white, wet, freezing, sleds, snowman, mittens, scarf, hat, slush, skiing, ice skating, snowballs, fireplace, and *snowflakes*

Classify the words on the list into how winter feels, looks, smells, sounds, and tastes, or what you can and cannot do in winter. List the words on a chart, and hang the chart in the room. Leave the chart hanging when you go to the next unit. When the wall gets too crowded, compile the charts in a class book.

Pictures: Provide pictures of winter scenes for discussion, each depicting different information about the season

Sharing Time (Show and Tell): Hold a sharing period during which children bring things from home related to the topic. Give all the children an opportunity to share if they wish, but assign different children for different days, because sharing by more than five or six children in one period can become tedious. Sharing objects from home is an important activity. It gives children confidence because they are talking about something from their own environment. Even the shyest children will speak in front of a group if they have the security of sharing something familiar from home. Encourage children to relate the items to the unit topic, if they can. Model language for children to encourage them to speak in sentences. Coordinate the activity with parents, informing them of their children's scheduled sharing and the general topic under discussion.

Experiments: Carry out a science experiment related to the topic being studied. Involve the children actively. Discuss the purpose and hypothesize what

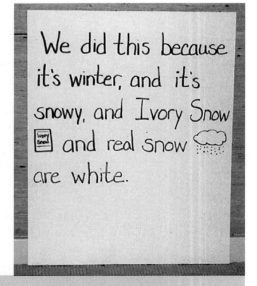

Experiences related to themes generate oral language that can be written down and then read.

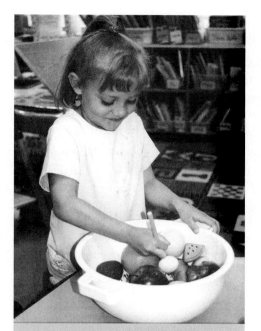

Food preparation can be a source of new vocabulary, especially because many of its terms take on special meanings—*stir, blend, boil, measure.*

is likely to happen. Encourage children to discuss what they are doing while they are doing it. When the experiment is complete, discuss the results with the class. (Example: Allow water to freeze, then melt. In warm climates use the refrigerator for freezing the water.)

Art: Carry out an art activity related to the topic. Allow children to create their own work rather than making them follow specific directions that yield identical results. Discuss the project and the available materials before the activity. Provide materials that children will want to touch, describe, and compare. While children are creating, encourage conversation about what they are doing. For example, provide blue construction paper, tinfoil, white doilies, cotton, wool, tissue paper, and chalk for a winter collage. Discuss why these colors and objects were selected. What is there about them that makes people think of winter? Suggest creating a picture that makes one think of winter. Discuss the textures of the materials and what can be done with them.

Music: Sing songs about winter, such as "It's a Marshmallow World in the Winter." Music is enjoyable, and lyrics help build vocabulary and sensitivity to the sounds and meanings of words. Listen to music without words, music that creates images concerning the topic. Ask the children for words, sentences, or stories that the music brings to mind.

Food Preparation: Prepare food related to the unit. Make hot soup, flavored snowballs, or popcorn. Discuss food textures, smells, taste, and appearance. Follow recipe directions, thus learning about sequencing and quantity. Allow children to help prepare the food, enjoy eating it together, encouraging discussion and conversation throughout. Food preparation can be a source of new vocabulary, especially because many of its terms take on special meanings—*stir, blend, boil, measure, dice,* and so on.

Dramatic Play: Add items related to the topic to the dramatic-play area—mittens, hats, scarves, boots for dress-up—to encourage role-playing and language about winter. Introduce the items by placing each in a separate bag and asking a child to reach in, describe what it feels like, and identify it without peeking. The sense of touch elicits descriptive language.

Outdoor Play: Encourage spontaneous language and frequent problem-solving situations during outdoor play. For example, provide snow shovels, sleds, pails, and cups during playtime in the snow. Discuss outdoor play before going out, and again after coming in.

Morning Message: Discuss weather and the calendar in a daily morning message. Encourage children to share news about themselves: a new pair of sneakers, a birthday. Make plans for the school day.

Class Trips: Take the class on a trip, bring in a guest speaker, or show a film. All three activities can generate language and encourage its use.

Read Stories: Read stories to the children about the topic under study. Books such as *Katy and the Big Snow* (Burton, 1943) enhance information and expand vocabulary.

Create Stories: Provide the children with a title, such as "The Big Winter Snowstorm," and let them think of a story about it.

Retell Stories: Ask children to retell stories. This activity encourages them to use book language and incorporate it into their own. Retelling is not always an easy task for young children, so props can be helpful—puppets, felt boards and felt characters, roll movies, and pictures in a book. With these same props, children can make up their own stories as well.

Very Own Vocabulary Words: In any of these activities, children should be encouraged as often as possible to select their favorite Very Own Words about winter. Favorite Very Own Words can be selected from discussions, art lessons, science experiments, songs, books, poems, cooking experiences, or any other activity. After a particular experience, ask children to name a favorite word. Record children's favorite Very Own Words for them on three-by-five cards and store them in each child's own file box or on a binder ring. When children are capable of recording their own words, assist them with spelling when they ask for help. Favorite Very Own Words enhance vocabulary and are a source for reading and writing development.

Word Walls: As the class learns new words that are especially related to themes, the teacher can place them on a word wall for use. Word walls have many purposes. They are mostly for reading grade-level high-frequency words. These words should be separated from the new vocabulary-themed words by color. That is, all high-frequency words may be in red, all new thematic words in blue. The new vocabulary on the word wall is used in different activities, such as alphabetizing words or using them in sentences and stories.

Summary of the Day: Summarize the day's events at the end of the school day, encouraging children to tell what they liked, did not like, and want to do the next day in school.

 CHILDREN'S LITERATURE AND LANGUAGE DEVELOPMENT. Among more general suggestions, select and offer children's literature that represents varieties of language and experience. Some children's books, such as *Too Much Noise* (McGovern, 1967), feature the sounds of language; they aid auditory discrimination or incorporate additional phonemes into a child's language repertoire. Others help develop the syntactic complexity of a child's language through embeddings and transformations and the use of numerous adjectives and adverbs—for example, *Swimmy* (Lionni, 1963). Craft books require children to follow directions. Wordless books encourage them to create their own stories from the pictures. Concept books feature words such as *up, down, in, out, near,* and *far,* or involve children in mathematical reasoning. Realistic literature deals with death, divorce, loneliness, fear, and daily problems; discussion of such themes leads to sociopsychological language, interpretation of feelings, sensitivity to others, and problem solving. Books of riddles, puns, jokes, and tongue twisters show children how language plays on meaning in certain situations. Poetry introduces children to rhyme, metaphor, simile, and onomatopoeia, and encourages them to recite and create poems. (Children's books are listed by these and other categories in Appendix A.) When children hear and discuss the language of books, they internalize what they have heard; the language soon becomes part of their own language. Research studies have found that children who are read to frequently develop more sophisticated language structures and increased vocabulary (Beck & McKeown, 2001).

Two anecdotes illustrate how children incorporate into their own language the language of books that have been read to them. My kindergarten class was playing on the playground one early spring day. A few birds circled around several times. Melissa ran up to me and said, "Look, Mrs. Morrow, the birds are fluttering and flapping around the playground." Surprised at first by Melissa's descriptive and unusual choice of words, I thought for a moment, then remembered. The words that Melissa was using came directly from a picture storybook we had read shortly before, *Jenny's Hat* (Keats, 1966). In the book, birds *flutter* and *flap* around Jenny's hat. Melissa had internalized the language of the book and was able to use it in her own vocabulary.

One day after a big snowstorm, my daughter asked, "Mommy, can I go out and play? I want to build a smiling snowman." I was surprised and pleased with this sophisticated language being uttered by my four-year-old. *Smiling snowman,* after all, represents a participle in the adjective position, a syntactic structure usually not found in the language of children before the age of seven or eight. Then I noticed that Stephanie had a book in her hand, *The Snowy Day* (Keats, 1962). In it Peter goes outside and builds a *smiling snowman.* Stephanie had used the book's language and made it her own.

The activities just suggested can be repeated throughout the school year with each new theme that is studied. Such adaptation and repetition make it possible to introduce children to hundreds of new vocabulary words, concepts, and ideas. They will assure children of opportunities to participate in new kinds of spontaneous language as topics and structured experiences change. Word lists and other materials produced during each unit can be maintained and made available for review and reuse.

Most of the suggestions can be followed at home as well as at school. Parents should not be expected to create elaborate centers or carry out units of instruction. But daily living offers holidays, seasons, family events, and other topics and events of special interest. Parents can tap such meaningful occasions for their potential enhancement of language development. They can discuss events, list

A felt board with story characters helps children use book language as they retell stories.

words, help children collect favorite Very Own Words, involve children in cooking and household chores, take trips, read stories, sing songs, and generally encourage the use of language as a pleasurable activity and a useful skill.

In the learning environment described throughout this chapter, language development is spontaneous and also encouraged. Modeling, scaffolding, and reinforcement make this environment interactive between child and adult, and they guide and nurture language development to an extent that children are not likely to achieve on their own. The strategies discussed are appropriate for children who have language differences and minimal language disorders. These youngsters, however, may need additional attention on a one-to-one basis from the classroom teacher or a resource room teacher.

Expanding Vocabulary and Word Meaning in Second and Third Grades

I have suggested many strategies to develop vocabulary for children from birth through the early childhood grades. Following are strategies for children in second and third grades to help them increase their vocabulary and make connections with the meaning of words when reading text. These strategies also should enhance vocabulary used in their writing.

Semantic Maps: Semantic maps are diagrams that help children see how words are related to one another (Johnson & Pearson, 1984). To enrich vocabulary development and the meaning of words try the following:

1. Choose a word related to a student's interests or a theme that is being studied.
2. Write the word on a chalkboard or a piece of experience chart paper.
3. Brainstorm other words that are related to the key word.
4. Create categories for the new words that emerge and classify them into those categories (see Figure 4.1).
5. Use the words to create a story (Cox, 2002).

Context Clues: Using clues from surrounding text is an important way of figuring out word meanings. Leaving blanks in sentences for children to determine

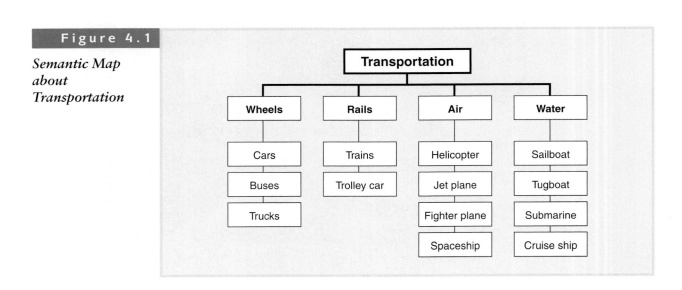

Figure 4.1

Semantic Map about Transportation

the appropriate word is an activity that helps them understand how to use context to find word meanings. Just looking to other words in a sentence to determine meaning is helpful as well. Students need to know that this is one of the best ways to learn new words because they are embedded in meaningful text. The clues they use are other words or phrases in the sentence that tell something about unknown words. Clues can be before or after the unknown word and are usually close to the word. They could also be in sentences before or after. Have students guess the meaning of the word from the clues, then discuss if the guesses are correct. The following sentence is from the book *Swimmy* by Leo Lionni. There are unusual words used that can be grasped from the words surrounding the more difficult ones:

> *"One bad day a tuna fish fierce swift and very hungry came _____ through the waves."*

> *The teacher left a blank in the sentence for a word that was difficult, but could be figured out. It was for the word* darting. *She read the sentence to the children with the blank and asked what word they thought fit there. They suggested that the word could be* swimming, rushing, shooting out, jumping, pushing. *None said* darting, *since it was not familiar to them. The teacher praised their choices and put in the word* darting *from the story. She asked the children what they thought it meant. They agreed it meant* pushing, shooting out, *and maybe* rushing, *which were words that they had already generated and that defined the unknown word* darting.

Vocabulary Books: Children can keep a new vocabulary book for the school year. There is a pattern to the book. The new word is written in the middle of the page. A synonym for the word is written in the upper right-hand corner, its definition in the upper left-hand corner. The student writes a sentence using the word, along with an illustration, in the lower left-hand corner. In the lower right-hand corner, the student chooses a classification for the word (e.g., a *poodle* is a dog, *orange* is a color). This book grows throughout the year as new words are added

Word Parts: Learning word parts is a way for second and third graders to build vocabulary and meaning. Choose word parts that are well-known prefixes and suffixes and commonly used roots of words. With knowledge of a few of these, children can begin to build their own words. Teach children to talk through the use of word parts to get the meaning. For example, when students learn word-part meanings they can talk through their word building as follows: "I know that the prefix *dis* means "not," and I also know that the word *content* means to be happy or pleased. If I add *dis* to the word *content* it would be *discontent*. Now it would mean that someone was not happy.

The Dictionary: Using the dictionary is another way to add to a student's repertoire of strategies to find and check meanings. Students must learn that words have many meanings, and they may all be listed in the dictionary. Therefore, when using the dictionary, they need to select the meaning for the word that makes sense in the context in which it occurs. Dictionaries prepared for young children should be used in the primary grades (Graves, Juel, & Graves, 1998).

Vocabulary-rich second- and third-grade classrooms have many materials to enrich language and vocabulary development. These classrooms, like those in earlier grades, should display new words and have many dictionaries. In the library corner, there are riddle books, joke books, and books with puns. There are many genres of children's literature, such as fiction and nonfiction. There are word games such as Boggle, Pictionary, Scrabble, and crossword puzzles (Blachowicz & Fisher, 2002).

Formats for Promoting Language and Vocabulary Development in the Classroom

By the time children come to school, they have had varied opportunities for talk in their daily lives. Most of the talk is spontaneous and deals with real-life experiences. With their parents, talk has included questions and answers, with parents directing the discussion or the children playing a more active role. I have discussed strategies that initiate talk. Here I will offer organizational structures in classrooms that will provide different types of talk experiences. These include teacher-directed question and answer discussions, small-group conversations to give and receive information, and spontaneous discussions that are led by the teacher or children in social settings. In addition, conversations that include different types of talk will be described.

In **structured question and answer discussions**, teachers need to provide open-ended questions that will encourage talk such as, "What would happen if?" "What would you do if?" and "Tell us why?"

Conversations occur best in small-group settings that include three to six children. Any number beyond that can no longer be considered a conversation but rather a large-group discussion. Guidelines, such as those below, need to be established for conversation to be productive.

Informal Conversations without the Teacher

Children need time to talk without leaders or specific outcomes. This type of conversation is likely to occur during free-play periods, center time, or outdoor play. Although classrooms that encourage this type of talk can be noisy, it is important for children to have the opportunity to use language in social settings at school.

Guidelines   *Small-Group Conversations with the Teacher*

1. **Children should listen to others during conversations.**

2. **Children need to take turns talking.**

3. **Students should raise hands, if necessary to ensure everyone gets a turn, and individuals do not interrupt each other.**

4. **Everyone should keep talk relevant to the topic of conversation.**

5. **Teachers need to help redirect conversation to its stated purpose, should it stray.**

6. **Teacher talk should be kept to a minimum as the teacher becomes a participant. Teachers should follow the same rules as the children: Listen to others when they are talking, take turns, do not do all the talking, and so on.**

☀ Guidelines *Formal Conversations without the Teacher*

A group leader needs to be selected to help direct the conversation when children are in charge of their own discussion. All of the same guidelines for productive conversation when the teacher is present apply when children direct conversations themselves.

1. **Children should listen to others during conversations.**

2. **Children need to take turns talking.**

3. **Students should raise hands, if necessary.**

4. **Everyone should keep the talk relevant to the conversation's purpose.**

In addition to learning the types of organizational structures in which talk should take place, students need to engage in different types of talk including aesthetic talk, efferent talk, and talk in dramatic activities.

Aesthetic talk typically revolves around children's literature. In this talk children have the opportunity to interpret what they have read or listened to. Children can participate in aesthetic talk when discussing literature, telling stories, and participating in Readers Theater. These activities will be discussed further in Chapter 8, which deals with using children's literature in the classroom.

Efferent talk is used to inform and persuade. Efferent talk occurs in discussion of themes being studied. It also occurs in situations such as show-and-tell, oral reports, interviews, and debates. These types of interchange are more formal than previously discussed and often require preparation on the part of the child.

Dramatic activities provide another avenue for different types of talk. When children participate in dramatic activities, they share experiences, explore their understanding of ideas, and interact with peers. Dramatic experiences can include informal role playing in dramatic-play areas of the classroom. Use of props and puppets to act out stories provides another avenue for talk.

A teacher who uses these organizational frameworks for language and has children engage in the types of activities that motivate talk will be providing a classroom rich in experiences and topics to talk about. In turn, language development will be enhanced.

Assessment of Children's Language Development

It is important to assess children's language to determine if it follows expected stages of development. Assessment also determines how much a child has progressed. The word *assessment* suggests several rather frequent measures by which to judge progress. Assessment should reflect instructional objectives and

Children should be encouraged to engage in conversation as they work together in small groups.

strategies. It should include evaluation of a wide range of skills used in many contexts. A certain child, for example, may perform better in an interview than on a pencil-and-paper test. Both kinds of evaluation, therefore, should be used. Literacy includes a wide range of skills; it is important to evaluate a child for as many as possible to determine strengths and weaknesses. Unfortunately, many assessment instruments are quite narrow in scope and frequently do not measure a child's total abilities.

There are several ways to measure children's language development in early childhood, which are similar to these used for measuring literacy development described in Chapter 2. *Checklists* are practical because they provide concise outlines for teachers and appropriate slots for individual children. They are most effective if used periodically during the school year. Three to four evaluations during the year can provide sufficient data to determine progress. Program objectives offer criteria to include on checklists.

✔ **C h e c k l i s t**   *Assessing Language Development*

Child's name _____   **Date** _____

	Always	Sometimes	Never	Comments
Makes phoneme sounds				
Speaks in one-word sentences				
Speaks in two-word sentences				
Identifies familiar sounds				
Differentiates similar sounds				
Understands the language of others when spoken to				
Follows verbal directions				
Speaks to others freely				
Pronounces words correctly				
Has appropriate vocabulary for level of maturity				
Speaks in complete sentences				
Uses varied syntactic structures				
Can be understood by others				

Teacher Comments:

Anecdotal records are another form of language assessment. They tend to be time consuming but can reveal rich information. Loose-leaf notebooks and file cards offer two means for keeping anecdotal records. These records require no particular format. Rather, the teacher or parent simply writes down incidents or episodes on the days they occur. Samples of a child's language and situations involving language can be recorded. Like checklists, anecdotal samples are necessary periodically to determine growth over a school year.

Tape recordings are another means of evaluating language. The process can take the form of an open interview or a hidden recording. (Videotaping equipment can serve the same purpose but may not be readily available in most early childhood classrooms.) Children who are unaware that their conversation is being recorded are likely to be more spontaneous and uninhibited (Genishi & Dyson, 1984). It is often difficult, however, to place a tape recorder where it will record language clearly enough to transcribe and analyze. Interviews with children can be more natural when an adult familiar to the child does the interviewing. Or it is also helpful to allow the tape recorder to become such a familiar tool in the classroom that the child uses it often in the language arts center. Under such circumstances the machine is not threatening when used in an assessment interview.

To record samples of natural language, discuss the child's experiences. Ask about home, favorite games or toys, favorite TV programs, brothers and sisters, trips taken, or birthday parties recently attended. You should try to collect a corpus of spontaneous language that provides a typical sample of the child's ability with language.

Tape assessment samples three or four times a year. Let children hear their own recorded voices and enjoy the experience. Then, for assessment purposes, transcribe the tapes and analyze them for such items as numbers of words uttered and numbers of words spoken in a single connected utterance (for example, "Tommy's cookie" or "Me want water"). The lengths of such utterances can be averaged to determine mean length. Length of utterance is considered a measure of complexity. When children begin to speak in conventional sentences, such as "That is my cookie," measure the length of the t-units. A **t-unit** is an independent clause with all its dependent clauses attached, assuming it has dependent clauses. It can be a simple or a complex sentence. Compound sentences are made up of two t-units. Length of t-units, like length of utterances, is a measure of language complexity. It typically increases with the user's age, and usually the more words per unit, the more complex the unit (Hunt, 1970).

Further analysis of taped utterances and t-units can determine which elements of language a child uses—number of adjectives, adverbs, dependent clauses, negatives, possessives, passives, plurals, and so on. The more complex the transformations, embeddings, and syntactic elements used, the more complex the language overall (Morrow, 1978). Data from several samples over a year can be most revealing.

The following is a verbatim transcription of a taped language sample from a seven-year-old boy in the second grade. The child was presented with a picture book and asked to tell a story from the pictures.

he's getting up in the morning and he's looking out the window with his cat and after he gets out of bed he brushes his teeth then when he gets done brushing his teeth, he eats he eats breakfast and then when he after he eats breakfast he he gets dressed to play some games then in the afternoon he plays with his toys then in the afternoon he plays doctor and early in the day he plays cowboys and Indians then when it's in the afternoon close to suppertime he plays cops and robbers when he's playing in his castle he likes to dream of a magic carpet he's driving his ship on the waves he's uh circus uh ringmaster he's lifting up a fat lady I mean a clown is standing on a horse a clown is on a high wire somebody fell and then hurt their head the cowboy is bringing some ice cream to the hurt man that night he goes in the bathroom and gets washed and then he goes to bed then he dreams I don't know what he's dreaming I will think of what he's dreaming he's dreaming of going to play and he's playing the same things over

After the sample is transcribed, the language is segmented into t-units. Following is a sample of the segmented sample of t-units:

1. He's getting up in the morning.
2. And he's looking out the window with his cat.
3. And after he gets out of bed, he brushes his teeth.
4. Then when he gets done brushing his teeth, he eats.
5. He eats breakfast.
6. And then (when he) after he eats breakfast he (he) gets dressed to play some games.
7. Then in the afternoon he plays with his toys.
8. Then in the afternoon he plays doctor.
9. And early in the day he plays cowboys and Indians.
10. Then when it's in the afternoon close to suppertime he plays cops and robbers.
11. When he's playing in his castle he likes to dream of a magic carpet.
12. He's driving his ship on the waves.
13. He's (uh) circus (uh) ringmaster.
14. He's lifting up a fat lady.
15. I mean a clown is standing on a horse.
16. A clown is on a high wire.
17. Somebody fell and then hurt their head.
18. The cowboy is bringing some ice cream to the hurt man.
19. That night he goes in the bathroom and gets washed.
20. And then he goes to bed.
21. Then he dreams.
22. I don't know what he's dreaming.
23. I will think of what he's dreaming.
24. He's dreaming of going to play.
25. And he's playing the same things over.

I have discussed oral language separately from the other communication skills in this chapter in order to describe its developmental stages and the theories of how it is acquired. This separation is somewhat artificial, however, because oral language is as important to literacy development as are reading and writing. We know that communication skills develop concurrently, each helping the growth of the others. Coordination and integration of the several communication skills in a single program are described in Chapter 9.

■ Monthly Poetry Recital

My kindergarten class always enjoys our poetry recitals, which vastly improve their oral language skills. For this activity, select a poem from a themed poetry book like *Chicken Soup with Rice* (Sendak, 1962). Copy the poem onto chart paper or onto an overhead transparency. Recite the poem for the children while encouraging them to read along. Repeat short phrases of the poem in order to help them memorize the words. Have the children practice the poem each day for one week using expression and volume appropriate for public speaking. Have the students create props to go along with the poem. For example, for the February poem in *Chicken Soup with Rice,* have the children make soup bowls, cakes, boys, and snowmen. After they have colored and cut out their props, attach craft sticks in order to use them as stick puppets. When the poem has been practiced with the puppets, have the children visit the classrooms of one grade level in your school to share the poem. Each month the children can learn a new poem and visit a different grade level to share their poem.

Kimberly Knarr, Kindergarten Teacher

■ Using Props for Oral Language Development with English Language Learners

Children's books that lend themselves to storytelling with props are always beneficial to ELL students because the props make the language visual, hands-on, and specific. Some good stories to use with a first-grade class include *The Jacket I Wear in the Snow* (Neitzel, 1991), *A Letter to Amy* (Keats, 1968), and *Peter's Chair* (Keats, 1967). After first reading one of these stories aloud, have the children create or gather the props needed to tell the story. For example, after reading *The Jacket I Wear in the Snow* (Neitzel, 1991), discuss the articles of clothing that were mentioned in the story, and add to the list if necessary. Distribute the articles of clothing to the students so that each has one item. Read the story a second time. This time, pause when an article of clothing is mentioned in the story. Encourage the children to hold up their item and name it when it appears in the story. For example, you will read, "This is the (sweater) I wear in the snow." The child who has the sweater will hold it up and say "sweater." Encourage the children to join in by chanting the repetitive phrases and the names of the articles of clothing as they are repeated in the story. This activity can be adapted for any story that provides opportunities for hands-on materials and repetition. The class participation using these props allows ELL students to make a connection between a tangible, familiar object and its English name.

Gina A. Goble, ESL Teacher, Grades K–3

Activities and Questions

1. Answer the focus questions at the beginning of the chapter.

2. What strategies are good for teaching language and literacy skills to English language learners?

3. What cultural concerns do teachers need to recognize when teaching English language learners?

4. Select an objective for language development listed in the chapter. Prepare a lesson that will help a child achieve the goal. Identify the theories of language acquisition used in your lesson.

5. Tape-record children at play or working in a group. Identify which characteristics of their language can be described by various theories of language acquisition. For example, imitation could be explained by the behaviorist theory.

6. Begin a thematic unit that you will continue as you read this book. Select a social studies or science topic. Select three objectives for language development, and describe three activities that will satisfy each of the objectives using your theme. An example follows:

Content Area: Science

Theme: Creatures That Live in the Sea

Objective for Language Development: Develop new vocabulary

Activity: Read *Swimmy* by Leo Lionni. Ask the children to remember two new words they hear in the story. After reading, list words that the children mention on a chart, and discuss their meaning.

7. Observe a preschool, kindergarten, or first- or second-grade class for about three hours. Note the amount of time children are given to talk, the amount of time the teacher talks, and the amount of time during which there is no verbal interaction. Compare the three figures. Then classify talk in the classroom into the following categories:

    a. Questions and answers

    b. Whole-class discussion

    c. Small-group discussion led by the teacher

    d. Interactive discussion among children

    e. Interactive discussion between teacher and children

Based on the results of this ministudy, determine how often we allow children to use language, and in how many different contexts or situations.

8. Plan an activity that will elicit aesthetic talk and one that will involve efferent talk. How is the language in each setting the same, and how is it different?

9. Continue the collection of assessment materials for the child for which you began a portfolio in Chapter 2. Collect one language sample from a child age two through seven. Elicit the language by showing a picture to discuss or asking the child to talk about favorite TV shows, pets, friends, family members, or trips. Tape-record the sample and transcribe it.

a. Check the characteristics of the child's language development according to the descriptions in this chapter and the checklist provided to decide whether the child is above, below, or at a level appropriate to his or her age. Compare with other members of the class who have studied different age groups.

b. Divide your language sample into t-units and determine the average length per t-unit; then count the number and type of syntactic elements used. Compare your sample to someone else in the class who is working with a child of a different age.

c. Collect three additional language samples for the same child at different times in the year. Evaluate the new samples as you did the first time and check for growth.

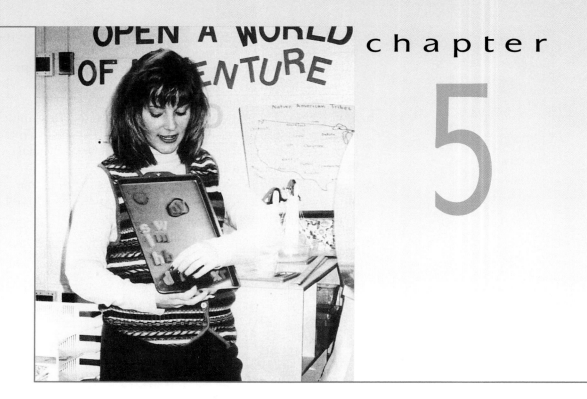

Strategies to Figure Out Words

*Phonological Awareness,
Phonemic Awareness,
and Phonics*

Young children are more interested in the functions *of literacy first and the form* later. *The first words a child says, reads, and writes are those with meaning and function in his or her life, such as family names, food labels, and road signs. After function, the child becomes interested in the* forms *of print, which includes names of letters and their sounds. Finally children learn* conventions *of print. This is the recognition that punctuation serves a purpose in reading and writing, and that spaces demarcate letters and words and words are written and read from left to right.*

—Frank Smith (1971)

Focus Questions

- Children demonstrate an interest in function, form, and then conventions of print. Discuss the implication of this statement for classroom instruction.
- Describe the concept of reading readiness.
- Define and describe how the use of the following strategies enhances a child's knowledge about print: (1) environmental print, (2) Very Own Words, (3) language experience approach, (4) context and picture clues, and (5) high-frequency words
- Define the following terms: (1) phonemic awareness, (2) phonological awareness, (3) alphabetic principle, (4) phonics, (5) phoneme–grapheme correspondence, (6) digraphs, (7) consonant blends, (8) long and short vowel sounds, and (9) inflectional endings.
- Describe the characteristics of commercially prepared materials designed for literacy instruction.

M rs. Abere's class was studying nutrition. The dramatic-play area was set up like a supermarket with products displayed separately in food groups: dairy products; breads and cereals; meat, poultry, and fish; and fruits and vegetables. To connect the learning of sound–symbol relationships and letter names with the unit, three letters were featured: *m* for meat, *f* for fish, and *d* for dairy. In addition to creating funny stories using the featured letters such as *Fanny the Fish was a Friendly Flounder who liked to Flip her Flippers as she Fluttered through the waves,* the children were to collect things that began with the featured letters and place them in boxes labeled with the appropriate symbol. These experiences caused them to talk about letters, sounds, and words in spontaneous play. Kathy and Kelly were pretending that they were shopping in the dramatic-play store. Kathy picked up a can of tuna fish and said, "Kelly, let's see how many foods we can find that begin with the letter *f*." They looked around, and Kathy found a box of Frosted Flakes and some French Fries. Kelly found a can of Fruit Cocktail, Fruit Loops cereal, and a container of Frozen Yogurt. The girls were excited when each found some food that began with the letter *f*. They said each word with a strong emphasis on the beginning *f* sound. Another activity the children were asked to do was to copy the names of the food that began with *f*. Mrs. Abere told them to do the same activities for the other featured letters in the unit, *m* for meat and *d* for dairy.

Developmental Trends in Literacy Acquisition

Becoming literate is a process that begins at birth and continues throughout life. Children differ in their rates of literacy achievement; they must not be pressured into accomplishing tasks or placed on a predetermined time schedule. Researchers have found that children learn that print has *functions* as a first step in reading and writing (Goodman, 1984; Mason, 1980; Smith, 1971). The first words a child says, reads, and writes are those with meaning, purpose, and function in his or her life, such as family names, food labels, road signs, and names of fast-food restaurants.

After function, the child becomes interested in the *forms* of print. Details about names, sound, and configurations of letters and words now serve the child's learning more than simple understanding of how print functions.

A child then learns the *conventions* of print. This process involves recognition that we read and write from left to right, that punctuation serves a purpose in reading and writing, and that spaces demarcate letters and words. Although recognition of the function of print dominates the first stages of reading and writing development, children acquire an interest in and notions about the form and conventions of print at the same time, but to a lesser degree.

Sulzby (1986a) warns that children do not systematically go from one developmental stage to the next in early reading and writing; they can take one step forward and the next day, one step backward. For example, if you test a child's knowledge of the alphabet and she can identify 15 letters, the next day she may only identify 12.

In a study of what children know about reading and of their skill in letter and word recognition, McCormick and Mason (1981) established three developmental levels in word recognition. Children first identified words through context, then used letter-sound cues, and finally relied on sounding out words.

As children gain experience with story readings, their questions and comments begin to focus on names of letters, the reading of individual words, or attempts to sound out words.

Studies of young children's responses to story readings also reveal developmental trends that follow McCormick and Mason's basic three-strand paradigm. Children's initial questions and comments during story readings are related to the pictures and the meanings of the stories. As they gain experience with story readings, their questions and comments begin to concern the names of letters, the reading of individual words, or attempts to sound out words (Morrow, 1987a; Roser & Martinez, 1985; Yaden, 1985). The function of print dominates early responses; the form of print becomes more important in later responses.

Acquiring Literacy Skills That Have a Purpose and Deal with Real-Life Experiences

Some children have considerable information about reading and writing before they enter school for formal instruction. Some can read and write before they come to school; others have had little exposure to literacy. There are children who come to school who have had almost no exposure to print and have no books in their home. Children who have had exposure to print and a literacy-rich environment know the difference between drawing and writing, and they associate books with reading. They can read environmental print, and they realize the functions of reading and writing. Because their knowledge about literacy to this point is based on meaning and function, they expect that reading and writing will be activities that make sense. Children without this exposure do not have these concepts about books and print.

Efforts to expand children's reading abilities into reading fluency initially need to build on their strengths and on what they already know and expect of reading (Harste, Woodward, & Burke, 1984). Early writing, similar to early reading, is embedded in real-life experience. Many families do things together that involve meaningful literacy. They write each other notes, lists, holiday greetings, and directions. Many children, however, do not have these same opportunities and therefore will not have the same skills developed at the same age.

Children are likely to become involved in literacy activities if they view reading and writing as functional, purposeful, and useful. Studies of early reading and writing behaviors clearly illustrate that young children acquire their first information about reading and writing through their functional uses (Goodman, 1980; Mason & McCormick, 1981; Taylor, 1983). Grocery lists; directions on toys, packages, household equipment, and medicine containers; recipes; telephone messages; school-related notices; religious materials; menus; environmental print inside and outside the home; mail; magazines; newspapers; storybook readings; TV channels; telephone numbers; conversation among family members; and letters represent but a sample of the functional literacy information with which a child comes in contact daily. Children are familiar with these forms of literacy, they participate in them, they pretend to use them at play, and they understand their purposes. Parents and child-care providers, preschool, and kindergarten teachers need to provide experiences with reading similar to experiences children have already had. In her research with preschool and kindergarten children, Goodman (1984) found that some already knew certain things necessary for reading. These children knew the difference between letter characters and pictures in books, how to handle a book, and how to turn pages. And they knew that books are sources of meaning through printed words. Her work also concerned children's awareness of environmental print in familiar contexts and suggested that literacy-rich environments can make learning to read as natural as language acquisition.

Reading Readiness

As noted in Chapter 1, early childhood researchers and teachers believed in the natural unfolding of the child. At a certain level of maturity, they felt, a child was ready to read, instruction was then appropriate, and the child would learn to read. Some educators became impatient with the notion of simply waiting for maturation, even though they thought that certain levels of maturation were necessary before reading could be taught formally without detriment to the child. This attitude led to instructional programs in reading readiness.

In general, reading readiness programs viewed getting ready to read as a set of social, emotional, physical, and cognitive competencies. If a child possessed these competencies, adherents said formal reading instruction could take place. Conversely, a child who had not mastered particular tasks was not considered ready for reading instruction. Strategies for readiness instruction depended on lists of skills in the four areas of development. The skills list provided an outline of activities to be designed to help develop the skills. Typically, these lists included characteristics such as those listed in the checklist on page 113, on which children were tested.

In programs that followed a **reading readiness** perspective, teachers prepared instruction to encourage social, emotional, physical, and intellectual development as outlined on the checklist and described in the following paragraphs.

✔ Checklist *Reading Readiness*

Child's name _____ **Date** _____

Social and Emotional Development	Always	Sometimes	Never	Comments
Shares				
Cooperates with peers and adults				
Demonstrates confidence, self-control, and emotional stability				
Completes tasks				
Fulfills responsibilities				

Physical Development	Always	Sometimes	Never	Comments
Demonstrates large motor control by being able to run, hop, skip, trot, gallop, jump, throw, and walk a straight line				
Demonstrates fine motor control by being able to hold a pencil properly, color within lines, and cut with scissors				
Demonstrates eye–hand coordination				
Can write name, copy letters, and draw a human figure				
Is generally healthy and vigorous				
Shows no visual or auditory defects				
Has established dominance (hand, eye, foot)				

Cognitive Development	Always	Sometimes	Never	Comments
Demonstrates auditory discrimination by identifying familiar sounds, differentiating sounds, recognizing rhyming words, identifying initial and ending consonant sounds, and possessing an auditory memory				
Demonstrates visual discrimination by understanding left to right eye progression; recognizing likenesses and differences; identifying colors, shapes, letters, and words; possessing visual memory; and showing a sense of figure–ground perception				

Teacher Comments:

Social and emotional development was and still is enhanced with periods of play during which children can select from materials placed in classroom centers. Centers may be for dramatic play, art, science, library, or outdoor play, and may contain blocks and manipulative toys. The goal is for children to learn to share and cooperate, to develop self-control and a good self-concept, and to learn about appropriate school behavior. Discussions often will focus on the topic of sharing and getting along with others. There will almost always be a unit focused on "All about Me," which emphasizes building self-confidence and positive self-esteem. Food plays an important role in the curriculum; a healthy snack is served daily, and snack time is considered a time to socialize and learn to get along with others.

Physical development of large and fine motor control was and is seen as a factor in literacy development. Teachers should have indoor and outdoor periods designed specifically to teach children to hop, skip, trot, gallop, jump, throw a ball, and walk a straight line. Often there is music to accompany these activities and specific pieces of equipment such as a balance beam.

To develop fine motor coordination, children can use clay and play with toys that require fitting pegs into holes or snapping things together. These activities supply the strength that little hands need to develop the coordination necessary to write letters. Teachers ask children to trace around lines of a particular illustration to develop eye–hand motor control. Children also trace pictures and letters with their fingers. Children practice cutting to enhance fine motor ability, which is needed to write letters.

Cognitive development is equally important to social, physical, and emotional development. In a reading readiness program, cognitive development meant working on auditory and visual discrimination skills in preparation for reading. To do this, children participated in **auditory** and **visual discrimination** activities. Some of these activities are still useful.

Visual discrimination activities involve children in seeing likenesses and differences in shapes and pictures. In the past worksheets were used to help children develop this skill. For example, a worksheet may picture a line of flowers that all look the same with one slightly different from the rest. Children are to find and circle or color the flower that is different. An occasional worksheet such as this can be useful in helping children follow directions. The activity is more useful with real objects in which we discuss similarities and differences. Another visual discrimination activity is color identification. Here children are asked to classify objects into color groups, or to make a collage of pictures cut from a magazine that are all, for example, red, blue, or green. Identifying like and different shapes such as squares, circles, and rectangles is another activity used for developing visual discrimination. Finally, children are taught left to right eye progression because the skill is necessary for reading. After working with these visual discrimination skills, teachers ask children to identify letters of the alphabet. Children memorize the alphabet, trace and copy letters, and learn to identify upper- and lowercase letters. All of these activities are seen as preparation for reading. The skills mentioned are still relevant. In the past worksheets were used to develop the skills. The worksheets did not have much meaning for the children. Today we use real materials and involve children more actively.

Auditory discrimination prepares children for learning to use auditory decoding skills. Teachers ask children to identify sounds that are alike and different. In the past we asked children to circle pictures on a worksheet that represented animals that make different or like sounds. Listening to rhymes, identifying rhyming words, and creating rhyme word lists is another auditory discrimination activity. Again, worksheets with pictures of objects are provided, and children are asked to circle the ones that rhyme. From rhyme, the teacher progresses to associating letters with their sounds. Some activities that help children perform this task include collecting objects that begin with the sound featured, and teachers may ask children to cut pictures from a magazine to make into a collage for the letter *M,* for example. Figure 5.1 shows a typical reading readiness worksheet that asks the child to circle pictures that begin with consonant sounds *d, p,* and hard *c.* These worksheets can be confusing because the deer could be considered a moose or antelope, and the piano a baby grand or simply a piano. Based on their own experiences, children may identify an illustration as something different from what the artist had in mind and circle the wrong letter. Therefore, if this type of activity is used, teachers *must* identify picture names for children.

The list of reading readiness skills is long. Previously it was assumed that a child must master all behaviors on the list before being given a book to read or becoming engaged in what is called formal reading instruction. The activities associated with a reading readiness program do not really teach children much about the total act of reading. They engage them in a variety of abstract activities that are only a part of reading. There are many sad stories of kindergarten teachers who retained children who were unable to master skipping, trotting, or galloping. Parents have become frantic and children brought to tears by teachers' insistence on mastery of motor skills. It was not uncommon to see classes of kindergarten children undergoing skipping lessons to the teacher's cadence of "step-hop, step-hop, step-hop, step-hop."

At least two misguided assumptions lie behind the reading readiness approach: (1) children know nothing about literacy before coming to school; and (2) they therefore need an instructional program in readiness. Reading readiness has not included writing and awareness of book and print characteristics that

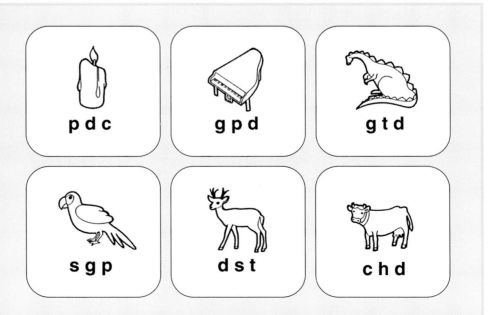

Figure 5.1

Reading Readiness Worksheet for Sound–Symbol Relationships

p d c   g p d   g t d

s g p   d s t   c h d

Directions: Circle the letter that each picture begins with, such as c̲ as in candle, p̲ as in piano, and d̲ as in dragon.

are necessary and important for reading. Instructional practices motivated by the readiness-skills approach often engage children in activities that do not seem very important to the total act of reading. There are children who have not accomplished many of the tasks on a list of reading readiness skills but nonetheless are able to read. Their ability to read goes unrecognized because reading readiness tests and activities never ask children to read. There are also children who can carry out the tasks on a list and experience difficulty learning to read. In today's classrooms, many readiness activities are still relevant. However, other experiences are also used to teach children about reading.

Psycholinguistic Cuing Systems and the Acquisition of Language and Literacy

According to psycholinguistic theory, language and literacy are acquired as a result of children having the ability to use three cuing systems to figure out new and unknown words to grasp meaning.

1. **Syntactic cues:** Using the grammatical structure or syntax of language
2. **Semantic cues:** Using the meaning of words and sentences
3. **Graphophonic cues:** Using the visual cues of letters and print and associating them with letters, letter clusters, and corresponding sounds

Along with these cuing systems, the psycholinguistic definition of reading also recommends capitalizing on children's prior strengths, knowledge, and past experiences. Goodman (1967) described reading as a psycholinguistic "guessing game" in which the child attempts to reconstruct, in light of his or her own knowledge, what the author has to say. Young children bring to school concepts and understanding from past experiences. Their awareness and use of oral language are particularly helpful.

Reading is an active process. Therefore, when children try to read, they need to anticipate what the written message is likely to say. They need to search the printed page for cues based on what they already know. They need to use the three cuing systems.

There are syntactic cues such as *The boy walked down the* _____. The child's internalized knowledge of syntax indicates that the word to place in the blank must be a noun such as *hill, stairs,* or *street.* A verb would make no sense: *The boy walked down the jumped.*

Semantic cues help children determine which words would make sense in a particular slot and which would not. Few would guess that the sentence reads, *The boy walked down the butter,* for example. It just doesn't make sense.

Graphophonic cues enable the child to determine words by looking at the visual cues of letters and letter clusters and associating them with their corresponding sounds.

Using the syntactic, semantic, and graphophonic cues, children can predict, guess, expect, make associations, and correct themselves to derive meaning from the printed page. The meaning comes from what they know about language and from their own experiences.

Theory and Research on Helping Children Figure Out Words

Word-study skills and knowledge about print involve learning strategies that will help children figure out words and become independent readers. Word-study skills for decoding words include the use of context and syntax, the development of a sight vocabulary, the use of the configuration or the shape of a word, and structural analysis (attending to different parts of words such as prefixes, suffixes, or the root). The most well known word-study strategy is the use of phonics, which involves learning letter sounds and combinations of letter sounds (referred to as phonemes) associated with their corresponding letter symbols (referred to as graphemes). One of the problems with phonics is that the English alphabet has at least 44 different sounds, and sound–symbol correspondence is not consistent—there are many irregularities and exceptions to many rules.

Phonemic awareness, which will be discussed in more depth in this chapter, is the ability to recognize that words are made up of individual speech sounds. This is different from phonics, which includes knowledge of the relationship between letters and sounds. **Phonological awareness,** which is different from phonemic awareness, involves identifying and manipulating larger parts of spoken language such as whole words, syllables, initial consonants, and word chunks at the end of words referred to as onsets and rimes. These are considered to be precursors to phonics—that is, they are needed in order to learn phonics. Phonics has received attention as an important skill for reading success to a greater and lesser extent over the years. There is no doubt that research has demonstrated its importance. However, it is the concurrent use of several of the word-study skills mentioned that creates a proficient reader (Reutzel & Cooter, 2004).

Research concerning early literacy has demonstrated the importance of meaningful experiences in instruction (Teale, 2003). We also have considerable research that demonstrates that to become a proficient reader, language codes need to be learned. This is true not only in English-speaking countries; there is considerable evidence from both experimental and longitudinal studies from many countries that phonemic and phonological awareness and knowledge of phonics are necessary for success in learning to read and write alphabetic languages (Adams, 1990; Juel, 1994).

Concerns about word study in early literacy deal with questions such as exactly what skills should be taught, when to introduce them, how to teach them, and how much time to spend dealing with them. Although there are no definitive answers to all these questions, we have found that teaching word-study skills in a variety of ways seems to be the best approach. For example, there should be some direct systematic instruction, some spontaneous instruction, and teaching and practicing skills in meaningful settings.

Skills and Objectives for Word Study

The following are objectives for word study to enhance literacy development. The child should be able to do the following:

1. Demonstrate that print is read from left to right.
2. Demonstrate that oral language can be written down and then read.
3. Demonstrate what a letter is and point to one on a printed page.

4. Demonstrate what a word is, point to one on a printed page, and know there are spaces between words.

5. Demonstrate that print in the environment has a message, and read some of this print on signs and logos.

6. Recognize high-frequency words and other words by sight.

7. Identify rhyming words he or she hears and make up a rhyme.

8. Identify and name upper- and lowercase letters of the alphabet.

9. Blend and segment phonemes in words.

10. Associate letters with their initial and final corresponding consonant sounds, including sounds of the same letter (Such as hard and soft *c*—cat, city; *g*—goat, George).

11. Associate letters with corresponding long and short vowel sounds (*a*—acorn, apple; *e*—eagle, egg; *i*—ice, igloo; *o*—oats, octopus; *u*—unicorn, umbrella).

12. Read fluently at instructional level.

13. Blend together consonant blends *bl, cr, dr, fl, gl, pr, st,* etc. (consonant blends are two or three letters that when placed together blend into one sound that represents the two or three letter sounds).

14. Identify consonant digraph sounds *ch, ph, sh, th,* and *wh* (digraphs are two letters that when placed together make a new sound unlike the sounds of either letter).

15. Use context, syntax, and semantics to identify words.

16. Divide words into syllables.

17. Attempt reading by attending to picture clues and to print.

18. Predict words based on a knowledge of phoneme–grapheme correspondence.

19. Identify different structural elements of words, such as prefixes, suffixes, and inflectional endings *-ing, -ed,* and *-s* at the end of a word.

20. Apply the following phonic generalizations:
    a. In a consonant–vowelconsonant pattern, the vowel sound is usually short (bat, bet, but, bit).
    b. In a vowel–consonant–e pattern, the vowel sound is usually long (cake, cute).
    c. When two vowels come together in a word, the first is usually long and the second is usually silent (train, receive, bean).

21. Identify common word families referred to also as rimes or phonograms, and build words by adding initial consonants (called onsets) to word families (*it, an, am, at, ite, ate,* and so on).

Standards and Word Study

State and U.S. national standards are concerned with word-study skills. Standards for kindergarten to third grade, as outlined by the National Center on Education and the Economy and the Learning Research and Development Center at the University of Pittsburgh (1999), talk about word study as *print-sound code.* In this area the standards are knowledge of letters and their sounds, phonemic awareness, and reading words.

Based on these standards, kindergarten through third-grade children should be able to do the following related to word study:

Have knowledge of letters and their sounds.

Segment and blend sounds (phonemic awareness).

Read words with more than one syllable.

Recognize or figure out irregularly spelled words and patterns.

Read words based on their knowledge of letters and their sounds and recognize a large number of high-frequency words.

Read text with accuracy and fluency at their own particular level. (Fluency suggests that reading is done in a smooth manner with appropriate intonation and pauses; accuracy refers to correct reading of words.)

Have self-monitoring and self-correcting strategies. (This means that children recognize when they need help and ask for it. They recognize when they have made a mistake and use strategies learned to try to correct their errors.)

Chapter 7 on writing discusses the development of spelling. Spelling also is learned as sound–symbol relationship patterns are acquired. As you use the strategies discussed for the acquisition of phonics, have children practice these word patterns frequently by using them in their writing to help with spelling.

Teaching Strategies for Figuring Out Words

Instructional activities designed to help youngsters learn about the function, form, structure, and conventions of print should involve a wide variety of learning experiences. Children need to be socially interactive when they are learning about print; they need direct instruction with models to emulate, and they need to learn through experiences that are meaningful, that are connected with real life, and that incorporate what children already know. If children see a need or usefulness attached to a reading skill, that skill probably will be learned without difficulty.

In the sections that follow, strategies are described to help children learn about print in direct, meaningful, and functional ways. Each strategy is appropriate for youngsters from preschool through third grade—teachers simply adjust the activity to the age groups they are working with. Learning these skills should be connected to content-area material and functional activities. Activities such as reading to children; pointing out words in the environment; noting their letters and sounds; taking a child's dictation; encouraging children to write in their own way; allowing youngsters to see the print as it is read from a Big Book and tracked from left to right across the page; and using predictable books that rhyme or have patterned language and that allow children to guess and share in the reading all help youngsters learn about print (Invernizzi, 2003). Through these experiences, children learn that print is read from left to right, that words in a book are oral language that has been written down and can be read, that letters have sounds, that letters make up words, that words have meaning, that pictures hold clues to what the print says, and that words can be predicted based on the meaning of the text. In addition, direct instruction in phonological and phonemic awareness, alphabetic knowledge, and phonics is needed.

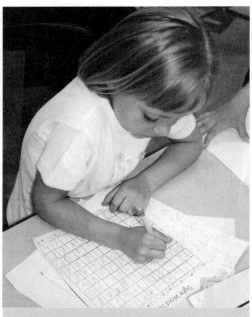

The use of an occasional worksheet will help to reinforce skills taught.

When explicit instruction is used, lessons need to teach skills as strategies for children to use. In these lessons the teacher does the following:

1. Begins with an explanation and rationale for the children by letting them know what is being taught and why it is being taught.

2. Models and demonstrates how to use the skill and when to use the skill.

3. Gives students the opportunity to practice the skill taught with the teacher's guidance.

4. Encourages students to practice and apply the skills.

The use of an occasional worksheet will reinforce skills taught. Children can read several words and simple books through their knowledge of syntax, semantics, and acquired sight vocabulary before phonics is emphasized. When youngsters have experienced success with initial reading, they will seek information about the forms of print because they will want to read independently.

Using Environmental Print

Several researchers have found that children as young as two can read familiar environmental print (Strickland & Snow, 2002; Hiebert, 1986). Others, however, have shown that a child often is reading the sign rather than its print. When the print is separated from its familiar environmental context, the young child sometimes can no longer identify it (Mason, 1980). Even so, when very young children associate the McDonald's logo with the word *McDonald's* and try to read it, they are learning that a group of letters makes up a word that can be read and thus provides information. The ability to read environmental print also gives the child a sense of accomplishment and usually elicits positive reinforcement of the child's achievement by caring adults.

As noted earlier, parents can make children aware of environmental print from the first year of life. During daily routines, parents need to point out and read words and labels on food boxes, road signs, stores, and restaurants. The world is filled with environmental print. Our early childhood classrooms need to have environmental print brought in from outside, and teachers need to label items in their child-care centers, nursery schools, kindergartens, and first and second grades. The print should be traced and copied. Such print, once familiar, becomes part of a child's sight vocabulary.

The environmental print that children tend to know best appears on food containers, especially those for cereal, soup, milk, and cookies, and on detergent boxes and bottles. Among common signs, they recognize fast-food logos, road signs, traffic signals, and names of popular store chains, supermarkets, and service stations. Collect such logos and trade names and make them available in your classroom by posting them on charts, pasting them onto index cards, and creating loose-leaf books of environmental print. Most firms distribute various printed materials free, complete with logos. Photograph environmental print in your neighborhood, and bring the photos to your classroom. Suggest that children read the words, copy them, and write them in a sentence or a story.

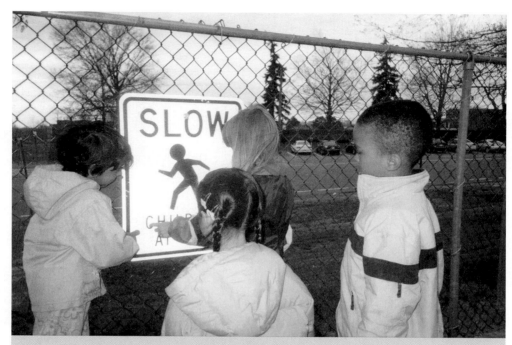

Photograph environmental print in your neighborhood, and bring the photos to your classroom. Suggest that children read the words, copy them, and write them in a sentence or a story.

Start including environmental print in your classroom at the beginning of a school year with only a few signs, such as children's names on their cubbies, and the word *Block Center* to identify that area of the room. Make labels with five-by-eight index cards and dark felt-tip markers. Begin each word with a capital letter and continue with lowercase manuscript, thus providing youngsters with configuration clues. Hang labels at heights easy for children to see. Point out the labels to the children, and suggest that they read them to friends and copy them. As the school year progresses, label new items that are added to the classroom. Refer to the labels as part of your normal routine so that they are used and will then add to the child's sight vocabulary. Label items because they are of interest to the class and serve a function such as identifying important classroom materials and learning centers. Use labels for relating messages such as *Wash Your Hands Before Snack*. Refer to the labels often so the children identify them as useful and functional.

Label items related to content-area topics. If you are studying dinosaurs—a popular topic in early childhood—display model dinosaurs and label each with its name. Even long, difficult words such as *Brontosaurus* and *Tyrannosaurus* immediately become sight words for many early childhood youngsters. It is not uncommon to observe preschool, kindergarten, first-grade, and second-grade children reading labels to themselves or to each other. I observed a kindergarten class after the teacher had posted two new labels in the science center, which featured a lesson on the sense of touch and focused on items that were hard and soft. I watched Josh take Jennifer by the hand and heard him say, "See, Jen. See this. This bunny is soft. This word says 'soft.' " Josh continued, "See this, Jen. This is a rock and this word says 'hard.' Touch it. It is hard." The two children stroked the bunny, pointed to the label, and said in unison, "soft"; they then touched the rock, pointed to the label, and said, "hard." They repeated the sequence several times.

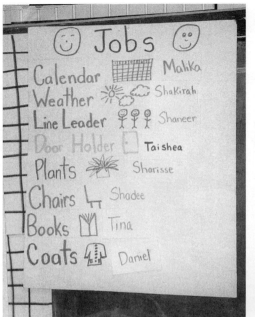

A chart with class jobs and a list of class rules provide important pieces of environmental print to early childhood rooms.

THE MORNING MESSAGE.   Another way to make print part of the classroom environment is to communicate with it, even with preschool children. Post messages and assignments for children daily. Select a permanent spot on the chalkboard or on chart paper. Use rebus or picture writing along with print to help children make sense of the message. Here are a few examples of appropriate messages:

> Happy Birthday, Tyrone
> Happy Flag Day
> Read a book to a friend.
> We are going on a trip to the town library today.

This routine will teach children to look automatically at the chalkboard each day for a special message. From the messages they will learn that print carries meaning that is interesting and useful. Some teachers refer to this practice as the **morning message** and have formalized it into a lesson when the school day begins (Morrow, 2003).

Morning messages are used at morning meetings, when the class gets together to discuss what will happen in school on that day. Write at least some of the message with the children watching, so that you provide a writing model for them. Use the message to develop various concepts about print. Emphasize specific words or letters, pursue questions about meaning, or let children add sentences to the original message.

When working with seven- and eight-year-olds, the contents of the morning message and the environmental print displayed in the room will be more sophisticated than when working with younger children. They can be used to point out sound–symbol relationships or phonic generalizations that are appropriate to deal with in first and second grade. For example, a morning message such as the following is a perfect opportunity to point out the *sh* digraph:

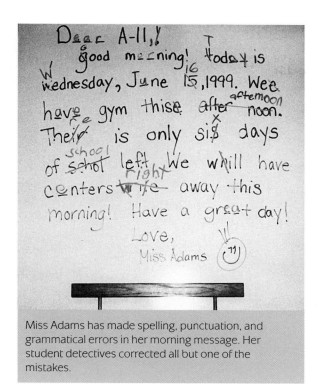

Miss Adams has made spelling, punctuation, and grammatical errors in her morning message. Her student detectives corrected all but one of the mistakes.

Shelly is wearing shiny new shoes.

In another message, such as the following, there are five examples of the phonic generalization that, in a vowel–consonant–*e* pattern, the vowel is usually long.

Kate told us that her birthday cake was made in the shape of a kite.

This is a perfect opportunity to observe and discuss this letter–sound pattern.

Teachers use morning messages to teach letter writing by writing some of the messages in the form of a letter and pointing out the elements of the format. Teachers also sometimes purposefully make spelling or punctuation errors in messages and ask the children to find the mistakes. Letters of the alphabet can be left out of words to be filled in, or complete words can be left out for children to figure out from the context of the sentence. Some teachers embed the class spelling words or new words into the message. They include words that demonstrate skills being taught, such as words with long *a* sounds or short vowel sounds, or words with digraphs or blends. Children are asked to identify and circle the featured words, vowels, and so on.

In Mrs. Youseff's kindergarten they had a morning message time daily. The children gathered around the experience chart, and her message was almost the same every day. It said:

Dear Boys and Girls,

   Today is Wednesday, September 8, 2005.
The weather is warm, and it is raining.
We are learning about reptiles. We talked about
snakes, lizards, and alligators.

   Love,
   Mrs. Youseff

Since the message is similar every day, the children begin to be able to read it. Soon Mrs. Youseff leaves out a word in the chart for the children to identify what is missing, as in this example:

Today is _____, September 22, 2005.

She will leave endings off of words such as *day* in the word *today*. She will leave off the year on the date, and so on.

Developing Sight Vocabulary

In *Teacher* (1963), Sylvia Ashton-Warner described Very Own Words as a method for developing sight vocabulary. She encouraged children to write their favorite words from a story or content-area lesson on three-by-five cards, each

Morning Message

Today is Tuesday November 26.
It is sunny and cold outside. Today
is Tom's birthday. In only two days
it will be Thanksgiving. I'm going to
my sister's house for Thanksgiving.
Her name is Tanya. We will eat
Turkey.

What will you do
for the holiday? What do we eat
on Thanksgiving? Why do we eat
these foods?

T   Th

This morning message is used to talk about an upcoming holiday and point out the initial consonant *t* and digraph *th*.

word on a separate card. Very Own Words are often from a child's home life—*Mommy, Daddy, Grandpa, Grandma, cookie.* They also reflect emotional feelings—*naughty, nice, good, no, punish.* After Very Own Words are recorded on index cards, they are stored in a child's file box, in a coffee can, in a plastic baggie, or on a loose-leaf ring hung on a bulletin board. Teachers have devised many other methods for storing Very Own Words. Helping children start their collections of Very Own Words is an exciting experience in school. Before an activity or exercise, let them know that at its completion you will ask them to name their favorite words from the activity. The activity should be a pleasant one that produces interesting language, perhaps popping corn or making play dough. Children also can choose a favorite word in a storybook or words generated

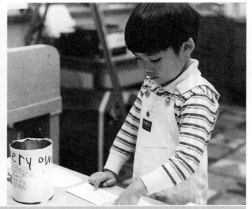

Very Own Words are a source for personal sight vocabulary. Teachers should encourage children to copy them, write them, and read them.

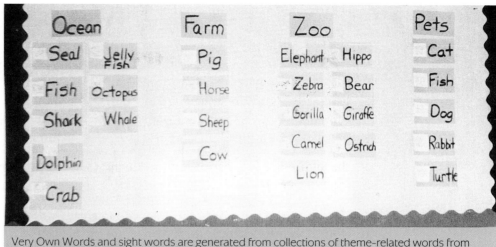

Very Own Words and sight words are generated from collections of theme-related words from specific units of study in science and social studies.

from the study of social studies and science units. Soon children will request their Very Own Words without being asked.

Encourage children to do things with their words—read them to friends or to themselves, copy them, dictate them to the teacher, and use them in sentences or stories. Because words are based on a child's expressed interests in situations at home and in school, the collection of Very Own Words is a powerful technique for developing sight vocabulary.

Seven- and eight-year-olds also enjoy and learn from collecting Very Own Words. They should alphabetize them and store them in a file box. Teachers can encourage children to study the letter patterns in their Very Own Words. They can discuss consonant and vowel sounds, blends, digraphs, and structural elements such as prefixes and suffixes, as well as phonic generalizations that may be evident. When a child studies letter patterns in words he or she has selected, it will mean more than doing the same task with words selected by the teacher or found in a textbook.

Very Own Words are also useful with bilingual children. The index card should include a child's Very Own Word in English and can have the word written in his or her native language as well.

HIGH-FREQUENCY WORDS AS SIGHT WORDS. There is a group of words that are found frequently in reading materials for young children that need to be learned for quick recall. They are words that do not carry meaning but that hold sentences together. They are often difficult to decode because they have irregular patterns in their spelling. It is helpful for children if they do not have to spend time segmenting these words as they read; they should be able to read them easily because they have been learned by memory or sight.

Sight words are often taught in a systematic and direct manner. The teacher selects a few of these words for the children to learn each week. To learn these words, the following activities are used:

Words are said aloud and used in a sentence.

The sentence is written on a chalkboard or flip chart and the sight word is
    underlined.

Features of each word such as the letters or its similarity to other words are discussed. The teacher also points out any regular or irregular patterns the word may have.

Children are asked to spell the word aloud, spell the word with their finger in the air, and write the word on paper.

Children chant the letters as they spell words.

The words can be written on index cards similar to Very Own Words and stored with the child's other cards.

In Figure 5.2 is a list of **high-frequency words** (Fountas & Pinnell, 1996). Teachers in grades K, 1, 2, and 3 need to make sure these are learned by sight over this period of time. According to Adams (1990), the following 13 words are 25 percent of the words children find in early literacy texts. These should be first on the list to learn: *a, and, for, he, in, is, it, of, that, the, to, was, you.*

WORD WALLS TO TEACH HIGH-FREQUENCY WORDS. A word wall typically has the letters of the alphabet posted across the wall. As high-frequency words are featured, they are posted under the letter where they belong in alphabetical order. The featured words are ones teachers select as being a priority to learn. Others may be ones that children are having difficulty with reading and spelling. The words are placed on index cards. Children are asked to spell each word out loud, trace it in the air, and copy it. Sometimes words are written and then cut out into the shape of the word, providing visual configuration clues for remembering it. Before putting words up, note their characteristics, such as their pronunciation, spelling, letter patterns. Suggest to children that the word wall can be used as a dictionary.

The word wall can be used to play word-study games. For example, if the teacher wants to work with rhymes, he or she can point to a word such as *went* and say, "The

Figure 5.2					
Frequently Used	a	came	her	look	people	too
Words	after	can	here	looked	play	two
	all	come	him	long	put	up
	an	could	his	make	ran	us
	and	day	house	man	run	very
	are	did	how	mother	said	was
	am	do	I	me	saw	we
	as	don't	I'm	my	see	went
	asked	down	if	no	she	were
	at	for	in	not	so	what
	away	from	into	now	some	when
	back	get	is	of	that	where
	be	go	it	old	the	will
	because	going	just	on	then	with
	before	good	keep	one	there	would
	big	had	kind	or	they	you
	boy	has	know	our	this	your
	but	have	like	out	three	
	by	he	little	over	to	

Source: Reprinted by permission from *Guided Reading: Good First Teaching for All Children* by Irene C. Fountas and Gay Su Pinnell. Copyright © 1996 by Irene C. Fountas and Gay Su Pinnell. Published by Heinemann, a division of Reed Elsevier, Inc., Portsmouth, New Hampshire.

Word walls can feature high-frequency words or words with short vowel sounds. Some teachers cut high-frequency words to illustrate their shape or configuration to help children remember them better.

word I am thinking of rhymes with *went* but begins with a *b*," or, "The word I am thinking of rhymes with *look* and begins with a *b*." Word-wall words also can be sorted by word families, word endings, and so on by moving the words around the wall and working on a sheet of paper. Many different lessons and directions for using the wall independently can be provided (Cunningham, 1995; Moustafa, 1997). With very young children the first words on the word wall will be their names.

To ensure that children are acquiring sight recognition of high-frequency words, they should be tested in their ability to read them. The teacher should ask them to identify the words with flash cards and find them in context within passages to read. This testing can be done several times during the school year (Allington & Cunningham, 1996).

Some additional word wall activities that the teacher can lead are as follows:

1. Have students sort words by pattern, that is words with the letters *an* or *at,* for example.
2. Classify words into colors, names, animals, etc.
3. The Secret Word game with the word wall provides the student with a series of clues such as these:

The secret word has an **at** *pattern at the end.*
It has three letters.
It is an animal.
It has fur and little pointy ears.
They live in people's houses.
The _____ enjoyed his dish of milk,

Using the Language Experience Approach

The **language experience approach (LEA)** has been used for many years in reading instruction. It can help children associate oral language with written language, teaching them specifically that what is said can be written down and read. It illustrates the left-to-right progression of our written language. In practice, it demonstrates the formation of letters plus their combination into words; it helps build sight vocabulary; it is a source for meaningful teaching of phoneme–grapheme correspondence as well as other knowledge about print; and it is based on the child's interest and experiences.

Many educators have been associated with developing and articulating the language experience approach, among them R. V. Allen (1976), M. A. Hall (1976), and J. Veatch et al. (1973). The LEA is based on the following premises, all from the learner's point of view:

> What I think is important.
>
> What I think, I can say.
>
> What I say can be written down by me or by others.
>
> What is written down can be read by me and by others.

The interests and experiences on which the LEA builds come from children's lives both at home and at school. The LEA is particularly suited for use with ELL students. It is about their lives; the vocabulary comes from them; they make their own books with their own words. In school, the teacher needs to plan experiences—for example, class trips, cooking projects, use of puppets, guest speakers, class pets, holiday events—or the study of topics that are exciting to young children, such as dinosaurs, outer space, and other cultures. The language experience lesson is usually carried out with an entire class, but it also can take place with a small group or an individual child.

An LEA lesson begins with oral language. A discussion is usually generated from an interesting or exciting class experience—for instance, a recent trip to the zoo or the pet gerbil's new litter. To begin the discussion, ask open-ended questions that will encourage descriptive responses rather than yes/no answers. For example, if the topic is a trip to the zoo, ask children to name their favorite animal. Why was it their favorite animal? What did the animal look like? What did the animal do while they were watching it at the zoo? It is important to accept all the children's responses. Accept nonstandard English without correction, but provide a language model by using standard English to paraphrase what the child has said.

After a discussion has generated several ideas, write them down. With a large group of children, write the ideas on a large sheet of paper (approximately 24 by 36 inches), which becomes an experience chart. It can be taped to the wall or mounted on an easel. Print with a dark felt-tip marker of medium thickness, allowing ample spacing between words and between lines so that the chart is very readable. Use manuscript in upper- and lowercase letters, following the conventions of regular print and thus giving configuration to words that the use of uppercase alone cannot give. Word configuration aids children in word identification.

In recording language on experience charts, teachers should write quickly and legibly, providing good manuscript samples for children to read and copy. As you write what children dictate, use their language unless it is difficult for others to understand. When dictation is difficult to understand, ask a child to restate an idea or, if necessary, help the child restate it. It is important to include the comments of as many children as possible. When creating a new chart, try to remember which children have not contributed in the past, and encourage them to contribute to the new chart. It is a good idea to identify who said what. The chart is more interesting to youngsters whose names are included. For example: Jacob said, "I liked the gorilla at the zoo. He jumped around and made funny faces." Jordanna said, "I liked the baby deer. They had big, bright, black eyes, wet black noses, and shiny brown fur." Try to accompany each sentence with an illustration; this will help children read the charts.

Experience charts should not be very long. Charts dictated by two- and three-year-olds can be simply lists of words, such as names of animals with illustrations next to them. Lists of words make appropriate charts for older children as well. They are a quick way to record and reinforce vocabulary associated with topics being studied. Small-group and individual dictations of experiences can be made into books by the teacher or the child. While writing a chart, take the opportunity to point out concepts about print: "Now I am writing the word *gorilla—g-o-r-i-l-l-a.* See, it begins here with a *g* and ends here with an *a.*" Mentally note which letters or sounds interest children. Ask children to point out on the chart where you should begin to write. Like directed listening (or reading) and thinking activities and the morning message, the LEA lesson should have a specific skill objective.

The last step in the LEA lesson is to read the chart to the class. Use a pointer to emphasize left-to-right progression. Let the class read the chart in unison, or ask individual children who contributed different sentences to read them. Leave the chart in a visible spot in the room, and encourage the children to read it and copy parts of it, copy words they like, or add to their Very Own Word collection from the chart. Vocabulary charts and experience charts representing different topics discussed in school can be left hanging in the room if space permits and then made into Big Books for children to look at throughout the school year. If a laminating machine is available, it is wise to preserve charts. Children's dictated stories also can be placed in the class library for others to read, as can books made by the entire class. Those made by the class often become the most popular books in the room. Class books can be made by having each child draw and write directly onto a duplicating master. This method allows easy production of multiple copies, one for each child.

Experience charts, dictated by the children and written by the teacher, develop oral language and encourage reading and writing.

Pocket chart activities are associated with the language experience approach. Words associated with experiences the class has had are featured in the chart. Short stories, poems, and songs that students chant together can be printed on individual sentence strips. Ask children to copy the charts to practice their writing. In addition, the sentence strips can be scrambled and sequenced into the pocket chart. Sentence strips are often cut up for students to work with on the word level, to help identify and practice new words and place them into sentences.

When teaching a unit on food and featuring the consonant *t* in all parts of words,

Ms. Macki selected *Potatoes on Tuesday* (Lillegard & McPhail, 1993) to read to her kindergarten class to reinforce this skill. The text of the book is as follows:

> *On Monday, cabbage,*
> *On Tuesday, potatoes,*
> *On Wednesday, carrots,*
> *On Thursday, tomatoes;*
> *On Friday, peas and green beans, too—*
> *On Saturday, a great big pot of . . .*
> *Stew! Mmmm.*

Source: From *Potatoes on Tuesday* by Dee Lillegard. © 1995, 1993 by Scott, Foresman and Company. Published by Good Year Books. Used by permission.

Ms. Macki wrote the words to the story on chart paper and then on sentence strips. She cut a second set of sentence strips into individual words. In this way she provided the children with activities to practice sequencing whole sentences into a story, building sentences from individual words by using the syntax and semantics of the text, and identifying of the consonant *t* within the context of a story. Children also were able to practice new vocabulary that appeared in the story. Pocket chart activities are often used to practice new skills during independent center time.

The language experience approach, which is appropriate throughout early childhood and beyond, can be used similarly to the morning message and Very Own Words for noticing phonic generalizations and sound–symbol correspondences. Learning about print in this situation is done with material that is familiar and meaningful. Occasionally prepare a chart in the language of bilingual children in your class. If necessary, solicit help from bilingual parents or colleagues. This strategy will guide bilingual youngsters in making connections between their language and English.

LEA materials are inexpensive and easy to use. They include chart paper, markers, colored construction paper, white paper, index cards, scissors, staplers,

Ms. Berk wrote the words to the little story on chart paper and then on sentence strips for children to sequence. She cut a second set of sentence strips into words for children to sequence.

pencils, and crayons. With directions from the teacher, these simple classroom materials record the precious words and pictures created by children from their own meaningful, real-life experiences. The LEA should be central, not supplemental, to literacy instruction in early reading programs.

Using Context and Pictures to Figure Out Words

Experiences with literature can lead children to use contextual clues and illustrations to recognize that words have meaning. Literature experiences can take place in whole-class, small-group, or one-to-one settings, using directed listening (or reading) and thinking activities, shared book experiences, and repeated readings of stories. For example, select a story that is predictable, in which the text and illustrations are closely related. Ask children to look at the pictures on a page before reading it to them. Ask them what they think the words will say. Then read the page to demonstrate that print and illustration are closely related and that the pictures provide information that can help the children as they read the story.

The syntax and semantics of a sentence (its grammatical structure and meaning) also help children identify words. Encourage children to use these elements of written language by stopping your oral reading at predictable points in a story and asking them to fill in words. For example, when reading *The Little Engine That Could* (Piper, 1954), first read the complete repetitive phrase "I think I can," then, the second time say, "I think I _____," the next time "I think _____," and last "I _____." This technique is most effective with a Big Book because you can point to the words as the children say them. As the children begin to understand the concept of filling in words, choose more difficult passages for your pauses. Prepare charts and sheets with predictable text, and leave out words to be filled in as you read. Children use their prior knowledge of syntax and context in predicting words. They assimilate and use the strategy when they read themselves.

In addition to these general suggestions, specific experiences to figure out words can be varied so that students have many different strategies for using context. A common way to determine words from context is through the meaning of the text. For example, in the sentence that follows, it is apparent that the missing word is *Queen*. We need to show children how to use the meaning of the text to figure out a word that might be unknown to them.

> *The King and _____ lived in the castle together.*

Another context clue exercise involves a series of related words. To help with this exercise or other context clue exercises, the initial consonant can be included. For example:

> *My favorite kinds of fruit are apples, b_____, pears, and oranges.*

A gamelike context clue activity involves the use of scrambled letters, as in the following sentence:

> *I am always on time, but my sister is always_____ (alte).*

When working with context clues, teachers can choose to omit all nouns, verbs, every fourth word, and so on. There are endless ways to use this strategy, and each contributes to helping children figure out unknown words. This approach is referred to as the cloze procedure as well.

Phonological Awareness and Phonemic Awareness

Phonological-awareness and phonemic-awareness instruction in early literacy lead toward helping students to become independent readers. Teaching these skills to children should be done concurrently with other strategies for learning to read, such as acquiring sight words and learning how to use context clues and picture clues. Children need to have a holistic view about books and reading as well as the more abstract skills as they work on decoding unknown words. As mentioned earlier, phonemic awareness is the ability to recognize that words are made up of individual speech sounds (Burns, Griffin, & Snow, 1999). The words *hat* and *chat* contain three speech sounds referred to as phonemes. The phonemes are not letters; they are sounds. This is different from phonics, which includes knowledge of the relationship between letters and sounds. Phonological awareness is different from phonemic awareness. It is the awareness of the sound structure of language. Phonological awareness involves identifying and manipulating larger parts of spoken language such as whole words, syllables, initial consonants, and word chunks referred to as onsets and rimes. The segmenting and blending of these sounds is the important skill children need to develop.

Phonemic awareness is a subset of phonological awareness. Phonemic awareness and phonological awareness are considered precursors to phonics and are needed to learn phonics. They are important to achieve successful reading ability. However, they are one part of a comprehensive program in learning to read (National Reading Panel, 2000). It is the concurrent use of several word-study skills that creates a proficient reader (Reutzel and Cooter, 2004). According to the National Reading Panel Report (2000), 18 hours of teaching phonemic awareness in the kindergarten year is needed for a child to learn the skills. In a 180-day school year, that would be about six minutes a day.

Phonemic and Phonological Awareness Instruction

Instruction in phonemic and phonological awareness should be playful as teachers read stories, tell stories, play word games, and use rhymes and riddles. Instruction in the area should be purposeful and planned; we cannot leave it to chance. In the past this instruction was spontaneous and incidental. Of course, it can still be spontaneous when the moment arises and should be; however, it must be systematically written into daily plans. Try as much as possible to make your instruction meaningful and with a purpose (Adams, 2001).

It is easiest for young children to learn to deal with larger parts of words or whole words first and then smaller parts. A skill to begin with in phonemic awareness is exposing children to rhyming activities. This is considered to be the easiest task, since it is deals with a whole word. Rhyming activities can be done in preschool and kindergarten. Simply chanting nursery rhymes or reading stories that rhyme helps children develop the skill. Next children can deal with segmenting sounds such as listening for and counting syllables in words. Have children learn about segmenting sounds in words by clapping the sounds in their name. The most difficult skill dealing with phonological awareness is segmenting and then blending words together using onsets and rimes. An onset is the beginning sound in a word; the rime is the ending chunk or group of letters in a word. Work in this area, for example, asks children to listen for the beginning sound in the word *cat,* which is *c,* and then to put it together with its ending chunk *at* to make the whole word *cat* (Yopp & Yopp, 2000). When teaching activities that help to learn rhyming, segmenting, and blending we ask children to match sounds, to work with sounds in isolation, and to make sound substitutions and sound deletions. These activities help children learn about sounds in words.

When asking children to match, we may ask them to identify whether two words start with the same sound, such as, *big* and *boy.*

When working with words in isolation, we will ask children what sound they hear at the beginning of the word *cow.* We are not asking for the letter name; we are asking for the sound.

When we ask children to substitute sounds, we change the beginning sound of a word like *bat* to *mmm,* and ask what the word is now, *mat?*

When we ask children to delete, we might say, tell me what word we have when we say the word *snowman* without the *man,* or *hat* without the *h.* Remember that phonological awareness involves saying sounds and not identifying them with the letters. They are oral exercises.

The easiest phonemic awareness task is working with rhymes. Teachers can help children to hear, identify, and match to similar word patterns such as rhymes. Early work in this area should be playful. Exposing children to books that contain rhymes such as *Green Eggs and Ham* (Seuss, 1960), *Goodnight Moon* (Brown, 1947), and *The Queen of Hearts* (Hennessy & Pearson, 1989) helps develop the skill. Teachers can recite rhyming and nonrhyming words from the books and ask children to differentiate between them. For additional practice with rhyme, children can do the following:

Make up words that rhyme with their names.

Sing songs that rhyme and separate out the rhyming words.

Act out well-known nursery rhymes such as Jack and Jill.

Make up new rhymes in a story such as *I Know an Old Lady.* Let the children decide what else she could swallow and what would happen to her if she did. For example, "I know an old lady who swallowed a frog, she began to jog when she swallowed a frog."

It is a good idea to have some routine rhymes and songs that the class chants repeatedly. The chant should allow children to change the rhymes and to match and substitute rhymes. The following chant will allow children to make up rhymes and substitute rhymes:

Let's Make a Rhyme

When it's cold outside, and you want to play,
Let's make a rhyme, my teacher would say.
    Did you ever see a dog
    Pushing a log
On a cold and winter's day?

When it's cold outside, and you want to play,
Let's make a rhyme, my teacher would say.
   Did you ever see a moose
   Pushing a goose
On a cold and winter's day?

The next step is for each child to think of an animal to make a rhyme with, for example:

   Did you ever see a cow
   Saying bow wow
On a cold and winter's day?

Segmenting is an important skill that is more difficult than rhyming for children. It is easier for a child to segment the beginning sound or onset, and then the ending chunk or rime. If this is done with the word *man,* for example, the child should be guided to say *mmm* for the onset /m/ and then *annn* for the rime /an/.

Syllabication is a way of segmenting words or working on phonological awareness. Children can clap the syllables in their names and in the names of their friends.

Name Chant

If your name has a beat and the beat is one,
   Say and clap your name and then run, run, run.

If your name has a beat and the beat is two,
   Say and clap your name and hop like a kangaroo.

If your name has a beat and the beat is three,
   Say and clap your name, then buzz like a bee.

If your name has a beat and the beat is four,
   Say and clap your name and stamp on the floor.

After segmenting words, ask children to blend them back together again. The goal is for children to be able to identify each sound within a word, know the number of sounds heard, and blend the word back together. We can ask then to stretch the word out like a rubber band, which would be asking them to segment, and then say it really really fast as the elastic springs back to blend. The following are some activities that will help children learn to segment and blend:

Sing the song "Bingo." In the song each letter is chanted and then blended together. Change the words from "There was a farmer had a dog and Bingo was his name," to "There is a pretty girl (or handsome boy) that I know and Jenny is her name-o, J-e-n-n-y, J-e-n-n-y, J-e-n-n-y, and Jenny is her name-o."

Play a riddle substitution of onsets game. Say, "I'm thinking of a word that sounds like head, *but begins with the /b/ sound," or, "I'm thinking of a word that sounds like* fat, *but has an /mmm/ sound at the beginning."*

A good song for segmenting and blending goes to the tune of "This Old Man." You can use the name of the letter featured or use the letter sounds.

This Old Man

This old man sings N songs
He sings N songs all day long
With a Nick, Nack, Nakie Nack
He sings his silly song
He wants you to sing along

This old man sings B songs
He sings B songs all day long
With a Bick, Back, Bakie Back
He sings his silly song
He wants you to sing along

Now make up your own verse with a new sound.

Elkonin boxes are used to engage children in segmentation and blending (Figure 5.3). Select and write words on a piece of paper. Draw square boxes next to each word. Have chips for students to put into the squares. Say the word on the paper, such as duck, and have the children put the number of chips in the boxes that represent the number of sounds in the word. For the word duck, children would put three chips into the boxes because the second ck in the word has one sound (Invernizzi, 2003; Fitzpatrick, 1997; Johns, Lenski, & Elish-Piper, 1999).

Learning About the Alphabet

 Many young children who cannot yet identify individual letters of the alphabet are able to read. As noted, they read sight words from environmental print, from classroom labels, and from Very Own Words lists. They learn other sight words from repeated readings and shared book experiences. It is not necessary to be able to identify and name the letters of the alphabet in order to develop an initial sight-reading vocabulary. It is easier for a young child *initially* to learn

Figure 5.3

Word-Study Game

Directions: Let's figure out how many sounds in the word "bell." I'm going to say it again, B-E-LL. Put a chip in the squares for each sound you heard in the word BELL. How many chips did you use? Now look at the letters in the word BELL. How many do you count (4)? A word can have different numbers of letters and sounds.

whole words already familiar through oral language, rather than learn abstract letters. Familiar words carry meaning for them, whereas isolated letters do not.

Children, of course, need to learn the alphabet to become independently fluent readers and writers. However, there is no evidence that alphabet identification should be treated as the first skill in early literacy; it makes more sense for children to learn to identify letters after they have learned several sight words. Traditionally, the alphabet has often been the first thing parents try to teach their children at home, and it is usually high on any list of reading readiness skills in preschool and kindergarten curricula. Because it is difficult to depart from deeply rooted tradition, learning the alphabet will always be prominent in early literacy programs.

Allow children to explore letters by using manipulative materials available in the literacy center. Be sure to include in the center alphabet puzzles, magnetic upper- and lowercase letters with an accompanying magnetic board, a set of wooden upper- and lowercase letters, tactile letters made of sandpaper, alphabet games, felt letters and an accompanying felt board, letter stencils, alphabet flash cards, and a long alphabet chart posted along the wall of the classroom at the children's eye level. In addition to these materials, a large supply of alphabet books and taped songs about the alphabet should be in the classroom library. (See Appendix A for a list of alphabet books.) Encourage children to explore these materials first through play. Later, they will begin to identify the letters they are playing with and teach letters they know to other children. Provide chalk and a chalkboard so they can make letters themselves. Children also enjoy finger-painting letters, painting them on easels, and shaping them out of clay. They like to eat alphabet soup or alphabet cookies or pretzels. Shaping letters with their fingers and whole bodies is an activity often used in early childhood rooms.

Systematic teaching of the alphabet, one letter per week, is not as successful as teaching children letters that are meaningful to them. Many teachers help children identify the letters in their own names first. When teaching thematic units, select a few letters to feature that are used in the context of the theme. For example, in a unit on transportation, feature *b* for boat and *t* for train. When children have learned to identify several different letters, ask them to look for the same letters in other contexts, such as magazines, newspapers, and books. Check children individually by using flash cards to determine which letters they know and which they do not know. Ask children which letters they would like to learn next from their Very Own Words. Give children flash cards of the letters they choose to learn, and encourage them to use those letters in all the activities just mentioned. Letters also need to be practiced all year through.

Additional ideas for learning and reinforcing what is known about the alphabet include the following:

Sing the alphabet song often and point to the letters on a poster as they are sung.

Play letter bingo, which involves cards filled with letters and markers to cover them. Call a letter and hold up a card with the letter on it to help children with letter identification. When a child covers one row of letters on the card, he or she gets bingo.

Provide children with alphabet journals. On each page is another letter of the alphabet. On the different letter pages children can trace the letter, write the letter, and find words in a magazine that use the letter and paste them on the page.

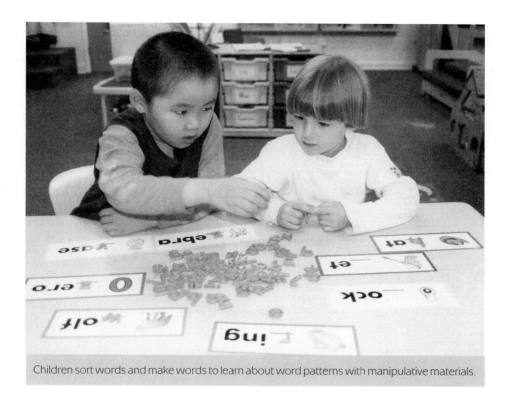

Children sort words and make words to learn about word patterns with manipulative materials.

Create an alphabet center with many different alphabet materials such as those already mentioned (magnetic letters, wooden letters, matching letter games, alphabet puzzles, alphabet books, alphabet stamps, alphabet flash cards). Children will identify this area with the alphabet and should be encouraged to use the materials often.

State standards expect children to be able to name and recognize the letters of the alphabet by the end of kindergarten. Teachers need to check children's knowledge of the alphabet and provide instruction based on the findings. If more direct instruction is needed to help students, then it should be provided. The letters of the alphabet must be practiced regularly. Students should be exposed to letters on a daily basis and in different settings. Figure 5.4 illustrates a commonly used form to record children's letter knowledge. Eventually children need to learn the alphabetic principle—knowing that words are composed of letters and that there is a systemic relationship between the letters and the sounds they hear.

Strategies for Teaching Phonics

Phonics is the most well known word-study strategy. Quite simply, phonics is the connection of sounds and symbols. The use of phonics requires children to learn letter sounds and combinations of letter sounds (referred to as phonemes) associated with their corresponding letter symbols (referred to as graphemes). In the English language there are 26 letters in the alphabet; however, there are at least 44 different sounds. Sound–symbol correspondence is not always consistent in English; there are many irregularities and exceptions to many rules, which are difficult for children to learn. Therefore, we must help children learn

| Figure 5.4 | *A Form to Record Children's Letter Knowledge* |

Letter Identification Score Sheet

Child's name _____   Age _____   Date _____

Recorder _____   Date of birth _____

	A	**IR**		**A**	**IR**
A			a		
F			f		
K			k		
P			p		
W			w		
Z			z		
B			b		
H			h		
O			o		
J			j		
U			u		
C			c		
Y			y		
L			l		
Q			q		
M			m		
D			d		
N			n		
S			s		
X			x		
I			i		
E			e		
G			g		
R			r		
V			v		
T			t		

Confusions:

Letters unknown:

Comments:

A = Alphabet response: (✓); IR = Incorrect response: record what the child says.   **Test Score:** ☐

words by sight that cannot be sounded out, and we need to give them strategies for figuring out words.

There is a recommended sequence for teaching phonics. However, when teachable moments occur, teachers should take advantage of them whether or not they are within recommended sequences.

Consonants

We begin teaching phonics with most commonly used initial consonant sounds such as *f, m, s, t,* and *h,* and then use these same sounds in ending word positions. The next set of initial and final consonant sounds usually taught are *l, d, c, n, g, w, p, r, k,* then *j, q, v,* final *x,* initial *y,* and *z.* Consonants are quite regular and represent one sound. Some consonants have two sounds such as *g* as in the word *garage, go,* and *girl,* often referred to as the hard *g,* and *g* as in *George, giraffe,* and *gentleman,* referred to as the soft *g.* Other consonants with two sounds are *c* as in *cookie, cut,* and *cost,* the hard *c* sound, and *c* as in *circus, celebrate,* and *ceremony,* the soft *c* sound. The letter *x* has a *z* sound at the beginning of a word, as in *xylophone,* but has the *x* sound as in the word *next.* The letters *w* and *y* say their names at the beginning of a word and act as consonants, as in *was* and *yellow.* In the middle or at the end of a word, *w* and *y* act as vowels, as in *today* and *blow.* Learning the consonant sounds begins in preschool in a limited way; more instruction occurs in kindergarten; and they are mastered in first grade.

Consonant blends and consonant digraphs are pairs of consonants that make new sounds. The blends are clusters of two or three consonants in which the sounds of all the consonants are heard but blended together, as in the words *blue, true, flew,* and *string.* Consonant digraphs are composed of two consonants that when put together do not have the sound of either one but rather an altogether new sound, such as *th* in *three, sh* in *shoes, ch* in *chair, ph* in *photograph,* and *gh* at the end of a word as in *enough.*

Vowels

The next phonic elements we teach are called vowels, which are *a, e, i, o,* and *u.* We teach short vowels first: *a* as in *cat, e* as in *bed, i* as in *hit, o* as in *hot,* and *u* as in *cut.* Next we teach long vowels, *a* as in *hate, e* as in *feet, i* as in *kite, o* as in *boat,* and *u* as in *cute.* Long vowels have the sound of the name of the letter. As mentioned earlier, *w* and *y* act as vowels in the middle and at the end of words. The letter *y* has the sound of a long *e* when it comes at the end of a word as in *baby.* The *y* has the sound of a long *i* when it is at the end of a one-syllable word such as *cry, try.*

Vowels change their sound when they are *r*-controlled. They become neither long nor short, as in *car* and *for.* As with consonants, there are vowel pairs that we teach. The first vowel pair is called a vowel digraph (two vowels represent a single sound such as *ai* in *pail* and *ea* in *seat*). The next vowel pair is called a diphthong. Diphthongs are a combination of two vowels that form a gliding sound as one vowel sound blends into the other, such as *oy* in toy and *oi* in oil.

Vowels can be difficult for children to learn, since they have many sounds and combinations of sounds that make the sounds change. The vowel sounds can begin to be taught in kindergarten; however, direct and systematic instruction occurs in first grade.

The phonic elements to deal with next include some structural aspects of words. At each grade level, teachers should review what has been learned and add on additional work in medial consonants, variant consonant sounds and blends, compound words, syllabication, contractions, prefixes, suffixes, synonyms, antonyms, and homonyms.

Children find it easier to learn about word patterns or chunks rather then individual sounds. Word patterns help in decoding many different words that contain the same patterns but may have a different beginning or ending sound. Teachers should help students to learn familiar word patterns, often referred to as phonograms, chunks, or word families. These groups of letters when at the end of a word are referred to as rimes. There are many common rimes. A list is provided in Figure 5.5.

There are many phonic generalizations or rules. Most of them only apply to a few words and therefore are not worth learning. There are three that are consistent and therefore are worth teaching:

> When a one-syllable word has only one vowel and the vowel comes in the middle of two consonants, the vowel is usually short, such as *hot, cut,* and *bet.* This is called the CVC pattern rule.
>
> When there are two vowels in a word with one syllable, and one of them is an *e* at the end of the word, the first vowel is long and the *e* is silent. This is called the CVCe pattern or the final *e* rule. Some words that demonstrate the rule include *plate, cute,* and *bone.*
>
> When a consonant is followed by a vowel, the vowel is usually long, as in *be, go,* and *because.* This is called the CV rule.

Earlier in the chapter I discussed the necessity for teaching phonics within meaningful contexts, along with a systematic and direct presentation of skills. It is also important that children have continual practice to learn sound–symbol relationships; rarely is a single lesson sufficient. Therefore, teachers should provide several experiences with letter and letter–sound combinations, and review with children as often as possible.

Meaning-Based Strategies

How can we help children recognize the sound–symbol relationships of consonants and vowels in a meaningful context? Science and social studies themes lend themselves to featuring letters that appear in units. For example, when studying farm, pet, and zoo animals, feature the letter *p,* because it is used frequently with this context. The following types of activities can follow:

1. Read *The Pig's Picnic* (Kasza, 1988), *Pet Show* (Keats, 1974), and *The Tale of Peter Rabbit* (Potter, 1902) during the unit, and point out words that begin with the letter *p* in these books.
2. Make word charts using words from the books that begin with the letter *p.*
3. On a field trip, bring peanuts to the zoo to feed the animals.
4. Make lists of animals that begin with the letter *p.*
5. Read the book *Animalia* (Base, 1987) and point out the *p* page, which says "Proud Peacocks Preening Perfect Plumage."
6. Collect sensory items about animals that begin with the letter *p,* such as Puppy Chow to smell, peanuts to eat and to feed to elephants when you visit the zoo, peacock plumes to touch, a purring kitten to listen to, and the book *Petunia* (Duvoisin, 1950) to look at and read.

7. List words from the unit that begin with the letter *p*.

8. Write an experience chart of activities carried out during the unit, and highlight the letter *p* when it appears in the chart.

9. Ask children to add to their Very Own Word collection with favorite words from the unit that begin with the letter *p*.

10. Make a collage of pictures featuring things from the unit, and mark those that begin with the letter *p*.

11. Print on a chart the song "Peter Cottontail." Sing the song and highlight the letter *p* when it appears.

12. Have children help you make up nonsense rhymes for featured letters and chant them, such as the following:

    My name is Penelope Pig.
    I pick petals off of petunias.
    I play patty-cake
    and eat pretzels with pink punch.

13. Add a page for the letter *p* to a class Big Book entitled *Our Own Big Book of Letters, Sounds, and Words.* Have children draw pictures or paste in pictures of words that begin with the letter *p*. (Directions for making a Big Book are in Chapter 6, page 160.)

14. Complete a worksheet for the letter *p* that requires students to trace the letter, write the letter, and circle pictures that begin with the letter *p,* such as *pig* and *popcorn.*

15. Encourage children to write about their experiences during the unit, such as their visit to the zoo, the books they read, and the songs they sang. In their writing they will be using the letters emphasized, and, although their writing may not be conventional, through the use of their invented spellings they are indirectly enhancing their phonemic awareness. When children write, they have to face the problem of mapping spoken language into written language. This process can lead to an understanding of the structure of spoken language. The more children write, the better they become at segmenting sounds in words. This point is demonstrated in the following example of Zach's story about *The Pig's Picnic.* He wrote, "Pig wanted the picnic to be perfect," as follows:

Pg wtd tha pcnc to be prfkt

Children's literature is an excellent source for featuring letters attached to themes. Be careful not to abuse the stories by overemphasizing the sounds featured; however, do not pass up the opportunity to feature letters in this natural book setting. For example, in a unit on food, Ms. Fino, a first-grade teacher, featured the letter *b* and read *Blueberries for Sal* (McCloskey, 1948), *Bread and Jam for Frances* (Hoban, 1964), and *The Berenstain Bears and Too Much Birthday* (Berenstain & Berenstain, 1987).

These and similar activities can be carried out for any initial consonant. Whenever letters being featured in a thematic unit appear in a language experience chart or a piece of children's literature, point them out to the children. Alphabet books generally use sound–symbol relationships as they introduce each letter, as do picture storybooks that use a particular letter prominently. (See Appendix A for children's literature for building sound–symbol relationships.)

When we read, we use several skills concurrently to decode and derive meaning from the printed page. We therefore need to encourage children to use multiple rather than isolated skills in their approach to reading. Children should be taught to use context clues and phonic clues simultaneously. One strategy that accomplishes this goal has already been suggested—reading a sentence in which you pause and leave a "blank" to be filled in by the child. For example, say, "The b_____ flew up to the tree and landed on a branch." Supplying the initial consonant for the word, either by sound or by sight, draws on a child's skills with phonics, context, syntax, and semantics.

Whenever possible take advantage of spontaneous situations to help children learn about print, such as the following example:

> *Christopher, a child in first grade, had just written his name on a picture he drew and exclaimed, "Wow, the word* STOP *is right in the middle of my name. See Christopher." He pointed to the letters in his name that spelled* STOP. *He continued, "But that doesn't make sense, then I should say my name Chri-STOP-her." The teacher immediately seized the opportunity to point out the* ph *digraph and explain to Christopher that the word* STOP *was in his name but when the letters* p *and* h *come together, they make a new sound as heard in Christopher, like the sound of* f. *She mentioned other words such as* photograph *and* phantom *that illustrated the* ph *sound.*

Explicit Word-Study Activities

Based on research about how children learn and how the brain works, activities with word families, also called *phonograms* and *word chunks,* that include building words and sorting words into different patterns help children learn letter–sound relationships and consequently how to decode unknown words. Word sorts and word building with *onsets* (the initial letter or letters before the first vowel) and *rimes* (the vowel and what follows), allow children to look at bigger chunks of words. When children learn how to figure out new ones by looking at and using the patterns in words, they have developed a strategy to deal with other unknowns. According to research, the brain looks for known patterns when involved in learning. It takes what is known and tries to apply it to the unknown. Patterns such as familiar word endings help children deal with unknowns (Strickland & Snow, 2002).

MAKING WORDS. Making words is a gamelike activity in which children learn to look for patterns in words and ways to make new words by changing one letter or more. Children use magnetic letters, wooden letters, felt letters, or letter tiles. In this activity, the teacher asks children to make words from a real word selected from a story, new vocabulary, themed words, and the like. The word can be scrambled or spelled correctly (Gunning, 2003)

Another popular type of word-making activity uses onsets and rimes. With younger children, the teacher provides a few well-known rimes such as *at, an,* or *in* and asks the children to make as many words with these endings as they can think of by adding different initial consonants or consonant blends to the beginning of the rimes. With the rime *at,* for example, children could create the following words: *cat, sat, mat, rat, hat, fat, nat, pat,* and *bat*. With the letters *a, d, n, s,* and *t,* children can be asked to do the following:

> Use two letters to make *at*
> Add a letter to make *sat*
> Take away a letter to make *at.*

Figure 5.5

Common Rimes Used in Early Literacy

ack	al	ain	ake	ale	ame	an	ank	up	ush
at	ate	aw	ay	ell	eat	est	ice	ick	ight
id	ill	in	ine	ing	ink	ip	ir	ock	oke
op	ore	or	uck	ug	ump	unk			

Change a letter to make *an*
Add a letter to make *Dan.*
Change a letter to make *tan*
Take away a letter to make *an*
Add a letter to make *and*
Add a letter to make *sand* (Cunningham & Cunningham, 1992)

Change a letter to make **word sorts.** After words have been made, they can be sorted in many different ways, or teachers can provide words for sorting. For example, if children make little words from the bigger word *Thanksgiving,* such as *thanks, giving, sing, sang, hang, king, thanking,* and *having,* they can be asked to sort the words that all have the *-ing* ending, words that rhymed, words ending with the consonant *g,* words beginning with the consonant *s,* and so on. Sorting words for blends, digraphs, and numbers of syllables are other ways to help students see patterns. Words also can be sorted for meaning by categories such as colors and types of food.

Using phonograms, or rimes, is an important way for children to sort and make words. A list of the most commonly used rimes for children to learn is presented in Figure 5.5 (Wylie & Durrell, 1970).

TEACHING CHILDREN HOW TO DEAL WITH NEW WORDS. When children learn new words, they need to look at the elements within the word to help them understands its parts. Figure 5.6 is a word-study guide for young children to use when they are introduced to new vocabulary.

Figure 5.6

Tell It to Yourself and a Friend Word-Study Guide

- The word is ___Hat_____

- When I say and stretch the word, it sounds like this _____

- The numbers of letters I see in the word is _____

- I hear this number of sounds in the word _____

- The spelling pattern in the word is _____

- This is what I know about the vowel in the word

_____

- Other words with the same sounds are

_____

- A sound box for this word looks like this:

_____

A Center for Word-Study Activities

A center that contains materials for word study is necessary in early childhood classrooms. The activities for making and sorting words discussed earlier can be gamelike if they are presented with interesting manipulative materials. With onsets and rimes as well as scrambled words, teachers can have children use magnetic letters and a magnetic board for making words. Students can use movable wooden letters, rubber foam letters, or flash cards with letters on them. Flash cards can have word endings on them or initial consonants or consonant blends. All onsets can be written in one color and rimes in another. The flash cards can be used to make words on a table or a pocket chart. To make this activity even more interesting, letter stamps and white slates with magic markers will work for making words. Some teachers make manipulatives such as movable wheels for making words. Board games such as bingo, lotto, concentration, and Candyland and card games can be constructed so that children have to make words within the rules of the game. Figure 5.7 illustrates some sample word-study games to place in centers.

Games for centers can be purchased from stores for teachers and large school supply companies. Teachers also can create numerous word-study activities that children learn from, use to reinforce what they know, and use independently when teachers are engaged in small-group instruction. Teachers can make materials and seek the help of parents, aides, and upper-grade children to make materials. Following is a list of books that contain ideas for word-study center materials:

Bear, D. R., Invernizzi, M., Templeton, S., & Johnston, D. (1996). *Words their way.* Englewood Cliffs, NJ: Prentice Hall.

Cunningham, P., & Hall, D. (1994). *Making words.* Torrance, CA: Good Apple.

Cunningham, P. (1995). *Phonics they use.* New York: HarperCollins.

Hill, S. (1997). *Reading manipulatives.* Cypress, CA: Creative Teaching Press.

Marriott, D. (1997). *What are the other kids doing?* Cypress, CA: Creative Teaching Press.

Morrow, L. M. (2002). *The literacy center: Contexts for reading and writing.* Portland, ME: Stenhouse.

Rosencrans, G. (1998). *The spelling book: Teaching children how to spell, not what to spell.* Newark, DE: International Reading Association.

USING A WORD-STUDY CENTER. From this rich collection of ideas and materials, Mr. Rosen assigned word-study activities for students to work on while he worked with small groups in guided reading instruction. The following explains the activities the children engaged in during center time.

Four children made as many words from the word *Thanksgiving* as they could. The letters of *Thanksgiving* had been cut up and placed in plastic baggies for each child. In addition to manipulating the letters to create words, the children wrote the words on an activity sheet.

With magnetic letters and their own individual magnetic slates children created word ladders. They started with one-letter words, then two, then three, and so on. Each child also had a five-by-eight index card to write his or her word from the bottom of the card up the ladder. A partner checked the words.

Figure 5.7 *Word-Study Games*

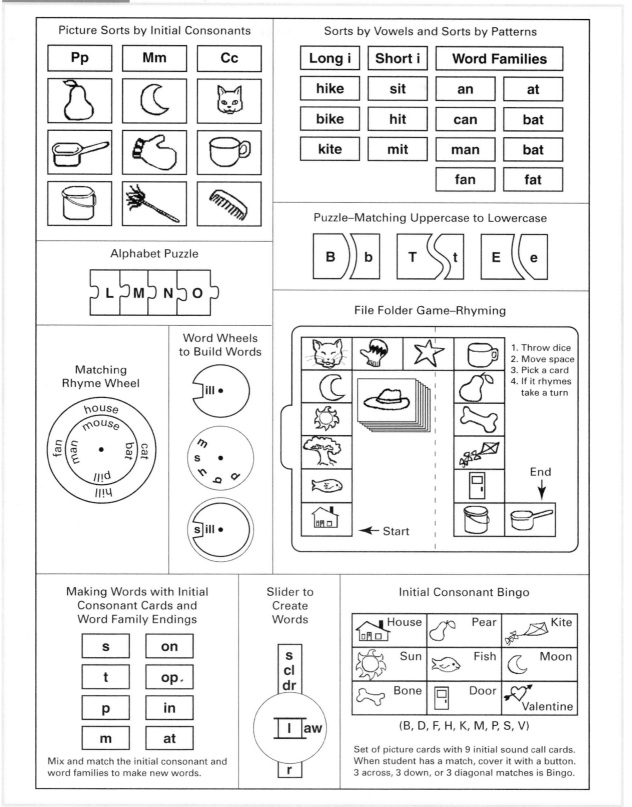

Source: Words Their Way: Word Study for Phonics, Vocabulary, and Spelling Instruction by D. R. Bear,
M. Invernezzi, S. Templeton, & D. Johnson, © 1996. Adapted by permission of Pearson Education, Inc.,
Upper Saddle River, NJ.

Another group of four children worked with ending phonograms or chunks, as Mr. Rosen called them, by creating words with onsets or initial consonants. He had prepared sliders, which are oak tag circles that have ending phonograms, with a slide of onsets to create words. Children created words with the sliders and wrote them down. They wrote additional words thought of as well.

Finally children created sentences with letter and word stamps. The stamps had familiar words for the children to create into sentences.

All these activities were manipulative. They involved children working with words from individual letters, to letter chunks, beginnings and ends of words, and total sentences. They also required children to work together, check each other's work, and collaborate. All the activities had a pencil-and-paper component for recording what was done; for example, the little words made from the big word *Thanksgiving* were written on a sheet of paper provided. This way the teacher has a record of work done with manipulatives and students are responsible for completing tasks. All children have the opportunity to use every material during this period.

Concerns about Phonics

There are several concerns about teaching phonics. A major problem is that so many rules for the English language have exceptions. For example, the sound of *k* in the word *kite* is its usual sound, but when *k* is followed by *n* it becomes silent as in the word *knot*. I believe that we should teach fewer rather than more rules because the ability to apply them is so limited for young children. Exceptions can be dealt with when they occur in print, or be treated as sight words when they are uncommon. In early childhood, our main concern should be with sound–symbol relationships and generalizations that rarely have exceptions.

Another problem when dealing with sound–symbol relationships is dialects. If a teacher from upstate New York taught in South Carolina or Georgia, he or she would teach long and short vowels with different sounds than those taught by a teacher who was from the South. Children in most parts of the United States live in communities comprising youngsters who speak many different dialects and attend the same school. These children may have difficulty dealing with sounds regardless of where their teacher is from.

In addition, there are different types of learners. There are auditory learners and visual learners. A child who is weak in auditory discrimination is not likely to master phonics and is best taught to his or her strength rather than to a weakness. The skills a child acquires as a result of learning phonics are important for becoming a proficient reader; alternatively, it is just one strategy within the total picture of literacy development, and we need not overemphasize it.

Oral Reading

We ask children to read orally in early literacy classrooms for many reasons. We can determine their reading level, the types of strategies children have for decoding and comprehending text, the types of errors they make, and strategies they need to develop. Oral reading tells us about children's reading **fluency,** which is determined by the rate of reading, accuracy, expression used, and phrasing. Children who are fluent readers use verbal expression and intonation that conveys the meaning of the text, and they attend to punctuation.

The accuracy with which children read particular passages determines their reading level. Reading level indicates which materials should be used for instructional purposes, which used for independent reading, and which will be too difficult. When children read orally, we can also find out if they self-monitor their own reading. For example, when they make an error, do they correct that error on their own? Do they search through the text to figure out words?

When we listen to children read orally, we can provide needed strategies for independent reading. The following are prompts for strategies students can use when they have difficulty decoding. The prompts should help children gain meaning from the text. These prompts are adapted from those presented by Fountas and Pinnell (1996).

Prompts to support the reader's use of sources of information:

Check the pictures.

Does that make sense?

Does that word sound right?

What's wrong with this? (Repeat what the child said.)

Try that again and think of a word that makes sense.

Do you know a word that starts with those letters?

Do you know a word that ends with those letters?

Prompts to support the reader's use of self-monitoring or checking behavior:

Were you right?

Why did you stop?

Would _____ fit here?

Would _____ make sense?

Check it. Does it look right and sound right to you?

You almost got that. See if you can find what is wrong.

Try that again.

Prompts to support the reader's self-correction behavior:

I liked the way you worked that out.

You made a mistake. Can you find it?

You're nearly right. Try again.

What else can you do to try and get the words right?

Prompts to support phrased, fluent reading:

Can you read this quickly?

Put your words together so it sounds like talking.

Source: Adapted by permission from *Guided Reading: Good First Teaching for All Children* by Irene C. Fountas and Gay Su Pinnell. Copyright © 1996 by Irene C. Fountas and Gay Su Pinnell. Published by Heinemann, division of Reed Elsevier, Inc., Portsmouth, New Hampshire.

Published Materials for Literacy Instruction

When we discuss development of skills, it is natural to talk about published materials. Published materials have been available for many years and have played an important role in literacy instruction. The materials have been referred to as basal readers. In the early 1990s when whole language was the model for instruction and children's literature the main source for literacy development, basal readers were referred to as anthologies of children's literature. These prepared reading instructional materials have been more popular at some times than at others, depending on the focus for literacy instruction. The programs are used by most school districts, and probably will continue to be used because they provide a complete package of instructional materials and are revised to include new findings in early literacy development. Some general rules should be applied to the selection and use of materials.

Study the objectives for the published program and determine if they incorporate the latest findings on strategies for nurturing early literacy.

Determine if the program matches the goals for standards set forth by the district or state where the material will be used.

Determine if the program includes developmentally appropriate practice as you view it in your district.

Ensure that the materials suit the needs of the children you teach.

Urban and rural children may need materials different from children in suburban settings. Are there materials suited for children who speak English as a second language?

Examine the materials for clarity, appeal to children, and durability.

Analyze the teacher's editions for clarity of objectives, descriptions of plans, suitability of lesson content, and flexibility for teachers in using the material. The program should put the teacher in charge of the materials; the materials should not dictate to the teacher.

Ensure that leveled little books to match instruction to children's reading ability are included.

In addition, ask the following questions about the published materials:

Are technology components available?

Are there practice materials?

Do the books have adequate multicultural representation?

Are a variety of genres presented in stories?

Do the stories link to other content areas?

Are there manipulative independent activities for centers and independent work?

Does the assessment component meet district's needs?

Are there plans for organizing and managing the delivery of the program?

Does the publishing company provide adequate staff development with the program?

Published materials have changed from text developed to help children acquire specific skills to become fluent readers, to real literature to help children learn to read from authentic meaningful text. The issue of the type of text to use for literacy instruction has always been of concern. Texts developed to teach specific skills often lack meaning and literary qualities. They do, however, provide a sequenced plan for helping young children understand what they read, with repeated vocabulary, limited vocabulary, phonetic elements, picture clues, and so on. Another type of text proposed by some educators is called "decodable text," which has several definitions. Some suggest that with decodable text all skills needed to read are taught before giving a child the material to read. In this text about 75 percent of the words include letter–sound patterns that are familiar to children and are taught until the text is given to the child to read. The main focus of the text is phonetically regular patterns. When introducing phonetic elements such as initial consonants *D, R,* and *M* and the *an* phonogram, decodable text might read:

Dan ran after the man.

Before reading the text, the word *the* would be taught as a high-frequency word and the word *after* as a sight word.

Basal materials always have had grade designations. One of the problems with grade designations is that, although the material is probably appropriate for instructing most children in a particular grade, some students will be reading above the level or below the level of their designated grade. For instruction to be useful, the level of the material is critical.

Many teachers figure out the difficulty level of books and select them to match the instructional level of the small groups they teach. Commercial publishers also level their materials. The leveled books are typically little paperbacks. Publishers may designate the grade level, or give them a letter level such as A, B, or C books. The purpose of leveled books is to disregard the grade assignment completely and to determine a child's level of reading and then select the appropriate book for instruction. Books are leveled for difficulty based on the following factors (adapted from Fountas & Pinnell, 1996):

The length of a book, including number of pages and words

The size and layout of the print

The patterns, predictability, and structure of language

Text structures and genres used

Phonetic patterns in the words

How well the illustration supports the text

Teachers working together have leveled collections of their books based on these criteria. They test the books by having children read them to determine how difficult or easy they are to read. To enhance collections teachers use central areas for storing leveled books so they have access to those needed for their students.

Publishers also create sets of leveled books, making purchasing easier for teachers if funds are available. Publishers level books based on many different criteria. One publisher may level books with specific repeated vocabulary, introduction of specific phonetic elements, and the like. Some companies that create leveled books for instruction are the following:

Benchmark Word I.D., 2107 N. Providence Road, Media, PA 19063

Rigby, 500 Coventry Lane, Suite 200, Crystal Lake, IL 60014

Scholastic, Inc., 555 Broadway, New York, NY 10012-3999

Sundance Publishers, 234 Taylor Street, Littleton, MA 01460

The Wright Group, 19201 120th Avenue NE, Bothell, WA 98011-9512

William H. Sadlier, 9 Pine Street, New York, NY 10005-1002

Selecting the appropriate book for instruction also can be done with the use of the running record described in Chapter 2 about assessment. The test is administered with leveled material. When a child scores 90 to 95 percent with a particular book, the level of that book is his or her reading instructional level. If the child scores higher than 95 percent, the book is for independent reading, and a score below 90 percent indicates the book is too difficult for the child to read.

Each teacher needs to make critical decisions about the use of materials in his or her instructional program. You should be in control of published materials and not allow the materials to dictate to you, as mentioned. For example, select sequences to use from the material that seem most appropriate. You need not start at the beginning of a book and follow it page by page to the end. Eliminate sections that you feel are inappropriate for your children. Repeat material when necessary. We have not found one published program that will determine the success or failure of literacy development with all young children. It is how you use the materials along with your basic philosophy and organization of the entire literacy program that will determine success. Commercially prepared instructional materials are only one part of literacy development. Many school districts use published materials, and many teachers depend on them as organizational tools. As a teacher you must decide on the design of your literacy instruction, the materials you use, and how you use them. Over and over again in research investigations, when the teacher is included as a variable when testing different types of methods, he or she is found to be the most important element for literacy success.

Assessing Knowledge of Word-Study Skills

There are numerous word-study skills discussed in this chapter. Initially, teachers should be concerned with a child's phonemic awareness. The Yopp-Singer Test of Phoneme Segmentation (Yopp, 1992), in Figure 5.8, is widely used to determine how well children can segment phonemes in words. The directions specify to ensure that the child says the sounds, not the letters in the word, because these are two different skills.

Fluency, self-monitoring, accuracy, level of text, knowledge of basic phonics when reading, and types of errors made all can be determined with the running record. A description of the purpose of a running record and how it is administered and scored is in Chapter 2.

| **Figure 5.8** | *Yopp-Singer Test of Phoneme Segmentation (Yopp, 1992)* |

Child's name _____ **Date** _____

Score (number correct) _____

Directions: Today we're going to play a word game. I'm going to say a word and I want you to break the word apart. You are going to tell me each sound in the word in order. For example, if I say "old," you should say /o/-/l/-/d/." (*Administrator: Be sure to say the sounds, not the letters, in the word.*) Let's try a few together.

Practice items: (*Assist the child in segmenting these items as necessary.*) ride, go, man

Test items: (*Circle those items that the student correctly segments; incorrect responses may be recorded on the blank line following the item.*)

1. dog _____	12. lay _____
2. keep _____	13. race _____
3. fine _____	14. zoo _____
4. no _____	15. three _____
5. she _____	16. job _____
6. wave _____	17. in _____
7. grew _____	18. ice _____
8. that _____	19. at _____
9. red _____	20. top _____
10. me _____	21. by _____
11. sat _____	22. do _____

Source: The author, Hallie Kay Yopp, California State University, Fullerton, grants permission for this test to be reproduced. The author acknowledges the contribution of the late Henry Singer to the development of this test.

In addition to daily performance samples of children's writing and activity sheets, observations and descriptions of children's reading behaviors should be included in word-study assessment. Checklists (like the one on pages 152–153) are also important materials for testing children on word-study skills. For example, to test for knowledge of the alphabet, the teacher can name particular letters and ask a child to circle them on a sheet of paper containing upper- and lowercase letters. Teachers can also use flash cards of letters for students to identify. Basic sight words are checked similarly to alphabetic knowledge by circling on a sheet of paper or with flash cards. To determine the ability to rhyme, the teacher says pairs of words and asks children to identify which do and which do not rhyme. Knowledge of phonetic sounds such as consonants is checked by having the child circle a picture that begins with a particular letter. Sometimes the teacher will say a word and ask the child to identify the letter it begins with. When asking children to determine the beginning letter of an object in a picture, ensure that the object is clear and easy to identify. For example, some children may mistake a donkey for a horse and choose the initial letter *h,* instead of *d.* Besides the assessments mentioned, some of the same gamelike activities used for instruction and practice materials for reinforcement are used for assessing children's knowledge of word-study skills.

✓ Checklist *Assessing Concepts about Print and Word Study*

Child's name _____ **Date** _____

	Always	Sometimes	Never	Comments
Knows print is read from left to right				
Knows that oral language can be written and then read				
Knows what a letter is and can point one out on a page				
Knows what a word is and can point one out on a printed page				
Knows that there are spaces between words				
Reads environmental print				
Recognizes some words by sight and high-frequency sight words				
Can name and identify rhyming words				
Can identify and name upper- and lowercase letters of the alphabet				
Can blend phonemes in words				
Can segment phonemes in words				
Associates consonants and their initial and final sounds (including hard and soft *c* and *g*)				

Checklist

	Always	Sometimes	Never	Comments
Associates consonant blends with their sounds (*bl, cr, dr, fl, gl, pr, st*)				
Associates vowels with their corresponding long and short sounds (*a*—acorn, apple; *e*—eagle, egg; *i*—ice, igloo; *o*—oats, octopus; *u*—unicorn, umbrella)				
Knows the consonant digraph sounds (*ch, ph, sh, th, wh*)				
Uses context, syntax, and semantics to identify words				
Can count syllables in words				
Attempts reading by attending to picture clues and print				
Guesses and predicts words based on knowledge of sound–symbol correspondence				
Can identify structural elements of words such as prefixes and suffixes, inflectional endings *-ing, -ed,* and *-s,* and contractions				
Demonstrates knowledge of the following phonic generalizations:				
a. In a consonant–vowel–consonant pattern, the vowel sound is usually short				
b. In a vowel–consonant–*e* pattern, the vowel is usually long				
c. When two vowels come together in a word, the first is usually long and the second is silent (train, receive, bean)				
Uses word families often referred to as rimes and phonograms such as *an, at, it,* and *ot,* and initial consonants to build words, e.g., *man, can, fan, ran.*				

Teacher Comments:

■ Alphabet Photos

I have a collection of alphabet books I find very useful for teaching the alphabet with my kindergarten children. I read different books throughout the year, and we do different activities based on the book. One of my favorites is *Chicka-Chicka-Boom-Boom* (Archambault & Martin, 1989). To help my students with learning the alphabet they each make a sign for one letter of the alphabet. They write both the upper- and lowercase letter. When I read the story, the children put their signs around their neck and pop into the story when their letter is called. Each letter is mentioned in the story twice. When we read the book again, the children trade signs. I have photographed as the story is read and then made a book of the photos for them to read their own live version of *Chicka-Chicka-Boom-Boom*. Some other alphabet books I find terrific to use with my students are the following:

> *The Handmade Alphabet* (Rankin, 1991) is an alphabet book in which hands sign each letter. I do the same with the children I teach.
>
> *Potluck* (Shelby & Travis, 1991) is about children going to a picnic and each bringing something. It starts with Acton who appears with asparagus soup, and then Ben who brought bagels. It ends with Yolanda bringing yams and yogurt and Zeke and Zelda zooming in with zucchini casserole. We make food in our class based on the book.
>
> *Where Is Everybody* (Merriam, 1989) is about different animals in different familiar places in the neighborhood doing different familiar things. For example: "Bear is in the bakery, Cat is at the computer, Dog is at the daycare center." We act out what the letters and animals are doing.
>
> *All Aboard ABC* (Magee & Newman, 1990) is an informational alphabet book with every page teaching us something about trains. For example: A is for all aboard and Amtrack trains that carry passengers from city to city all across the United States, B is for the boxcar which gets its name from its shape, C is for caboose, which is the last car of the freight train and is used by the train crewmen. I read this book to my class when we are learning about different forms of transportation.

Ruth Mandel, Kindergarten Teacher

■ Rolling Words

For a second-grade activity, place students into groups of four at the Working with Words Center. The students play a game in which they make a variety of words from different letter combinations. This activity is beneficial for diverse learners because it is hands-on and collaborative, and it allows for children of different ability levels to participate at the appropriate level. Using blank wooden or foam cubes, prepare four letter dice for each group. Use a permanent marker to write letters on the cubes. At least one die should display the vowels *a, e, i, o, u,* and *y.* One die should have the letter combinations that reflect spelling patterns or sounds that are being studied. For example, if the class is studying *r*-controlled vowels, the six sides of one cube may be labeled *ar, or, ir, er, ur,* and "Roll Again." The other two dice may have the consonant and/or vowel combination of your choice.

In their groups, the children will take turns rolling the dice using plastic cups. If a player lands on "Roll Again," then he or she rolls that particular die again. The object of the game is to try to create words using the faces of the four dice that are showing on top. After a word is formed, the student records the word under his or her player number on the group's score sheet. (Players can "challenge" each other if they think that a word is not legitimate.) The player loses a turn if he or she cannot create a word using the four faces on top. The students earn points based on the number of letters in each word created. A student who creates a two-letter word earns two points; a student who creates a three-letter word earns three points; and so on. The game ends and points are tallied after either a set amount of time or number of turns.

Joanne Jacobson, Second-Grade Teacher

Activities and Questions

1. Answer the focus questions at the beginning of the chapter.

2. Observe the environmental print in an early childhood classroom. Note what you think could be added to it, both from within the classroom and from the outside world.

3. Select three children from prekindergarten through second grade whose scores on standardized tests are available. Observe the children for oral language ability, competence in comprehension, and print knowledge. Compare what you observe concerning the children's literacy ability with their test results.

4. Write an experience chart dictated to you by children in an early childhood classroom. If you do not have access to children, do this exercise in your college classroom with your peers dictating the contents for the chart. Critique the appearance of your chart and note problems you encountered while writing it. Use your self-evaluation for ideas for improvement.

5. Select five children from an early childhood classroom in which the students have collected Very Own Words. List all the words in the children's collections. Compare the list with the words found in basal reading material for the age children you selected. How closely do the basal words and the children's Very Own Words match each other?

6. Select three initial consonants other than *p*. Design classroom experiences that will teach and reinforce the sound–symbol relationships of each. Connect the letters to a thematic topic that is commonly studied in science or social studies in early childhood classrooms. Use traditional and authentic experiences.

7. Create a lesson to teach high-frequency words using a word wall.

8. Create lessons to teach phonic skills using your morning message words. With a pocket chart and word cards, have children
   a. make words from onsets and rimes.
   b. sort words with similar patterns into piles.
   c. make little words from a big word.

9. Continue the portfolio assessment for the child you selected to assess for language development in Chapter 4. Observe the child using the assessment checklist provided in this chapter concerning the evaluation of concepts about print. Check for phonemic awareness and reading level using a running record.

10. Continue the thematic unit that you began in Chapter 4. Select three objectives in the area of concepts about print, and describe three activities that will satisfy each of the objectives using your theme. (You dealt with sound–symbol associations earlier; select other concepts about print to emphasize.)

Developing
Comprehension of
Text and Concepts
about Books

Few children learn to love books themselves. Someone must lure them into the wonderful world of the written word, someone must show them the way.

—Orville Prescott
A Father Reads to His Child (1965)

Focus Questions

- What are the objectives for teaching concepts about books and comprehension of text for young children?
- What experiences enhance a child's concepts about books?
- Define the term *comprehension of text.*
- Describe types of read-aloud experiences and how they are effectively carried out to promote comprehension.
- Identify and describe strategies that develop comprehension, such as the use of graphic organizers and summarizing techniques.
- How should comprehension strategies be taught?
- List and define the structural elements in good narrative text.
- What are the structural elements found in good expository text?
- What is meant by an aesthetic stance and efferent stance when discussing text?

For several months, Mrs. Johnson has been discussing different authors and illustrators with the children in her first-grade class. There is a class chart in the room with their favorite authors and illustrators listed. Today Mrs. Johnson asked the children to add names to the list because they had recently read stories by authors and illustrators who were new to them. First she asked for authors, and the following names were mentioned: Ezra Jack Keats, Tomie dePaola, Leo Lionni, and Arnold Lobel. Next she asked if they could name some illustrators, and students came up with the following names: Dr. Seuss, Eric Carle, Maurice Sendak, and Crockett Johnson. Jamie raised her hand and said, "Hey, something weird just happened. I noticed that all of the authors named are also illustrators and all of the illustrators are all authors too." Christopher raised his hand and said, "That's not so weird, I know a bunch of people who are authors and illustrators at the same time. There's me, and Josh, Jennifer, and Patrick." Christopher was looking around the room and naming all the children in the class. When he finished naming his classmates, he continued, "We're all authors and illustrators. We all write books and illustrate them. They are published and they are in our classroom library. How could we forget that?"

Mrs. Johnson made a **T-chart** on the whiteboard. On one side she wrote "Dr. Seuss," and on the other side, "Ezra Jack Keats." She explained to the children that the T-chart would help them to compare and contrast the characteristics of the authors and illustrators to find out what they had in common and what characteristics were different. She then guided the children by modeling how to use the T-chart. She asked them to list characteristics of each of the author's illustrations first and then list characteristics of their stories. When they finished, they looked for characteristics in common and those that were different. On another day, Mrs. Johnson did this activity with the whole class again with two of the other author/illustrators. She then had pairs of children work on another author/illustrator pair doing their own T-chart as she walked around the room to help. Finally, for the fourth pair of author/illustrators, children were expected to do a T-chart on their own during independent center work. When completing this task, children were encouraged to use the books of the author/illustrators to help with the characteristics list. As she taught this comprehension strategy, Mrs. Johnson first explained the strategy and what it was for. Next she modeled the use of the strategy. The third step was to have the students use the strategy in a cooperative setting with a partner, and Mrs. Johnson walked around the room to answer questions and generally help to guide the students as they practiced the new strategy. Finally, she gave the students the opportunity to perfect the skill and practice it more in independent application.

Figure 6.1	Authors		Illustrators	
T-Charts	**Dr. Seuss**	**Ezra Jack Keats**	**Dr. Seuss**	**Ezra Jack Keats**
	Rhymes	No rhymes	Bold colors	Bright colors
	Characters	Real characters	Watercolor	Collage
	Imaginary	Real-life story	Cartoons	Realistic
	Made-up words	Real words		

Concepts about Books

When children are very young, teachers discuss how to handle books, the parts of a book, and the difference between pictures and print. Children with early book experience are aware of many of these concepts. Those who are not need to be taught. Knowledge of concepts about books is important along the road toward becoming literate.

Objectives for Developing Concepts about Books

A child who has a good concept of books

1. knows that a book is for reading.
2. can identify the front and the back of a book as well as the top and the bottom.
3. can turn the pages of a book properly in the right direction.
4. knows the difference between print and pictures.
5. knows that pictures on a page are related to what the print says.
6. knows where one begins reading on a page.
7. knows what a title is.
8. knows what an author is.
9. knows what an illustrator is.

Activities That Develop Concepts about Books

We often assume that children know the concepts about books just outlined. However, to many two- to six-year-olds these concepts are totally unfamiliar. About 1000 books need to be read to a child before he or she enters kindergarten to help the child acquire concepts about books so he or she is ready for experiences in reading and writing. To help children learn concepts about books, point the concepts out at every opportunity when you read to them. You can introduce a story, for instance, by pointing appropriately as you say,

> *"The title of the story that I'm going to read is* Mr. Rabbit and the Lovely Present *(Zolotow, 1962). This is the title on the front of the book. The author of the book, the person who wrote it, is Charlotte Zolotow. Here is her name. And the illustrator, the person who drew the pictures, is Maurice Sendak. Here is his name. All books have titles and authors, and if they have pictures they also have illustrators. The next time you look at a book, see if you can find the title. It is always on the front cover."*

The repetition of such dialogue familiarizes children with the concepts, which they assimilate easily. Similar dialogue helps to explain other concepts. Point to a picture, then point to the print. Identify each, then ask,

> *"Which do we read, the picture or the print?"*

As you get ready to read to them, ask children to point out the top and bottom of the book, and where you should begin reading on a page. Not only will you give the children the opportunity to learn the concepts, but at the same time you can determine which children understand the concept and which need help.

These discussions can be carried out during story readings to small groups or to individual students. A child's independent exploration of books will reinforce what you have pointed out or explained. As a result of this type of teacher behavior, the following will begin to happen when reading stories to children.

After I read *The Little Engine That Could* (Piper, 1954) to a four-year-old, she said to me, "Show me where it says 'I think I can, I think I can.' I want to see it in the book." When I showed her the words, she repeated them while pointing to them and then asked to see them again in another part of the book. She proceeded to search through the rest of the book, reading with great enthusiasm each time she found the line "I think I can, I think I can."

Big Books are an important part of early literacy instruction. They are oversized picture storybooks that measure from 14 by 20 inches up to 24 by 30 inches. Holdaway (1979) suggested that the enlarged print and pictures in these books help get children involved with concepts about books, print, and the meaning of text. Big Books are appropriate from preschool through third grade. Active involvement is encouraged when using Big Books in small- and large-group settings. When using a Big Book, a teacher places it on a stand because it is difficult to handle otherwise. An easel is usually used for a Big Book stand and makes the print and pictures visible for the children. Class Big Books can be made as well as purchased. When they are made, children become even more aware of book concepts because they are engaged in creating a book. Figure 6.2 provides directions for making a Big Book.

Figure 6.2

Instructions for Making a Big Book

Materials

- 2 pieces of oak tag for the cover (14″ × 20″ to 20″ × 30″)
- 10 pieces or more of tagboard or newsprint the same size as the oak tag used for the cover to be used for the pages in the book
- 6 looseleaf rings (1¼″)
- Holepunch

Directions

- Punch three sets of holes in top, middle, and bottom of the cover and paper that is to go inside of the book.
- Insert a looseleaf ring in each hole. The Big Book should have a minimum of 10 pages.
- Print should be 1½ to 2 inches high.

Big Books are effective for developing concepts about books mainly because of their size. As the teacher reads the book and tracks the print from left to right across the page, children see that books are for reading, and they see where a person begins to read on a page. They also learn to differentiate the print from the pictures. The connection is made that the oral language they hear from their teacher is being read from the print on the page in the book. The correct way to turn pages is easy to see with Big Books because they are so enlarged. The title of the book is prominently displayed on the front of the book and on the title page, as is the name of the author and illustrator.

In Mrs. Johnson's room, children are always encouraged to read the title of a book and the name of the author and illustrator before starting to read the text. One day during an independent reading and writing period, Damien placed the Big Book *Chicken Soup with Rice* (Sendak, 1962) on the Big Book stand. He had gathered three children to sit in front of him to read to. He started by saying, "The title of the book I'm going to read is *Chicken Soup with Rice*." He turned the first page and began reading the text. Patrick popped up and said, "Damien, you can't read the book yet; you forgot to read who the author and illustrator are." Damien pounded his fist to his forehead, looked somewhat annoyed with himself, and said, "How could I forget that. Let's see, the author of this book is Maurice Sendak and he is the illustrator too."

Theory and Research on Comprehension of Text

Comprehension is the ability to read or listen and understand text. Understanding what is read is one of the major goals for reading instruction. The English poet Samuel Taylor Coleridge wrote the following short piece entitled *On Reading Comprehension:*

> There are four kinds of readers. The first is like an hourglass, and their reading being as the sand, it runs out, and leaves not a vestige behind. A second is like the sponge, which imbibes everything and returns it in nearly the same state, only a little dirtier. The third is like a jelly bag, allowing all that is pure to pass away, and retaining only the refuse. And the fourth is like the workers in diamond mines, who cast aside all that is worthless and retain only pure gems.

How do we get children to cast aside unnecessary information and retain only the pure gems when reading or listening to a passage?

Pressley and Afflerbach (1995) have outlined characteristics of the kind of skilled readers who comprehend well, the kind of readers we hope to create:

■ Good comprehenders read materials from the beginning to end, and also jump around looking for information that might help with clarification.

■ Good comprehenders slow down their reading when they come to information that is relevant to what they want to remember.

■ Good comprehenders anticipate the content of the text based on prior knowledge about the topic.

■ Good comprehenders reflect on ideas in the text by creating summaries about what they have read.

■ Good comprehenders refer to the text about important information to clarify issues.

Definitions of comprehension emphasize that it is an active process. In this process, the reader or listener interprets and constructs meaning about what he or she reads or listens to based on prior knowledge about the topic, thereby making connections between the old and the new (Pressley & Hilden, 2002). This concept arises from research on schema theory that suggests that we have schemata (background knowledge) for certain information based on prior experience with a given topic. That schema is never complete because more can always be learned about a subject. For example, if someone told us something about the circus, we would gain one bit of information; if we saw pictures of the circus, we would have additional information; and if we went to see the circus, we would know even more. Then when we read about the circus or listened to a story about it, the new information would expand and refine what we already know. Comprehension of a narrative or expository piece that is read or listened to involves a child's integration of his or her prior knowledge concerning a topic with the new text to create new knowledge (Pressley & Hilden, 2002).

Teale (1984) suggests that comprehension development is enhanced as a result of children's social interactions with others during reading and writing experiences. For example, children benefit from early experiences with books that are mediated by an interactive adult who provides problem-solving situations. The child is asked to respond, and the adult offers information when necessary. In such situations, children and adults interact to integrate, construct, and make relationships with printed text.

Comprehension greatly depends on how the difficulty of the text matches the ability of the listener or reader. Therefore, it is important to keep in mind when reading to children, or when they read themselves, the following characteristics about the text that will determine how well they will comprehend:

■ The familiarity of the content in the text
■ The background knowledge required to understand the text
■ The quality of the writing
■ How interesting the topic is to the listeners or readers
■ The syntactic complexity of the sentences
■ The amount and difficulty of vocabulary included
■ The length of a selection that is read or listened to (Graves, Juel, & Graves, 1998)

Developing metacognitive abilities is an aid to comprehension. Metacognition is one's own awareness of how his or her learning is taking place. When it comes to comprehension, it means that students can articulate how they are able to comprehend and the problems they have comprehending, and then discuss how the problems might be solved. When students engage in metacognition, or self-monitoring, they can choose the appropriate comprehension strategy for the text and can regulate, check, and repair their reading processes as they go (Gunning, 2003).

In an important and well-known piece of research by Dolores Durkin (1978–79), it was found that comprehension was rarely taught in the primary

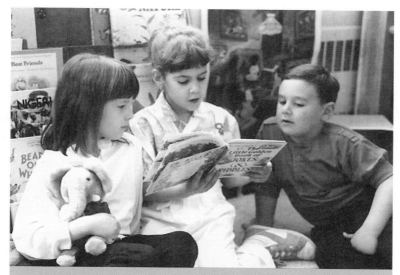

Comprehension is an active process where readers and listeners interpret and construct meaning about what they read or listen to.

grades. During the 1980s a great deal of research about comprehension was carried out by the Center for the Study of Reading at the University of Illinois in Urbana, and as a result of that work and other work that followed, more attention has been paid to teaching comprehension in the primary grades. A report entitled *Reading for Understanding: Toward a Research and Development Program in Reading Comprehension* created by the Rand Reading Study Group (2002) and published by the U.S. Office of Educational Research and Improvement in Washington, DC, and the National Reading Panel Report (2000), discusses the comprehension strategies that need to be taught to students and how they should be taught. Both reports draw on research about successful comprehension practice. The objectives and strategies discussed in this chapter to a large extent reflect the findings of these reports.

Objectives for Developing Comprehension of Text

A child is developing comprehension of narrative and informational text when he or she does the following:

1. Attempts to read well-known storybooks that results in the telling of a well-formed story.
2. Participates in story reading by saying words and narrating stories as the teacher reads.
3. Participates in cooperative learning activities to construct comprehension of text.
4. Monitors his or her comprehension (metacognition):

   Think about your thinking;
   Know what you understand;
   Know what you don't understand;
   Use strategies to help understand what you don't know.

5. Answers questions and participates in discussions and activities involving
   a. literal thinking that asks the reader to identify details such as who, what, when, where, and to classify, sequence, and find the main idea.
   b. inferential and critical thinking that asks the reader to predict, interpret (put yourself in the place of the characters) draw from background knowledge, evaluate, compare and contrast, determine cause and effect.

6. Generates questions, discussions, and activities involving
   a. literal thinking that asks the reader who, what, when, where; to classify and sequence.
   b. inferential and critical thinking that asks the reader to: predict, interpret (put yourself in the place of the characters), draw from background knowledge, evaluate, compare and contrast, determine cause and effect, apply information and problem solve.

7. Uses graphic organizers:
   a. Maps
   b. Webs
   c. KWL
   d. T-charts
   e. Venn diagrams
   f. Graphs
   g. Charts

8. Recognizes and understands features of and structures in expository text such as the following:
   a. Features in expository text
      (1) Table of contents
      (2) Headings
      (3) Glossary
      (4) Index
      (5) Diagrams
   b. Structures in expository text
      (1) *Description:* Gives the reader a picture of the subject based on story observation.
      (2) *Sequence:* Explains the steps that produce a certain product or outcome.
      (3) *Comparison and contrast:* There are comparisons that include items with a similar classification that are compared first and then contrasted. Point-by-point comparisons describe similarities and differences alternately.
      (4) *Cause and effect:* Causality tells why something happens.
      (5) *Problem–solution:* A problem is presented, followed by its solution. An understanding of chronology is necessary to comprehend this structure.
      (6) *Exemplification* (reason and example): The main idea is printed with supporting details (Vukelich, Evans, & Albertson, 2003).

9. Recognizes and understands features of and structures in narrative text such as
   a. *Setting:* beginning, time, place, characters.
   b. *Theme:* main character's problem or goal.
   c. *Plot episodes:* events leading to solve the main character's problem or reaching his or her goal.
   d. *Resolution:* problem solution, goal achievement, ending.

10. Engages in summarizing activities:
    a. Retelling
    b. Drawing conclusions

11. Engages in mental imagery.

12. Engages in cooperative activities such as the following:
    a. Collaborative response groups
    b. Think-pair-share
    c. Think-alouds
    d. Literature circles
    e. Buddy reading
    f. Partner reading

13. Uses references and study skills that involve the following:
    a. The dictionary
    b. Internet searches
    c. SQ3R: survey, question, read, recite, review

14. Participates in fluency training:
    a. Echo reading
    b. Choral reading
    c. Tape-assisted reading
    d. Antiphonal reading
    e. Paired reading
    f. Reader's theater
    g. Repeated reading

Standards and Comprehension

The standards that deal with comprehension of text from the National Center on Education and the Economy and the Learning Research and Development Center at the University of Pittsburgh (1999) are referred to as "Getting Meaning from Text." When getting meaning from text, children are expected to have competence in self-monitoring and self-correcting strategies.

When children self-monitor their reading,

- they notice when sentences or paragraphs are incomplete or when texts do not make sense.
- they use syntax to help figure out the meaning of new words.
- they raise questions about what the author was saying.

When children demonstrate comprehension,

- they can comprehend text when reading books that have subplots as well as a main plot.
- they understand nonfiction that contains concepts with subordinate and co-ordinate structures presented in complex and compound sentences.
- they grasp meaning from figurative language such as similes and metaphors.
- they compare one text to another text they have read or heard.
- they explain motives of characters.

How Comprehension Strategies Are Taught

When learning strategies, children must play an active role as they respond to literature in different ways. Select narrative or informational text that relates to a child's real-life experiences and that is well structured. Narrative material contains clearly delineated settings, themes, episodes, and resolutions. Quality expository text presents nonfiction content-area information to children in the following structures: description, sequence, comparison and contrast, cause and effect, problem–solution, and exemplification.

Comprehension instruction is effective when students engage in learning in cooperative settings at least some of the time. It gives them the opportunity to discuss with each other and learn from each other. Teaching comprehension strategies has been found to be most effective when using the following steps:

Direct explanation: The teacher explains what the strategy is, why it is important, and when it is used.

Modeling: The teacher demonstrates the use of the strategy by using it with the children.

Guided practice: The teacher provides an opportunity for the students to practice using the strategy. The teacher guides the students in how and when to use the strategy. Guided practice is a good time for students to work together so they can help each other learn.

Independent application: The teacher provides time for students to practice the strategy without guidance so they can carry it out without assistance (CIERRA, 2001).

Reflection: The child thinks about how the strategy can be used in other situations. The child thinks about how good he or she is at using the strategy (McLaughlin, 2003).

The teacher provides time for students to practice comprehension strategies through partner reading so they can carry them out without assistance.

In the vignette at the beginning of the chapter, Mrs. Johnson uses parts of the format described over a period of time when teaching her children about comparing and contrasting characteristics of authors and illustrators.

Comprehension Strategies

In this section, several strategies to enhance children's concepts about books and comprehension development will be described. These strategies can be introduced in whole-group settings and used repeatedly with new materials. They are appropriate for small-group instruction, often referred to as guided reading lessons, when explicit teaching takes place. Teachers decide which strategies to use in these reading groups based on the needs of the children involved.

All the strategies can be used with preschool-age children through third graders.

They need to be adapted to the age of the children with whom they are being used.

The Directed Listening and Thinking Activity and Directed Reading and Thinking Activity

When children are read to or they read themselves, there should always be a purpose for the reading. The format of the **directed listening and thinking activity (DLTA)** and the **directed reading and thinking activity (DRTA)** sets a purpose for reading, thus helping to direct thought. This strategy, when internalized by children as a result of frequent use by the teacher, will be transferred and used by students when new material is read or listened to (Morrow, 1984; Stauffer, 1980). Whatever the DLTA or DRTA specific objectives may be, its framework offers the listener or reader a strategy for organizing and retrieving information from the text. In the following DRTA/DLTA for *The Little Red Hen* (Izawa, 1968b), there are two main strategies in which children are asked to participate:

1. Sequencing the events of the story
2. Making inferences and judgments related to the text

In the lesson that follows, when using the DLTA, the children listen to the story; with the DRTA, the children read the story.

PREPARE FOR LISTENING OR READING WITH PREQUESTIONS AND DISCUSSION. Build a background by introducing the story: "Today I'm going to read a story (or, you will be reading a story) entitled *The Little Red Hen*. Let's look at the pictures to see if you can tell what the story is going to be about."

Directed listening and thinking activities set a purpose for reading or listening and help focus students' thoughts.

Encourage children to respond as you turn the pages of the book. After they have offered their ideas, say, "The story is about a hen who wants to bake some bread and asks her friends for some help." This activity has been referred to as a "walk through the book" or a "book walk."

Ask prequestions that build additional background that sets a purpose for listening or reading. Relate the questions to real-life experiences whenever possible: "Have you ever asked people for help? What kind of help? Did they help you? Has anyone ever asked you for help? What kind of help? Were you able to help the person? How? This story is about a little red hen that needed and asked for help while baking bread. While I'm reading (or, while you are reading), try to decide if you think the little red hen did the right thing with her bread at the end of the story. Think of reasons why you think she was right or wrong. As I read (or, you read) try to remember what happened first, second, third, and at the end of the story."

When the children have gained enough experience with your prequestions, you can ask them to think of their own: "Now that I've told you a little about the story, what do you want to find out when I read it to you (or, when you read it)?"

READING THE STORY.   Be sure to show the children the pictures as you read the story. Stop just one or two times for reactions, comments, or questions from the children. Don't interrupt the story for lots of discussion. That will come at the end. If the children are reading the story, remind them to study the pictures. Model or scaffold responses to guide them in their thinking, keeping in mind the objectives for this particular DLTA or DRTA: "Can you remember what help the little red hen has asked for so far? How have the other animals acted about giving help?" If the children do not respond, scaffold or model responses by changing questions to statements: "These animals aren't very helpful to the little red hen. Each time the hen asks for their help, the animals all answer, 'Not I.'" Also ask for children's predictions of what will happen next. Have only one or two stopping points for discussion during the story.

DISCUSSION AFTER READING.   The postdiscussion should be guided by the objectives or purpose set for listening and reading: "What did the little red hen want help with first? second? and so on." Ask children to retell the story; retelling will demonstrate their knowledge of sequence. Allow children to use the pictures in the book to help them follow sequence. Finally, focus on the second goal, making inferences and judgments: "What would you have done if you were the little red hen? Do you think she did the right thing with her bread, and why? What lesson can we learn from this story?"

A DLTA or DRTA can have many different objectives. The framework, however, is always basically the same: (1) preparation for listening or reading—prequestions and discussion; (2) reading the story with few interruptions; and (3) discussion after reading. All three steps are focused on the DLTA's or DRTA's specific objectives. A DLTA or DRTA can focus on literal responses (such as recall of facts and sequencing), inferential responses (such as interpreting characters' feelings, predicting outcomes, and relating the story to real-life experiences), and critical responses (such as evaluating, problem solving, and making judgments). It can focus on identifying elements of story structure whether narrative or expository text. It helps youngsters draw meaning from the print. Research has demonstrated that a DLTA can increase the story comprehension of young listeners (Morrow, 1984), just as a DRTA can increase the story comprehension of young readers (Baumann, 1992; Pearson et al., 1992).

Developing Comprehension with Shared Book Experiences

The **shared book experience** (Holdaway, 1979) is usually carried out in a whole-class setting, although it may be carried out in small groups as well. During this activity, teachers model fluent reading for children. They also help children to develop listening skills, since during the reading the children are asked to participate in some way.

Shared book reading often involves reading from a Big Book designed so that everyone in the group can see the pictures and the words clearly while it is being read. If the book is a new one for the class, the children are asked to listen during the first reading. If it is being read for the second time or is already familiar, immediate participation is encouraged. Often the teacher uses a pointer during the reading to emphasize left-to-right progression with younger children and the correspondence of spoken and written words.

Children's participation could include: chanting together repeated phrases in the story, stopping at predictable parts and asking children to fill in words and phrases, or reading key words that are special to the story. Shared book experiences could include echo reading, where the teacher reads one line and the children repeat it. Big Books and regular-size copies of the same book should be available for children to use independently after a first Big Book reading.

Shared book readings can be tape-recorded and made available in the listening station. This activity provides a familiar and fluent model for reading with good phrasing and intonation for children to emulate. Shared book experiences can be adapted to the DLTA format, with one of the objectives being to provide a participatory and enjoyable read-aloud event.

Research indicates that shared book reading benefits the acquisition of reading and writing. It enhances background information and sense of story structure, and familiarizes children with the language of books (Cullinan, 1992; Morrow, 1985). A well-structured story has a setting (a beginning, time, place, and introduction of characters), theme (the main character's problem or goal), plot episodes (a series of events in which the main character attempts to solve the problem or achieve the goal), and a resolution (the accomplishment of the goal or solving of the problem and an ending). From hearing many well-formed stories, children can predict what will happen next in an unfamiliar story on the basis of their awareness of its structure. Hearing stories with good plot structures also helps children write and tell their own stories (Morrow, 1985). The language of books is different from oral language and provides a model for their writing and speaking. The following sentences from two picture storybooks make this evident:

> One bad day a tuna fish, fierce, swift and very hungry, came darting through the waves. (Lionni, *Swimmy,* 1963)

> The wild things roared their terrible roars, gnashed their terrible teeth, and rolled their terrible eyes. (Sendak, *Where the Wild Things Are,* 1963)

This next piece is from E. B. White's *Charlotte's Web* (1952) and is appropriate to read to first and second graders.

> At last Wilbur saw the creature that had spoken to him in such a kindly way. Stretched across the upper part of the doorway was a big spiderweb, and hanging from the top of the web, head down, was a large grey spider. She was about the size of a gumdrop. She had eight legs, and she was waving one of them at Wilbur in friendly greeting. "See me now?" she asked.
>
> "Oh, yes indeed," said Wilbur. "Yes indeed! How are you? Good morning! Salutations! Very pleased to meet you. What is your name, please? May I have your name."
>
> "My name," said the spider, "is Charlotte."

Predictable stories are ideal for shared book experiences because they allow children to guess what will come next, thereby encouraging participation. Predictability takes many forms. The use of catch phrases, such as "'Not I,' said the dog," "'Not I,' said the cat," and so on, in *The Little Red Hen* (Izawa, 1968b) encourages children to chant along. Predictable rhyme enables children to fill in words, as in *Green Eggs and Ham* (Seuss, 1960). Cumulative patterns contribute to predictability. For example, new events are added with each episode, then repeated in the next, as in *Are You My Mother?* (Eastman, 1960). This book repeats phrases and episode patterns as its central character, a baby bird, searches for his mother by approaching different animals and asking the same question, "Are you my mother?"

Conversation can contribute to predictability, as in *The Three Billy Goats Gruff* (Brown, 1957) or *The Three Little Pigs* (Brenner, 1972). All books become predictable as children become familiar with them, so repeating stories builds a repertoire for shared book experiences. Books that carry familiar sequences, such as days of the week, months of the year, letters, and numbers, are predictable— *The Very Hungry Caterpillar* (Carle, 1969), for instance. Books gain predictability through good plot structures and topics familiar to children. Books in which pictures match text page by page tend to be predictable to children, especially if everyone in the group can see the pictures as the story is being read.

Predictable books are excellent for emergent and conventional readers in shared book experiences as well as in independent reading. They allow the child's first experience with reading to be enjoyable and successful with minimal effort. Such immediate success encourages the child to continue efforts at reading. (A list of predictable books is provided in Appendix A.)

We often stop reading to children as they begin to read themselves. It is crucial to continue reading to them as they get older. Reading to them in a shared book setting enhances skills already learned and motivates interest in the books featured in the classroom.

Repeated Book Readings to Enhance Readers' Comprehension

Children enjoy repetition. Being familiar with an experience is comfortable, like singing a well-known song. Besides offering the pleasure of familiarity, a repeated story helps develop concepts about words, print, and books. In a study with four-year-olds, one group listened to three repeated readings of the same story and the other group listened to three different stories. After stories were read, each time the discussions revealed that the children in the repeated-reading group increased the number and kind of responses made, and their responses differed significantly from those of the different-story group. Their responses became more interpretive, and they began to predict outcomes and make associations, judgments, and elaborative comments (Morrow, 1987a).

They also began to narrate stories as the teacher read (their first attempts at reading) and to focus on elements of print, asking names of letters and words. Even children of low ability seemed to make more responses with repeated readings than with a single reading (Ivey, 2002).

Repeated readings are important to youngsters because they can engage in the activity on their own. Children who are able to read themselves or participate in pretend reading behaviors often will select the same book to look at or read over and over again. Teachers should repeat readings of stories to children and encourage youngsters to read stories more than once. They should carry out discussions about books that have been read and discussed previously.

The following dialogue is from a transcription of a child's responses to a third reading of *The Little Red Hen*. This excerpt includes primarily the child's comments and questions and the teacher's responses; most of the story text has been omitted.

Teacher: Today I'm going to read the story *The Little Red Hen*. It is about a hen who wanted some help when she baked some bread. (The teacher begins to read the story.) Who will help me to cut this wheat?

Melony: "Not I," said the cat. "Not I," said the dog. "Not I," said the mouse.

Teacher: That was good, Melony. You are reading. (The teacher continues reading.) Who will take this wheat to the mill to be ground into flour?

Melony: "Not I," said the cat. "Not I," said the dog. "Not I," said the mouse with the whiskers.

Teacher: Very nice, Melony. (The teacher continues to read.)

Melony: I want to read that part, but I don't know how.

Teacher: Go ahead and try. I bet you can. I'll help you: The cat smelled it.

Melony: The cat smelled it and she said umm that smells good, and the mouse smelled it, and it smelled good.

Teacher: (The teacher continues reading.) Who will eat this cake?

Melony: The mouse, the doggy, the kitty!

Teacher: You're right again, Melony. (The teacher reads to the end of the story.) Did you want to say anything else about the story?

Melony: He was bad so he couldn't have no cake. (Melony searches through the pages.) That's the wrong part.

Teacher: Show me the part you are talking about.

Melony: There it is, almost at the end. She's going to make a cake and she'll say who's going to bake this cake for me. And the cat says, "Not I," the dog says, "Not I," the mouse says, "Not I." And then when she's cooking it they smell a good thing and then they wanted some, too, but they didn't have any, 'cause they didn't plant the wheat.

Teacher: You're so right. They didn't help do the work, so they didn't get to eat the cake.

Melony: Where does it say, "Not I"? Show me the words in the book.

Teacher: Here it is. Can you find it again?

Melony: (She flips through the pages.) I'm looking for where she bakes the cake. Here it is. Yea. And he smelled it. And he smelled it. And the mouse smelled it. (She turns pages.) They're going in the kitchen. And she said, "All by myself, I cut the wheat. All by myself, I took it to the mill to get it into flour. All by myself I baked the cake. All by myself I'm going to eat it."

Teacher: That's terrific, Melony. That's what the hen said.

Melony: (She points to the dog.) The dog was not happy. Where does it say dog?

Teacher: You're right. He doesn't look happy. Here is where it says dog (pointing).

Melony: There's the word, dog, dog, dog. How does that dog look?

Teacher: He looks hungry and mad because he can't have any bread.

Melony: You're right. But it's his fault. He didn't help. And that's the end. (Morrow, 1987a)

This type of sophisticated response can only happen when a child has heard a story that has been repeated many times.

Children enjoy hearing the same book read to them over and over again. As adults we often tire of the repetition, but it has great value in early reading development. There should be a repertoire of books considered favorite stories that are read repeatedly to children at home and in school. To study emergent reading behaviors, Sulzby (1985) observed children from ages two to six attempting to read favorite storybooks. They could participate in the activity because they knew the stories so well. Although they were not yet readers in the conventional sense, the children were asked, "Read me your book." Sulzby found that, in their "reading," the children produced speech that could indeed be categorized as a first act of reading; that the speech they used as they "read" was clearly differ-

---

Figure 6.3 | *Sulzby's Classification Scheme for Children's Emergent Reading of Favorite Storybooks*

1. *Attending to pictures but not forming stories.*
   The child "reads" by labeling and commenting on the pictures in the book but does not "weave a story" across the pages.

   yes ☐   no ☐

2. *Attending to pictures and forming oral stories.*
   The child "reads" by following the pictures but weaves a story across the pages through wording and intonation like those of someone telling a story. Often, however, the listener too must see the pictures in order to understand the story the child is "reading."

   yes ☐   no ☐

3. *Attending to a mix of pictures, reading, and storytelling.*
   The child "reads" by looking at the pictures. The majority of the child's "reading" fluctuates between the oral intonation of a storyteller and that of a reader.

   yes ☐   no ☐

4. *Attending to pictures but forming stories (Written language–like).*
   The child "reads" by looking at the pictures. The child's speech sounds like reading, both in wording and intonation. The listener rarely needs to see the pictures in order to understand the story. With his or her eyes closed, the listener would think the child was reading print. The "reading" is similar to the story in print and sometimes follows it verbatim. There is some attention to print.

   yes ☐   no ☐

5. *Attending to print.*
   This category has two divisions:

   a. The child reads the story mostly by attending to print but occasionally refers to pictures and reverts to storytelling.

   b. The child reads in a conventional manner.

   a ☐   b ☐

Source: Adapted from E. Sulzby, "Children's Emergent Reading of Favorite Storybooks: A Developmental Study." *Reading Research Quarterly,* 20(4), 458–481. Copyright © 1985 by the International Reading Association.

ent in structure and intonation from their typical conversation; and that different developmental levels could be observed in these "oral readings."

From children's attempts at storybook reading, then, we can develop and determine particular characteristics of reading behavior. Because the activity is developmental and leads to literacy, teachers should ask children to participate in it to encourage their emergent literacy behaviors and to evaluate it as well.

Small-Group and One-to-One Story Readings

The importance and benefits of reading to small groups and to individuals must not be overlooked. Too often considered impractical in school settings, one-to-one and small-group readings yield such tremendous benefits that they must be incorporated into school programs. The most striking benefit of one-to-one story readings at home—often called the lap technique—is the interactive behavior it involves, along with the direct channels of information it gives the child. It also provides the adult with insight into what the child already knows and wants to know. Very young children for the most part can only participate in small-group and one-on-one readings, since they need the attention that this setting offers.

In one study (Morrow, 1988), it was determined that one-to-one readings in a school setting had positive results with preschoolers from lower socioeconomic backgrounds, even though the youngsters had little previous experience with storybook reading or interacting with adults during this time. Teachers in the study practiced the same interactive behaviors identified by researchers who had studied home storybook readings (Applebee & Langer, 1983; Cochran-Smith, 1984; Roser & Martinez, 1985). These teacher behaviors included managing storybook reading by introducing the story and providing background information.

Frequent readings by teachers who followed the guidelines outlined on page 174 increased the number and complexity of the children's responses. The youngsters offered many questions and comments that focused on meaning. Initially, they labeled illustrations. Later, they gave increased attention to details, their comments and questions became interpretive and predictive, and they drew from their own experiences. They also began narrating—that is, "reading" or mouthing the story along with the teacher. As the program continued, some children focused on structural elements, remarking on titles, settings, characters, and story events. After many readings, the children began to focus on print, reading words and naming letters and sounds (Morrow, 1987a). Compared with one-to-one readings, reading to small groups of children seems to encourage more and earlier responses. Children tend to repeat one another's remarks, and they are motivated to respond to and elaborate on what their peers have said.

The following segments from transcriptions of small-group story readings illustrate the various questions and comments children make when they are involved in the activity, and the wealth of knowledge and information they receive from the responding adult. The transcriptions also illustrate what the children already know and what their interests are and therefore help us design instruction.

Story: *The Very Hungry Caterpillar* (Carle, 1969)
(The child asks questions about book concepts.)

Jerry: (He points to the picture on the front of the book.) Why does it have a picture on it?

Teacher: The cover of the book has a picture on it so you will know what the story is about. Look at the picture. Can you tell me what the book is about?

✹ G u i d e l i n e s *Teacher Behavior during Storybook Reading*

1. Manage
   a. Introduce story.
   b. Provide background information about the book.
   c. Redirect irrelevant discussion back to the story.

2. Prompt Responses
   a. Invite children to ask questions or comment throughout the story when there are natural places to stop.
   b. Scaffold responses for children to model if no responses are forthcoming. ("Those animals aren't very nice. They won't help the little red hen.")
   c. Relate responses to real-life experiences. ("I needed help when I was preparing a party, and my family shared the work. Did you ever ask for help and couldn't find anyone to give it to you? What happened?")
   d. When children do not respond, ask questions that require answers other than yes or no. ("What would you have done if you were the little red hen and no one helped you bake the bread?")

3. Support and Inform
   a. Answer questions as they are asked.
   b. React to comments.
   c. Relate your responses to real-life experiences.
   d. Provide positive reinforcement for children's responses.

Source: From L. M. Morrow, "Young Children's Responses to One-to-One Story Readings in School Settings." *Reading Research Quarterly,* 23(1), 89–107. Copyright © 1988 by the International Reading Association.

Jerry: Ummm, I think that's a caterpillar. Is it about a caterpillar?

Teacher: You're right, very good. The book is about a caterpillar, and the name of the story is *The Very Hungry Caterpillar.* When you look at the pictures in a book, they help you find out what the words say.

Story: *Caps for Sale* (Slobodkina, 1947)
(The child asks for a definition.)

Teacher: I'm going to read a story today called *Caps for Sale.*

Jamie: What are caps?

Teacher: A cap is a little hat that you put on your head. See, there is a cap in the picture.

Jamie: I never knew that before. I knew about hats, but I never heard about caps.

Story: *Chicken Soup with Rice* (Sendak, 1962)
(The child attends to the print.)

Chris: Wait, stop reading. Let me see this again. (He turns back to the page that talks about the month of June.) How come they're the same? (He refers to the words of June and July.)

Teacher: What do you mean?

Chris: Look at the letters, J–U, J–U. They look alike.

Teacher: Look more closely at the ends of the words. Are they the same?

Chris: Ohh, nooo, just the front part.

Story: *Caps for Sale* (Slobodkina, 1947)
(The child predicts.)

Colleen: I wonder why those monkeys took the caps?

Teacher: I don't know. Can you think why?

Colleen: Well, the peddler was sleeping and those monkeys looked at the caps, and maybe they think they're for them. Or, I know! Maybe they're cold so they want a cap.

Teacher: Those are good ideas, Colleen.

Story: *Madeline's Rescue* (Bemelmans, 1953)
(The child relates the text to real-life experience.)

Jamie: What's the policeman going to do?

Teacher: He's going to help Madeline. Policemen are nice; they always help us.

Jamie: Policemans aren't nice. See, my daddy beat up Dominic and the policeman came and took him away and put him in jail for no reason. And my daddy cried. I don't like policemans. I don't think they are nice.

The children's comments and questions relate to literal meanings, raise interpretive and critical issues by associating the story with their own lives, make predictions of what will happen next in a story, or express judgments about characters' actions. In these examples the children's comments and questions relate to matters of print, such as names of letters, words, and sounds. The same types of questions and comments occur when small groups of children read together without the presence of a teacher. Recording and then analyzing one-to-one and small-group story readings reveal what children know and want to know (Morrow, 1987a). The coding sheet in Figure 6.4 aids such analysis.

Although whole-class readings are more practical and have tremendous value in simply exposing children to literature, the interactive behavior between adult and child in one-to-one readings and small-group readings does not occur in the large-group setting. If we review transcripts of story readings in all three settings, several things become apparent. In whole-group settings, a child cannot ask questions or comment throughout the story, since it would interfere with the story line for the other children. In addition, the teacher might never get through a coherent reading. In a whole-group setting, the discussion has to be managed by the teacher to such an extent that he or she often says more than the children. A truly interactive situation does not exist because of the size of the group. In small-group and one-to-one readings, by contrast, a teacher initially may manage and prompt often, but only to encourage and model responses for children. The roles reverse in a

Small-group storybook reading with the teacher encourages interesting responses and elaboration of text by children.

Child's name _____ Date _____

Name of story _____

(Read one story to one child or a small group of children. Encourage the children to respond with questions and comments. Tape-record the session. Transcribe or listen to the tape, noting each child's responses by placing checks in the appropriate categories. A category may receive more than one check, and a single response may be credited to more than one category. Total the number of checks in each category.)

1. Focus on story structure _____
   a. Setting (time, place) _____
   b. Characters _____
   c. Theme (problem or goal) _____
   d. Plot episodes (events leading toward problem solution or goal attainment) _____
   e. Resolution _____

2. Focus on meaning _____
   a. Labeling _____
   b. Detail _____
   c. Interpreting (associations, elaborations) _____
   d. Predicting _____
   e. Drawing from one's experience _____
   f. Seeking definitions of words _____
   g. Using narrational behavior (reciting parts of the book along with the teacher) _____

3. Focus on print _____
   a. Questions or comments about letters _____
   b. Questions or comments about sounds _____
   c. Questions or comments about words _____
   d. Reads words _____
   e. Reads sentences _____

4. Focus on illustrations _____
   a. Responses and questions that are related to illustrations _____

short time, when most of the dialogue is initiated by the children (Morrow, 1987a).

Children who do not experience one-to-one readings at home are at a disadvantage in their literacy development. It is necessary to carry out such strategies in school to compensate for what is not provided at home. Gains in both literacy skills and positive attitudes toward books can occur. To learn to associate books with warmth and pleasure, children who have not had the benefit of the lap technique at home can experience it at school. It is difficult to provide one-to-one and small-group readings in school because of time limitations and the number of children. Asking aides, volunteers, and older children to help can solve the problem. Many school districts have federal funding for work with young children identified as having potential learning problems. Ratios in such programs may be as low as five children per teacher. Those settings also allow one-to-one readings as part of a literacy development program.

Answering Questions and Participating in Discussions Generated by Teachers and Students

The benefits of reading aloud come from the interaction between adult and child. Studies carried out in school settings illustrate that active participation in literacy experiences enhances comprehension of and sense of text structure (Morrow, 1985; Pellegrini & Galda, 1982).

As children discuss text with others, at first they are interested in the illustrations and label items pictured or repeat words said by the adult who is reading (Yaden, 1985). Such interactive behavior leads children to respond with questions and comments, which become more complex over time and demonstrate more sophisticated thinking about printed material. Eventually, children's remarks about the content of the text demonstrate their ability to interpret, associate, predict information, and elaborate. Their remarks focus sometimes on title, setting, characters, and story events (Morrow, 1988; Roser & Martinez, 1985), and at other times on print characteristics, including names of letters, words, and sounds (Altwerger, Diehl-Faxon, & Dockstader-Anderson, 1985). Teachers help students to discuss and thus respond to text by

1. prompting children to respond before they do on their own.
2. scaffolding responses for children to model when they are not responding themselves.
3. relating responses to real-life experiences.
4. answering student's questions.
5. asking questions.
6. offering positive reinforcement for children's responses.

GENERATING QUESTIONS.   Productive discussions result from good questions. Discussions from questions must include more than a few words by participants and include questions that ask for clarification, explanations, predictions, and justifications. The following is a list of categories for asking questions:

1. Literal questions identify details such as who, what, when, and where, and ask students to
   a. classify ideas.
   b. sequence text.
   c. find the main idea.
2. Inferential and critical questions ask students to
   a. draw information from their background knowledge.
   b. relate text to life experiences.
   c. predict outcomes. (What do you think will happen next?)
   d. interpret text. (Put yourself in the place of the characters.)
   e. compare and contrast.
   f. determine cause and effect.
   g. apply information.
   h. problem solve.

Discussion questions should reflect children's interests and have many appropriate responses rather than just one correct answer. Occasionally questions with one correct answer can be asked. Most questions, however, should stimulate discussion and elicit responses that reflect what children think and feel about what has been read. These questions are asking for an aesthetic response because children have to synthesize ideas, sensations, feelings, and images. The questions provide a model for children to pose their own. The following questions will enable children to participate in an aesthetic discussion:

> How did you feel about the story?
>
> What did this story mean to you?
>
> What questions do you have about the story?
>
> What did you learn from what you read?
>
> How will that information be useful to you?
>
> Do you agree with what the characters did in the story? Why? Why not? (Gambrell & Almasi, 1994)

The efferent stance is usually taken with expository text that offers content information. Questions that ask for an efferent response require students to remember and analyze details and descriptions, sequences, and cause and effect. Some questions that will elicit efferent responses (Gunning, 2003; Rosenblatt, 1988) include the following:

> What is the main thing that the author is trying to tell you?
>
> What details, facts, happenings, or examples are used to explain the main idea?
>
> What idea did you find most interesting?
>
> What new ideas did you learn?
>
> How could you find out more about these ideas?
>
> If you could speak with the author, what would you like to ask him or her?

When asking questions, instruct students to look back into the text to find the answers to questions they cannot answer themselves. We need to help students know where to find answers that are explicit; that is, the answer to a question is stated in the text. Students need to be able to find implicit answers to questions when the answer is not exactly stated but can be found within a few sentences in the text. Finally students need to be able to answer scriptal questions. These answers are not in the text but are a part of the child's background knowledge (CIERA, 2001).

STUDENT-GENERATED QUESTIONS. When they are able, we need to encourage students to engage in asking questions similar to those posed by the teacher. When they do so, they can find out if they can answer their own questions, they can practice looking for the answers, and they can work with others to find the answers.

 ## Graphic Organizers

Graphic organizers are visual illustrations or representations of text information that help readers see relationships between concepts or events in a narrative or expository writing. They can help teach many elements needed for comprehension, such as vocabulary, cause and effect, problem solving, and so on. Following are some well-known types of graphic organizers.

WEBBING AND MAPPING. Webs and maps are graphic representations, or diagrams, for categorizing and structuring information. They help students see how words and ideas are related to one another. Webs tend to be drawn using a spiderlike effect, and maps may have boxes with labels in them that connect in different places. **Mapping and webbing** strategies build on children's prior knowledge. They help the child retrieve what is known about a topic and use the information in reading and listening to text. Research has demonstrated that the use of webbing and mapping strategies is successful in the development of vocabulary and comprehension. This research has also shown the effectiveness of the strategies with struggling readers, minorities, and bilingual children (Pittelman, Levin, & Johnson, 1985; Pittelman et al., 1991).

When webbing or mapping is used to develop vocabulary concepts and definitions related to a word, the word is written on the board or chart paper. Children are asked to brainstorm ideas related to the word. For example, after reading *The Snowy Day* (Keats, 1962), the teacher asks the children to provide words that describe what snow is like. The word *snow* is written in the center of the chart or chalkboard, and the words given by the children are attached to it. A sample of a snow web done by a kindergarten class is shown in Figure 6.5.

Another web about the same story could be used to expand ideas about activities to do in the snow. In Figure 6.6 a first-grade class generated the things that Peter did in the snow in the story and then other things that we can do in the snow.

A map provides a different format for graphically presenting materials before and after listening to or reading a book. Maps deal with more complex representations; therefore, boxes for different categories are needed to present the ideas graphically. Story structures can be mapped to help children learn about the structural elements in the text. Sequences of events or studies of individual characters can be mapped also. Figure 6.7 is a map of the story *Mr. Rabbit and the Lovely Present* created by a second-grade class. The map illustrates the structural elements in the story.

K-W-L. K-W-L is a cognitive strategy to enhance comprehension. It is used mainly with expository text and can be adapted for use with narrative stories. It shares some similarities to a DRTA and a DLTA. **K-W-L** stands for *What We **Know**, What We **Want** to Know,* and *What We **Learned*** (Ogle, 1986). With this technique students use prior knowledge to create interest about what is to be

Figure 6.5

A Web for Expanding Vocabulary

Figure 6.6

*A Web for
Expanding Ideas*

Figure 6.7

*A Story Structure
Map*

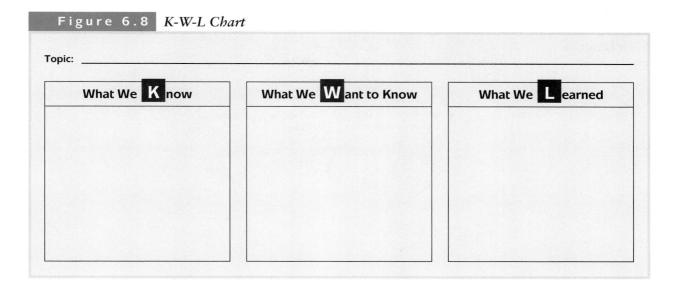

Figure 6.8 *K-W-L Chart*

read. It helps set a purpose for reading to direct thinking, and it encourages sharing of ideas. The K-W-L chart (Figure 6.8), which lists items generated in a K-W-L discussion, is particularly useful when reading material for thematic instruction (Sampson, 2002). The following are the steps involved in putting the strategy into practice. Before reading expository text,

1. children brainstorm what they think they know about a topic. For example, if the book they are going to read is entitled *Volcanoes* (Branley, 1985), the class would list *What We **Know*** about volcanoes.

2. children list questions about *What We **Want** to Know* before reading the book about volcanoes.

3. after reading the text, children make a list of *What We **Learned*** about volcanoes.

After reading the book, children can compare information learned from the text with what they already knew before reading the book. They can determine what they learned as a result of reading the text and, finally, what is still on the list of what they would like to learn because it was not included in the book.

VENN DIAGRAMS.   A **Venn diagram** is a graphic organizer that uses two overlapping circles to show relationships between ideas. The Venn diagram helps to compare two or three concepts in a text (Nagy, 1988). When comparing two concepts, we list the main characteristics of each in the outer circles and the characteristics in common in the intersection. The Venn diagram can be used with expository or narrative text.

Ms. Anastasi read the book *Frogs and Toads and Tadpoles, Too* (Fowler, 1992) to her class. This scientific trade book highlights the similarities and differences between frogs and toads. After the read-aloud, she drew two big intersecting circles on chart paper, labeling one "frogs" and the other "toads." Ms. Anastasi labeled the space created by the intersecting circles "similar characteristics." She asked the children to name traits from the book that were specific to frogs and then to toads. As the children responded, Ms. Anastasi wrote the responses in the appropriate areas of the diagram. Then Ms. Anastasi asked the

Figure 6.9

Venn Diagram

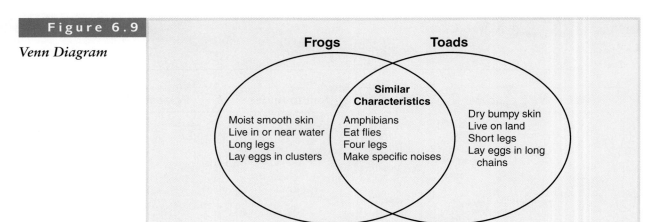

children if any of the traits were the same. If they were, she put them in the space labeled "similar characteristics." Ms. Anastasi looked back into the text with the children to look for words that would help them know that similarities or differences were being discussed. For example, words like *similarly, likewise, as,* and *nevertheless* indicate sameness, while words and phrases like *in spite of, still, but, even though, however, instead,* and *yet* indicate differences (Vukelich, Evans, & Albertson, 2003). As an extension activity, Ms. Anastasi had the students work with partners to create Venn diagrams using another expository text that included ideas to compare and contrast.

GRAPHIC ORGANIZERS FOR EXPOSITORY TEXT. Graphic organizers can help children learn text structures as well. In Figure 6.7 we illustrated a story structure map for a narrative text. Children need to learn the structures of both narrative and expository text and to summarize both. To give students more help with expository text structure, the following text structure sentences can be used over and over again:

> **Description:** A _____ is a kind of _____ that . . .
> An apple is a kind of fruit that is red and juicy and sweet.
> **Compare and Contrast:** _X_ and _Y_ are similar in that they both . . . , but . . .
> _X_ . . . , while _Y_ . . .
> Rain and snow are similar in that they both fall from the sky and they are both wet, but rain doesn't stick to the ground and has no color, while snow does stick to the ground and is white.
> **Sequence:** _____ begins with . . . , continues with . . . , and ends with . . .
> Flowers begin as seeds, we water them, and they will grow; they continue to grow a stem and leaves, and end with the flower.
> **Problem–Solution:** _____ wanted . . . , but . . . , so . . .
> The children wanted to play outside but couldn't because of the rain, so they played in the school gym instead.
> **Cause and Effect:** _____ happens because . . .
> The car got stuck and wouldn't go because it was out of gasoline.

Figure 6.10

*Graphic
Organizer
for Sequence
of Events*

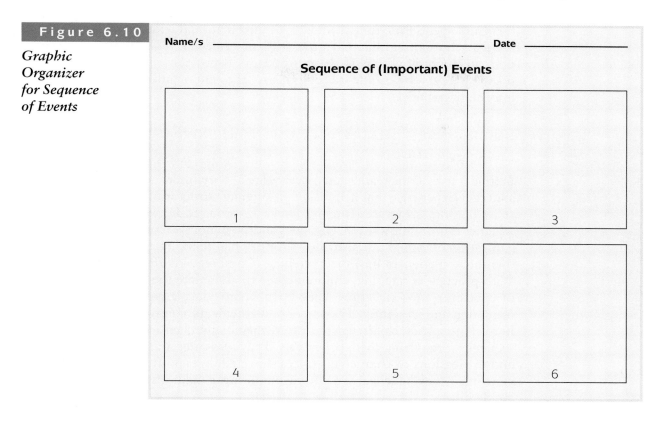

Figures 6.10 and 6.11 provide graphic organizer outlines for sequence-of-events and cause-and-effect structures in expository text. According to Duke & Kays (1998; Duke, 2000), early childhood classrooms have very few nonfiction

Figure 6.11

*Graphic
Organizer for
Cause and Effect*

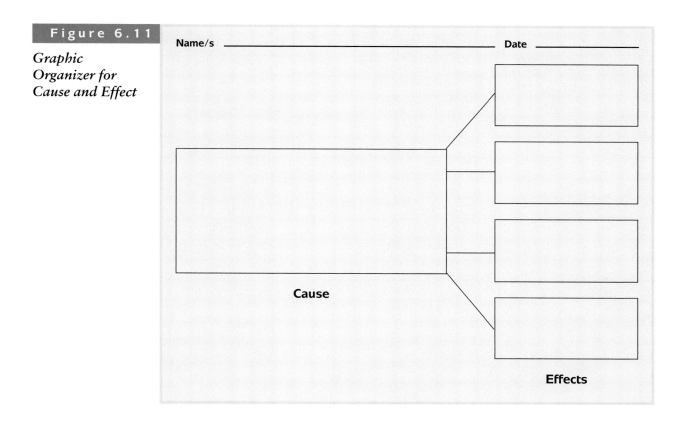

texts and spend little time dealing with informational text. Informational texts are read more often than narrative texts in adult life. It is important that children be taught how to read them. Appendix A provides an extended list of expository texts by grade to emphasize the importance of working with informational text.

Summarizing Strategies: Story Retelling and Rewriting

Letting a listener or reader retell or rewrite a story offers active participation in a literacy experience that helps develop language structures, comprehension, and sense of story structure (Ritchie, James-Szanton, & Howes, 2003). Retelling, whether it is oral or written, engages children in holistic comprehension and organization of thought. It also allows for original thinking as children mesh their own life experiences into their retelling (Gambrell, Pfeiffer, & Wilson, 1985). With practice in retelling, children come to assimilate the concept of narrative or expository text structure. They learn to introduce a narrative story with its beginning and its setting. They recount its theme, plot episodes, and resolution. In retelling stories, children demonstrate their comprehension of story details and sequence, organizing them coherently. They also infer and interpret the sounds and expressions of characters' voices. In retelling expository text, children review what they have learned and distinguish the main ideas from the supporting details.

Retelling is not an easy task for children, but with practice they improve quickly. To help children develop the practice of retelling, tell them before they

Guidelines *Story Retelling*

1. Ask the child to retell the story. "A little while ago, I read the story [name the story]. Would you retell the story as if you were telling it to a friend who has never heard it before?"

2. Use the following prompts only if needed:
   a. If the child has difficulty beginning the retelling, suggest beginning with "Once upon a time," or "Once there was . . ."
   b. If the child stops retelling before the end of the story, encourage continuation by asking, "What comes next?" or "Then what happened?"
   c. If the child stops retelling and cannot continue with general prompts, ask a question that is relevant at the point in the story at which the child has paused. For example, "What was Jenny's problem in the story?"

3. When a child is unable to retell the story, or if the retelling lacks sequence and detail, prompt the retelling step by step. For example:
   a. "Once upon a time," or "Once there was . . ."
   b. "Who was the story about?"
   c. "When did the story happen?" (day, night, summer, winter?)
   d. "Where did the story happen?"
   e. "What was [the main character's] problem in the story?"
   f. "How did [he or she] try to solve the problem? What did [he or she] do first [second, next]?"
   g. "How was the problem solved?"
   h. "How did the story end?" (Morrow, 1996)

read or listen to a text or story that they will be asked to retell or rewrite it (Morrow, 1996). Further guidance depends on the teacher's specific purpose in the retelling. If the immediate intent is to teach or test sequence, for instance, instruct children to concentrate on what happened first, second, and so on. If the goal is to teach or assess the ability to integrate information and make inferences from text, instruct children to think of things that have happened to them like those that happen in the selection. Props such as felt-board characters or the pictures in the text can be used to help students retell. Pre- and postdiscussion of text helps to improve retelling ability, as does the teacher's modeling a retelling for children. With written retellings, a teacher may prefer to have children write the entire piece first and then confer with them afterward.

Retellings can be used to develop many types of comprehension. The prompts should match the goals. In addition to its usefulness as a learning technique, retelling also allows adults to evaluate children's progress. If you plan to evaluate a retelling, tell the child during your introduction of the selection that he or she will be asked to retell it after the reading. During the evaluative retellings, do not offer prompts beyond general ones such as "Then what happened?" or "Can you think of anything else about the selection?" Retellings of narrative text can reveal a child's sense of story structure, focusing mostly on literal recall, but they also reflect a child's inferential and critical thinking ability. To assess the child's retelling for sense of story structure, first parse (divide) the events of the story into four categories: setting, theme, plot episodes, and resolution. Use a guide sheet (see Figure 6.12) and the outline of the parsed text to record the number of ideas and details the child includes within each category in the retelling, regardless of their order. Credit the child for partial recall or for recounting the "gist" of an event (Pellegrini & Galda, 1982). Evaluate the child's sequencing ability by comparing the order of events in the child's retelling with the proper order of setting, theme, plot episodes, and resolution. The analysis indicates which elements the child includes or omits and how well the child sequences, and also where instruction might be focused. Comparing analyses of several retellings over a year will indicate the child's progress.

The following example uses a parsed outline of the narrative story, *Jenny Learns a Lesson* (Fujikawa, 1980). The parsed outline is accompanied by transcriptions of two children's retellings of the story. A retelling guidesheet follows with a quantitative analysis of the first transcription told by a child named Beth (Morrow, 1996).

Parsed Story

Setting

1. Once upon a time there was a girl who liked to play pretend.
2. Characters: Jenny (main character), Nicholas, Sam, Mei Su, and Shags, the dog.

Theme

Every time Jenny played with her friends, she bossed them.

Plot Episodes

First episode: Jenny decided to pretend to be a queen. She called her friends. They came to play. Jenny told them all what to do and was bossy. The friends became angry and left.

Second episode: Jenny decided to play dancer. She called her friends and they came to play. Jenny told them all what to do. The friends became angry and left.

Figure 6.12

*Story Retelling
and Rewriting
Evaluation
Guide Sheet:
A Quantitative
Analysis*

Child's name _____ Beth _____   Age _____ 5 _____

Title of story _____ Jenny Learns a Lesson _____   Date _____

General directions: Give 1 point for each element included as well as for "gist." Give 1 point for each character named as well as for such words as *boy*, *girl*, or *dog*. Credit plurals (*friends*, for instance) with 2 points under characters.

Sense of Story Structure

Setting

a. Begins story with an introduction   _____ 1 _____

b. Names main character   _____ 1 _____

c. Number of other characters named   _____ 2 _____

d. Actual number of other characters   _____ 4 _____

e. Score for "other characters" (c/d):   _____ .5 _____

f. Includes statement about time or place   _____ 1 _____

Theme

Refers to main character's primary goal or problem to be solved   _____ 1 _____

Plot Episodes

a. Number of episodes recalled   _____ 4 _____

b. Number of episodes in story   _____ 5 _____

c. Score for "plot episodes" (a/b)   _____ .8 _____

Resolution

a. Names problem solution/goal attainment   _____ 1 _____

b. Ends story   _____ 1 _____

Sequence

Retells story in structural order: setting, theme, plot episodes, resolution. (Score 2 for proper, 1 for partial, 0 for no sequence evident.)   _____ 1 _____

Highest score possible: _____ 10 _____   Child's score: _____ 8.3 _____

Source: From L. M. Morrow, "Story Retelling: A Discussion Strategy to Develop and Assess Comprehension." In *Lively Discussions!: Fostering Engaged Reading,* ed. L. B. Gambrell & J. F. Almasi, 265–285. Copyright © 1996 by the International Reading Association.

Third episode: Jenny decided to play pirate. She called her friends and they came to play. Jenny told them all what to do. The friends became angry and left.

Fourth episode: Jenny decided to play duchess. She called her friends and they came to play. Jenny told them all what to do. The friends became angry and left.

Fifth episode: Jenny's friends refused to play with her because she was so bossy. Jenny became lonely and apologized to them for being bossy.

Resolution

1. The friends all played together, and each person did what he or she wanted to do.
2. They all had a wonderful day and were so tired that they fell asleep.

Verbatim Transcriptions

(Beth, age five) Once upon a time there's a girl named Jenny and she called her friends over and they played queen and went to the palace. They had to . . . they had to do what she said and they didn't like it so then they went home and said that was boring. It's not fun playing queen and doing what she says you have to. So they didn't play with her for seven days and she had . . . she had an idea that she was being selfish, so she went to find her friends and said, I'm sorry I was so mean. And said, let's play pirate, and they played pirate and they went onto the ropes. Then they played that she was a fancy lady playing house. And they have tea. And they played what they wanted and they were happy. The end.

This retelling by five-year-old Beth was transcribed when she was in the first part of her kindergarten year. To demonstrate how retellings can become more sophisticated and improve with practice and time, another retelling by this same child when she was at the end of her kindergarten year follows. The story is called *Under the Lemon Tree* (Hurd, 1980). It is about a donkey who lives under a lemon tree on the farm and watches out for all the other animals. A fox comes in the night to steal a chicken or duck and the donkey hee-haws loudly to protect them. He scares the fox away but wakes the farmer and his wife who never see the fox. This happens frequently until the farmer can no longer take the noise and moves the donkey to a tree far from the farmhouse where he is very unhappy. The fox comes back and steals the farmer's prize red rooster. The other animals quack and cluck and finally wake up the farmer who chases after the fox. When the fox passes him, the donkey makes his loud noises again, frightening the fox, who drops the red rooster. The farmer realizes that the donkey has been protecting his animals and moves him back to the lemon tree where he is happy again.

Here is five-year-old Beth's retelling of *Under the Lemon Tree:*

Once upon a time there was a donkey, and he was in a farm. He lived under a lemon tree close to the animals on the farm. In the morning all the bees buzzed in the flowers under the lemon tree. He was next to the ducks, the chickens, and the roosters. It was night time. The red fox came into the farm to get something to eat. The donkey went "hee-haw, hee-haw" and then the chickens went "cluck, cluck" and the ducks went "quack-quack." Then the farmer and his wife waked up and looked out the window and saw nothing. They didn't know what came into their farm that night. They said, "What a noisy donkey we have. When it gets dark we will bring him far away." So when it get darker and darker they brang the donkey over to a fig tree. And he had to stay there. He couldn't go to sleep alone. That night the red fox came into the farm again to try and get something to eat. All the ducks went quack-quack and the turkeys went gobble-gobble. The farmer

Figure 6.13

A Qualitative Analysis of Story Retelling and Rewriting

Child's name _____ Date _____

Name of story _____

	Yes	No
Setting		
a. Begins story with an introduction	☐	☐
b. Names main character	☐	☐
c. List other characters named here: _____		
_____		
d. Includes statement about time and place	☐	☐
Theme		
a. Refers to main character's primary goal or problem to be solved	☐	☐
Plot Episodes		
a. Episodes are recalled	☐	☐
b. List episodes recalled	☐	☐
Resolution		
a. Includes the solution to the problem or the attainment of the goal	☐	☐
b. Puts an ending on the story	☐	☐
Sequence		
a. Story is told in sequential order	☐	☐

Interpretive and Critical Comments: Read through the retelling or rewriting and list comments made or written by students that are of an interpretive or critical nature.

and his wife woke up and said, "Is that noisy donkey back again?" They rushed to the window and saw the fox with their red rooster in his mouth and yelled, "Stop thief, come back." The fox passed the donkey and shouted "hee-haw, hee-haw." The red fox heard it and dropped the rooster and ran away. The farmer and his wife said, "Aren't we lucky to have the noisiest donkey in the whole world." And they picked up the rooster and put one hand around the donkey and they all went home together and tied the donkey under the lemon tree.

Retellings can be evaluated for many different comprehension tasks. The directions to students prior to retelling and the method of analysis should match the goal. Figure 6.13 provides an analysis form for evaluating oral and written retellings in which checks are used instead of numbers for a general sense of elements a child includes and to determine progress over time. Also provided in the form is a qualitative evaluation of interpretive and critical responses. Figure 6.14 provides a student evaluation form for oral and written retellings. Self-evaluation with a teacher, with a child, or alone is an important part of the learning process.

Figure 6.14

Student Oral or Written Retelling Self-Evaluation Form

Name _____ Date _____

Name of story _____

Setting	Yes	No
a. I began the story with an introduction.	☐	☐
b. I talked about the main character.	☐	☐
c. I talked about other characters.	☐	☐
d. I told when the story happened.	☐	☐
e. I told where the story happened.	☐	☐

Theme

	Yes	No
I told about the problem in the story or the main goal of the characters.	☐	☐

Plot Episodes

	Yes	No
a. I included episodes in the story.	☐	☐

Resolution

	Yes	No
a. I told how the problem was solved or goal achieved.	☐	☐
b. I had an ending on the story.	☐	☐

Sequence

	Yes	No
My story was retold or rewritten in proper order.	☐	☐

Comments for Improvement:

Next time I need to include in my retelling:

Collaborative Response Groups

Strategies discussed for enhancing comprehension thus far are done in whole-group, small-group, or one-to-one settings with the teacher as director. In the following strategies, students participate in collaboration with one another, independent of the teacher. The National Reading Panel suggested that collaboration is an important strategy for developing comprehension (2000). These strategies are often referred to as **response groups.** Response groups have many different names and formats. They all enable children to engage in productive conversations about text eliciting personal responses. Response groups allow students to exchange ideas, refine ideas, and think critically about issues related to what they read or listened to. In these groups they learn to offer responses and to listen to what others have to say. Because young children need the teacher to model behavior for response groups before they are able to participate in them with peers, the groups are introduced in teacher-directed settings first. A brief description of types of response groups follows.

LITERATURE CIRCLES. Literature circles are formed for children to discuss books they have read with one another. The children have these discussions independently of the teacher. Children can be discussing the same or different books. Most often, however, the group discusses the same story. Teachers need to model literature circle activities so they can be carried out successfully. The steps in organizing literature circles include the following:

> The teacher provides a list of books that students select from to carry out their literature circle discussions.
>
> Small groups are formed by the teacher, and they select one book from the list of books that they will read and discuss. Groups meet regularly for their discussions.
>
> The teacher helps students with discussion using prompts similar to those reviewed in previous sections dealing with promoting conversations about books.

Students are given jobs within the group, for example:

- *The discussion director* is responsible for the opening and closing remarks, reminding members to refer to their books to find support for their comments, and ensuring that everyone participates. The discussion director asks questions that the group will discuss.
- The *literary luminary* is responsible for selecting parts of the book for the group to read aloud. The selection should be funny, sad, or interesting, and so on.
- The *illustrator* draws something related to the reading.
- The *creative connector* finds the connection between the book read and the outside world. The connections are to the students, the book, the classroom, and their families and friends.
- The *vocabulary enricher* looks for words that are important to the book. They could be new words.
- The *summarizer* writes a summary of the reading. It should be short and to the point.
- The *investigator* finds more information about the topic of the book. (Daniels, 1994)

With young children, literature circles will be more successful if topics are raised for discussion by the discussion director, such as these:

- Telling the parts of your story you liked best
- Telling the parts of the story you did not like
- How you might have ended the story if you were the author

Children can place sticky notes on pages to remember issues to discuss. They ask the group to turn to the page as they refer to it. Children can comment on an issue, ask a question of others, or ask for clarification to help them better understand. This type of exercise requires guidance from the teacher and practice on the part of children.

BUDDY READING.   **Buddy reading** is usually a situation in which a child from an upper grade is paired with a child in kindergarten or first or second grade.

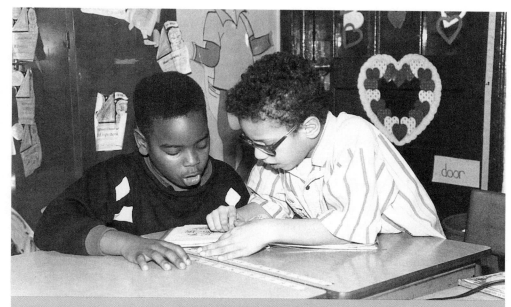

Cooperative strategies—when children read together as in partner reading and think, pair, share—enhance comprehension.

The child in the upper grade is instructed how to read to children. At specified times during the school week, buddies get together for storybook reading and discussions.

PARTNER READING.   **Partner reading** involves peers reading together. This may simply mean that the children take turns reading to each other, or that they read sitting side by side. Teachers can structure partner reading similar to literature circles with topics posed for partners to discuss after reading to each other.

THINK, PAIR, SHARE.   The **think, pair, share** strategy involves teacher-posed questions, which students are asked to think about before answering. Students are then paired with peers to discuss their answers to the questions. They then return to a larger group to share the answers they have discussed among themselves (Gambrell & Almasi, 1994).

MENTAL IMAGERY AND THINK-ALOUDS.   **Mental imagery** and **think-alouds** involve children in several strategies, alone, together, and with and without the teacher. Mental imagery asks children to visualize what they see after they have been read to or have read a passage themselves. We ask children to "Make a picture in your minds to help you remember and understand what you read or what was read to you." After the mental imagery, we ask children to "think aloud" and talk about their images to peers or to the teacher. We also ask children to predict what will happen next in the story. We tell children to ask themselves questions about the story, and to reread when they need to clarify ideas or remember forgotten details. We often ask them to personalize the text by asking them if they have ever been in a similar situation as the main character and what did they do. Visualizing ideas, and relating those visualizations orally, helps clarify information and increase understanding (Gambrell & Koskinen, 2002).

Fluency

A skill that needs more emphasis in literacy instruction is fluency. According to the National Reading Panel Report (2000), helping children to become fluent readers is crucial for literacy development. Fluency is a combination of accuracy, automaticity, and prosody when reading. More simply, a child who reads fluently is able to decode text automatically and accurately. He or she does not have to labor over every sound. In addition, the child reads with the appropriate pace and expression. This aspect of language is referred to as prosody. Prosody suggests that the student is comprehending text, since he or she is reading with appropriate expression and rate (Kuhn & Stahl, 2003). The ultimate goal for reading instruction is that students be fluent readers.

Research has shown that the following strategies are useful in helping to develop fluency:

ECHO READING. When we involve children in echo reading, the teacher or more able reader reads one line of text, and the child then reads the same line. The number of lines read is increased as the child's reading improves. When reading, be sure to model with good accuracy, pace, and expression. To be sure the children are looking at the words and reading the words, instead of just listening and repeating. Ask them to look at and follow the print on the page with their finger. Try to echo read a few times a week.

CHORAL READING. When choral reading, the entire class or a small group of children read an entire passage together along with the teacher. The teacher ensures that he or she provides a model for pace and expression. Short passages and poetry are good for choral reading. When choral reading, the child feels the correct pace and expression necessary in reading fluently. Try to choral read a few times a week.

PAIRED READING. Paired reading involves a more able reader in the same classroom or from another classroom as a model of fluent reading for less fluent readers. When they read together, the more able reader acts as the tutor. The children should read material that is easy for the child who is less fluent. The readers should take turns; for example, the tutor can read a page and then the less fluent reader repeat the same page. They can also alternate reading page by page. The tutor helps the less able reader with accuracy, rate, and expression.

READER'S THEATER. Reader's theater is the oral reading of a short play. The children have assigned parts and practice the parts for the presentation. This provides a model of what good fluent reading sounds like. Invite parents to school to hear the class perform a reader's theater piece, and take the opportunity to introduce them to the concept of fluency. Teach them some of the strategies by having them participate with you and their children. These activities are easy, they don't take much time, and they are effective.

ANTIPHONAL READING. Antiphonal reading is a choral reading in which parts are taken by groups. Poetry, especially poetry with conversation, lends itself to antiphonal reading. Divide your class into two, three, or four groups. Assign each group a different part to read. Practice each part and then read together (Johns & Berglund, 2002).

TAPE-ASSISTED READING. Listening to fluent reading samples on audiotapes while following the written text is an excellent model for children. Tapes can be either purchased or made by teachers, parents, and other students who present fluent models for reading.

REPEATED READING. Read the same book three or four times a week. When a story is repeated and known, it offers the opportunity for fluent reading just because of its familiarity. When children can read a text fluently, they get the feeling for what it sounds like. On the first day read the text to the children. On the second day do an echo reading. On the third day do a choral reading, and on the fourth a partner reading. Because you are supporting the reading of the text, use challenging books with rich vocabulary.

Children should participate in fluent reading activities daily. They are easy to do, they don't take much time, and they are fun. Fluency can be worked on with children from preschool through grade three. Preschoolers can participate in all the fluency activities, but as listening activities rather than reading. They are exposed to the rhythm, pace, and expression involved in fluent reading. They can echo speak instead of echo read. The teacher recites, and they repeat. Choral speaking can be done with memorized pieces of poetry. They can be involved in paired listening with an older child, listening to excellent models of storybook reading on tape, and repeated readings.

EVALUATING FLUENCY. Listen to a child's reading of a passage that is at his or her instructional level. The child can read it to you, or you can tape-record the passage and evaluate it later.

1. Check the number of words read per minute in comparison with expectations at the child's grade level.
2. Do a running record or miscue analysis to determine types of errors being made that disrupt fluency.
3. Use an informal fluency tool that describes the reading, such as the following:
   - Reading is word by word.
   - There are long pauses between words.
   - Many words are missed.
   - The reading is in a monotone with little evidence of use of punctuation or sense that the text is understood.
   - The rate is slow and laborious.

The following are appropriate recorded reading rates for first, second, and third graders:

The mean number of words read per minute for first graders in December is 54, in February is 66, and in May is 79.

The mean number of words typically read by second graders is 53 in the fall, 78 in the winter, and 94 in the spring.

For third graders, the mean number of words read in a minute is 79 in the fall, 93 in the winter, and 114 in the spring.

Have students evaluate their own fluency. They can listen to the taped reading and evaluate the reading as follows:

Okay: Reading is word by word, slow, and choppy with some words missed and not enough expression to show an understanding of the text.

Good: The pace of the reading is slow but not choppy. Most words are pronounced properly with enough expression to show some understanding of the text.

Wow: Reading flows smoothly at a good pace. All words are decoded properly and expression demonstrates an understanding of what is being read.

Have the children evaluate their fluency about four times a year.

MATERIALS FOR FLUENCY TRAINING. Reading materials for reading instruction such as basal selections or leveled books are good for fluency training. They can be read using echo and choral reading as part of the instructional routine when new text is introduced. Books with conversation, such as fables, are good for reader's theater, since the characters provide parts for children to read. Short pieces of text and poems are best for choral, echo, repeated, and paired reading. A book of poems by Mary Ann Hoberman called *You Read to Me, I'll Read To You* (2001) has delightful poems with at least two characters talking to each other in every poem. The poems are in different colored print for the different characters. It is perfect for reader's theater, echo and choral reading, antiphonal reading, paired reading, and repeated reading. A portion of one poem entitled "I Like" is colored in purple for one character and pink for another, and blue represents reading all together.

I like soda.
　　I like milk.
I like satin.
　　I like silk.
I like puppies.
　　I like kittens.
I like gloves.
　　I like mittens.
I like to slide.
　　I like to swing.
We don't agree on anything!

From *You Read to Me, I'll Read to You* by Mary Ann Hoberman. Copyright © 2001 by Mary Ann Hoberman. By permission of Little, Brown and Company.

Assessment of Concepts about Books and Comprehension of Text

The techniques described in this chapter are designed to develop concepts about books and comprehension of story through the use of expository and narrative text. The skills listed in the Checklist for Assessing Concepts about Books and

Comprehension of Text can be developed and assessed by a broad range of strategies used in various contexts. To determine how much children know about books, such as their front, back, top, and bottom; which part is print and which parts are pictures; how pages are turned; where reading begins; and what titles, authors, and illustrators are, one can observe regularly how youngsters handle books; hold one-to-one interviews with children; question and encourage response in whole-group, small-group, or individual interaction; or use any of the several other techniques described in this chapter. Children's responses can be literal, interpretive, or critical. They can reflect simple recall, detail, sequence, association, prediction, judgment, and evaluation. Children's comprehension of story can be demonstrated and evaluated through their story retelling, story rewriting, attempted reading of favorite storybooks, role-playing, picture sequencing, use of puppets or felt-boards to reenact stories, and questions and comments during storybook reading. When possible, keep periodic performance samples of activities, such as a story rewriting and audio- or videotapes of retellings.

Throughout this chapter, assessment tools for evaluating strategies have been provided. These materials should be placed in a child's portfolio to evaluate his or her concepts about books and comprehension of text. Baseline data from children should be collected early in the school year with assessment measures repeated every six to eight weeks.

☑ **Checklist**   *Assessing Concepts about Books and Comprehension of Text*

Child's name _____   **Date** _____

Concepts about Books	Always	Sometimes	Never	Comments
Knows a book is for reading				
Can identify the front, back, top, and bottom of a book				
Can turn the pages properly				
Knows the difference between the print and the pictures				
Knows that pictures on a page are related to what the print says				
Knows where to begin reading				
Knows what a title is				
Knows what an author is				
Knows what an illustrator is				

(continued on next page)

✔ **Checklist** *(continued from previous page)*

Comprehension of Text	Always	Sometimes	Never	Comments
Attempts to read storybooks resulting in well-formed stories				
Participates in story reading by narrating as the teacher reads				
Retells stories				
Includes story structure elements in story retellings:				
Setting				
Theme				
Plot episodes				
Resolution				
Responds to text after reading or listening with literal comments or questions				
Responds to text after reading or listening with interpretive comments or questions				
Responds to text after reading or listening with critical comments or questions				

Participates and Responds During

	Always	Sometimes	Never	Comments
Partner reading				
Buddy reading				
Literature circles				
Mental imagery				
Think-alouds				
Discussions				
Think, pair, share				

Vocabulary Development

	Always	Sometimes	Never	Comments
Learns new words daily in oral language				
Uses new words in writing				

Teacher Comments:

An Idea for the Classroom from the Classroom

■ Visualizing

This third-grade activity helps develop the effective comprehension strategy of visualizing. Choose a passage or full text (either narrative or expository) that contains vivid descriptions. Have the students sit in a circle on the floor. Start the lesson by writing the word *visualizing* on chart paper or on the board. Ask students what they know about visualizing and write down their responses. Explain that visualizing involves making a picture in your mind that connects to the words you hear or read. Describe a situation in which you used visualization to understand and remember something, and ask the students to provide their own examples. Next, read the chosen text, but do not show any of the pictures. Ask the students to listen carefully and to make a picture in their minds that helps them remember the story. They can close their eyes if it helps them. After the read-aloud, have the students return to their seats and illustrate the "pictures they made in their minds," or their interpretation of the text. The students can then share their illustrations with their classmates and explain their individual interpretations. Lead a discussion of the similarities and differences in the students' various interpretations. Compare the students' illustrations with those in the actual text.

Heather Casey, Third-Grade Teacher

An Idea for the Classroom Suited for Diverse Learners

■ Graphic Organizers

This activity, appropriate for second or third grade, works with a variety of text structures, both narrative and expository. The creation of graphic organizers is useful for all students, especially ELL students, because it provides a concrete, visual, simplified representation of the text. I begin by reviewing different text structures and the appropriate graphic organizers that help us summarize and understand the text. I explain that the students will make their own creative graphic organizers to help them understand, organize, and remember what they read.

Students select a book from a set of texts with varied reading levels. If you are studying a particular theme, the books may all be related to that theme. The teacher helps each student select a text at the appropriate reading level. There should also be a variety of text structures, especially sequence, main idea/supporting details, cause/effect and problem/solution, represented by the students' selections.

The students read their text and decide which structure it seems to best fit. Examples of multiple graphic organizers are written on the board. The students will need plenty of writing and drawing materials. Once the students choose the structure, they summarize the text using an appropriate graphic organizer. For example, a student who reads a narrative text may do a story map with the setting, characters, problem, plot episodes, and resolution. A student who reads an expository text with a main idea/supporting details structure will put the main idea at the top of the paper, with all of the important supporting details written in boxes underneath. As the students work, I circle around the room and meet briefly with each student to make sure they are on the right track. The students might want to write out a rough draft before they finalize their graphic organizer design. They can draw pictures next to the few sentences of text that they include in their graphic organizers. The students are not limited to standard graphic organizers. They are free to create a modified design if it makes sense to them and if they can explain their reasoning to the teacher. Also, students may choose to work in pairs, an activity which provides the added benefit of collaboration.

Julie Anastasi, Third-Grade Teacher

Activities and Questions

1. Answer the focus questions at the beginning of the chapter.

2. Ask a two-, four-, and six-year-old to read a favorite storybook. Describe the reading behaviors they attempt. Are developmental differences evident among their performances?

3. Meet with one child between the ages of three and eight years old. Each time you meet let the child practice retelling a story. Tape and transcribe each session. Using the forms provided in Figures 6.3 and 6.4, analyze the tapes for the elements of story structure, details, and sequence. Did the child improve from the first to the third retelling?

4. Select a piece of informational text and narrative text. Prepare discussion questions that will involve children in literal, interpretive, and critical thinking. Then change those questions into activities (such as role-playing stories or felt stories) that enable children to demonstrate their comprehension of the story.

5. Prepare two different directed listening and thinking and directed reading and thinking activities, including pre- and postdiscussions. Select different objectives for each DLTA or DRTA. Use your plans with small groups of children.

6. Using another comprehension strategy such as graphic organizers, create a lesson to teach the strategy with both expository and narrative texts.

7. Select a strategy to enhance fluency and create a lesson to teach the strategy. Identify selections you will use for reading.

8. Continue your portfolio assessment for the child you selected to assess for language development in Chapter 4. Observe the child using the assessment checklist provided in this chapter concerning the evaluation of concepts about books, comprehension of text, and other measures provided.

9. Continue the thematic unit that you began in Chapter 4. Select two objectives in the area of concepts about books, two in comprehension of text, and two for fluency. Describe activities that will satisfy each of the objectives using your theme.

10. The following passages describe a guided reading lesson in a small group taught by three different first-grade teachers. Each uses strategies to promote comprehension. While reading these passages, think about the following questions:

a. Do the questions posed by the teachers foster factual or interpretive thought?

b. Is there an emphasis on specifics or understanding of issues raised?

c. Is the plan flexible or predetermined?

d. Is there time for problem solving in an interactive manner with peers?

e. Is the atmosphere constricted, controlled, supportive, warm, or rewarding?

f. Can children raise questions?

g. Are students asked to predict and analyze?

h. Is there an emphasis on higher order thinking or literal levels of thought?

Read Teachers A and B and then answer the questions. If you had to select just one of these teachers to be, which one would you choose and why? After answering the questions, read Teacher C and then go back and answer all the questions again.

Teacher A

Teacher A begins her lesson by introducing to the group, the story they will be reading, Goldilocks and the Three Bears. *The teacher guides the children through a book walk, looking at the pictures and discussing what is happening on each page to become familiar with the story in advance of reading. Before reading the story, she tells the children she will want them to remember, after reading the story, the important details of the story such as the main characters, where the story takes place, what happened first, second, and so on, and how the story ends. She writes this information on an experience chart.*

The teacher asks the children to read the story orally together. At the end of the reading, she has the children do their own book walk to review the text. To check their comprehension, the teacher asks factual questions about the text such as, "Who are the main characters in the story?" and "What did Goldilocks do first when she got to the bears' house?" She asks similar questions all the way through the passage.

After the discussion the children are given a worksheet to complete. The worksheet is designed to reinforce the details of the story and enhance vocabulary. It includes questions that require the children to circle the correct answer. When the children are finished with the worksheet, the lesson is over.

Teacher B

Teacher B begins her guided reading lesson by asking the students to share things they have done that they knew were wrong. After the children describe their experiences, the teacher asks why they did these things. She then introduces the children to the story they will read, Goldilocks and the Three Bears. *Before reading, she has the children take a book walk by looking at the pictures in the book. She asks the children to predict what they think is happening on the different pages and what the story is about. The teacher asks the class to think about who does bad things in the story while they read. The class then reads the story orally together from beginning to end. Afterward, the teacher asks questions designed to elicit information about the students' comprehension of the story theme by asking, "What are the main events in the story? Who does good things in the book and who does things that are wrong in the book and why? Why were they wrong or right? Was it okay for Goldilocks to go in the bears' house uninvited? Why yes or why no?" Children are asked to discuss favorite parts of the story and read these parts to the class. A discussion follows about the illustrations in the book. "Are the pictures important to the story? Do they help tell parts of the story?"*

The teacher offers the children three choices for extended activities they would like to do related to the story, for example, draw a picture about the story, act out the story, or make a felt story and tell it. The children decide to draw pictures about the story and make a class book. Different parts of the story are given to each child. They write what is happening on their page. The book is put together for the class to read.

Reminder: Answer the questions posed at the beginning of the case study activity, and then read Teacher C.

Teacher C

Teacher C begins his guided reading lesson by asking the students if they have any special things at home that they like very much. He asks how they might feel if someone came and took or used their special things without asking and ruined them. He introduces the story Goldilocks and the Three Bears *and has the children do a book walk looking for how the bears' special things were used and ruined. Before reading, Teacher C asks the children to think about what special things were used and ruined. They read the book aloud together. The teacher asks the class to discuss how they think the bears felt when they got home and found someone had been in their house. All suggestions are accepted as the teacher explains that there are no right or wrong answers.*

The teacher asks the children to create an entirely new story about Goldilocks. The teacher allows the children to decide which students they would like to work with. In pairs they brainstorm and create their new story with illustrations and text. When they complete their work they share their stories.

Now answer the questions at the beginning of this case study activity for Teacher C, and decide which teacher you would like to be now that you have read Teachers A, B, and C. Support your answer.

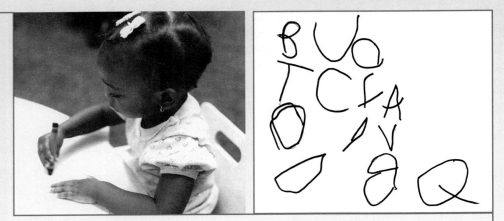

Writing, Spelling, and Literacy Development

Children want to write. They want to write the first day they attend school.
This is no accident. Before they went to school they marked up walls,
pavements, newspapers with crayons, chalk, pens or pencils . . . anything
that makes a mark. The child's marks say, "I am."

—Donald Graves
Writing: Teachers and Children at Work

Focus Questions

- Describe theories concerning how early writing is acquired.
- Describe the categories that reflect children's early attempts at writing and compare them to the stages of spelling development.
- What objectives are appropriate for promoting writing development in early childhood?
- What strategies can be used for writing development from birth to two years of age?
- What strategies can be used for developing writing in preschool through third grade?
- What steps are involved in the process approach to writing?
- What mechanical aspects of writing are important for children to learn?
- What strategies will promote achievement in spelling?
- How can writing be assessed?

At the beginning of an interactive writing session, Mrs. Callister read the story *I Know an Old Lady*. It is a nonsense tale that is read and also sung. The story is composed of rhymes, and each segment is repeated to make it predictable. The purpose of the lesson is to have children engage open-ended, problem-solving thinking, to develop vocabulary, and to use rhyme. A portion of the story follows:

> I know an old lady who swallowed a fly,
> I don't know why she swallowed a fly, perhaps she'll die.
> I know an old lady who swallowed a spider
> That wiggled and jiggled and tickled inside her,
> She swallowed the spider to catch the fly,
> I don't know why she swallowed the fly, perhaps she'll die.
> I know an old lady who swallowed a bird,
> How absurd to swallow a bird
> (the refrain is repeated)
> I know an old lady who swallowed a cat,
> Now fancy that she swallowed a cat
> (the refrain is repeated)
> I know an old lady who swallowed a dog,
> What a hog to swallow a dog
> (the refrain is repeated and additional verses are chanted).

After the story, Mrs. Callister asked her second-grade children to think of other things the old lady might swallow and what would she do or say as a result.

Tasha said, "I got one, I know an old lady who swallowed a snake, ummm, ummm, she got a big ache when she swallowed the snake." Mrs. Callister suggested she come up to the flip chart to write her idea down on the chart paper. After she wrote it Jason said, "I think it might sound better if we said what a mistake to swallow a snake." Mrs. Callister asked the class which idea they thought was best for the poem. They all agreed that they liked Jason's idea. The teacher gave Tasha the white correction tape to put over the sentence so she could write it again the way the class wanted it.

Christopher raised his hand and said, "I know an old lady who swallowed a frog, what a hog to swallow a frog." Molly said, "We can't do that, because in the real story when she swallows a dog, they say what a hog to swallow a dog." Christopher thought and said, "I know—I know an old lady who swallowed a frog, she started to jog when she swallowed a frog." "That's great," said Molly. Mrs. Callister asked Christopher to come up and write his rhyme on the chart paper.

Many of the children had ideas that were written down. Several of the ideas were improved by the group. Numerous new words popped up, and there were discussions about how to spell them and their meanings. The class agreed upon ten lines to the poem they liked for their story. Each child had paper on a clipboard to write on that they used during interactive writing. They wrote the poem on their paper as it was being created. When the chart was complete the class chanted the poem together. When they were done, Michael said, "You know, I think what we wrote is better than the original one." Everyone nodded and agreed.

Theory and Research about Writing Development

Relationships between Reading and Writing

The purposes for reading and writing are similar. We read and write to construct meaning. Readers deal with meaning by responding to what has been read. Writers deal with meaning by constructing text (Bromley, 2003). When reading and writing, children engage in similar activities. Readers and writers

- organize ideas.
- generate ideas.
- monitor their thoughts.
- problem solve.
- revise how to think about the ideas.

Children learn about reading and writing in similar ways. They experiment and pretend play at reading and writing and engage in trial and error as they practice literacy skills they have learned. Children are inventive when learning to read and write—they decorate letters, symbols, and words; they mix drawing and writing; and they invent messages in various forms and shapes (see Figure 7.1). Similarly when they read, they invent what they think the text may say by reading the pictures; they invent the voices of the characters in the books; and they predict outcomes in stories and create their own endings. We teach children phonics skills so they can decode text independently. When children write they need to use the same phonic skills to create their writing pieces. It is important to realize how similar reading and writing are and to engage children in both

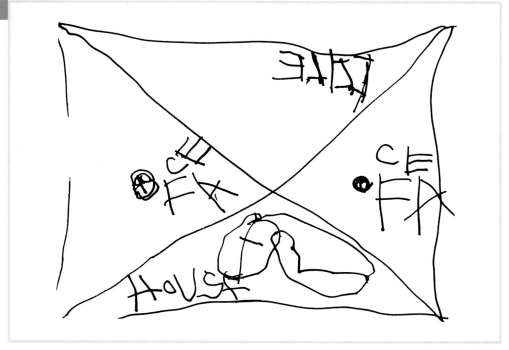

Figure 7.1

In this writing sample, Max, age five, uses his writing almost as a decoration for the drawing.

reading and writing daily. When children read they are strengthening writing skills, and when children write they are strengthening reading skills.

How Early Writing Is Acquired

Children's early literacy experiences are embedded in the familiar situations and real-life experiences of family and community (Ritchie, James-Szanton, & Howes, 2003). In fact, we have discovered that, because these literacy events are so natural, many parents do not know about their children's writing and reading experiences until they are pointed out to them (Taylor, 1983). Many things family members do on a regular basis involve literacy. They write each other notes, they make to-do lists, they send greeting cards, and they write directions.

Early writing development is characterized by children's moving from playfully making marks on paper, to communicating messages on paper, to creating texts. Children are at first unconcerned about the products of their "writing"; they lose interest in them almost immediately. However, once they begin to understand that the marks made can be meaningful and fun to produce, they are determined to learn how to write (Tompkins, 2000).

Children learn the uses of written language before they learn the forms (Bromley, 2003; Gundlach et al., 1985). In observing children scribbling and inventing primitive "texts," researchers have noted that children seem to know what writing is *for* before they know much about how to write in correct forms. The letters to friends or relatives, the greeting cards, and the signs they produce are not conventional forms of writing. Yet, the children seem impelled by an understanding of the function of written texts (see Figure 7.2).

Children's writing develops through constant invention and reinvention of the forms of written language (Dyson, 1986; Graves, 1994). Children invent ways of making letters, words, and texts, moving from primitive forms to closer approximations of conventional forms (Hansen, 1987). Parents and teachers of preschool children need to show an interest in children's early writing and accept and support their youngsters' production of the primitive forms. Children invent writing forms from their observations of environmental print and their observing, modeling, and interacting with more literate individuals who write in their presence.

Figure 7.2

Jay, age five, attempts functional writing in a letter to his friend, Peter.

Children learn about writing through explicit instruction from teachers, and by observing others more skilled than themselves. Children need to be guided and taught about writing by supportive adults, and they need to observe adults participating in writing. People who are more proficient writers play an important modeling role in children's writing development (Temple et al., 1988).

Children need to write independently. When they write independently, they are involved in practicing aspects of writing—letter formation and differentiation, similarities or differences between drawing and writing, spelling, punctuation, and so forth. When children engage in independent writing they become more conscious of what they know (see Figures 7.3 and 7.4).

Children need to write in social settings. When children write with each other or with a teacher or a more literate other, they talk about what they write, they share each others' writing, and they imitate the more literate other. Social interaction is crucial to learning to write.

Figure 7.3

Jennifer, age three and a half, practices writing through the repetition of similar letter patterns from left to right across the page.

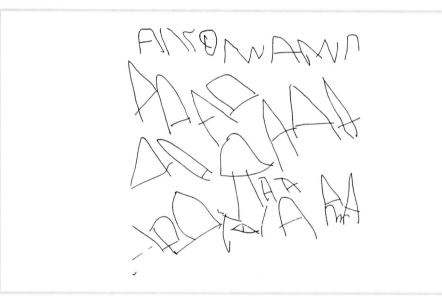

Figure 7.4

Three-year-old Robert separates his writing from his drawing by enclosing each in a circle during self-initiated practice.

Writing development is a part of a child's journey to literacy development. Literacy learning starts with drawing, then writing, and next reading (Vygotsky, 1978). Children's main resource for literacy learning is their knowledge of ways to symbolize experience and to communicate through those symbols. This theoretical framework can be summarized as follows:

1. Literacy development encompasses the development of reading, writing, listening, speaking, and viewing.
2. Literacy development involves learning to use the symbols involved in reading, writing, listening, speaking, and viewing.
3. The symbols in literacy development also include the development of social and cultural meanings.

For most children, the process for writing development occurs as a continuum. Under normal circumstances, children's early literacy development begins with learning to communicate—first nonverbally, then by talking, next with symbolic play, and finally by drawing. Each new phase is rooted in earlier phases and forms a new network of communication resources.

Literacy learning begins to develop in the interactions of family and community life. In the process, children move from playing with written language to using it to communicate. They invent and reinvent forms. When children first begin making marks on paper, most do so with no knowledge of the alphabetic nature of the written language's symbol system. Shortly thereafter, they view letters as referring to actual people or things. It is quite a bit later when children realize that writing represents language (Spandel, 2001).

The Development of Writing Ability

Children learn a lot about literacy through play, especially in literate societies where they imitate adult models by making their own pretend play marks on paper. Soon the marks become written messages, from which children achieve a sense of identity in their own eyes and in the eyes of others. The continuum from playing with drawing and writing, to communicating through written messages, to writing narrative and expository text, reflects the basic theories of early literacy development (Dyson, 1993; Halliday, 1975; Parker, 1983; Sulzby, 1986a).

Researchers have recorded varied descriptions of developmental stages of writing in early childhood (Dyson, 1985; Sulzby, 1986b; Teale, 1986). Most agree, though, that if there are stages, they are not well defined or necessarily sequential. Dyson (1986) describes children's writing development as having two broad phases. From birth to about age three, children begin to explore the form of writing by scribbling. Then, as children progress from three to six, their "controlled scribbling gradually develops into recognizable objects that they name, and similarly, the scribbling gradually acquires the characteristics of print, including linearity, horizontal orientation, and the arrangement of letterlike forms" (p. 2).

Sulzby (1985) identified six broad categories of writing in kindergarten children, cautioning that these should not be considered a reflection of developmental ordering. They do, however, describe children's early attempts at writing.

1. *Writing via Drawing*. The child will use drawing to stand for writing. The child is working out the relationship between drawing and writing, not confusing the two. The child sees drawing/writing as communication of a specific and

Figure 7.5

Writing via drawing: When asked to write something, Brad (age four) drew a picture. The same request over time yielded the same response, a drawing for writing.

purposeful message. Children who participate in writing via drawing will read their drawings as if there is writing on them (Figure 7.5).

2. *Writing via Scribbling.* The child scribbles but intends it as writing. Often the child appears to be writing and scribbles from left to right. The child moves the pencil as an adult does, and the pencil makes writinglike sounds. The scribble resembles writing (Figure 7.6).

3. *Writing via Making Letterlike Forms.* At a glance, shapes in the child's writing resemble letters. However, close observation reveals that they only look like letters. They are not just poorly formed letters, though; they are creations (Figure 7.7).

4. *Writing via Reproducing Well-Learned Units or Letter Strings.* The child uses letter sequences learned from such sources as his or her own name. The child sometimes changes the order of the letters, writing the same ones many different ways, or reproduces letters in long strings or in random order (Figure 7.8).

Figure 7.6

Writing via scribbling: When asked to write, Katie (age three) scribbled randomly. She eventually progressed to a left-to-right scribble and then purposeful marks that could be periods to end the sentence.

Figure 7.7 *Writing via making letterlike forms: Olivia (age four) wrote letterlike forms from left to right.*	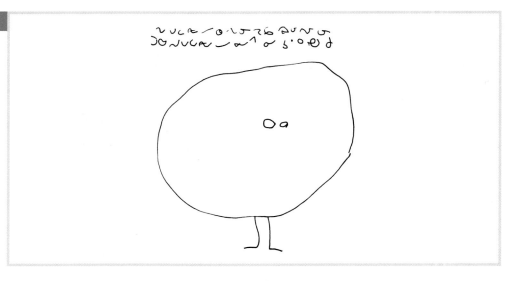

5. *Writing via Invented Spelling.* Children use many varieties and levels of **invented spelling.** Children create their own spelling for words when they do not know the conventional spellings. When using invented spelling, one letter may represent an entire word, and words sometimes overlap and are not properly spaced. As the child's writing matures, the words look more like conventional writing, with perhaps only one letter invented or left out (Figure 7.9).

6. *Writing via Conventional Spelling.* The child's writing resembles adult writing (Figure 7.10).

Sulzby's general description of early writing is helpful for teachers and parents when they are observing and describing children's writing. As noted,

Figure 7.8 *Writing via reproducing well-learned units or letter strings: Written by Brian (age four) these letters go from left to right across the page.*	

Figure 7.9

Writing via invented spelling: "I love cats because they are so pretty and I like other animals too. I love my family and they love me back." This was written by Jenny in the spring of her kindergarten year.

I Love cat's Bcuz Thea are So Prety (no) and I lik uther anmlz I Love mi famle and Thea Love me bac.

however, Sulzby emphasizes that these categories are not necessarily developmental or sequentially invariant.

Objectives for Promoting Writing Development

Thinking about writing development changed enormously in the 1970s. We always encouraged children to use crayons and paper to develop motor coordination in preparation for writing, but we never thought of writing to convey meaning as being an integral part of an early literacy program for children as young as two. We now integrate strategies for writing into the daily routines of babies, toddlers,

Figure 7.10

Conventional spelling: This story was written by Kevin, who was in third grade.

Little Red Riding hood

Once upon a time there was a little girl named little red riding hood. No one knew why she always walked, she should be riding something. The next morning Mrs. Shobert asked little Red riding hood why are you always walking? Then she walked away and she was thinking "hmm" that gave her an idea to buy something. She went to a toyota deler, she didn't like anything. Then she went to a bike place and said, "I think I like that one." Now Red riding hood rides.

preschoolers, kindergartners, and first graders. We consider even the youngest child's marks on paper as early attempts at writing, rather than as random marks. This perception is necessary in programs for early literacy development.

Generally, the best way to assist young children in language and literacy development is to provide instruction and create situations that are meaningful. This principle applies equally in the home, child-care center, preschool, kindergarten, and first, second, or third grade. The following objectives for promoting writing development are posed from the perspective that children learn language, including writing and reading, by using it purposefully in many situations (for example, in playing or communicating).

Objectives for Writing Development

1. Children will be provided with an environment in which they are regularly exposed to many kinds of print.
2. Children will experience print as a source of pleasure and enjoyment.
3. Children will regularly observe adults writing for work and for leisure.
4. Children will be given opportunities and materials for writing.
5. Children will be assisted in deciding what to write about, but left alone to make such decisions.
6. Children's attempts at writing, whatever the form, will be responded to as meaningful communication (e.g., scribble writing, letterlike forms, random letters, invented spelling).
7. Children will be taught manuscript and cursive writing.
8. Teachers will take the opportunity through children's writing to point out sound–symbol correspondences as the spoken word is transformed into the written.
9. Children will be exposed to and taught the use of some aspects of punctuation: periods, commas, and quotation marks.
10. Children's invented spelling will be accepted as working toward conventional writing.
11. Teachers will provide instruction in spelling.
12. Students will participate in evaluating their own work.
13. Children will be instructed in and encouraged to use writing for a wide range of purposes, such as creating stories, expository text, persuasive writing, descriptive writing, journal writing, and functional writing such as lists, letters, signs, and announcements.
14. Children will be taught about and read narrative and expository text in a variety of structures, to serve as models for their writing.
15. The use of writing will be integrated throughout the curriculum.
16. Children will experience constructivist activities prepared for them when writing in school and explicit instruction of skills in writing.

Strategies for Writing Development from Birth to Two

Earlier chapters have described strategies that parents can use to help children with oral language development and early reading. Some of those strategies can be applied directly to children's early writing development; others can be adapted. Some strategies are helpful specifically with writing development. It is crucial to remember, though, that speaking, reading, and writing are dynamically linked in children's development. When we help children with oral language, we also contribute indirectly to their literacy development by increasing their language experience. Similarly, reading development contributes to speaking and writing, and writing to speaking and reading. This understanding forms the basis for the integrated language arts approach.

I've watched my grandson begin his adventure into the world of literacy. We have large newsprint in the house and fat crayons for him to use that are always placed in the same spot. At 15 months he began to make marks on the paper. When he began scribbling, his productions sprawled all over the page. At 20 months we saw more controlled sprawls, dots, and wavy lines. He watched his parents writing often, and by 23 months his writing began to resemble cursive writing. The length of time he was able to engage in writing increased as he reached two years. Now he could spend 10 minutes writing. He also began to babble in his own way while he wrote as if he was telling a story about what he was writing. Next he began to attempt to write letters to familiar words such as the M in McDonald's or in Mommy. It is important to observe the literacy development of a child so we can remember milestones for future reference. This attention is important for parents, child-care providers, and preschool teachers to adopt.

If we interact with children in this way, especially from their second year on, we are ready to support them when, as a part of their scribble writing, they try to write one or more of these environmentally learned letters. In fact, some children may make their first such attempts between 18 and 24 months, though most children will not begin until they are two or three.

We can assist children in their first attempts to make marks on paper. Often, when children begin scribbling (some at 18 months), they bang on the paper with their writing implements. As they become more familiar with writing, they will begin using smoother, more deliberate and coordinated movements to make their marks. When children are in their first, primitive stages of scribbling, we can show them how to hold markers or crayons. We can guide their hands to paper, not making marks for them but helping them understand that the paper is the place for writing.

Our responses to children's early scribbling are important. It is better not to urge children to write particular things. They should make marks spontaneously and decide for themselves when these marks are intended to represent something. It is important not to press them to tell us what their marks mean or represent. It is better to say, "I like that," than to ask, "What is it?" "Can you write some more?" is also a helpful response, but do not insist if the child says no. Expressing genuine pleasure in children's early markings, whether they resemble writing or not, and seeing them as an important step in a long developmental process are positive responses that will encourage children to continue. By continuing their "writing," they will incorporate in it what they are learning about print from daily literacy events.

Beyond responding supportively to children, we can model writing for them. We can let them see us writing letters, lists, and notes and filling out forms, and we can interact with them about what we are doing. For example: "I'm writing a letter to invite your parents to school. Do you have ideas of what I should say? Do you want to write something on the paper to them?" When writing, invite the youngsters to sit with you, watch you, ask questions, and try their own hand

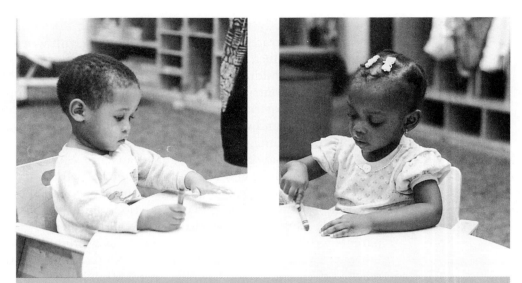

Some children may make their first attemps at scribble writing between 18 and 24 months, though most children will not begin until they are two or three.

at writing. This gives children opportunities to see how we go about writing and to begin to understand that the marks we make convey meaning.

An important way that we can support children's writing development is to provide experiences with environmental print, including print they see on television, on food cans and boxes, on signs, in stores, and on the computer. We need to talk with children about their experiences with environmental print by commenting, asking questions, and encouraging them to identify and remember signs, letters, and bits of print out of their normal contexts (for instance, an *M* used somewhere other than in a McDonald's sign).

Junk mail is a form of environmental print that can arouse interest in writing. Children enjoy writing or making marks on flyers, brochures, ads, announcements, and forms. They will write over the print and in the blank spaces. Apparently, the look and arrangement of the print gives them the model and inspiration to make their own marks.

Repeating rhymes and singing songs also can contribute to children's early writing. So can using hand puppets and playing with toys and games, such as puzzles that can be taken apart and put back together. Manipulative toys that require dexterity help with the motor development needed to shape letters. Playing with clay or play dough, finger painting, using chalkboards, and painting on easels help build motor coordination as well. Of course, reading to children not only develops oral language and promotes early reading attempts, as discussed earlier, but it also can motivate children to emulate the writing or to make their own books, no matter how crude the first attempts. Parents and caregivers in child-care centers can display children's early writings on walls, doors, and appliances, to be enjoyed and not judged or corrected.

Homes, child-care centers, and preschool should provide environments for writing—comfortable spots with rugs and child-size tables and chairs—and storage for writing materials. The latter should include felt-tip markers, pencils, crayons, and chalk. There should be ample supplies and varied sizes of large unlined paper (newsprint works well) and a chalkboard. Materials should be stored consistently in the place provided for writing so that the child can learn how to select materials and put them away independently.

Standards for Writing in Kindergarten through Third Grade

Policy makers, educators, and others are concerned about expectations for children to accomplish specific goals at specific grade levels. The International Reading Association/National Council of Teachers of English *Standards for the English Language Arts* (1996) outline the following general standards for writing that are not grade level specific:

> Students employ a wide range of strategies as they write and use different writing process elements appropriately to communicate with different audiences for a variety of purposes.

> Students apply knowledge of language structure and language conventions (e.g., conventions, style, vocabulary) to communicate effectively with a variety of audiences and for different purposes. (p. 3)

Throughout this book I have referred to the *Primary Literacy Standards for Kindergarten through Third Grade* (1999) prepared by the National Center on Education and the Economy and the Learning Research and Development Center at the University of Pittsburgh. In the standards for writing in this document, each grade has similar headings. The outcomes for the grade levels, however, increase in difficulty.

The first standard listed for writing in the primary grades is called *Writing Habits and Processes*. This standard provides for children's exploration and experimentation. It suggests that students write daily in kindergarten through grade three to develop the desire and need to write regularly. Children should be given the opportunity to select their own topics and experiment with writing.

The next standard in the document involves *Writing Purposes and Resulting Genres*. It notes purposes for young children's writing such as telling stories through narrative writing, informing others with information reports or expository text, using functional writing, and responding to literature.

The third standard discusses *Language Use and Conventions*. It concerns style of writing and syntax, vocabulary and word choice, spelling, punctuation, capitalization, and other conventions.

These standards suggest some explicit and systematic instruction for the specific outcomes desired. The following section outlines strategies that can be used to accomplish these outcomes.

Writing in Early Childhood Classrooms

Parents and teachers can expect to see rapid development in writing in children from two to eight years of age. As we have seen, it is during this period that most children move from scribbling to producing random letters, to writing letters, to writing words with invented spellings, to beginning to use conventional writing. They will begin to space properly between words and use some marks of punctuation. They tend to write longer pieces, and their productions often represent wider ranges of functions and forms. This is a time when children show intense bursts of writing activity, perhaps alternating these with intense bursts of reading activity. It is important, therefore, that teachers have a sense of children's writing needs and interests at this time and know how to interact with them to support their efforts, learning, and growth.

Like younger children, preschoolers and kindergarteners take more pleasure in the *process* of writing than in its *products*. The act of writing is their center of interest, although they gradually develop concern for the products. When they play waiter or waitress, for example, and take an "order," they may be concerned that others can "read" it. The same thing might happen with notes or greeting cards sent to relatives or friends. Children begin to evidence concern that recipients are able to read their messages—perhaps so they can write back. Children who have had little experience pretending to write might be reluctant to make marks on paper even by kindergarten age, possibly because they have become aware that their marks are not conventional writing and thus might not be accepted. It is important to let them know that writing that is not conventional will be accepted. Some children may request conventional spellings and will not write unless they know it is correct. They should be given the help they request.

We must realize that what young children write about and how they approach writing is more important initially than their mechanics of writing (spelling, handwriting, punctuation, and spacing). Learning to write involves learning to compose texts that convey meaning. As children gain experience with writing, they will learn the skills and mechanics of writing through practice and instruction.

When children are free to write in unconventional ways, such as using invented spellings as illustrated in Figure 7.9, they are enhancing phonemic awareness and eventually knowledge of phonics. When children write, they have to transform the spoken word into written language. This process fosters understanding of the structure of spoken language and how it is related to written language. The more children write, the better they become at segmenting sounds and blending them into words, which develops not only their ability to write, but also their ability to read independently.

Young children choose to write if a situation has meaning for them. If we impose upon them our selection of what they should write about all the time, we are not likely to see positive results. With these basic ideas in mind, we can create strategies and appropriate environments for helping children write.

The Writing Center

The literacy area in the classroom should include a place designated for writing. It should be easily accessible, attractive, and inviting. This area can be a part of the library corner. It should be furnished with a table and chairs, plus a rug for youngsters who want to stretch out and write on the floor. Writing implements should include plenty of colored felt-tip markers, large and small crayons, large and small pencils (both regular and colored), and chalk and a chalkboard. Various types of paper should be available, lined and unlined, plain white or newsprint, ranging from 8 by 11 inches to 24 by 36 inches.

Index cards for recording Very Own Words should be stored in the writing area, as should the children's collections of Very Own Words. Each child should have a writing folder to collect samples of his or her written work during the school year. Several computers for word processing are also necessary. Materials for making books should be available, including colored construction paper for covers, plain white paper for inside pages, a stapler, and scissors.

Teachers can prepare blank books, keyed to special occasions, for children to use. For example, a blank Valentine's Day book shaped like a heart and made of red construction paper with five or six sheets of plain white paper stapled inside provides inviting space that children can fill with their written greetings. (See Figures 7.11, 7.12, 7.13 on preparing blank books.) Stock *bare books* (books with hard covers but no print inside) for special projects and blue books used for examinations are perfect for young children's writing. They can be purchased inexpensively from school supply companies. They come with 12 or 16 pages, which is usually just right for an original story by a young child. Try to purchase blue books with the name of a university or college that is close to your school or select a university well known to your students. It makes children feel special about writing in them. Keep a supply of interesting pictures, posters, magazines, and newspapers; these can stimulate, decorate, or illustrate children's writing.

An alphabet chart in easy view helps children identify and shape letters they may need while writing. Plastic, magnetic, wooden, and felt letters should be among the language arts manipulatives. These help develop eye-hand coordination and aid in letter recognition and formation. Small white slates are good for practicing new words learned and writing sentences that feature these words. A bulletin board should be available for children to display their own writing with a space for posting notices or sending and receiving private messages. "Mailboxes" for youngsters' incoming and outgoing "mail" can be placed in the writing center. The mailboxes for a pen pal program are discussed later in the functional writing section. The writing center should be labeled with a sign that says "Author's Spot" or with a name selected by the children.

Basic implements and supplies for writing should be stocked in every other learning center in the room as well. The accessibility of these materials will encourage writing (Bromley, 2003). A child might want to record the outside temperature on a chart in the science center, protect a construction of blocks with a "Do Not Touch" sign, or copy a Very Own Word in the social studies or science area. A group might decide to turn the dramatic-play corner into a dentist's office, including in it an appointment book for recording dates, times, and patients' names; appointment cards; patients' records; and a prescription pad for medication.

The activities described for the writing center should be introduced to the entire group. They are used during writing workshop and at center time for

Figure 7.11

Stapled Book. Cut colored construction paper and white writing paper into a desired shape. Staple at the side.

Figure 7.12

Folded, Stitched, and Glued Book

a. Sew a running stitch down the center of eight to ten sheets of eight-and-a-half-by-eleven plain white writing paper backed with a piece of nine-by-twelve colored construction paper.

b. Place an eleven-by-fourteen piece of contact paper or wallpaper face down. Paste two pieces of six-by-nine oaktag or cardboard on the peeled contact paper a quarter inch apart, leaving about a one-inch border. Fold each corner of the contact paper onto the oaktag to form a triangle (glue if using wallpaper).

c. Fold the edges of the contact paper onto the oaktag (paste down if using wallpaper). Place a twelve-inch piece of Mystic Tape down the center of the contact paper and over its edges. Put glue on the two exposed pieces of oaktag and on the quarter-inch space between them.

d. Place the folded and stitched edge of the construction paper and plain white paper in the quarter-inch glued space. Paste the construction paper onto the oaktag and over the contact-paper border to make the inside covers.

Figure 7.13

Sewn Book. Punch holes into oak tag and white writing paper. Sew together with yarn.

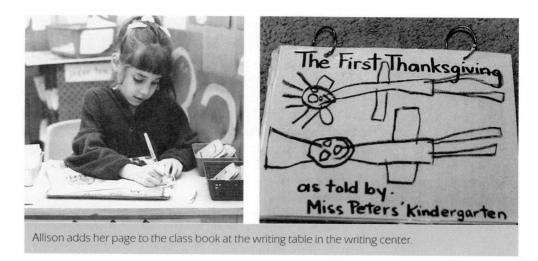

Allison adds her page to the class book at the writing table in the writing center.

independent writing. Since the activities are done independently, the teacher has modeled for the children how to use the materials. With this preparation, students will participate in the writing activities as a means of communication quite naturally.

The Writing Workshop

A **writing workshop** is a period of time set aside for writing instruction of any kind, such as independent writing, interactive writing, or journal writing. During writing workshop the teacher will provide a minilesson, a time for writing, and a time that writing is shared. At least 30 minutes a day should be allocated for writing workshop. As children get older they should spend more time writing.

- **Minilesson.** The teacher holds a whole-class or small-group lesson to teach a particular type of writing skill, such as letter writing or writing expository text. The lesson lasts from five to ten minutes. It prepares the children so they can then practice writing of the new skill.
- **Writing time.** The children are then given an assignment to write alone or sometimes with a peer. The writing assignment is tied to the minilesson skill. While the children are writing, the teacher meets with children or pairs of children for a conference about the writing they are doing to help with the new skill learned. When working with a peer, children are encouraged to conference with each other about their work.
- **Shared writing.** Writing workshop ends with children completing a written product, sharing their finished work with a partner or small group, or sharing a piece of writing with the class. With the sharing comes constructive comments such as "I really like the way you described that horse in your story. I could actually picture him in my mind." The comments should relate to the skill that was emphasized in the minilesson. In this case it was descriptive language.

Teachers may hold writing workshops with small groups of children based on need for the development of different writing skills. This type of arrangement is similar to guided reading lessons described in Chapter 9.

Teaching Children to Write in Different Genres

Children need to learn to write for many purposes. The following are types of writing that should be taught, along with experiences to help practice each writing genre.

Narrative writing involves writing original stories or retelling a story that was read to children or that children read themselves. Narrative stories could be about incidents in a child's life as well. Good narrative stories have a beginning, a middle, and an end. They follow a basic story structure with a setting at the beginning that introduces the characters, time, and place. The theme, which is the problem or goal of the main character, comes next. Then there are the plot episodes, or the events that help the main character solve his or her problem or accomplish his or her goal. Finally there is the resolution, which involves the solving of the problem or the accomplishing of the goal and an ending to the story. Activities that provide practice in narrative writing include rewriting a story (which had been read to the child or read by the child), writing an original story, writing a script for a story that includes conversation, or writing another episode for a story.

Descriptive writing involves writing with language that describes precisely. When we help children to describe, we ask them to be involved in using their senses—listening, seeing, smelling, touching, and tasting. We practice using many different words to tell about the same thing. Asking children to describe a flower, to compare two things, or to use their five senses when writing about a particular topic will help with descriptive writing.

Persuasive writing involves trying to get someone to have your point of view. We write persuasively when we write in an emotional or factual manner. For example, a book review may try to persuade someone to read a book. Other activities include creating a poster or advertisement for a product or writing a movie review.

Expository writing includes many types of experiences. Expository writing is usually about information that might come from content-area subjects such as social studies or science. In this type of writing children need to collect information and summarize it. The reports do not include personal views; they are factual. This type of writing could include providing directions to complete a task or discussing cause and effect. When we ask children to engage in this type of writing, we might ask them to write up an interview with someone, prepare a report about an informational text, summarize a unit of study, or write a biography. Expository text structures are discussed in Chapter 6. These structures—such as description, sequence, comparison, cause and effect, and problem solving—need to be taught and practiced in children's writing.

Journal writing is a personal type of genre. It is considered to be an informal type of writing. For the most part children write about themselves in journals. Journals can take many forms, some of which are described later in this chapter.

Poetry writing. Poems can be rhymes or can follow a formula. For example, an acrostic poem uses the letters of a name, place, or thing as the outline for the poem.

Functional writing is writing that serves clear, real-life purposes. Class writing projects that are particularly purposeful include *greeting cards* for birthdays, holidays, and other occasions to parents, grandparents, sisters, brothers, friends, and relatives. Write *thank-you notes* to guest speakers who come to class, to adults who help on class trips, to the director of the zoo you visited, or to the librarian who spent time with the class at the public library. Prepare lists of things to remember to do in preparing a party, a special program, or a class trip. Make *address and telephone books* with entries from class members. Write notes to parents about activities in school. Encourage individual children to write to their parents about specific things they are doing in school.

Collecting and using Very Own Words offer opportunities for writing and copying. Using classroom environmental print in one's own writing is another good writing task. Some preschools and kindergartens, as well as elementary classrooms, have established *mail service* and *pen pal* programs (Edwards, Maloy, & Verock-O'Loughlin, 2003; Martinez & Teale, 1987). Children are offered pen pals to write to regularly (once a week is reasonable). Teachers or aides may have to help children write their letters or may have to take dictation. Encourage children to use the writing capabilities that they have, even if they cannot produce conventional writing. Teachers also may have to read the incoming letters to students who cannot yet read conventionally.

The use of e-mail for pen pals (called "key pals") is another way for children to communicate with others for functional reasons. E-mail gives children the opportunity to write to others around the world, and the sending and receiving of messages is almost immediate.

A *notice board* for exchanging messages also motivates functional writing (Newman, 1984). Children can tack up pictures for each other as beginning messages. The teacher needs to provide a model by leaving messages for individuals and for the entire class. Notices about school or class events are appropriate. It is important to draw attention to the board when posting a class message or when leaving messages for individuals, so children get into the habit of looking for messages and leaving them themselves. There also needs to be a place for private messages. These can be posted on the notice board in an envelope or in student mailboxes. Some teachers have taped brown bags to each child's desk for them to receive private messages. Occasionally, the teacher should check the messages to see that children are writing. One teacher found the note in Figure 7.14, written by Asia, a first-grade girl, to Andra, a boy in first grade.

Writing Strategies

TAKING DICTATION. Taking dictation from children was a common language-experience-approach strategy that was used before we realized that young children could and should write in their own unconventional way. Taking dictation, however, does play an important role in writing development. We model reading for children by reading to them before they read conventionally; we should also model writing for them by taking dictation some of the time. When teachers take dictation, children have the opportunity to grow more in their writing ability as they watch an adult model. The following ideas are important when teachers take dictation:

1. Begin with discussion to encourage ideas.
2. Write exactly what the child says, using standard spelling.
3. Make sure the child can see you write.
4. Write legibly.
5. Read the dictation back to the child when finished, tracking the print as you read it.
6. Encourage children to read the dictation by themselves, to another child, or to an adult.

Figure 7.14

A Private Message Sent by a First-Grade Girl to a First-Grade Boy

Dear Andra
look I am triing
to make this
relashtoin ship work.
I no that you are
mad at me but I
did not do anyting
to you. All I did was
trie to take the
paper away from
you and you ript
it and you no that
you did. And if you
didthn wi didyou.
blame it all on me. Love Asia

INTERACTIVE WRITING. Interactive writing provides a model for children so they will know what to do when writing on their own. Interactive writing is a joint effort as the teacher and the children create the writing together. The teacher guides the lesson and writes on large chart paper in a whole-group or small-group setting. Sometimes the children are writing as the text is being created either on regular lined paper or on their own whiteboards. Whiteboards work well in this activity, since there is editing along the way, and it is easy to edit on a whiteboard. Any type of writing can be done in the interactive setting, such as writing a letter, a narrative piece, or an informational piece (McCarrier, Pinnell, & Fountas, 2000). Interactive writing is for the purpose of instruction, so the goal is to end up with a well-written text in content and form.

The topic for writing is decided upon by the teacher with some input from the class. It is good to select writing that has a purpose for the class and that includes a part of the writing curriculum. If the class is studying *water* for example, they might want to make a list of the uses of water as a summary of the unit. In addition to recording what they learned, they will also learn about writing lists.

Anyone can begin the writing. When a student contributes an idea it is written by that child on the chart and then discussed afterward. The teacher guides students almost word by word if they need help with spelling, an idea, or a better way to say something. The entire class can contribute to the conversation to

Teachers may need to take dictation for journal writing, for writing to pen pals, and so on. Eventually children should be encouraged to do their own writing.

improve the writing. White correction tape is used during interactive writing for errors that are made. Instead of crossing out a misspelling or incorrect form of a word, the teacher just puts the white tape over the error where the correction is made. When a child notices an error in the writing, he or she can use the tape as well.

Mrs. Jenkins wanted to teach her first-grade students about being courteous and writing thank-you notes. She wanted to teach them about the content of thank-you notes and the format. As part of their study of good health habits, a mother in the class, who was a nurse, was invited to be a guest speaker. Mrs. Jenkins used this talk as the reason for writing a thank-you note to the nurse and decided to present the lesson in an interactive writing experience. While writing the letter there was a discussion about the indentation of the first word in the paragraph. They discussed other things to say in a thank-you note besides thanking the person. They decided they could say what they liked about the presentation, and they thought they could ask her if she might come again. They discussed different ways to end the letter, such as using the word *Love* or *Sincerely,* and when to use one or the other. The activity accomplished two tasks, the need to teach courteous behavior and the need to learn about the content and format for thank-you notes. Another example of an interactive writing experience is on page 204 of this chapter.

 INDEPENDENT WRITING. Chapter 8 discusses periods of time for independent reading and writing, which give children the opportunity to participate in literacy activities. During independent reading and writing children can choose activities based on several options, and they choose to work alone or in collaboration with others. Chapter 8 also emphasizes pleasurable experiences with reading and writing. It is difficult to separate reading and writing, especially during this independent time when children direct their own behavior. However, it is interesting to note when observing children during independent reading and writing periods that equal time is spent at both these literacy activities. When children decide to engage in reading and writing, it is often a cooperative effort. During this period, children have the opportunity to select from a list of literacy activities, such as the following:

Read a book, magazine, or newspaper alone or with a friend.
Listen to a story on the headsets at the listening station.
Read or tell a story using a felt-board and story characters.
Read or tell a story using puppets.
Prepare a tape story by recording your reading of a book.
Write a story alone or with a friend.
Write a story and make it into a felt story.
Write a story and record it for the listening station.
Write a story and perform it as a puppet show.

Present a play based on a story you wrote or read.

Bind a story you have written into a book and place it in the library corner for others to read.

Participate in content-area activities that involve reading and writing.

The following anecdotes describe the writing that took place during my observations of independent reading and writing periods in a second-grade classroom. It is evident how closely reading and writing are linked. So many of the things children chose to do were motivated by what they had read or what was read to them. When writing, they often looked for additional information by reading more in other sources.

After listening to the teacher read *The Magic School Bus inside the Earth* (Cole, 1987), Stephanie, Jason, Kevin, and Nicky decided to make an advertisement poster for the book that showed key pictures with captions for each picture. They had learned about persuasive writing in writing workshop and were putting these skills to practice. The children delegated responsibilities. They made up a title for the poster and called it, *Scenes from the Magic School Bus inside the Earth.* They drew episodes from the story and wrote their own captions for the pictures. The poster took several days to complete. (One of the characteristics of independent reading and writing is that projects can be worked on over a long period.) When the poster was complete, the children presented their work to the class. Stephanie and Jason held the poster, and Kevin and Nicky were the spokespersons. Kevin explained how the group wanted to illustrate the story in an unusual way and decided on a poster. Kevin and Nicky took turns pointing to the pictures they had all drawn and reading the captions they had written for each.

Motivated by a story about magic, Zarah and Shakiera decided to write their own about a magical fish called Alexander. Shakiera asked Zarah to write the story, and Shakiera suggested that she would draw the pictures. Shakiera also offered to help think of the words to write. Zarah began to write the first line: "A fish called Alexander was a talking fish." Shakiera told Zarah to add to the sentence, "and he had magic."

Zarah said, "Magic, I don't know if that's the right word. I think he had powers." Shakiera said, "I think that magic and power are the same thing." The girls agreed and went on to write the rest of the story. These children were writing narrative text and discussing vocabulary issues.

Television shows, rock stars, and current events also motivated writing during independent reading and writing. Three girls created a roll movie that included biographies of each member of well-known singing group. They used very descriptive language that they had learned about in writing workshop.

Current events and books children read motivated writing. Joey was reading a book about the U.S. Civil War. He asked the teacher to read it to the class, which she did. Joey decided to write his own book about the Civil War, and Christopher joined him. Christopher called the book "U.S. Saratoga." As they were drawing pictures, they made bombing sounds. Suddenly Joey said, "Wait a minute, this is weird. We're making airplane carriers fighting in the Civil War." The two boys changed their minds and decided to do a book about a war that could be happening now. These boys were sorting out, collecting, and organizing their ideas, which are skills they learned about writing informational text.

Julia and Katie wrote a script for a play they were going to have some children act out. It was a wedding ceremony, and their text is reproduced in Fig-

Figure 7.15

A Play Written by Julia and Katie during an Independent Writing Period

We are gathd her today to jon thes two wondrfal pepel in holey matramony. Silvea Do you tak Gim to be yor offl weded hasbind, I do. Gim do you tak Silvea to be yr offel weded wife. I do. Ma we have the rins. Silvea pot this ring on Gims Finger. Gim pot this ring on Silveas finger. I now prnawns you man and wife. Yo may now kis the brid

ure 7.15. Conversation is another skill being practiced here, which the students have been taught about during journal writing and narrative writing.

These episodes during independent reading and writing reveal a wide variety of topics that children focused on. We would probably never think to ask children to write about some of them. If we did, the children would never have the enthusiasm they demonstrated because they had not selected the topics themselves. We also don't know all the interests of students. Some of the topics they might select to write about are very sophisticated. Children have original ideas that they can draw from their varied and rich life experiences. The topics they select have meaning and function for them, and therefore they write freely and enthusiastically about them.

Independent writing activities can be adapted for children with special needs. Children can write to other youngsters who may share their problems. As teachers have said, "There is something for everyone during independent reading and writing—the gifted, the child who attends basic skills classes, and youngsters who are English language learners."

Children need to participate in many types of writing experiences. A center time when children write independently is an important experience for practicing writing skills learned. Children practice different types of writing such as functional writing, journal writing, narrative and expository text writing, and writing using the process approach. Before children engage in any type of writing, the teacher should know what is expected of them.

JOURNAL WRITING.   **Journal writing** can be carried out successfully in early childhood rooms, with entries made daily or at least several times a week. Journals can be written in notebooks or on pages stapled together to create a book. Children are encouraged to write freely in their journals at times and to write at their own developmental levels. Thus, some children's journals might include pictures and no writing, scribble writing, random letters, or invented spelling. The teacher models journal writing, perhaps with a personal message such as, "I'm very excited today. My daughter is going to be in a play tonight, and I'm going to watch her." By example children are given an idea about the kinds of entries that are appropriate. Some children draw or write stories in their journals, others write about personal experiences, and others write about information they have

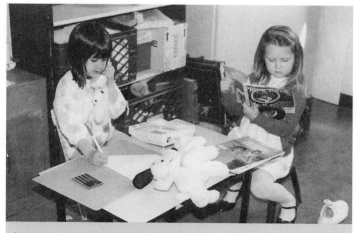

Melissa pretends to be a nurse and writes down an appointment in the dramatic-play center designed to be a doctor's office when the class was involved in a thematic unit about good health.

learned. Journals entries can be related to topics studied such as recording the growth of a seed that was planted, charting daily temperature, or reacting to a story that was read. From time to time the journal can also take dialogue form, with the teacher responding to a child's journal entry with a comment. If the child writes, "I had a picnic," the teacher might respond, "That sounds like fun. What did you eat?" The length and fluency of children's journal entries show great gains when the activity is continued regularly throughout a school year (Gunning, 2003).

Because there are different names for journals, it often becomes confusing as to which one should be used. It is the concept of journal writing that is important, that is, putting one's thoughts and early writing attempts down on paper without concern for the mechanics of writing. To help differentiate the different uses of journals, several are mentioned in the following paragraphs:

Personal journals are private journals in which children write about their lives or topics of special interest to them. These are shared only if a child chooses to do so. These are never subject to correction for spelling, punctuation, and so on.

Dialogue journals can be written about any topic, but they are shared with teachers or peers. The journal is similar to a conversation, except that the conversation is done in writing instead of speaking. A dialogue journal could be shared with the teacher or a peer responding to a journal entry that is written. It can also be an actual conversation between two people where one is writing to the other and a response is expected. The written dialogue provides students with feedback about their thoughts.

Reading response journals are those in which children respond to narrative or informational text read. They write their feelings concerning responses to the story or information. Teachers do read response journals.

Learning logs usually involve content areas, such as social studies or science. Children record information being learned, such as charting the progress of a setting hen's eggs. The more children learn about content area subjects the more they will have to write. The writing can take many forms such as charting or summarizing information.

Juan keeps a learning log about a science experiment he is doing.

There are many other titles for journals—family journals, journals about themes, and so on. Journal writing helps students become more fluent writers, choose topics to develop, learn the mechanics of writing, reflect on ideas, and articulate them. Whatever they are called, some journal experiences should include private reflections about the life of the child, others should include responses to a child's journal writing by the teacher or peers, some should be written in response to literature, and some should be written in relation to information learned.

Children's Literature and Writing

CHILDREN'S LITERATURE MOTIVATES WRITING. Children's literature is as natural a medium for encouraging writing as it is for encouraging oral language and reading (Vukelich, Evans, & Albertson, 2003; Tompkins, 2000). Reading several books by the same author or illustrator can prompt a class letter asking the author how he or she gets ideas to write or asking the illustrator what kind of art materials he or she uses. It is best to identify authors or illustrators who are likely to respond, for it is important to receive a response, even if it comes from a publisher's representative.

Old favorites and series books—those that use the same character in several different books, such as *Madeline* (Bemelmans, 1939), *Curious George* (Rey, 1941), and *Harold and the Purple Crayon* (Johnson, 1955)—can motivate children to write their own books or a class book about the character. Books such as *Swimmy* (Lionni, 1963) and *Alexander and the Terrible, Horrible, No Good, Very Bad Day* (Viorst, 1972) involve the main character in a series of adventures or incidents as the story proceeds. Children can be asked to write still another episode or adventure for the character. Some stories, such as *Alexander and the Terrible, Horrible, No Good, Very Bad Day,* lend themselves to writing about personal experiences. (Figure 7.16 illustrates one child's response to this task.)

Shared book experiences and small-group story readings (described in Chapter 6) all can lead to writing experiences. Predictable books provide patterns that

---

Figure 7.16

An Example of Writing Motivated by Children's Literature

children can imitate in their own writing through cumulative patterns, as in *I Know an Old Lady* (Westcott, 1980); repetitive language, as in *Are You My Mother?* (Eastman, 1960); familiar sequences, as in *The Very Hungry Caterpillar* (Carle, 1969); or catch-phrases, as in *Horton Hatches the Egg* (Seuss, 1940). (See Appendix A for a list of such books.)

Heather, Kim, and Tina decided to write their story about a baseball hero they particularly liked. Heather was concerned that the information they had from a magazine was not enough. She suggested that they look in the dictionary. Kim told Heather that dictionaries are for finding out how to spell words and getting their definitions, and encyclopedias are for finding out information. The girls found additional information in the encyclopedia, copied it, and continued with their work. These students were collecting information that they would have to organize and summarize. These were skills they had learned in writing workshop about writing expository text.

SHARING WRITING MOTIVATED BY CHILDREN'S LITERATURE. Children need to share their writing with an audience. When they know they will be sharing their work, they will write for that audience and have a greater purpose for writing. At a designated time during the day, usually at the end when the class gets together to review the day's happenings, a child can be selected as Author of the Day to share something that he or she has written (Graves & Hansen, 1983). More than one piece can be read, and more than one child can be Author of the Day. Those authors who read their writings in a particular week should display them on a bulletin board in the writing center along with photographs of themselves. When sharing work, the child can sit in a chair marked "**Author's Chair.**" Children in the audience should be encouraged to comment about their friends' work with such statements as "I like what you wrote" or "I fell and cut my knee once, too." Because at first the children may not comment readily, the teacher needs to model comments for the audience, whose young members will soon emulate the behavior.

It was Steven's turn in the Author's Chair. He sat down, organized his materials, and said:

> *I've been working on a series of stories. They are all about the same character, and in each one he had another adventure. It is sort of like the books about* Clifford the Big Red Dog. *My stories are about a cat, and the first one is called* The Cat Named Buster. *I call that Part I; I already have Part II and Part III. Part II is called* Buster Meets Pretzel. *Pretzel is a dog. Part III is called* Buster Gets Lost. *I'll read Part I to you.*

After reading Part I of his stories, Philip said, "Can I read one?" Steven replied, "Sure, but you should read all of them. They go together." Philip continued, "I just want to read the first one now." Steven said, "OK, but you don't know what you're missing."

Writing Poetry

Another form of writing enjoyed by young children is poetry. With very young children, the class can write the poetry together in a shared writing experience on chart paper. Poetry that rhymes is probably the most well-known type. There are many types of formula poetry enjoyed by children. Acrostic poems are quite popular. They begin with a topic word that is written vertically on the page. The word could be a child's name, a season, a place, or a thing. The poem uses the letters of the topic being written about. You can use just a word, a phrase, or a sentence. For example, here is an acrostic poem I wrote about my grandbaby James:

James

Jolly
Adorable
Messy
Enthusiastic
So sweet, so silly, so special

Triangle poems have a specific formula to them. The first word and first line is a noun, the second line is made of two adjectives, the next two words are "ing" words, and the fourth and last line is a sentence. Here is a triangle poem about spring:

Spring
New pretty
Dancing playing
It's so nice to be outdoors

Haiku is a form of formula poetry that comes from Japan. The topics of haiku are often related to nature. There are three lines in a haiku and 17 syllables in the entire poem. The first line has five syllables, the second line seven syllables, and the third line five syllables. Here is a haiku about trees:

The trees above me
Swaying across the blue sky
Make a pretty sound

An activity that develops vocabulary and syntax and can create poems follows. Select a topic about something you are studying—for example, the rain. Make that the topic word in the poem. Brainstorm what rain is like and what it does, for example:

Rain
Heavy
Light
Cold
Warm
Falling
Blowing

This is a poem that can be chanted. To take it one step further, put the word *rain* with the words listed and chant

Heavy rain
Light rain
Blowing rain
Cold rain
Warm rain
Falling rain

Stephanie made her story into a roll movie.

Stephanie puts the finishing touches on the cover of a book she has written.

Publishing Children's Writing

Children's work should be published. "Why publish?" almost answers the question "Why write?" "Writing is a public act, meant to be shared with many audiences" (Graves, 1983, p. 54). When children know their work will be published, they write for a defined purpose. When work is to be published, it becomes special; it needs to be done carefully. Children can publish their work in many ways. The most popular is to bind writings into books, which are placed in the literacy center and featured on open bookshelves for others to read. (Three ways of making a book are illustrated earlier in this chapter in Figures 7.11, 7.12, and 7.13.)

Other means of publishing include creating felt-board stories or roll movies, telling stories to classmates, role-playing what has been written, or presenting the story in a puppet show. A computer can be used to type, save, and print original material.

The Process Approach to Writing in Early Childhood

The process approach makes children realize that writing involves thinking, organizing, and rewriting before a piece is complete. They become aware that a first writing rarely constitutes a finished product. Typical steps in this approach include prewriting, drafting, conferencing, revising, and editing (Fletcher & Portalupi, 2001; Calkins, 1986).

Prewriting is probably the most important part of the writing process. It helps students select a topic to write about, it helps to figure out the purpose of a piece, and it helps to decide for whom the piece is being written. In prewriting activities a decision can be made about the form that the writing will take, such as a poem, letter, or narrative. Prewriting also can involve getting the information needed to write and organizing the writing (Tompkins, 2003). Prewriting activities could involve brainstorming related to the topic, webbing ideas, and making outlines. Prewriting can take place with the entire class, a friend, or the teacher, or alone.

Drafting is the second part in the process. The author makes a first attempt at writing the piece by getting the words down on paper. The lists prepared in the prewriting phase are used as a guide. During drafting, getting the ideas written is more important than spelling, punctuation, correct grammar, and so on. Rough drafts can be done on the computer or by hand. When writing by hand, write on every other line of the paper so there is space for editing.

Conferencing can be done with a teacher or a friend. This is a time to reflect on what has been written to see whether changes are needed. The discussion about changes has mostly to do with content. To get the conference going the teacher can say, "Tell me how your writing is coming along?" "What will you write next in this piece?" "Can you think of another way of describing the character in your writing?" "I like the way you say your character is funny; could you write some examples of how he is funny?" Children should be taught to reflect on their own work and work of their peers. We can teach them to use some of these questions with each other.

Revision constitutes making substantive changes in ideas and finding ways to make the piece more descriptive or informative. It means changing things around, trying different ways to make them better. It means sharing the writing with a friend or a group, and reading it over again and again.

Editing, the last part of the process approach, requires making minor changes to the piece, mostly attending to mechanics such as punctuation, grammatical corrections, spelling, and handwriting.

Process-writing self-planning sheets for prewriting guidance and revising are helpful for students in late first grade and beyond; see Figures 7.17 and 7.18.

Figure 7.17

Prewriting Guidance Sheet

Author _____

Who am I writing this for?

Why am I writing this?

What is being explained?

What happens:
- First
- Second
- Third
- Then
- Finally

Source: Adapted from Thomas Gunning, *Creating Literacy Instruction for All Children* (4th ed.) (Boston: Allyn & Bacon, 2003).

Figure 7.18

Revising Guidance Sheet

Author _____

What do I like about my writing?
- Why?

Did I:
- Tell what was being explained?
- Change the parts that needed changing?

What are the changes made?
- Make a list.

Source: Adapted from Thomas Gunning, *Creating Literacy Instruction for All Children* (4th ed.) (Boston: Allyn & Bacon, 2003).

CONCERNS ABOUT THE PROCESS APPROACH. The process approach should be used cautiously and only occasionally with children in the early childhood years. The prewriting phase may be accomplished through discussion and word lists with very young children and throughout the grades. Prewriting often involves the selection of a topic to write about. We want to allow children to select topics themselves as often as possible. Many children just cannot seem to make such choices. Having a purpose for a writing activity is helpful when trying to select a topic. For example, the writing activity should have a particular form such as writing an acrostic poem, or the activity could be to learn about writing a well-formed expository piece. After the type of writing is identified, it is easier to select the topic. With students who are still having trouble, it is helpful when the writing revolves around a very general topic that is being studied in class, such as the rain forest. Children can then select their particular topic more easily. With this type of support students will eventually become more capable of selecting topics on their own.

Drafting can also be done by very young children and throughout the grades, but the products of drafting will be different depending on the development of the students. A draft could be an entire written story or a series of letter strings. Conferencing, where the teacher asks children to discuss their work, can also be done at all ages and stages. Older children can be asked how they think they can change their piece to make it better. Most younger children should not be asked to revise. Editing might be too tedious for many students. It is up to the teacher to understand the developmental level of the children with whom she is working. Some children may be frustrated by revisions and editing, particularly by having to copy their work over. Be selective in choosing students with whom to use the process approach. Involve only those who seem capable of handling it. Try only one or two of the steps in the process. As children increase their skills, more of the steps can be used.

Writing conferences between a teacher and a child are times to discuss what the child has written, to encourage the child in writing, and to assess progress by observing and reviewing the writing products gathered in the child's folder. During the conference the teacher can take dictation or help the child with a word, a caption, a picture, or a publishing activity. This is an especially good time to work with students who are capable of dealing with any of the steps in process writing and to encourage reluctant writers.

Writing programs in early childhood should be initiated at the beginning of the school year. Teachers should refer to children as authors and writers so that they perceive themselves as such. Teachers need to model writing through messages on the message board, notes to parents, thank-you notes to children, and experience charts dictated by the class. They must be supportive when working with young writers. Reluctant writers need to be encouraged to write in "their very own way" (Bromley, 2003; Martinez & Teale, 1987; Sulzby, 1986b). Youngsters need to know that their work does not have to look like adult writing. Showing them samples of other children's writing, including drawings, scribble writing, and random letters, helps them see that they can do the same thing. Adults need to facilitate young writers' attempts by taking dictation if children cannot or will not write themselves, spelling words, showing children how to form letters when asked, and answering questions that arise during writing. Like other areas of literacy, writing requires social interaction if it is to promote development. Therefore, teachers need to offer young writers feedback, encouragement, and positive reinforcement.

The Mechanics of Writing: Spelling and Punctuation

Thus far this chapter has emphasized the importance of promoting children's interest in writing and giving them opportunities to write that will prove to be enjoyable. This section deals with the *mechanics of writing*.

HANDWRITING. Writing requires dexterity. Although it is unnecessary and often unwise to teach preschoolers and kindergarteners the particulars of proper letter formation, they can be encouraged to use manipulatives such as puzzles and sewing cards that strengthen their fine motor coordination. In the earlier discussion of the literacy center, other materials that help with writing and identifying letters were mentioned, including magnetic letters, letter forms to trace and copy, and whiteboard slates to practice writing letters, words, and sentences. The letters of the alphabet should be displayed at eye level for children, and the teacher can model the correct formation of upper- and lowercase manuscript (Figure 7.19). Legibility needs to be the main goal for handwriting. Learning about spaces between words is important so that words will not run into each other. There are only a few lines and shapes to learn when writing manuscript. They include a vertical line, a horizontal line, diagonal lines, a half circle with

Figure 7.19

Forming the Letters of the Alphabet

Figure 7.20

Manuscript Forms

the opening on the left, right, top, or bottom, and a full circle (Figure 7.20). The straight lines in manuscript are called sticks. All lines are written from the top to the bottom. All circles and half circles are written from the top to the bottom. The letters *h, m, n, r,* and *u* are written without lifting the pencil off of the page beginning with the stick. So to make the *h,* you start at the top of the stick and go down to the line and go back up half of the stick to make the half circle with the opening on the bottom. The letters *b, d, g, p,* and *q* are made with a circle first and then the stick is attached.

Teach children about putting spaces between letters and words. A good rule is that one figure space will help to separate words. Children can and will develop their own handwriting style, but they need to learn that whatever their style, neat handwriting is a form of courtesy for those who will be reading what they write.

Initial writing will be on unlined paper. When children have developed sufficient dexterity, they can begin to use lined paper. This level will be reached at the end of kindergarten and into first grade.

SPELLING AND PUNCTUATION. Spelling and punctuation should be taught when the need arises, and in a systematic fashion during minilessons. Opportunities for dealing with commas, question marks, periods, and capital letters occur when reading a morning message, for example, and then the mechanics of writing are being discussed in a natural setting. Spelling and punctuation have become areas of concern with the acceptance, for example, of invented spelling in the early stages of writing. Many teachers are not sure when to begin formal teaching of spelling and punctuation and to begin correcting invented forms. Children should be encouraged to write in any way that they can in their first attempts. However, they need to know that it is "a child's way of writing and not grown-up writing." When children are comfortable writing, and do so freely in their own style of early attempts, teachers should begin to point out elements of spelling and punctuation that will help them make the transition from invented spelling and punctuation to conventional forms. Figure 7.21 outlines stages of spelling development.

The following are some suggestions for encouraging conventional forms of spelling and punctuation:

- When you take dictation from a child, you can comment on the spelling of some unusual words and appropriate punctuation.
- When children use certain consistent invented forms of spelling and punctuation in their writing, put the correct form on a 3 by 5 Very Own Word card for them to copy the next time they use that word or punctuation. Get children in the habit of asking for words they do not know how to spell on index cards to help them develop their own spelling word list.

Figure 7.21

Stages of Spelling Development

Precommunicative Spelling

- Children use scribbles.
- Children are developing a sense of directionality with scribbles.
- Children write some letters.
- Children write random strings of letters and numbers mixed with no association of the letters, marks, or numbers to sounds (e.g., L4TZMP for house).

Semiphonetic Spelling

- Consonants begin to represent words and are related to the sounds of the words (e.g., TIMGTAK—Today I am going to the Park.).
- Beginning and ending consonant sounds may be included (b for bug; bd for bed).
- One or two sounds may be correct in a word.

Phonetic Spelling

Children spell words as they sound (e.g., sokar for soccer).

Transitional Spelling

Children use a high percentage of correctly spelled words, and the remaining words are spelled using some type of spelling generalization (e.g., afternewn for afternoon).

Conventional Spelling

Children apply the basic rules of English to spelling and correctly spell 90 percent of the words they write.

Source: Adapted from J. Johns, S. D. Lenski, and L. Elish-Piper, *Early Literacy Assessments and Teaching Strategies,* Dubuque, IA: Kendall/Hunt, 1999, pp. 139–140.

- When using Big Books, and tracking print, emphasize the spelling of words or types of punctuation used.
- Use the **morning message** for teaching spelling and punctuation. Write new spelling words in the message for children to copy in their writing. Leave blanks for children to fill in words from a choice of the new spelling words for the week. You also can use incorrect spelling and punctuation so children act as detectives to correct the errors. Or, a message can be written in all lowercase letters for children to correct with appropriate capitals put in the right place. Use incorrect spacing between words and sentences to provide for conversation about these mechanics of writing. This activity leads to an opportunity to help children with spacing in their own writing by telling them how one finger space is used between words and two finger spaces between sentences.
- Encourage children to do free writing, which will result in improved spelling and punctuation.
- Phonics lessons, which teach about word families and sound–symbol relationships, will help with spelling. Make children aware that they should be using their knowledge of sound–symbol relationships when they spell words, and that phonograms or chunks or digraphs such as *ch* and *sh* are spelling patterns to learn.
- In writing conferences with children, take the opportunity to make them aware of editing, which includes correct spelling.
- Make children aware of spelling resources, such as the dictionary.

- Teach the children how to use spell checks on the computer.
- Use word lists of common but difficult words to spell, such as *the, this,* and *but,* for children to memorize. A few words a week should be part of a spelling list to learn. The older the children, the more words can be assigned per week. (Figure 5.2 is a list of high-frequency words.)
- Add words from theme units to spelling lists.
- Encourage children to help each other with spelling words and punctuation.

As mentioned, it is important to free children to write their thoughts on paper without concern for the mechanics of writing. When they are ready, it is also important to make them aware of writing that is mechanically correct. There are times for free writing and times for edited pieces. Children should know that each type of writing is acceptable, but they occur in different settings. The word-study discussion in Chapter 5 about phonics provides activities that will help with spelling through word building. The following are some spelling games that are easy to use in the classroom to reinforce spelling words being taught (Rosencrans, 1998):

Letter Box: Put five or six letters that make up the week's spelling words in a box. Students will arrange letters to make spelling words.

Mixed-Up Scrambled Words: Write spelling words with the letters mixed up, and ask children to write each word correctly.

Spelling Collage: Ask children to write their spelling words randomly on a 9 by 12 paper covering as much an area as possible with the words. With markers and crayons have the students trace over the spelling words in different colors in a decorative manner. Display the spelling collages on a bulletin board.

Spelling Detectives: In various communications such as on word walls, morning messages, center activity directions, or job descriptions, make errors in spelling words. It is the children's job to find the errors daily.

Word Hunt: Have students look regularly for spelling words that appear in all that they do at school and at home, for example, in a math book, a science book, the newspaper, a book they are reading for pleasure, on food lists at home, and so on.

Trace a Word: Have students "write" spelling words on a partner's back using their pointer finger. The partner has to guess the word.

Hidden Words: Prepare a list of spelling words that are surrounded by other letters. Have students find then circle or color the spelling words embedded within (example: ovisrm mx**the**uv qr**but**zi).

Transitions

Throughout this chapter theories and strategies for helping children develop the desire to write have been discussed. All the strategies are appropriate for preschool through third grade, with adaptations based on the particular age group. Teachers often want to know how children move from one level of writing ability to another or from unconventional writing to conventional. It is somewhat individual for every child, but trends do emerge. First and foremost we want to provide an atmosphere in which children will write. Children who are reluctant to write, because they think they cannot, can be shown work done by others of their own age so that they see that unconventional writing is acceptable. We foster acceptance so that children will attempt writing. As youngsters learn more about phoneme–grapheme correspondence, they begin to realize that their invented spelling is not conventional spelling. At this point, they begin to ask for correct spelling as they move into the conventional stage of writing. It may seem as if they are taking a step backward because suddenly they will not be writing as much or as spontaneously as they did in the past. Their concern for writing correctly has that effect on their performance. This will last for a short time as their spelling vocabulary increases, they learn to use the dictionary, and they seek help from friends and the teacher. Conventional writing is a gradual process in which a child often goes back and forth from conventional to unconventional writing until sufficient proficiency is gained for the writing to be considered completely conventional.

Assessment of Children's Writing Development and the Writing Environment

As in other areas of literacy, assessment of a child's writing should take place throughout the school year. That way the teacher can determine a child's level of development, monitor progress, and plan programs accordingly. The checklists on pages 238 and 239 provide a resource for the teacher to evaluate characteristics of a child's writing development and the classroom writing environment.

The assessment checklist is used to analyze individual writing samples collected through the school year for the specific characteristics outlined in the measure. Figure 7.22 provides another means of evaluating children's written original stories and oral dictations of stories for sense of story structure as well as the inclusion of interpretive and critical thoughts. Qualitative and quantitative assessment measures for narrative story rewriting after reading or listening to a story read are found in Figures 6.12 and 6.13. Assessment of children's expository writing is found in Figure 7.23.

The measures for evaluating writing and the checklists in this chapter provide the teacher with information about the language the child uses, the concepts included in the writing, the purpose for writing, and the writing mechanics used. The checklists provide information about the conventions of writing. They will indicate the stage of writing or spelling that a student is demonstrating, as well as the mechanics of writing used such as capitalization and punctuation. The measures for story rewriting and writing of original stories will determine how well the child uses meaning and structure in his or her writing. All these assessment tools will help determine appropriate instruction and practice a child needs in order to progress in writing development.

Teachers should maintain a portfolio of materials related to a child's writing development, such as observation notes as the child writes, samples of the child's writing over a period of time, notes from conferences with the child, notes from conferences with the child's parents, and completed checklists. The portfolio should include the best of the child's work and samples showing need for improvement as well. The portfolio can be used during parent conferences and

✓ Checklist *Assessing Writing Development*

Child's name _____ **Date** _____

	Always	Sometimes	Never	Comments
Explores with writing materials				
Dictates stories, sentences, or words he or she wants written down				
Copies letters and words				
Independently attempts writing to convey meaning, regardless of writing level				
Can write his or her name				
Collaborates with others in writing experience				
Writes in varied genres:				
narrative (stories)				
expository (personal and informational reports)				
Writes for functional purposes				
Check (√) the level or levels at which the child is writing				
_____ uses drawing for writing and drawing				
_____ differentiates between writing and drawing				
_____ uses scribble writing for writing				
_____ uses letterlike forms for writing				
_____ uses learned letters in random fashion for writing				
_____ uses invented spelling for writing				
_____ writes conventionally with conventional spelling				

Mechanics for Writing

	Always	Sometimes	Never	Comments
Forms uppercase letters legibly				
Forms lowercase letters legibly				
Writes from left to right				
Leaves spaces between words				
Uses capital letters when necessary				

	Always	Sometimes	Never	Comments
Uses periods in appropriate places				
Uses commas in appropriate places				

Spelling Development

Check (√) the level or levels at which the child is spelling				
_____ precommunicative spelling				
_____ semiphonetic spelling				
_____ phonetic spelling				
_____ transitional spelling				
_____ conventional spelling				

Teacher Comments:

Checklist *Assessing the Classroom Writing Environment*

	Yes	No
Space provided for a writing center		
Tables and chairs included in center		
Writing posters and bulletin boards for children to display their writing themselves		
Writing utensils (pens, pencils, crayons, magic markers, colored pencils, etc.)		
Typewriter and/or computer		
Writing materials (many varieties of paper in all sizes, booklets, pads)		
A message board or private message area for children to leave messages for the teacher and other members of the class		
A place to store Very Own Words		
Folders for children to place samples of their writing		
Materials to make books		

Figure 7.22

*Evaluating Oral
and Written
Original Stories*

Child's name _____ Date _____

Name of Story _____

Setting	**Yes**	**No**
a. The story begins with an introduction.	☐	☐
b. One or more main characters emerge.	☐	☐
c. Other characters are talked about.	☐	☐
d. The time of the story is mentioned.	☐	☐
e. Where the story takes place is mentioned.	☐	☐

Theme

a. A beginning event occurs that causes a problem for the main character or goal to be achieved.	☐	☐
b. The main character reacts to the problem.	☐	☐

Plot Episodes

An event or series of events is mentioned that relates to the main character solving the problem or attaining the goal.	☐	☐

Resolution

a. The main character solves the problem or achieves the goal.	☐	☐
b. The story ends with a closing statement.	☐	☐

Sequence

The four categories of story structure are presented in typical sequential order (setting, theme, plot episodes, resolution).	☐	☐

Interpretive and Critical Comments

Read through the oral taped story and the written original story and record comments and responses that demonstrate interpretive and critical thought.

can accompany a child to his or her next teacher. Children should have their own writing folders in which they keep samples of their writing throughout the year. They also should be involved in the assessment process by participating in parent and teacher conferences, and in conferences with the teacher alone. Figure 7.24 provides a general way for children to assess their own writing interest and ability. For kindergarteners and young children, something simpler for self-evaluation can be used. The children can evaluate with a friend or the teacher whether their work is *Wow, Good,* or *Okay.* The teacher says *Wow* with a very enthusiastic voice; *Good* is much more toned down; and *Okay* is said just that way, *Okay.* When they evaluate they discuss why one of these words was used. The evaluation is based on their ability as well. When evaluating together, look and see whether children took time with their illustrations. Was their writing done to the best of their ability? All these suggestions support the purpose of assessment to (1) enhance the teacher's understanding of children's writing ability, (2) aid in program planning, and (3) help children and parents understand a child's progress and the processes involved to help gain more competence in writing.

Figure 7.23		Yes	No
Evaluating Expository Text	The expository text includes some of these characteristics:		
	1. **Comparing and contrasting** Noting similarities and differences	☐	☐
	2. **Sequencing** Listing factual information that happened in proper sequential order	☐	☐
	3. **Cause and effect** Describing how something happened and why	☐	☐
	4. **Exemplification** Providing a reason and an example	☐	☐
	5. **Description** Giving a good picture of what specific information looks like	☐	☐

Figure 7.24

Self-Assessment about Writing for Children

Name _____

The good things about what I wrote are:

The things I don't like about what I wrote are:

I could make this writing better if I:

I used correct spelling:

I used my best handwriting:

Is writing hard or easy for me?

For me writing is (a) fun, (b) not so much fun.

Writing could be better if:

Next time I write something, I will try to do the following things to make it better:

An Idea for the Classroom from the Classroom

■ Preschool and First-Grade Pen Pals

Children from a nearby preschool wrote to my first graders to find out what the elementary school was like. We wrote a class letter back answering their questions and included our pictures. One week later, we received a response. Now we had established a letter-writing routine. The children in my class took turns writing parts of each letter on chart paper. We went through the writing process steps of brainstorming, revising, editing, and rewriting for our new audience. Three children acted as scribes, while the rest of the class developed the letter. Later, three new children were chosen to revise and edit. Finally, three more children rewrote the letter. We also used e-mail to send messages to pen pals that need quick responses. Being pen pals became a part of our writing curriculum. We invited the preschoolers for a snack and a paired-reading session, and to our end-of-the-year play. In turn, the preschoolers invited our class for a picnic at the preschool. We developed a friendship with the younger students, and our first-grade class learned the purposeful and very rewarding skill of letter writing. In addition, the preschoolers became familiar with our school, which most of them would be entering soon.

Donna M. Ngai, First-Grade Teacher

An Idea for the Classroom for Diverse Learners

■ Writing across Genres

One of the best ways to help students learn about the styles and purposes of different genres is to read a variety of genres and discuss the characteristics. The students should also have plenty of practice writing in different genres. In my second-grade class, we study metamorphosis, and we have caterpillars living in our classroom. I read a variety of nonfiction texts about caterpillars and metamorphosis to the class. My students brainstorm what they notice about these nonfiction texts, in terms of style and content. These expository texts are sometimes easier for ELL students to understand because they are not culturally specific and they lack English idioms. Also, big words like *metamorphosis* and *chrysalis* are often easier for students to remember because they are so distinct. I ask the students to observe the caterpillars on a daily basis and to take notes in their science journals. After their observation period, I ask them to expand on their notes and to write "as scientists" to document what they have noticed. If a student starts to write something like "Pedro was taking a nap. Pedro was happy," I explain that scientific writers need to use the word *caterpillar* instead of a first name, and that they also must write only what they observed, without interpretation. I say to the student, "We are not sure if the caterpillar is happy, so let's try to think of something that we know for sure because we observed it." With guided conversations like this one, the students start to understand the differences in various genres, and their writing becomes much more specific and purposeful.

Joanne Jacobson, Second-Grade Teacher

Activities and Questions

1. Answer the focus questions at the beginning of the chapter.

2. Ask three children of different ages, for example, three, five, and seven, to write about their favorite food, television show, storybook, or game. Take notes on their behavior during writing, and analyze the sample of their writing to determine each child's writing developmental level.

3. Many functional and meaningful writing experiences are related in this chapter. Try to think of writing experiences not dealt with in the chapter that you could suggest for children to participate in.

4. Think of several dramatic-play themes that you could create in an early childhood classroom, such as a restaurant. For each theme, think of the writing materials you could provide for that play area for children to use.

5. Continue the portfolio assessment for the child you selected to assess for language development in Chapter 4. Observe the child using the assessment checklist provided in this chapter concerning the evaluation of writing development. Collect writing samples from the child over the course of several months. Evaluate them to determine the child's development in writing over time.

6. Continue the thematic unit that you began in Chapter 4. Select three objectives in the area of writing development and describe three activities that will satisfy each of the objectives using your theme. Be sure that your activities reflect functional and meaningful writing tasks.

7. Create an activity to enhance spelling and punctuation for young children.

*Motivating Reading
and Writing*

Children who read and write only when they have to are not being taught a love of reading. The best index of the success of literacy instruction is the eagerness with which children approach reading and writing.

Love of reading and writing is not taught, it is created.

Love of reading and writing is not required, it is inspired.

Love of reading and writing is not demanded, it is exemplified.

Love of reading and writing is not exacted, it is quickened.

Love of reading and writing is not solicited, it is activated.

—Russell Stauffer
Adapted from *Wilson Library Bulletin*

Focus Questions

- What objectives and standards help guide the development of positive attitudes toward literacy activities, thus motivating reading and writing?
- What are the physical characteristics of well-designed literacy centers that motivate children's use of these spaces?
- Name and define different genres of children's literature.
- Describe strategies using children's literature that motivate interest in reading and writing.
- Describe literacy center activities and explain how they are organized to promote independent reading and writing.
- How can technology enhance literacy development?
- How can play enhance literacy?

During a period for independent reading and writing, second graders Trisha and Jessica chose a felt story of the book *Are You My Mother?* (Eastman, 1960). The following transpired as they worked together reading the story and manipulating the felt characters:

Jessica: Can I read the story?

Trisha: OK.

Jessica: (She begins reading with enthusiasm as Trisha works the felt pieces on the board.) The baby bird asks the cow, "Are you my mother?"

Trisha: (She puts the cow on the felt-board.) Mooooooo.

Jessica: Moooooooo. (Jessica continues to read the book.)

Trisha: Look at this picture. (She points to the baby bird. Both start to giggle.)

Jessica: Here I am Mother! (She reads in a high-pitched voice.) Mother, mother, here I am!

Trisha: I like it when he says to the tractor, "You are my mother, Snort, Snort."

Jessica: Snort, Snort! I thought I had a mother. (She puts her hand to her head as she says this, using a baby bird voice and swaying back and forth pretending she is crying.)

Trisha: (She imitates Jessica by putting her hands on her head.) I thought I had a mother!

Jessica: (She points to the felt-board.) Can I do this now and you read? (They trade places, and Trisha starts reading. She speaks in dramatic and different voices for the two birds. Trisha is reading too fast for Jessica to put the characters on the board.)

Jessica: Wait, wait, will you wait a minute Trisha. (She puts the dog on the felt-board, and Trisha continues.) Wait, Wait, Wait! (She puts the mother bird on the felt-board.)

Two second graders reading and performing a felt story together.

This dialogue was between two second-grade children engaged in a literacy center activity. The children were practicing literacy skills in a classroom atmosphere that promotes the desire to read and write through the use of motivating literacy activities.

Strategies for Motivating Reading and Writing

A survey of classroom teachers concerning priorities for research indicated that motivating children to want to read and write was ranked high on the list of suggestions (O'Flahavan et al., 1992). Teachers recognize the importance of motivation in the development of children's literacy skills. They are interested in learning new ways to promote their students' interest in reading and writing. An entire chapter about this topic has been included because I believe it is an integral part of teaching children to read. I begin with motivation theory and then go to selected topics I believe to be particularly motivating for children in classrooms that utilize the theory. The areas discussed in the chapter are designing literacy centers and using them in classrooms, using children's literature in the classroom, technology and literacy, and literacy and play.

Motivation is defined as initiating and sustaining a particular activity. It is considered the tendency to return to and continue working on a task with sustained engagement (Wittrock, 1986). A motivated reader chooses to read on a regular basis, and for many different reasons. Researchers have found that experiences that offer students (1) choice, (2) challenge, (3) social collaboration, and (4) success are likely to promote motivation.

Choice

Providing children with the opportunity to make choices about which literacy tasks they will participate in gives them responsibility and control over the situation. Choice needs to involve multiple modalities for learning; that is, the development of literacy skills may combine traditional activities that use pencil and paper experiences with modalities that use technology, drama, or the visual arts. Choice instills intrinsic motivation (Guthrie, 2002; Gaskins, 2003).

Challenge

Students must perceive that there is some challenge to an activity, but that it is one that they can accomplish. Tasks should be perceived as not too hard but not too easy. When tasks are viewed as too easy, children become uninterested, whereas if tasks are too difficult, they become frustrated (McKenna, 2001; Stahl, 2003).

Social Collaboration

Motivation is increased through activities that offer opportunities for *social collaboration*. When children have the opportunity to learn in social situations involving collaboration with the teacher or peers, they are likely to get more done than they could do alone (Guthrie, 2002).

Success

When students complete a task they must consider it a *success*. Often children finish a task that is not completely correct, but if they perceive themselves as

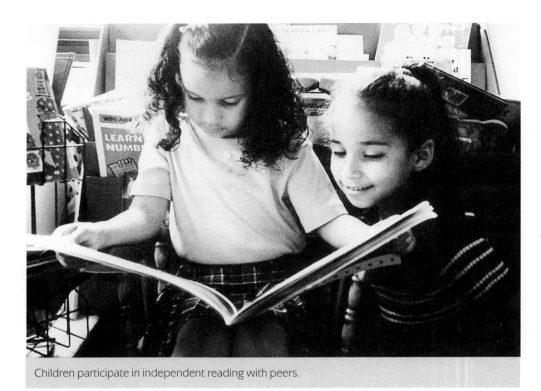

Children participate in independent reading with peers.

being successful, intrinsic motivation is enhanced (Ritchie, James-Szanton, & Howes, 2003). When a child has met with some but not total success, such as spelling the word *read* as *reed,* he or she should be acknowledged for the part of the spelling that is correct. After all, three of the four letters are right. The child's success should be noted at the same time that he or she is helped with the conventional spelling of the word.

The information presented in this chapter is based on motivation theory. Following are objectives to help motivate the desire to read and write.

Objectives for Motivating Reading and Writing

1. Children should be provided with an environment that is literacy rich, with choices of literacy materials that are challenging but will bring success.
2. Teachers should provide models of literacy behavior for children to emulate.
3. Children need to be given the opportunity to participate in social collaborative settings when reading and writing as well as opportunities for reading and writing alone.
4. Children should be able to choose literacy activities in which to participate.
5. Children should have the opportunity to listen to stories read by their teachers and peers in a pleasant, relaxed atmosphere.
6. Teachers should allow for response to literature through discussion, role-playing, the use of puppets to retell stories, and so on.
7. Children need the opportunity to take books home from the classroom literacy center.
8. Children should experience varied genres of children's literature.

9. Teachers should help children enhance word-analysis skills and comprehension skills using children's literature.

10. Teachers need to provide literacy experiences that involve technology and play.

Theory and Research on Motivating Reading and Writing

Standards for literacy achievement generated by various groups, states, and school districts often appear to be skills based. However, most standards are concerned with developing readers and writers who do not learn just the skills of reading and writing, but also the joys of reading and writing. The focus is on the need for children to be motivated to read and write for pleasure and information. The standards in different states and from different groups have included sections about reading and writing habits and expectations for how students will acquire these habits in kindergarten through third grade. The following are standards for reading and writing habits from the National Center on Education and the Economy and the Learning Research and Development Center at the University of Pittsburgh (1999).

Reading Habits

Good reading habits will be established with children having opportunities to read independently often. Books that are of high literary quality and interest, represent multiple genres, and are at a greater difficulty level than children could read on their own should be read to children. It is expected in the early childhood grades that in order to develop the reading habit, children will have the opportunity to

- read a wide range of genres in literature, such as poems and stories, functional text (signs, messages, and labels), and narrative and expository texts.
- read several short books a day at school during independent reading periods.
- listen to books read to them each day at school and discuss the books.
- listen and read books with parents.

Writing Habits

Good writing habits will be established with children having opportunities to write independently often. Children should listen to each other's writing. Many different forms of writing should be practiced, such as functional, informational, expository, and narrative writing.

To develop good writing habits and thus enhance motivation to write, it is expected that in the early childhood grades children will

- write a lot and listen to what others write.
- write independently.
- write in a wide range of genres, such as poems and stories, functional text (signs, messages, and labels), narrative texts, and expository text.

- listen to others' writing and discuss each other's work.
- write at home.

Standards for literacy achievement are important goals to attain. It is particularly important to include the standards just discussed so that we create students who not only can read but also choose to read for pleasure and for information. Time for independent reading and writing has been criticized as wasted time, since children can be off task. It is important to structure these periods to help children reap the benefits of the activities. Ideas for structuring independent reading and writing are discussed later in this chapter.

Preparing a Literacy-Rich Environment

Plato said, "What is honored in a country will be cultivated there." Teachers who honor the development of literacy demonstrate that attitude by providing within their classrooms a rich environment where the use of books can be cultivated. Their students honor literacy development by assimilating the attitudes and atmosphere presented by the teacher.

A classroom **literacy center** is essential for children's immediate access to literature. Children in classrooms with literature collections read and look at books 50 percent more often than children in classrooms without such collections. The efforts spent in creating an inviting atmosphere for a classroom literacy center are rewarded by increased interest in books (Guthrie, 2002). Morrow (1987b) found that well-designed classroom literacy centers significantly increased the number of children who chose to participate in literature activities during free-choice periods. Literacy centers in preschools, kindergartens, first and second grades that were identified as having specific design characteristics correlated with children's use of the centers during free-choice periods. Conversely, poorly designed literacy centers were among the least popular areas during free-choice periods in early childhood rooms (Morrow, 1982). Suffice it to say, the physical features of a classroom literacy center can play an important role motivating children to use the area.

Features of Well-Designed Literacy Centers

Classrooms need multiple centers for children to practice skills learned and to work independently. Chapter 4 describes content-area centers to meet this need. Classrooms should have literacy centers that include a library corner and writing area. The library corner in the literacy center will be described in this chapter. In Chapters 7 and 9 the writing area is discussed.

Physical Space

A classroom literacy center should be a focal area, immediately visible and inviting to anyone entering the classroom. To provide privacy and physical definition, it should be partitioned on two or three sides with bookshelves, a piano, file cabinets, or freestanding bulletin boards. The dimensions of the literacy center will vary with the size of the classroom. Generally, it should be large enough to accommodate five or six children comfortably (Figure 8.1).

Figure 8.1 *A Classroom Literacy Center*

Bulletin Board

Private Spot

Writer's Workshop

Computers

Author's Spot

Listening Station

Bulletin Board

Read and Write

Get Carried Away

Story Puppets

Featured and Themed Books in Open Bookshelves

Check Books IN OUT

Journals

Magazines

Writing Paper

Colored Paper

Roll Movie

THE THREE PIGS

Felt-Board Story

Word Study and Comprehension Manipulatives

Books by Level

A B C D

Poetry Fables Bugs Space Animals Weather

Word Sorts Word Building Story Retelling

Themed Books

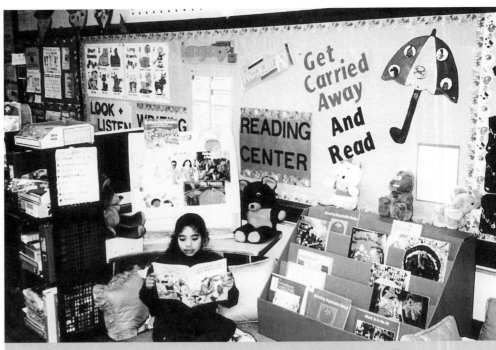

A classroom literacy center is crucial for children's immediate access to books.

The literacy center should be furnished with an area rug and pillows or bean-bag chairs because much of the activity there takes place on the floor. If possible, it should also include a small table and chairs where children can use headsets to listen to taped stories and make their own books. A rocking chair allows comfortable reading: a place for teachers to read to children and children to read to their classmates. They read their original stories and present literacy projects to the group while sitting in the rocking chair. It is the chair that invited guests use to read or present other information to the class. The rocking chair is the Literacy Chair of Honor.

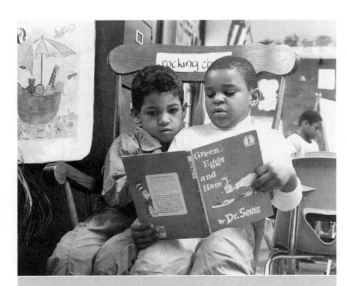

The rocking chair is the Literacy Chair of Honor.

Children have little privacy in school. Many children relish being alone and sometimes read in coat closets and under shelves. Because it is partially partitioned from the rest of the room, the literacy center provides some privacy. Listening to recorded stories on headsets offers even more privacy, and an oversized carton, painted or covered with contact paper, makes a cozy separate reading room.

The Author's Spot is an integral part of the literacy center. It usually consists of a table and chairs with various writing materials available. There are colored felt-tip pens, crayons, and lined white paper ranging in size. It is necessary to include at least one computer in the Author's Spot. Materials for making books also should be present, including colored construction paper for covers, plain white paper for inside pages, a stapler, and scissors. (The Author's Spot, or writing center, is described more thoroughly in Chapter 7.)

Children should be involved in the planning and design of a literacy center. They can develop rules for its use, be in charge of keeping it neat and orderly, and select a name for it, such as the Book Nook.

The Library Corner

Well-designed library corners within literacy centers have several ways for storing books. One type houses the bulk of the books, which are shelved with the spines facing out. Another type is open faced, allowing the covers of the books to be seen; this method is important for calling attention to special books. Featured books are changed regularly, and placed on the open-faced shelves for easy access. An alternative to open-faced shelving is the circular wire rack, commonly found in bookstores. These racks and open-faced shelving should highlight books with themes being studied. These books are changed with the theme and the shelving used to feature special new selections (Tafa, 2001).

Books in the collection should be shelved by category. They can be color coded according to the type of book. Identify all animal books, for example, by placing a blue dot on their spines and clustering them on a shelf marked "Animals," with a blue dot next to the label. An even simpler method is to store genres in plastic crates or cardboard boxes, with labels on the front naming the types of books in the container.

About five to eight books per child is appropriate in a classroom library, with three to four grade levels included. Books should include narrative and expository text. In the past collections for early childhood were almost exclusively narrative stories. Nonfiction expository text should comprise one-third to one-half of the total selections in a classroom library (Moss, Leone, & Dipillo, 1997).

Books are not difficult to accumulate. They can be purchased inexpensively at yard sales or flea markets. Teachers can borrow up to 20 books a month from most public libraries, ask for book donations from parents, and hold fundraisers for book purchases. In addition, children's paperback book clubs offer inexpensive books and free bonus books for bulk purchases.

Children's literature is stored by categories in baskets that are labeled for easy access.

Figure 8.2

Loose-Leaf Notebook Page for Checking Out Books

Name ⁀ldmika Jones

Name of book	Date out	Date in
Green Eggs and Ham	Feb 10	Feb 17
Carrot Seed	Feb 20	Feb 26
Curious George	March 3	March 9
Where the Wild Things Are	March 15	March 21

Children's magazines and newspapers belong in the classroom library, even if they are not current. For the cost of mailing and shipping, some publishers and local magazine agencies will donate outdated periodicals to schools.

To ensure continued interest, the teacher must introduce new books and materials and recirculate others in the library corner. Approximately 25 new books should be introduced every two weeks, replacing 25 that have been there for a while. In this way, "old" books will be greeted as new friends a few months later. Recirculation compensates for limited budgets as well.

Books from the library corner should be available for students to check out and take home for a week at a time. The check-out system should be simple. Young children should have specified times to bring books to borrow to the teacher, who notes the date, child's name, and book title. Some kindergarten children have been taught to check out books themselves by copying titles and recording dates on five-by-eight cards filed under their own names. Other youngsters enjoy keeping track of books borrowed and read by recording titles and dates on index cards held together with a key ring. Another method for checking out books is a loose-leaf notebook with a page for every child to record books taken out and returned. Figure 8.2 provides a sample check-out notebook page.

Books in the Library Corner

Books and other materials selected for the library corner should appeal to a variety of interests and span a range of grade levels. It is advisable to stock multiple copies of popular books. Children sometimes enjoy reading a book because a friend is reading it (Morrow, 1985). Several types of children's literature should be represented:

Picture storybooks are most familiar to us as children's literature. Their texts are closely associated with their illustrations. Picture storybooks are available on a wide range of topics, and many are known for their excellence. The Caldecott Medal is awarded annually to the illustrator of an outstanding picture storybook. Many of these books have become classics and their authors renowned—Dr. Seuss, Ezra Jack Keats, Tomie dePaola, Maurice Sendak, and Charlotte Zolotow, to name just a few. Every child should have the benefit of hearing some of these books read. However, emergent readers will often find the vocabulary and syntax too sophisticated to read on their own. Quality picture storybooks will include a setting, a well-defined theme, episodes closely tied to the theme, and a resolution of the story.

Informational books offer nonfiction for readers. For a while we did not include much expository text in our libraries, thinking that young children liked narratives more. As adults we read material that is mostly nonfiction; therefore, we need a lot of experience with this type of text. Informational text is about foreign countries, communities, dinosaurs, famous people, and so on. These texts broaden children's background information, help them to explore new ideas, and often stimulate a deep interest in a particular topic. Quality expository text will have a definitive structure. Good structures found in expository texts include description, sequence, compare and contrast, cause and effect, problem and solution, and exemplification.

Picture concept books are appropriate for the very young child. Most picture concept books do not have story lines, though they often have themes, such as animals or toys. Each page usually carries a picture identified by a printed word. Many picture books are made of cardboard, cloth, or vinyl to withstand rigorous handling. Alphabet and number books are also considered picture concept books.

Traditional literature includes nursery rhymes and fairy tales, familiar stories that are part of our heritage and originated in the oral tradition of storytelling. We assume that children are familiar with *Goldilocks and the Three Bears* (Izawa, 1968a) and *The Three Little Pigs* (Brenner, 1972), yet many youngsters have not been exposed to these traditional stories. Children who *do* know the stories welcome them as old friends.

Realistic literature is a category within picture storybooks that deals with real-life problems. *Tight Times* (1983) by Barbara Hazen, for example, describes how a family handles the problems that arise when the father loses his job. He tries to explain the situation to his son so he will understand when he calls it *Tight Times*. Books in this category deal with issues that many children face, such as bedtime fears or problems that arise when a new baby comes into the family. These books touch on very sensitive issues, such as divorce, drugs, alcohol, and death. Many can be read to the entire class if they address issues that all share. Teachers should use discretion as to what is read to the whole class. They can recommend specific titles to families of children who face difficult issues.

Easy-to-read books are designed to be read by emergent readers themselves. They have limited and repeated vocabularies, and many of them use rhyme, which makes them predictable and aids independent reading. Because of their limited vocabulary, few easy-to-read books rate as quality literature, but many preschool and kindergarten children begin to read independently with them.

Fables and folktales retell many of the myths and traditional stories that are available in picture-book style for the younger child. Many of these stories originate in other countries and cultures and therefore broaden a child's experience and knowledge base.

Wordless books carry definite story lines within pictures, but use no words. They are often thought appropriate for very young children and are confused with picture books. They are designed not for babies but for children three and older. The child creates the story by reading the pictures, some of which are intricate.

Poetry is too often forgotten in collections of children's literature at home and in school. Many themed anthologies have been compiled for young children, and they are an important part of the literacy center.

Novels are longer books with chapters. We can begin reading novels to young children to expose them to the genre. They are often quite attracted to them and eager to begin to read them. Children call novels chapter books.

Biography is another genre appropriate for young children. There are simple biographies of historical figures, popular figures in sports, and television performers.

Big books are usually large versions of smaller picture storybooks or original picture storybooks in this large format. They are oversized books that rest on an easel in order to be read. The purpose of the big book is for children to be able to see the print as it is being read, to make the association between oral and written language, and to see how the print is read from left to right across the page.

In addition to these categories of books, young children enjoy joke and riddle books, craft books, cookbooks, participation books, which involve them in touching, smelling, and manipulating, books in a series built around a single character, and books related to television programs appropriate for their age. As mentioned, magazines and newspapers should also be choices for reading in the library corner. They provide a nonthreatening format, different topics, and reading matter for diverse ability levels, and they include multicultural material. Newspapers and magazines appeal to parents as well.

Children particularly enjoy literature that is predictable because it helps them understand the story line more easily and enables them to read along with the individual reading to them. Predictable literature contains rhyme; repetition; catch phrases; conversation; familiar sequences, such as days of the week or numbers; cumulative patterns, in which events are repeated or added on as the story continues; stories about familiar topics; familiar or popular stories; uncluttered illustrations that match the text; and stories that have well-developed story structures (setting, theme, plot episodes, and resolution).

Listings of children's literature in several categories, including books for children with special needs and multicultural books, are in Appendix A. There is a special emphasis placed on informational books in the appendix, since we have neglected this type of text in the past. There is also a list of web sites for locating children's books.

Following are children's book clubs and children's book awards that provide additional literature resources:

Book Clubs

Scholastic Book Clubs, Inc., Firefly (preschool), SeeSaw (K–1), Lucky (2–3), 2931 East McCarty Street, PO Box 7504, Jefferson City, MO 65102-7504; 800-724-6527

TrollCarnival Book Club, PO Box 3730, Jefferson City, MO 65102-9610; 800-654-3037

Trumpet Book Club, PO Box 7511, Jefferson City, MO 65102; 800-826-0110

Children's Book Awards

Caldecott Medal. American Library Association, 50 East Huron Street, Chicago, IL 60611-2795

Children's Book Showcase. Children's Book Council, 12 W. 37th St., 2nd floor, New York, NY 10018-7480

Newbery Medal. American Library Association, 50 East Huron Street, Chicago, IL 60611-2795

Other Materials in the Literacy Center

The literacy center needs to contain language arts materials for skill development. Manipulatives that help children learn letters of the alphabet, rhymes, and sound–symbol relationships of consonants, digraphs, and long and short vowels should be included in a special section of the center. These manipulatives come in the form of magnetic letters, puzzles, bingo games, and board games, to name a few. Teacher-made materials can also be used. (These types of materials are described more fully in Chapter 5, which deals with skill development.) Materials to enhance comprehension must also be available in the literacy center. Techniques that will be described later in this chapter, such as using a felt-board and story characters for storytelling and organizing puppet presentations, engage children in demonstrating knowledge of story sequence and structure, classifying details, predicting outcomes, and interpreting text—skills that develop and enhance comprehension of text.

Elements of softness such as stuffed animals belong in a library, especially if they are related to books available in the corner—a stuffed rabbit next to *The Tale of Peter Rabbit* (Potter, 1902), for instance. Children enjoy reading to stuffed animals or simply holding them as they look at books. A felt-board, with figures of story characters from favorite books, is one of the more frequently used materials in a literacy center, as are roll movies, puppets, and headsets with taped stories. A roll movie consists of a box with a picture window cut out that makes it look like a television. A dowel is inserted at the top and bottom of the box. Shelving paper is written on and illustrated and attached to the dowels for presentation (see photograph on page 272). The center should also include

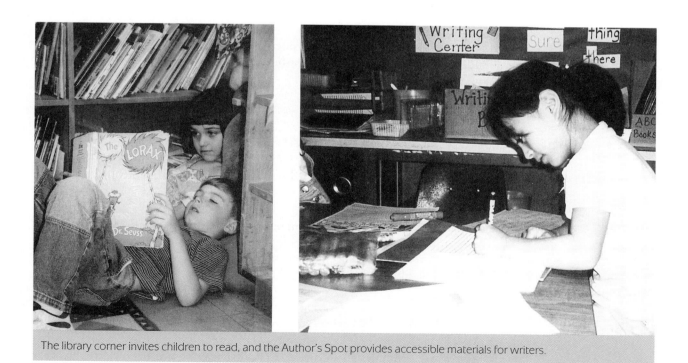

The library corner invites children to read, and the Author's Spot provides accessible materials for writers.

materials from which children can make their own books, felt stories, and roll movies. In addition, attractive posters that encourage reading are available from the Children's Book Council (568 Broadway, Suite 404, New York, NY 10012; www.cbcbooks.org) and the American Library Association (50 East Huron Street, Chicago, IL 60611; www.ala.org).

Reactions to Literacy Centers

Teachers and children had the following reactions to literacy centers in their classrooms that I had designed. Teachers said that they were originally concerned that there was not enough space in their rooms for literacy centers and were surprised that all the materials could fit. Eventually, teachers themselves provided more space for the literacy centers. Teachers commented that the physical presence of the literacy center made a statement to the children that literacy was valued because space was taken from the classroom to make room for the area. Teachers agreed that children were attracted to the area by the manipulative materials in the center, such as the felt-board stories and puppets. They found that the rocking chair, rug, pillows, and stuffed animals made the center relaxing and comfortable for reading. One teacher remarked:

The literacy center became a place where children of all reading and writing abilities mingled. . . . This social context seemed to provide an atmosphere for cooperative learning. The children looked forward to their time there each day.

A child commented:

I liked to cuddle up on the pillows with a book, or crawl into a private spot, or rock in the rocking chair and read. You get to take books home right from the classroom center.

Children referred to the center as a special place. They felt that the literacy center could be improved by adding more space, more books, and more time to use it. One child commented, "The only thing missing from the literacy center is a snack bar."

The Teacher as a Model to Motivate Interest

The teacher plays a critical role in influencing children's attitudes toward reading and their voluntary reading.

> One of the clear points to emerge from research into reading failure is that there was no association between reading and pleasure. . . . The role of teachers in stimulating voluntary reading among children and young people is . . . potentially the most powerful of all adult influences upon the young. (Irving, 1980, p. 7)

Programs that incorporate pleasurable experiences with literature create interest in and enthusiasm for books that in turn increase children's voluntary use of books (McKenna, 2001). Among other specific activities in early childhood classrooms, teachers should read or tell stories to children daily. Interest heightens when stories are discussed both before and after being read, especially if they are related to issues that reflect children's real-life experiences or current school topics. Literal and inferential discussions can be introduced even at the preschool level. Skill development can easily be incorporated into storybook-reading activities in pleasurable and meaningful ways. The following example describes a discussion about *Goldilocks and the Three Bears* in which inferential and critical comprehension is being developed with four-year-olds.

After reading *Goldilocks and the Three Bears*, I asked who were the good and the bad characters. Hands waved in the air, and Jennifer answered, "Goldilocks was good and the bears were bad." When I asked Jennifer why she thought that, she said, "Well, the bears scared Goldilocks."

Another hand went up and Tim said, "No, that's not right. The bears are good and Goldilocks is bad. Goldilocks went into the bears' house when they weren't home. She ate their food and didn't even ask."

"That's right," said Megan, "and she broke their chair and went to sleep in their bed and didn't even ask if it was okay."

Chris chimed in, "Yeah, Goldilocks was really bad. She did a lot of bad things because she didn't ask if she could."

"Would you go into a stranger's house and do the things Goldilocks did?" I asked. The whole group called out in unison "Nooooo." I asked why not. Sara answered, "Because that is bad. It's like stealing. She was naughty. If the cops found out, I bet they will arrest her."

Discussion about authors and illustrators also arouses interest. Reading different stories by the same author or a series of books about the same character, such as *Frog and Toad Are Friends* (Lobel, 1979) or *Amelia Bedelia* (Parish, 1970), increases interest as well. Read different kinds of literature to the class, and as often as possible coordinate stories with topics being discussed. If the topic is spring, bring a cocoon to class, discuss the life cycle of a butterfly, and follow the discussion with *The Very Hungry Caterpillar* (Carle, 1969), the story of the caterpillar's transformation to a butterfly. Read and recite poetry together regularly. Recruit older children, the principal, the custodian, the nurse, the librarian, parents, and grandparents to read to classes, to small groups, and to individuals. Encourage children to share books with one another. Books from home should be shared with the group and children encouraged to take books home from school.

Many popular folk songs have been made into picture storybooks, such as *Go Tell Aunt Rhody* (Quackenbush, 1973) and *Old MacDonald Had a Farm* (Quackenbush, 1972). These books are particularly good to read to children because the children are familiar with the words and want to pretend to read the books themselves. Cooking is another pleasurable activity that can be related to literature. Many picture storybooks feature food, such as *Bread and Jam for Frances* (Hoban, 1964). After reading the story the class can make bread and jam or whatever food is appropriate. Art activities also can be motivated by story readings. After reading *The Snowy Day* (Keats, 1962), have children create a winter collage from blue construction paper, white cotton, wool, doilies, chalk, and silver foil. After reading *Where the Wild Things Are* (Sendak, 1963), ask kindergarteners and first graders to think of a wild thing and draw a picture of it. Gather their pictures into a class book. Class books become favorites and are read frequently. Children also enjoy filmstrips and videos, which motivate their interest in reading the associated book.

Story Reading and Storytelling with Expository and Narrative Text

Making Story Reading Pleasurable

Being read to helps to create positive attitudes toward reading and writing. The warmth that accompanies storybook reading, by a caring adult, lasts beyond the experience. It involves ritual, sharing, and mutual good feelings. Certain books take on special meanings between an adult and child through repetition or because they are favorites of the one or the other. My daughter and I have a special relationship with the book *Alexander and the Terrible, Horrible, No Good, Very Bad Day* (Viorst, 1972). I first read it to Stephanie when she was four, and whenever things seemed to go wrong for her, I found myself saying, "I guess you're having a terrible, horrible, no good, very bad day." Soon, when things were not going well for me, she would say the same thing to me. When Stephanie was in the seventh grade, she came home from school one day, wearing only one sneaker, and looking generally distraught.

"What's the problem?" I asked.

She replied, "Someone stole one of my sneakers, I got yelled at for talking when my friend asked me a question in class and I answered her, I have tons of homework, and I lost my assignment notebook."

"I guess you're having a terrible, horrible, no good, very bad day," I said.

She smiled and said, "You're right, so I think I'll move to Australia."

"Some days are like that, even in Australia," I replied. We both laughed. The familiar words of a familiar book created a special ritual between us. Good feelings gained in story readings transfer to the act of reading itself (Hiebert, 1981; Taylor, 1983).

In the discussion that follows the word *story* refers to both the use of narrative and expository text. A story is the reading, telling, or reporting of an event or series of events whether fictitious or nonfiction. For quite a while narrative stories have been used almost exclusively with young children, with little exposure to expository text. Surveys of primary classrooms show that less than 15 percent of the read-aloud materials were expository (Yopp & Yopp, 2000). The concept has been that children must learn to read narrative text in the early grades before reading to learn information with expository text in the upper grades. This unnatural separation has caused difficulties for students when the focus shifts to expository text in fourth grade and children are unfamiliar with the genre. Adults read and write more nonfiction than narrative text. Yet in early childhood classrooms children are exposed to expository text infrequently. There is a misconception that three- to eight-year-olds are too young to understand and enjoy expository books. Therefore, in the discussion that follows we are talking about story reading and storytelling with both expository and narrative text.

To make story reading as enjoyable and pleasurable as possible, select good pieces of literature. Good narrative text includes the following:

- A **setting** with well-delineated characters, a time, and place described
- A well-designed **theme** concerning the problem or goal of the main character
- **Episodes,** which are a series of plot-related events that help the main character to solve his or her problem or achieve the goal
- A **resolution,** which discusses the solution to the problem or the achievement of the goal

Quality expository text should be selected for reading as often as narrative and include a definitive structure. The types of expository text that children should be exposed to include the following:

■ **Description:** Description gives the reader a picture of the subject based on story observation.

■ **Sequence:** Sequence explains the steps that produce a certain product or outcome.

■ **Compare and Contrast:** Comparisons are usually made in two ways. In block comparisons, two items (with a similar classification) are compared and then contrasted. In point-by-point comparisons, similarities and differences are compared alternately.

■ **Cause and effect:** Causality tells why something happens.

■ **Problem–solution:** A problem is presented, followed by its solution. An understanding of chronology is necessary to comprehend this structure.

■ **Exemplification** (reason and example): The main idea is printed with supporting details (Vukelich, Evans, & Alberson, 2003).

Good expository and narrative texts include clear and uncluttered illustrations, catch phrases, rhyme, and repetition.

A teacher should read to youngsters in a relaxed atmosphere in a location designated for such readings. Each day let a different child sit close to you while you are reading, with the other children in a single or double semicircle. If you have a rocking chair, use it as the place where you sit when you read. Because children enjoy seeing illustrations in books during story reading, hold the book so it faces the group or turn the book at appropriate pauses so its pictures can be seen. Before reading a story to a group, practice reading it aloud to yourself.

Be expressive in your reading, change your voice and facial expressions when a different character speaks, and highlight special events. A story reading is like a dramatic presentation. Read slowly and with a great deal of animation. Record or videotape your readings so you can evaluate and improve your technique. Begin a story with an introduction like the following:

"Today I'm going to read a story about a little girl who wants to get her mother a present for her birthday. She can't think of anything and asks a rabbit to help her. The title of the story is Mr. Rabbit and the Lovely Present *(Zolotow, 1962). The author's name is Charlotte Zolotow, and the illustrator is Maurice Sendak. While I read the story, think of which part of the present you like the best."* When you have finished reading the story, begin a discussion with a question such as *"Who would like to tell me which part of the present you liked best?"*

Creative Storytelling Techniques

Storytelling strongly attracts children to books (Ritchie, James-Szanton, & Howes, 2003). It has a power that reading stories does not, for it frees the storyteller to use creative techniques. It also has the advantage of keeping the storyteller close to the audience. Telling a story produces an immediate response from the audience and is one of the surest ways to establish a rapport between the listeners and the storyteller. Long pieces of literature can be trimmed so that even very young children can hear whole stories in one sitting. Considered an art, storytelling can be mastered by most people.

It is not necessary to memorize a story, but be sure you know it well. Use all the catch phrases and quotes that are important to the story. Use expression in your presentation, but do not let your dramatic techniques overshadow the story itself. Look directly at your audience and take their attention into consideration. Storytelling allows you to shorten stories as you go if attention spans seem to be short. It is important to have the original book at hand when you have finished telling a story so that the children can see it and enjoy it again through its pictures and printed text.

Creative techniques help storytelling come alive. They excite the imagination, involve the listeners, and motivate children to try storytelling themselves and create their own techniques. Take clues for creative techniques from the story. Some stories lend themselves to the use of puppets, others are perfect for the felt-board, and still others can be worked up as chalk talks.

Felt-boards with story characters are a popular and important tool in a classroom. You can make characters or purchase them. Prepare your own with construction paper covered with clear contact or laminate. Attach strips of felt or sandpaper to the backs of the cutouts so they cling to the felt-board. Narrative and expository texts that lend themselves to felt-board retelling are those with a limited number of characters who appear throughout the story or a limited number of ideas.

Puppets are used with stories rich in dialogue. There are many kinds of puppets, including finger, hand, stick, and face puppets. Shy children often feel secure telling stories with puppets. Such stories as *The Gingerbread Boy* (Holdsworth, 1968) and *The Little Red Hen* (Izawa, 1968b) are appropriately told with puppets because they are short, have few characters, and repeat dialogue. An informational book can be retold by a puppet.

Sound-story techniques allow both audience and storyteller to provide sound effects when they are called for in a book. The sounds can be made with voices, rhythm instruments, or music. When preparing to tell such a story, first select those parts of the story for which sound effects will be used. Then decide on each sound to be made and who will make it. As the story is told, students and storyteller chime in with their assigned sounds. Record the presentation, then leave

Children act out *The Three Little Pigs* using face puppets.

the recording in the literacy center with the original book. Among books that adapt easily to sound-story techniques are *Too Much Noise* (McGovern, 1967) and *Mr. Brown Can Moo! Can You?* (Seuss, 1970).

Prop stories are easy to develop. Simply collect stuffed animals, toys, and other articles that represent characters and objects in a story. Display the props at appropriate times during the storytelling. Three stuffed bears and a yellow-haired doll aid in telling *Goldilocks and the Three Bears* (Izawa, 1968a). Several toy trains aid in *The Little Engine That Could* (Piper, 1954) and could be used with an informational book about trains as well.

Chalk talks are another technique that attracts listeners. The storyteller draws the story while telling it. Chalk talks are most effective when done with a large chalkboard so that the story can keep going in sequence from beginning to end. The same technique can be carried out on mural paper hung across a wall; the storyteller simply uses crayons or felt-tip markers instead of chalk. The chalk-talk technique can also be adapted to easel and chart paper or an overhead projector. Choose a story with simple illustrations. Draw only a select few pictures as you tell the story. There are stories that have been written as chalk talks, including an entire series, *Harold and the Purple Crayon* (Johnson, 1955).

Headsets with taped stories are also popular materials in the literacy center. The stories are most often read but can be told on a tape for children to listen to and follow along in the text. They are helpful with English language learners because they provide a model for correct English. They are also good for struggling readers who can follow along in the text while listening to a fluent reader. Have parents, the principal, teachers, the nurse, the superintendent, and others record the tapes. Eventually children can make tapes for others as well.

Because numerous techniques for storytelling have not been mentioned, you can add to this list. All the materials discussed need to be modeled for children, who will then want to become storytellers themselves. After modeling children can do the following:

- Tell the story that the teacher modeled with one of the techniques the teacher used.
- Create a technique for presenting a piece of literature they know well that has been selected by the teacher.
- Children present the completed project to the class.
- Write an original story and create a technique for presentation. When it is complete, the children who worked on the project can present it to the class and then place in the literacy center for others to use.

Storytelling activities involve children in literal comprehension because they must know the sequence, details, and elements of the story. They must problem solve as they create the materials, deciding what parts of the story to include or delete. They interpret voices of characters as they make a presentation of their finished project to the class.

The teaching of specific skills can be embedded into teacher presentations of storytelling techniques. For example, if you need to teach letter-writing skills, the story *A Letter to Amy* (Keats, 1968) is a perfect selection. The story is about a boy who wants to invite a girl to his birthday party, but he worries that his friends might laugh. He sends her an invitation and wonders if she will come and what will happen. The book contains a lot of discussion about the letter. A student of mine taught letter writing and introduced it by telling a felt-board version of *A Letter to Amy.* One of the items in the story for the felt-board was an envelope with a well-written letter having the appropriate heading, format, and so on. Children used this model to write letters of invitation to others. Another story was used to reinforce the initial consonant *p.* The teacher told the story *The Pigs' Picnic* (Kasza, 1988) using a chalk-talk technique and asked the children to be detectives and listen for all the words that started with the letter *p.*

Story Reading and Storytelling: Vignettes from the Classroom

I had the opportunity to work with several first- and second-grade teachers who practiced sharing literature with children in pleasurable ways. The teachers read and told stories and made manipulatives for storytelling to use in their classrooms. These teachers incorporated many of the strategies discussed earlier, and one of them commented about these strategies:

> *The children enjoy being read to, and they never grow tired of this activity. I thought that in second grade, reading to youngsters wasn't that important anymore; however, the benefits of read-aloud sessions became quite evident as I involved my children in them more and more. The stories generated sophisticated discussion; we'd relate them to the students' own life experiences. We discussed authors, illustrations, and elements of story structure. Through these story readings and discussions, I found that my students seemed to appreciate literature more, they became more aware of the different genres of children's literature that exist, and vocabulary and comprehension were enhanced as well. I realized how important it was for me to model reading to children and in many different ways. I read using felt characters, roll movies, chalk talks, and so on. I learned how to make reading more appealing for the children. Consequently, I saw an increased desire in my children to read as they modeled my behavior in reading stories I had read to them and using the storytelling props.*

Second graders who listened to the teacher tell stories and use story techniques were asked what they learned and liked. They commented:

> *I like it when the teacher reads to us. She uses such good expression, you can learn to read better yourself by listening to her. . . .The teacher reads and tells stories in many different ways so it is always interesting, and you can learn to do it the way she does.*

One day during a story-reading session in a second-grade class with a focus on making comparisons between styles of illustrators, Ms. Payton told the children that she was going to read two picture storybooks that they had heard before. She asked the children to concentrate on the pictures or illustrations as she read the stories, to note their styles so the children could describe them. After she read the stories, she asked if the children thought that the books were illustrated by the same individual. They all said no because they looked very different. Ms. Payton identified the illustrators (and also authors) of the books, who were Ezra Jack Keats for *Peter's Chair* (1967) and Dr. Seuss for *Green Eggs and Ham* (1960). Then she asked the children to describe the illustrations for each book.

Tamika said, "Well in *Peter's Chair* the illustrations look like a painting. They are made like they are real. I think Ezra Jack Keats is a very good drawer. I like the colors he uses."

Ms. Payton explained that not only does Mr. Keats paint his pictures, but he also uses collage as a technique. When you look closely at his illustrations, you see bits of wallpaper, newspaper, doilies, and so on blended into his pictures.

Ms. Payton asked if someone would like to describe the style of the other book. Marcel raised his hand. He said, "Dr. Seuss is very different from Keats; he uses lots of lines and sort of fantasy little shapes. He uses colors on people and things that aren't what we usually expect. His drawings look like cartoons, and the other ones look like real things."

The discussion was followed by the children's illustrating stories they had written. They were told that their illustrations could be their own original styles or that they could use the style of an illustrator in a storybook that they knew. Ms. Payton walked around to talk about the work the children were doing. Magda decided to make her drawings similar to those of Dr. Seuss, and Ms. Payton said to her, "Magda, if Dr. Seuss came through our door he would think that he illustrated your story, your work looks so much like his." Magda is a child with limited English proficiency. The positive reinforcement in this situation started a conversation about her work with the teacher.

Reading and Writing Independently

Research has shown that the amount of free reading done by children, both in and out of school, correlates with reading achievement. In a large-scale investigation of elementary school children, it was found that students who reported reading two minutes outside of school scored at the 30th percentile on standardized reading tests. Children who read five minutes a day scored at the 50th percentile. Those who read 10 minutes a day scored at the 70th percentile, and children who read 20 minutes a day scored at the 90th percentile (Anderson, Fielding, and Wilson, 1988; Taylor, Frye, & Maruyama, 1990). Children who read voluntarily develop lifelong, positive attitudes toward reading.

Sustained silent reading and DEAR time (Drop Everything and Read) have been defined as a quiet time for children to engage in silent reading. Everyone in the classroom selects a book, sits alone, and reads. Silent reading is important because it allows children to practice skills learned and to concentrate on understanding what is read. However, these periods have been criticized because children spend a lot of time selecting a book, and when they finally sit down to read, they often flip through the pages and do not do much reading. In addition, there has been no accountability for what is read.

To be more productive, independent reading and writing periods can focus on a content-area theme that is being studied in the classroom, an author or illustrator, or a particular genre of children's literature. For example, if children are learning about animals, the teacher can designate that their book selection for independent reading and writing can only be about this topic. The teacher should separate these books from others on the shelf. There can be a special spot for independent reading books on the shelf, or they can be in a special basket. Limiting the number of books helps to make the task easier and quicker (Ritchie, James-Szanton, & Howes, 2003). For the purposes of accountability to help keep children on task, they can keep a log of pages read during independent reading and writing time, summarize what they read, or write the part of the book liked best. Teachers need to set rules and review before independent reading and writing begins. Some appropriate rules follow:

- Select your book quickly.
- Read only one book in a period.
- Record the name of the book and the date it was read in your log.
- Write a short note to the author about what you liked about the book.

Literature Activities Initiated by the Teacher

Literature activities need to be modeled and initiated by teachers to encourage children's interest. The following is a list of motivating suggestions to use on a regular basis:

Carry Out on a Daily Basis

1. Read or tell narrative and expository stories to children.
2. Discuss literal and interpretive issues in stories read.
3. Allow children to check books out of the classroom library.
4. Have children keep track of books read.
5. Have children keep the library corner neat and organized.

Do Several of the Following Each Week

1. Have the principal, custodian, nurse, secretary, or a parent read to the children at school.
2. Discuss authors and illustrators.
3. Write to authors.
4. Have older children read to younger children.
5. Have children read to each other.
6. Show videos and DVDs of stories.
7. Use literature across the curriculum in content-area lessons.
8. Use art to respond to books (e.g., draw a mural of a story, use art techniques modeled after a particular illustrator).
9. Tell stories using creative storytelling techniques.
10. Have children tell stories with and without props.
11. Have children act out stories.
12. Prepare recipes related to stories (e.g., make stone soup after reading the story of the same name).
13. Read TV-related stories.
14. Make class books and individual books; bind them and store in the library corner.
15. Sing songs that have been made into books and have the book on hand (e.g., *I Know an Old Lady*).
16. Make bulletin boards related to books.
17. Have children write advertisements for good books they have read.

18 Discuss proper ways to care for and handle books.

19. Read, recite, and write poetry.

20. Have a 10- to 20-minute independent reading and writing period a few times a week.

Carry Out on a Regular Basis

1. Feature and introduce new books on the open-faced bookshelves.

2. Introduce new books added to the library corner.

3. Circulate 25 new books into the library corner every two weeks.

4. Have a bookstore in the school where children can buy books regularly.

Carry Out a Few Times a Year If Possible

1. Give bookmarks to children.

2. Give each child a book as a gift.

3. Have a young authors conference (share books children have written; bind books; invite authors, illustrators, storytellers, poets).

4. Have a book fair for children to purchase books.

5. Have a book celebration day (e.g., dress up as book characters, tell stories to each other, show movie and filmstrip stories, have stories told creatively).

6. Have children order books from a book club.

Activities for Parents Related to the School Literature Program

1. Provide a newsletter a few times a year about book-related activities in school.

2. Ask parents to participate in some literature-related activity at school (e.g., reading to children, helping with book binding, raising money to buy books).

3. Have a workshop for parents that describes the importance, purpose, and activities of the school literature program.

4. Have a workshop for parents describing how they can participate in independent home reading programs.

5. Provide booklists for parents with suggestions for their home library.

Motivating Reading and Writing with Literacy Center Time

The literacy center is an important part of the classroom that acts as a source for motivating reading and writing. It is used in many ways.

1. The literacy center is used to engage children in productive literacy work as soon as they arrive at school.

2. The literacy center is used when children finish their work before others, in order to engage in interesting activities and reinforce strategies learned.

3. The literacy center engages students in productive independent work, freeing the teacher to work with small groups of students in guided reading instruction, one-on-one teaching, and assessment.

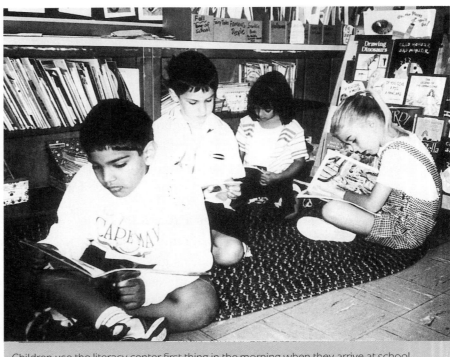

Children use the literacy center first thing in the morning when they arrive at school.

4. The literacy center allows students to select and enjoy literacy activities in a social setting during periods set aside to read and write for pleasure and for information. The purpose of these activities is to develop lifelong voluntary readers and writers.

As discussed earlier in this chapter, elements that help motivate children include choice, social interaction, challenge, and success. When children work in the literacy center, they have a choice of activity. These activities are most often done with peers in a social setting. The activities are challenging but designed to allow for success.

Organizing Literacy Center Time

During literacy center time, children make decisions about what they will do and with whom they will work. Some guidelines for children to follow are shown in Figure 8.3. These are posted in the classroom and reviewed before each session.

In addition to rules pertaining to use of materials, children are taught cooperative skills that are practiced and posted as shown in Figure 8.4. These include helpful things to say and to do for each other during literacy center time (Morrow, 1997).

When the literacy center is first used, some teachers assign children to groups of two or three, determine the activity in which children will participate, and appoint a leader to help organize the project. As a result of participating in the assigned groups with assigned tasks, children eventually can make these decisions about what to do on their own. To help children select activities, things to do

Figure 8.3

Rules for Using Materials during Literacy Center Time

1. Decide with whom you will work or if you will work alone.
2. Choose a reading or writing activity from the literacy center.
3. Do only one or two activities.
4. Use the materials in or outside of the literacy center.
5. Handle the materials carefully.
6. Speak in soft voices; people are working.
7. Put materials back in their places before taking others.
8. Try activities you haven't done before.
9. Try working with people you haven't worked with before.
10. Be ready to share completed activities with the class.
11. Record completed tasks in your log.
12. Keep the literacy center neat.

Figure 8.4

Rules for Cooperating in Groups during Literacy Center Time

Helpful Things to Do When Working in Groups

- Select a leader to help the group get started.
- Give everyone a job.
- Share the materials and take turns talking.
- Listen to your friends when they talk.
- Stay with your group.

Helpful Things to Say When Working in Groups

- Can I help you?
- I like your work.
- You did a good job.

Check Your Work

- Did you say helpful things?
- Did you help each other?
- Did you share materials and take turns?
- Did you all have jobs?
- How well did your jobs get done?
- What can we do better next time?

during literacy center time are posted and reviewed, as illustrated in Figure 8.5. In addition, cards that explain how to use each activity are also posted (see Figure 8.6).

For children who are beginning readers, teachers often include pictures representing activities to help with reading rules and roles on the activity cards. However, teachers need to review these lists, so children learn what they say and begin to read them.

At the literacy center children practice skills learned and learn to participate in reading and writing activities independently. Early in the program, some

Figure 8.5	
Things to Do during Literacy Center Time	1. Read or look at a book, magazine, or newspaper. 2. Read to or share a book with a friend. 3. Listen to someone read to you. 4. Listen to a taped story and follow the words in the book. 5. Use the felt-board with a storybook and felt characters. 6. Use the roll movie with its storybook. 7. Write a story. 8. Draw a picture about a story you read. 9. Make a book for a story you wrote. 10. Make a felt story for a book you read or a story you wrote. 11. Write a puppet show and perform it for friends. 12. Make a taped story for a book you read or a story you wrote. 13. Check out books to take home and read. 14. Use activity cards with directions for the task you select.

Figure 8.6	

Activity Card	**Tell a Story Using the Felt-Board**
	 1. Select a leader for your group.
	 2. Select a book and the matching felt-story characters.
	 3. Decide who will read or tell the story, and who will use the felt characters.
	 4. Take turns reading and placing the felt figures on the board.
	 5. Be ready to present the story to the class.
	 6. Record the activity in your log (see Figure 8.7 for a log sample).
	 7. Check your work:
	     How well was the story presented?
	     How well did the group work together?

children do not stay on task. Within a few weeks, most of the children will be able to complete activities.

Children often spend a good deal of time on projects from the literacy center which extend over a few days. When center time ends and a child has not completed an activity, a place is provided for projects to be stored. Each child fills in a log at the end of literacy center time to show what he or she accomplished during that period (Figure 8.7).

Teachers should share center materials from other classrooms to increase their supply. Children can be involved in making materials for the literacy center. They can record taped stories and make felt stories and roll movies for others to use in the listening center. They can create original stories and make them into books for the classroom library. Participation in these activities increases their feeling of ownership and respect for the area (Morrow, 1997).

The Teacher's Role during Literacy Center Time

Besides preparing the literacy center environment, the teacher also plays an important role before and during literacy center time. The teacher models the use of literacy activities before they are ever put into the center so children are familiar with them. He or she helps children to get activities started, and

Figure 8.7 *Log Sample*

Log: Circle, draw, or write about what you did during literacy center time

Name _____

Activity _____   **Date** _____

Read by myself   Read to a friend   Told a roll movie   Listened to a taped story

Told a felt story   Wrote a story   Made a felt story, roll movie, or picture   Other

Write or draw what you did:

Source: Adapted from *The Literacy Center: Contexts for Reading and Writing* by Lesley M. Morrow, copyright © 1997, reprinted with permission of Stenhouse Publishers.

participates along with the children in their activities when they need assistance. The goal for this period, however, is for the children to be self-directed in the activities undertaken.

The effort to help children be independent when using the literacy center will be extremely beneficial when teachers work with small groups for guided reading instruction. During guided reading instruction all children, except for a few who are working with the teacher, need to be productively involved in independent literacy activities.

Skills Developed during Literacy Center Time

The data collected in several research studies of students who participated in literacy center time revealed that students participated in many different activities (Morrow, Sharkey, & Firestone, 1994). The activities were self-directed and involved the children in making decisions about what work to do and how to carry through with their plans. Children read books and wrote stories and also engaged in projects, such as creating puppet presentations for pieces they had written or read. Most activities were done in groups of two to three and involved

During literacy center time, children may choose to tell a roll movie story or a felt-board story. All activities are literature related and are accompanied by the original book..

peer cooperation and peer tutoring. The groups were composed of single and mixed genders. Children took charge of their learning and demonstrated the use of oral reading, silent reading, and writing, while demonstrating their comprehension of text in literal and inferential discussions.

Literacy center activities expose children to reading and writing in many forms and give them the opportunity to make choices. These activities constitute a positive approach toward activating interest in reading and writing, and provide a time to practice and learn skills. Because of the element of choice, there is something for everyone: gifted, average, and special-needs children. Children from different backgrounds work together on similar interests. Children with language differences are welcomed as members of groups doing puppet shows and felt stories, and given roles in which they can participate.

I work with teachers regularly to implement programs with them similar to those described here. I visit the classrooms often. Mrs. Lynch had a second-grade class in an urban district that I had been working with for an entire school year. I visited her room on the last day of school to say good-bye to the children. Mrs. Lynch and I shared a sense of pride while observing the children during a literacy center time. We saw some children curled up on a rug or leaning on pillows in the literacy center with books they had selected themselves. Louis and Ramon were squeezed tightly into a rocking chair, sharing a book. Marcel, Patrick, and Roseangela snuggled under a shelf—a "private spot" filled with stuffed animals. They took turns reading.

Tesha and Tiffany were on the floor with a felt-board and character cutouts from *The Gingerbread Boy*, alternately reading and manipulating the figures: "Run, run as fast as you can! You can't catch me, I'm the Gingerbread Man!"

Four children listened on headsets to tapes of Maurice Sendak's *Pierre* (1962), each child holding a copy of the book and chanting along with the narrator, "I don't care, I don't care."

Tyrone had a big book and gave several other children copies of the same story in smaller format. Role-playing a teacher, he read to the others, occasionally stopping to ask who would like to read.

Leon read a story he had written to Tamaika. When he finished, she suggested acting out Leon's story with puppets, which they did. Throughout the dramatization, Leon behaved like the director of a play. He knew his story and his characters and wanted them to act in a manner that reflected his intent.

Much of the information discussed here represents the results of studies that involved classroom observation and intervention in kindergarten through second grade. Children in these classrooms participated in literacy programs that included activities that have been described in this chapter. These youngsters scored significantly better on tests of reading comprehension, the ability to retell and rewrite stories, and the ability to create original oral and written stories by including elements of story structure than children in classrooms that did not participate in the program. Children in the treatment classrooms also showed significant improvement in use of vocabulary and language complexity (Morrow, 1990, 1992; Morrow, O'Connor, & Smith, 1990).

Reacting to Literacy Center Time

Teachers and children were interviewed to determine their attitudes toward literacy center time and the program in general.

Teachers commented that the children particularly like literacy center time because they are able to

- choose activities they want to do.
- choose the books they want to read.
- choose to work alone or with others.
- choose manipulatives such as puppets and felt stories.

Teachers said that children learned the following during literacy center time:

- To work together and cooperate with each other
- To be independent and make decisions
- A sense of story structure from the stories they listened to and read
- New vocabulary
- A better understanding of what they read or what was read to them
- An appreciation for books and knowledge of different genres of children's literature
- That their peers could teach them and were willing to do so

By participating in the program teachers said they learned that

- the social family atmosphere created at center time was conducive to learning.
- children are able to collaborate and work independently.
- there is something for everyone, advanced and slower children, in the literacy center. Allowing children to work in the literacy center made the teachers more flexible and spontaneous. They became facilitators of learning rather than always teachers.
- children who do not readily participate in reading and writing did so during literacy center time. It may be because they are making the decisions about what they do.

In the student interviews, children were asked what they learned in the literature program, and they answered:

- You learn that reading can be fun.
- You learn to read and write better because you read a lot.
- You learn to understand what you are reading, and you learn a lot of new words.
- You get to learn how to read better because kids who know how to read well help you.
- You learn about authors and illustrators and that they are people like you, and you think that you could be one. (Morrow, 1992)

Evaluating Literacy Center Time

One of the major concerns about literacy center time is helping children who are not on task. Typically about 85 percent of a class will work well independently. One good thing about literacy center time is that you can see who is off task. When we teach whole groups, we never know. Children learn to look like they are involved. To help with on-task behavior, structure activities for those having difficulty. Be sure activities include a completed task to give to the teacher.

During literacy center time, teachers observed their classes to notice which children were on task, which children needed help getting started, and what activities the children were choosing to participate in. They periodically made changes in the management of literacy center time to help enhance productivity.

Teachers recorded anecdotes of activities and collected writing samples. They made audiotapes and videotapes of the groups at work and of performances of completed tasks. Children were involved in evaluating their literacy center time activities. They discussed how they cooperated and the quality of their completed tasks. When completed activities were presented, peers offered constructive criticism. Children were asked about their suggestions for improving the program and identified materials and books they wanted added to the centers.

Teachers discussed literacy center designs and how they might be improved to increase student productivity. Teachers moved the center from one area of the room to another, because they found a space that was bigger, brighter, or quieter. They added books and manipulatives to provide more choices for children. Figure 8.8 provides an evaluation form for assessing your literacy center.

Use of Technology to Motivate Literacy Development

Technology is important in the early childhood classroom. It is a source of motivation for literacy instruction. Technology offers young children opportunities to develop literacy skills. Computers allow children to construct knowledge in social or independent literacy settings in which they deal with word study or with meaning of text (Labbo & Ash, 1998). For example, electronic books have been found to motivate children to read and enhance their achievement in

Figure 8.8	*Literacy Center Evaluation Form*

	Yes	No
1. Children participate in some phase of the library corner design (develop rules, select a name for the area, develop materials, etc.).	☐	☐
2. The area is placed in a quiet section of the room.	☐	☐
3. The area is visually and physically accessible.	☐	☐
4. Part of the area is partitioned off from the rest of the room.	☐	☐
5. Bookshelves are available for storing books with spines facing outward.	☐	☐
6. There is an organizational system for shelving books (e.g., color coding by topic).	☐	☐
7. Open-faced bookshelves are available for new featured books.	☐	☐
8. Five to eight books are available per child.	☐	☐
9. Many books are available representing three to four grade levels and of the following types: a. picture books, b. picture story books, c. traditional literature, d. poetry, e. realistic literature, f. informational books, g. biographies, h. novels, i. easy-to-read books, j. riddle and joke books, k. participation books, l. series books, m. textless books, n. TV-related books, o. brochures, p. newspapers, q. magazines.	☐	☐
10. New books are circulated every two weeks.	☐	☐
11. There is a check-out/check-in system for children to check out books daily.	☐	☐
12. There is a rug.	☐	☐
13. There are throw pillows.	☐	☐
14. There is a rocking chair or beanbag chair.	☐	☐
15. There are headsets and taped stories.	☐	☐
16. There are posters about reading.	☐	☐
17. There are stuffed animals.	☐	☐
18. The area is labeled with a name selected by the class.	☐	☐
19. There is a felt-board and story characters and the related books.	☐	☐
20. There is a roll movie and related book.	☐	☐
21. There are materials for writing stories and making them into books.	☐	☐
22. There is a private spot in the corner such as a box to crawl into and read.	☐	☐
23. There is a system for children to keep track of books read.	☐	☐
24. The area occupies about 10 percent of the classroom space, and five to six children can fit comfortably.	☐	☐

analyzing words, recalling details of stories, and acquiring a sense of story structure (Kinzer & McKenna, 1999; Stine, 1993).

The Internet connects children to limitless sources of information from around the world. As teachers of young children, we need to be aware of what computers can do so that we can help our students use the technology to enhance their literacy development.

Computer Software

Software programs are one of the most common ways for teachers to use computers with children. Computers need CD-ROM drives for software programs.

The following general rules should be followed when selecting software for use (Wepner & Ray, 2000):

Instructions for children are concise, clear, and easy to follow.

The activities are engaging, promote active participation, and will hold the attention and interest of children.

The content matches and expands on what children are learning within their school curriculum.

The program provides practice for concepts being learned.

The text is narrated and highlighted for children to be able to deal with the activities independently.

There is a guide for teachers for introducing and using the software.

Assessment is provided.

Quality software is available for every type of literacy skill, such as the development of phonemic awareness, phonics, comprehension, writing, and vocabulary. According to Wepner and Ray (2000), the following criteria should be used to select quality software to develop reading skills such as phonics and phonemic awareness: (1) skills are introduced in a predictable sequence; (2) feedback is focused and immediate; (3) there is opportunity for repetitious feedback; and (4) children are engaged in an active manner with the software.

Another type of software is the electronic book. Electronic books use the best children's literature and present stories to children in a variety of ways. Images move on the screen, books are read aloud, and the text is clearly shown. Because these stories are animated, they are motivating to children.

Computers should be a part of early childhood equipment and provide a source for literacy development.

Another advantage to electronic books is that embedded in the book are skill development techniques such as K-W-L, emphasis on development of story structure, and the use of a directed-reading-and-thinking-activity format (Wepner & Ray, 2000).

Software to develop writing is helpful for beginning writers, children whose fine motor control is not well developed, and children with physical disabilities involving their hands. Quality software for writing development supports text that is generated by children and encourages students to expand on, revise, and edit what they have written.

When using software, be sure that you are familiar with it and that children know how to use the computer and the program. Software can be introduced to the whole class by projecting it onto a TV monitor or projecting with a data processor so that all can see. Your purpose will determine how you choose to use the software, but most of the time software is used for practicing skills already taught. The work is done alone or with a peer, independent of the teacher. Similar to a center activity, computer work is a perfect activity for children when teachers are engaged in guided reading groups for explicit instruction. There should be a time for students to discuss problems they may have with the software and to share accomplishments on the computer.

The Internet

Another way to use the computer in the classroom is with the Internet, which has endless possibilities. Pen pals correspond instantly all over the world using e-mail. The World Wide Web is an unlimited resource for information related to whatever children are studying. For example, for a unit about space, the teacher can collect fiction and nonfiction books about space for the room and locate an appropriate web site for children to use as a source for more information. There are sites for children on which to review books before reading them, review software they are using, and access electronic books. In addition, schools and classrooms can create their own web sites for various reasons. Figure 8.9 is an example of a web site prepared by a second-grade teacher to welcome her class at the beginning of the school year.

It is the teacher's responsibility to help students find web sites that will be useful for them, and to help them learn how to find others on their own. A helpful reference book is *101 Best Web Sites for Kids* (Meers, 1999). When selecting web sites for children, Wepner and Ray (2000) advise the following considerations:

- The web site loads quickly.
- The title page presents a thorough overview of the contents.
- The contents of the web site fit with your purpose.
- There are icons that link to pages on the site needed and possibly to other relevant sites.
- The graphics are attractive and enhance the concepts.
- The narration is clear and enhances the concepts to be learned.

The computer with software and the Internet with all its capabilities for correspondence and retrieval of information must be included in daily routines for learning. Children will need to function with a computer on a daily basis.

Figure 8.9

A Web Site Created by a Second-Grade Teacher

Welcome to Second Grade!

I Am So Excited to Begin Our Year Together!

We are going to have so much fun together! On our first day of school there will be many surprises for you! We have a special pet that can't wait to meet you! A yummy delicious treat will be on your desk! A bag of goodies will be waiting for you! I could go on and on, but I really want you to be surprised!

What Should You Bring On the First Day?

The first day is such a special day. It will be a day spent getting to know each other and the classroom. I thought that a fun way for us to get to know each other a little bit better is to make bags about ourselves. Let me explain. Take any bag that you have around your house. Fill it with things that would help us to get know you better. You might include a family picture, your favorite book, a special stuffed animal, or anything else that you dream up! We will each get a chance to share our special bags!

A Little Bit About Me

I have always wanted to be a teacher ever since I was in the second grade. I used to set up my dolls and pretend to teach them. Now I have real live students! (They are a lot more fun!) I am married and have three cats—Forest, Cleo, and Michina. I love to read, write my own stories, travel, cook, spend time with my family, go to the movies, rollerblade, and jog. I feel that I am the luckiest person in the world because I get to do my favorite thing every day—teach!

Source: Loredana McFadden, 1999, second-grade teacher, Colts Neck, New Jersey.

Appendix C provides a list of software and web sites designated for specific skill development.

Use of Play to Motivate Literacy Development

A curriculum area we must continue to use is motivating literacy learning through play. In play settings, children interact and collaborate in small groups. When designed to promote literacy behaviors, the dramatic-play area is coordinated with a social studies or science theme that is being studied to bring meaning to the experience. Materials for reading and writing are provided to support the play theme, and during play children read, write, speak, and listen to one another using literacy in functional ways.

Although early childhood educators have realized the value of play for social, emotional, and physical development, in the past it has not been viewed as a place or time to motivate literacy. Play has gained greater importance as a medium for practicing literacy behaviors because it provides repeated, meaningful, functional social settings. Literacy development involves a child's active engagement in cooperation and collaboration with peers, builds on what the child already knows, and thrives on the support and guidance of others. Play provides this setting. During observations of children at play, one can see the functional uses of literacy that children incorporate into their play themes. Children have been observed to engage in attempted and conventional reading and writing in collaboration with other youngsters (Morrow, 1990; Neuman & Roskos, 1992; Roskos & Christie, 2000).

To demonstrate the importance of the social, collaborative, and interactive nature of literacy development, let us visit a classroom where the teacher, Ms. Hart, has designed a veterinarian's office to go along with an animal theme with a concentration on pets. The dramatic-play area was designed with a waiting room; chairs; a table filled with magazines, books, and pamphlets about pet care; posters about pets; office hour notices; a no-smoking sign; and a sign advising visitors to "Check in with the nurse when arriving." A nurse's desk holds patient forms on clipboards, a telephone, an address and telephone book, appointment cards, a calendar, and a computer for recording appointments and patient records. Offices contain patient folders, prescription pads, white coats, masks, gloves, cotton swabs, a toy doctor's kit, and stuffed animals to serve as patients.

Ms. Hart guides students in the use of the various materials in the veterinarian's office, for example, by reminding the children to read to pets in waiting areas, fill out forms with prescriptions or appointment times, or fill out forms with information about an animal's condition and treatment. In addition to giving directions, Ms. Hart also models behaviors by participating in play with the children when the materials are first introduced.

The following anecdotes relate the type of behavior that was witnessed in this setting—a setting that provides a literacy-rich environment with books and writing materials; models reading and writing by teachers that children can observe and emulate; provides the opportunity to practice literacy in real-life situations that have meaning and function; and has children collaborating and performing reading and writing with peers.

Jessica was waiting to see the doctor. She told her stuffed animal dog Sam not to worry, that the doctor wouldn't hurt him. She asked Jenny, who was waiting with her stuffed animal cat Muffin, what the kitten's problem was. The girls agonized over the ailments of their pets. After a while they stopped talking and Jessica picked up a book from the table and pretended to read *Are You My Mother?* to her pet dog, Sam. Jessica showed Sam the pictures as she read.

Jennie ran into the doctor's office shouting, "My dog got runned over by a car." The doctor bandaged the dog's leg; then the two children decided that the incident must be reported to the police. Before calling the police, they got out the telephone book and turned to a map to find the spot where the dog had been hit. Then they called the police on the toy phone to report the incident.

Preston examined Christopher's teddy bear and wrote out a report in the patient's folder. He read his scribble writing out loud and said, "This teddy bear's blood pressure is 29 points. He should take 62 pills an hour until he is better and keep warm and go to bed." While he read, he showed Christopher what he

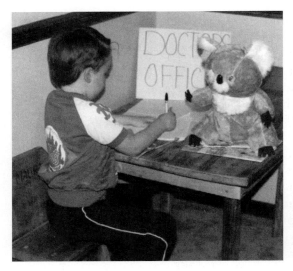

DOCTOR		SERVICE		ROOM	
	DATE			Note progress of case, complications, consultations, change in diagnosis, condition or discharge, instructions to patient.	

After examining the stuffed bear, this young veterinarian in the dramatic-play center wrote: "This teddy bear's blood pressure is 29 points. He should take 62 pills an hour until he is better and keep warm and go to bed."

had written so he would understand what to do. He asked his nurse to type the notes into the computer.

Figure 8.10 shows forms that may be used in the dramatic-play center when it is designed as a veterinarian's office during a unit on animals.

Additional play settings that encourage reading and writing at different grade levels follow:

1. *Newspaper Office:* Includes telephones, directories, maps, computers, paper, pencils, and areas that focus on sports, travel, general news, and weather.

Figure 8.10   *Forms to Write on for the Veterinarian's Office in the Dramatic-Play Center*

Appointment Card

Name: _____

Has an appointment on _____

☐ Mon. ☐ Tues. ☐ Wed. ☐ Thurs. ☐ Fri. ☐ Sat.

Date _____ at _____ a.m. p.m.

Prescription

Patient's Name: _____

Prescription:

Refills: Instructions:

                       Franklin A. Morrow, D.V.M.

Patient Record Form

Patient's Name: _____

Owner's Name: _____

Address: _____

     History and Physical Findings:

Type of Animal: _____

Date of Visit: _____

Telephone Number: _____

     Treatment:

2. *Supermarket or Local Grocery Store:* Can include labeled shelves and sections, food containers with their labels left on, a cash register, telephone, computers, receipts, checkbooks, coupons, and promotional flyers.

3. *Post Office:* Can be used for mailing the children's letters and needs to include paper, envelopes, address books, pens, pencils, stamps, cash registers, computers, and mailboxes. A mail carrier hat and bag are important for delivering the mail by reading names and addresses.

4. *Airport:* Can be created with signs posting arrivals and departures, tickets, boarding passes, luggage tags, magazines and books for the waiting area, safety messages on the plane, and name tags for the flight attendants. A computer is used to get onto the Internet to make plane reservations.

5. *Gas Station and Car Repair Shop:* Can be designed in the block area. Toy cars and trucks can be used for props. There can be receipts for sales, road maps to help with directions to different destinations, auto repair manuals for fixing cars and trucks, posters that advertise automobile equipment, and empty cans of different products that are sold in stations (Morrow & Rand, 1991).

For materials to be used for literacy to their fullest potential, teachers need to use props that are natural and from the child's environment. The materials in the setting created must serve a real function and be familiar to children. Do not set up several dramatic themes at once. Have the dramatic-play area match a theme being studied. Change the area when you begin to study a new theme. Teachers need to guide the use of materials initially by modeling their use (Neuman & Roskos, 1993).

The materials in dramatic-play areas should be clearly marked and be accessible. All levels of literacy development should be accepted, and reading or writing attempts should be recognized as legitimate literacy behaviors. Teachers might find it useful to record anecdotes about literacy activities engaged in by children.

In the discussion of play, I have concentrated on cooperative learning to encourage literacy development. Play is typically thought of as a preschool and kindergarten activity; however, play can be used with first, second, and third grades as well. Older children engage in more sophisticated literacy behaviors when participating in play. For example, the Internet can be used in many play settings as a source of information, for news stories, air travel routes, and so on.

Assessing Children's Attitudes toward Books

Direct observation of children's behavior while they are listening to stories, reading, or looking at books independently is an effective method for assessing their attitude toward books. How much attention do they give to the books they are looking at or reading? Do they simply browse? Do they flip through the pages quickly, paying little attention to print or pictures? Do they demonstrate sustained attention to pictures and print throughout (Martinez & Teale, 1988)? You should also note how frequently children select looking at books when faced with other options. In occasional interviews with individual children, asking what they like to do best in school and at home might reveal interest in reading. Dur-

✓☑ **Checklist**

Assessing Attitudes toward Reading and Writing and Amount of Voluntary Reading and Writing

Child's name _____ **Date** _____

	Always	Sometimes	Never	Comments
Voluntarily looks at or reads books at school				
Asks to be read to				
Listens attentively while being read to				
Responds during book discussions with questions and comments to stories read to him or her				
Takes books home to read voluntarily				
Writes voluntarily at home				
Writes voluntarily at school				

Teacher Comments:

ing conferences, ask parents if their children voluntarily look at books or pay close attention when they are read to. At the same time, ask parents how often they read to their children. Gather facts about the home literacy environment that will help you understand the child's attitude toward books.

A checklist for assessing attitudes toward reading and writing is provided above, and a motivation interview for a child's portfolio of assessment materials appears in Figure 8.11. They are useful tools concerning children's interest in reading and writing.

An Idea for the Classroom from the Classroom

I created the following experience when I was teaching children in a mixed-age-grouping primary classroom. The story is particularly suited to diverse classrooms because it deals with self-esteem, or liking who you are.

▨ Felt-Board Story

I wanted to introduce my students to the use of the felt-board as a means for retelling stories and creating their own original stories with characters. I selected

Figure 8.11   *Motivation Interview*

Directions: Tell the child that you would like to find out more about what kids like to do and how they feel about reading and writing. Ask each question in the interview and read the multiple-choice responses.

How often would you like your teacher to read to the class?

(2) every day   (1) almost every day   (0) not often

Do you like to read books by yourself?

(2) yes   (1) it's okay   (0) no

Which would you most like to have?

(2) a new book   (1) a new game   (0) new clothes

Do you tell your friends about books and stories you read?

(2) a lot   (1) sometimes   (0) never

How do you feel when you read out loud to someone?

(2) good   (1) okay   (0) bad

Do you like to read during your free time?

(2) yes   (1) it's okay   (0) I don't read in my free time

If someone gave you a book for a present, how would you feel?

(2) happy   (1) okay   (0) not very happy, disappointed

Do you take storybooks home from school to read?

(2) almost every day   (1) sometimes   (0) not often

Do you read books out loud to someone in your family?

(2) almost every day   (1) sometimes   (0) not often

What kind of reader are you?

(2) I'm a very good reader   (1) I'm okay   (0) I'm not very good

Learning to read is

(2) easy   (1) a little hard   (0) really hard

Do you like to write?

(2) yes   (1) it's okay   (0) I'd rather do something else

Do you write in your free time?

(2) a lot   (1) a little   (0) not at all

What do you like to read best?

(2) books and magazines   (1) schoolwork   (0) nothing

Source: Adapted from L. B. Gambrell, *Me and My Reading Scale,* 1993. In *The Impact of Running Start on the Reading Motivation of and Behavior of First-Grade Children* (Research Report). College Park: University of Maryland, National Reading Research Center.

a story that was easy to illustrate and a theme that would generate interpretive conversation, and I encouraged the opportunity to write additional episodes for it. The name of the story is *A Bunny Called Nat*, an anonymous tale. The story is about "a bunny named Nat, who was sassy and fat, and he could change his color, just like that." This is a repetitive rhyme in the story, and at the end of the rhyme fingers are snapped. The bunny in the story is a gray bunny who does not like his color because it is so plain. He is able to change his color, but each time he does, he has an unpleasant adventure.

When I introduced the story to the children, I asked them to listen for the different colors that Nat becomes and the problems he faces each time. I then told the story, using the different colored bunny characters on the felt-board to help. When the story was over, we discussed Nat and his different colors. We also discussed the ending of the story and its meaning, trying to relate it to the experiences of the children. We discussed whether they ever wanted to be anyone other than themselves and why, and whether it would really be better.

After the discussion, I asked the children to think of another color that Nat could become with an adventure attached to it as in the real story. I then asked them to write their story and draw and color a bunny to add to the felt story we already had. The bunnies were made of construction paper, and felt strips were glued onto the back to make them stick to the felt-board.

Seven-year-old Lindsey wrote the following:

> *"I'm a bunny named Nat, I'm sassy and fat, and I can change my color just like that." And suddenly Nat was a red bunny. Red like an apple, red like a cherry, and red like a fire truck. Suddenly a group of bees was coming. They saw Nat in the red color and they were thinking that Nat was an apple. The group of bees was going where Nat was sitting, they wanted to eat him. Then Nat saw the bees. He ran and ran but the bees followed him. So he said as he ran, "Being red is not so good, but I'm a bunny called Nat, I am sassy and fat, and I can change my color, just like that."*

In this activity children are involved in the discussion and the creation of a story. The theme of the story, concerning self-image, is an important topic for conversation and can help children understand each other's strengths, weaknesses, and needs. The story, *A Bunny Called Nat*, and a pattern for the bunny (Figure 8.12) follow:

■ Sample Felt-Board Story

A BUNNY CALLED NAT

(adapted version of an anonymous tale)
(As the story is being told, hold up and then place a new colored bunny on the felt-board as each bunny is named.)

Materials

Five bunny characters drawn identically but in the following colors: gray, blue, green, yellow, and orange. The bunny pattern is found in Figure 8.12.

Figure 8.12

Felt Figure for Story A Bunny Called Nat

Once upon a time there was a little gray rabbit and his name was Nat. One day he looked around and saw that all his brothers and sisters, cousins and friends were gray, too. He thought he would like to be different from them. So he said:

I'm a bunny called Nat,
I'm sassy and fat,
And I can change my color
Just like that. (Snap your fingers.)

And suddenly Nat was a blue bunny. He was blue like the sky and blue like the sea. He was blue like the twilight and blue like the dawn. It felt nice and cool to be blue. He decided to take a look at himself in the pond. He hurried to the edge and admired his reflection in the water. He leaned over so far that SPLASH! he fell into the pond. Nat fell deep into the blue water and he couldn't swim. He was frightened. He called for help. His friends heard him, but when they came to the pond they couldn't see him because he was blue just like the water. Fortunately a turtle swam by and helped Nat get safely to shore. Nat thanked the turtle. He decided that he didn't like being blue. So he said:

I'm a bunny called Nat,
I'm sassy and fat,
And I can change my color
Just like that. (Snap your fingers.)

And this time, what color did he change himself to? Yes, he was yellow—yellow like the sun, yellow like a daffodil, yellow like a canary bird. Yellow seemed like such a happy color to be. He was very proud of his new color, and he decided to take a walk through the jungle. Who do you think he met in the jungle? He met his cousins the lion and the tiger. The lion and the tiger looked at Nat's yellow fur and said, "What are you doing in that yellow coat? We are the only animals in this jungle that are supposed to be yellow." And they growled so fiercely that Nat the bunny was frightened and he ran all the way home. He said:

(Repeat poem.)

And this time what did he change his color to? Yes, he was green. He was green like the grass and green like the leaves of the trees. He was green like a grasshopper and green like the meadow. As a green bunny, Nat thought he'd be the envy of all the other bunnies. He wanted to play with his other bunny friends in the meadow. Since he was the color of the grass in the meadow, he could not be seen and his friends just ran and jumped about him not seeing him at all or mistaking him for a grasshopper. So Nat the bunny had no one to play with while he was green. Being green wasn't much fun. So he said:

(Repeat poem.)

And what color was he then? Right, he was orange. He was orange like a carrot, orange like a sunset, orange like a pumpkin—he was the brightest color of all. He decided he would go out and play with all his brothers and sisters and friends. But what do you suppose happened? When his friends saw him, they all stopped playing and started to laugh, "Ha-ha, whoever heard of an orange bunny?" No one wanted to play with him. He didn't want to be orange anymore. He didn't want to be a blue bunny because if he fell into the pond no one could see him to save him. He didn't want to be a yellow bunny and be frightened by the lion and the tiger. He didn't want to be a green bunny because then he was just like the meadow and none of his friends could see him. And so he said:

(Repeat poem.)

Do you know what color Nat the bunny changed himself into this time? Yes, you're right. He changed himself back to gray. And now that he was gray all of his friends played with him. No one growled or laughed at him. He was gray like a rain cloud, gray like an elephant, gray like pussy willows. It felt warm and comfortable being gray. From that time on, Nat the bunny was always happy being a gray bunny, and he decided that it's really best being just what you are.

Activities and Questions

1. Answer the focus questions at the beginning of the chapter.

2. Select a literacy skill to teach that is grade appropriate for you. Select a piece of children's literature that provides an example of that skill and choose a creative storytelling technique that seems appropriate for the story and skill (e.g., felt characters, chalk talk, sound-story). Create materials for the story and tell it to a group of children or to your peers. Evaluate your performance according to the criteria for storytelling discussed in the chapter and how well the skill was taught.

3. Evaluate the literacy center in an early childhood classroom using the form in Figure 8.8. List all the characteristics of the center that reflect criteria described in this chapter. List items that need to be included.

4. Observe an early childhood classroom on three different occasions. List all the literacy activities carried out by the teacher that you believe contribute to developing motivating positive attitudes toward reading and writing.

5. Continue your portfolio assessment for the child you selected to assess. Observe the child using the assessment checklist provided in this chapter con-

cerning the evaluation of his or her attitudes toward writing and reading. Interview the child using the motivation survey (Figure 8.9).

6. Create a play experience for second and third graders that will develop literacy.

7. Write a lesson plan that requires children to use the Internet to find information. Be sure that children are using literacy skills in the assignment.

8. Continue the thematic unit that you began in Chapter 4. Select three objectives for building positive attitudes toward reading, and describe three activities using your theme that will satisfy each of the objectives.

Organizing and Managing the Literacy Program

"What is honored in a country will be cultivated there." In classrooms
in which teachers honor literacy development, it will be cultivated as
an integral part of the school curriculum.

—Plato

Focus Questions

- Describe classroom environments that are rich in literacy materials and support optimal literacy instruction.
- What is meant by integrating literacy learning into content areas through the use of themed units?
- How can literacy development be integrated into the following content areas: art, music, math, science, social studies, and play?
- Identify different grouping methods, or organizational arrangements, for working with children to meet their individual needs.
- Describe a language arts block that incorporates all aspects of a balanced literacy program.
- How can literacy learning be integrated into activities throughout an entire school day?

Mrs. Youssef wanted to integrate literacy activities in content-area subjects. Her second-grade students often found science boring with only the textbook, because it did not feature real-life situations. She decided to use selections of children's literature that related to different topics in science to make them more relevant.

The children were learning about "The Changes in Our Earth," a unit that focused on topics such as hurricanes, glaciers, and the composition of the earth. Mrs. Youssef found several excellent selections of children's literature for this unit. Two of them were *How to Dig a Hole to the Other Side of the World* (McNulty, 1979) and *The Magic School Bus Inside the Earth* (Cole, 1987). Both books combined good literature with factual information about the topic. These books motivated a great deal of enthusiasm and discussion in class. Mrs. Youssef asked the children to write a narrative story similar to the literature she shared—that told a story, but included many science facts they had learned. This proved to be a difficult task for the children. Most of them wrote expository pieces that gave facts about the composition of the inside of the earth and what a volcano is and does. Those who wrote narratives did not include very many science facts. Mrs. Youssef decided to have the children write a whole-class science story by having the students generate science vocabulary and concepts they learned and use those ideas to write the story together. The story they wrote follows.

Our Class Adventure

One sunny day in Sacramento, California, our class went on a camping trip to a mountain. We put down all our bags and set up the tents. Kevin, Alex, Jason, and Keri went to the stream to catch fish for lunch. Antoinette and Emily went to get wood for a fire, since it was cold on the top of the mountain. While the other kids were setting up their tents, a bear came out. The bear saw the fish, ate them, and went away. Two hours later, our class decided to go for a hike. Along the way we saw a river and rocks that were weathered. We also saw two glaciers which were blocking a river. Suddenly, everything started to rumble and shake and everyone fell to the ground. Little and big rocks tumbled down the mountain. Smoke started coming out of the mountain and everyone started to yell. Amber started running around in circles. Then what we thought was just a mountain blew its top. Lava started coming down out of the volcano and an earthquake started. It was a good thing we brought our earthquake survival kits. We all ran to our camp for cover, but the camp was destroyed. The survival kits were fireproof and lava proof, so they were okay. Inside there were tools which we used to fix up the camp. We fixed it up so well that it looked like new.

The success of any program depends to a large extent on how it is organized, designed, and managed. Even creative and knowledgeable teachers have difficulty without careful planning, preparation of the environment, organization of lessons, and management of daily routines. This chapter ties together the prerequisites for successful implementation of the ideas described earlier in this book. Specifically, it focuses on (1) preparation of the physical environment, including selection of materials and their placement in the classroom; (2) integration of literacy activities throughout the school day in all content areas; (3) grouping practices to meet individual needs; and (4) a suggested outline for a school day that provides literacy experiences throughout. This chapter is concerned with the teaching of children from two and a half to eight—

preschoolers, kindergartners, and first, second, and third graders. (Chapter 10 addresses home literacy environments and daily routines appropriate for infants and toddlers. Child-care centers for children birth through age 2 need to organize rich literacy environments, routines, programs, and activities similar to those described for homes.)

Preparation of the Physical Environment

The physical design of a classroom has been found to affect the choices children make among activities (Morrow & Tracey, 1996; Morrow & Weinstein, 1986). The design of the room should accommodate the organization and strategies of the teaching that occurs there. Programs that nourish early literacy require a literacy-rich environment, an interdisciplinary approach to the development of literacy, and recognition of individual differences and levels of development.

The following example shows children participating in functional literacy activities in a classroom environment prepared with materials and space that stimulated reading and writing.

Mrs. Shafer's kindergarten is learning about workers in the community. While discussing news reporters, the children decided they would like to have a news office in the dramatic-play area where they could publish their own newspaper. Their teacher helped create the center where they placed writing paper, telephones, phone directories, a typewriter, and a computer. There were pamphlets, maps, and other appropriate reading materials for the different sections of the newspaper, such as sports, travel, weather, and general daily news. The class completed their first newspaper, and Yassin was in charge of delivering the paper the first month. He had a newspaper delivery bag, and each paper had the name of a child on it. As the delivery person, Yassin had to match the names on the papers to the names on the children's cubbies. Later, when the kindergartners read their newspapers, they shared them with great enthusiasm. Each child had contributed something to the paper, for example, a drawing, a story, or a group poem.

Theory and Research Concerning Literacy-Rich Physical Environments

Historically, theorists and philosophers who studied early childhood development emphasized the importance of the physical environment in learning and literacy development. Pestalozzi (Rusk & Scotland, 1979) and Froebel (1974) described real-life environments in which young children's learning could flourish. Both described the preparation of manipulative materials that would foster literacy development. Montessori (1965) depicted a carefully prepared classroom environment intended to promote independent learning, and she recommended that every material in the environment have a specific learning objective.

Piaget (Piaget & Inhelder, 1969) found that children acquire knowledge by interacting with the world or the environment. Ideal settings are oriented to real-life situations, and materials are chosen to provide opportunities for children to explore and experiment. Dewey (1966) believed in an interdisciplinary approach. In other words, learning takes place through the integration of content areas. He believed that storing materials in subject-area centers encouraged interest and learning.

Based on these discussions, any classroom designed to provide a literacy-rich environment and optimum literacy development will offer an abundant supply of materials for reading, writing, and oral language. These materials will be housed in a literacy center. Literacy development will be integrated with content-area teaching reflected in materials provided in content-area learning centers. Materials and settings throughout the classroom will be designed to emulate real-life experiences and make literacy meaningful to children. They will be based on information children already possess, and will be functional so that children see a need and purpose for using literacy. Careful attention to a classroom's visual and physical design contributes to the success of an instructional program. Preparing a classroom's physical environment is often overlooked in planning instruction. Teachers and curriculum developers tend to concentrate on pedagogical and interpersonal factors, but give little consideration to the visual and spatial context in which teaching and learning occur. They direct their energies toward varying teaching strategies while the environment remains unchanged. The environment needs to be arranged to coordinate with and support program activities; otherwise, instruction will not be as successful as it could be (Weinstein & Mignano, 2003).

When purposefully arranging the environment, teachers acknowledge the physical setting as an active and pervasive influence on their own activities and attitudes, as well as those of the children in their classroom. Appropriate physical arrangement of furniture, selection of materials, and the visual aesthetic quality of a room contribute to teaching and learning (Loughlin & Martin, 1987; Morrow, 1990; Morrow & Tracey, 1996; Morrow & Weinstein, 1986). For example, design of spatial arrangements alone affects children's behavior in the classroom. Rooms partitioned into smaller spaces facilitated verbal interaction among peers, fantasy, and cooperative play more than did rooms with large open spaces. Children in carefully arranged rooms showed more productivity and greater use of language-related activities than did children in randomly arranged rooms (Moore, 1986; Reutzel & Cooter, 2004).

Studies that investigated the role of literacy-enriched dramatic-play areas based on themes being used in the classroom found they stimulated increased language and literacy activity and also enhanced literacy skills (Morrow, 1990; Neuman & Roskos, 1993, 1997). These researchers also have found that dramatic play with story props improves story production and comprehension, including recall of details and ability to sequence and interpret.

Preparing Literacy-Rich Physical Environments

 Research that has investigated the physical design of classrooms strongly suggests that, by purposefully arranging the space and materials, teachers can create physical environments that exert an active, positive, and pervasive influence on instruction. Educators must think of their classrooms as places to project a visual atmosphere that communicates a definitive message. The following sections describe the visual presentation of a literacy-rich physical environment to motivate reading and writing based on the research discussed in previous chapters.

PRINT IN YOUR CLASSROOM. Literacy-rich classrooms are filled with functional print that can be seen easily. There are labels on classroom items and signs

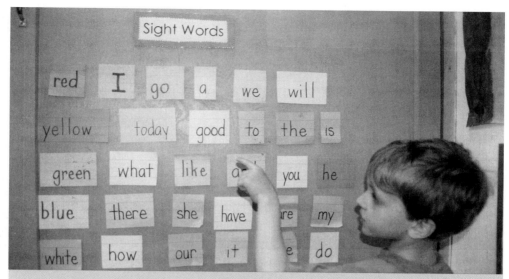

A sight-word chart of high-frequency words helps children to read and write independently.

communicating functional information and directions, such as *Quiet Please, and Please Put Materials Away after Using Them.* There are charts labeled *Helpers, Daily Routines, Attendance,* and *Calendar* to name a few (Schickedanz, 1993). Labels identify learning centers and each child's cubby. A notice board placed prominently in the room can be used to communicate with the children in writing. Experience charts and morning messages are used to display new words generated from themes, recipes used in the classroom, and science experiments conducted. Word walls display high-frequency words learned, new spelling words, sight words, and words that feature phonics elements being taught. Teachers discuss and use the print in the classroom with the children to ensure it is noticed. Children are encouraged to read and to use words from the print in their writing (Ritchie, James-Szanton, & Howes, 2003).

The outdoor environment also should accommodate literacy development. In addition to the usual playground equipment, new materials that reflect unit instruction add to the interest of outdoor play. Where climates are seasonal, for example, flowers should be planted in the spring; rakes provided in the fall for leaf gathering; and pails, shovels, and other digging and building equipment provided in winter for snow play. Creative materials such as crates, boxes, plastic containers, boards, ropes, and balls give children incentives to play creatively. The materials generate language during play and in class discussions, and provide information for writing experience charts and class books.

THE CLASSROOM LITERACY CENTER. The literacy center, which includes the library corner and a writing area, should be the focal point in a classroom. Children's immediate access to literature and writing materials increases the number of children who participate in literacy activities during the school day. Both areas in the literacy center need to be obvious and inviting but also should afford privacy and be clearly defined. The areas should accommodate four to five children comfortably. The center says to children that as teachers we value literacy by making it an important part of our classroom. The materials range in difficulty to meet individual needs and the different developmental levels of the children. Each set of materials has its own place and is to be respected. The literacy center includes materials for reading, writing, oral language development, and developing word-study skills. The different parts of the center have already been discussed in other chapters (the library corner in Chapter 8, the writing center in Chapter 7, oral language center materials in Chapter 4, and materials to develop word study in Chapter 5). The library corner and writing center will be described again here to pull the area together.

The Library Corner. The library corner should house books on traditional shelves with only their spines showing. Shelve books by category, and use some sort of coding system. Coding introduces the idea that books in regular libraries are organized systematically for easy access. Other shelves should be open faced to display full covers, thus calling attention to them. Use the open-faced shelving to feature books about themes being studied, and rotate new books in every few weeks. Books can be stored in plastic bins and labeled by genre. We also store leveled books in plastic bins and labeled by level of difficulty. To ensure there is something for everyone in the center, include five to eight books per child at three or four grade levels representing different genres of children's literature. Stock multiple copies of popular stories. Children enjoy reading the same book together.

Furnish the area with a rug and pillows. Include a rocking chair representing the Literacy Chair of Honor, where the teacher and others read to the children. This area is where children read for pleasure, read to other children, or present stories to the class that they have written. Provide a cozy private spot for reading. Teachers have used large cartons from household appliances, painted or covered with contact paper, where children can crawl inside and read.

Posters and bulletin boards that celebrate reading should be used to decorate the area. Devise a method for checking books out of the classroom library to take home and read. Provide materials for active involvement in storybook reading and storytelling, with storytelling manipulatives such as a felt-board with story characters, roll movies, puppets, and headsets for listening to taped stories. These materials deal mostly with language and comprehension skills. Provide manipulative word-study games and activities that include making words and sorting words based on letter patterns to help build independent readers.

The Writing Area. The writing area requires a table and chairs, plus colored felt-tipped markers, large and small crayons, pencils (both regular and colored), chalk, a chalkboard, and paper in a variety of sizes, kinds, and colors. Include unlined plain paper or newsprint of many different sizes. Have index cards available to record children's Very Own Words, high-frequency words, or word patterns they may need to practice. A writing folder for each child can be kept in a large box. Computers must be in the writing area as well. Book-making materials include paper, a hole punch, a stapler, and construction paper. Blank books prepared by the teacher and children can be keyed to special occasions and completed by youngsters. Display children's writing on a bulletin board. Equally valuable are *notice boards* on which messages can be exchanged among classmates or between teacher and students.

Involve children in designing and managing the literacy center. They can help develop rules for its use and keep it neat and orderly.

DESIGNING CONTENT-AREA CENTERS TO ACCOMMODATE INDIVIDUAL NEEDS. Programs that motivate early literacy development require literacy-rich environments that recognize the need for an integrated approach to literacy learning and awareness of individual differences and developmental levels. These classrooms are arranged in centers designed for particular content areas. Centers contain materials specific to topics currently under study and general supplies and resources. The materials are usually manipulative and activity oriented. They are also designed such that children use them independently or in small groups. Centers are partially separated from each other by furniture that houses their materials. Centers should be labeled and their materials stored on tables, on shelves, in boxes, or on a bulletin board. Each piece of equipment in a center should have its own designated spot so that teachers can direct children to it and children can find and return it easily. Early in a school year, a center need hold only a small number of items; new materials are gradually added as the year progresses. The teacher should introduce the purpose, use, and placement of each item added.

Content-area centers are dedicated to social studies, science, art, music, math, literacy, dramatic play, and block play. Centers contain materials pertinent to the content area, and materials are added that are specific to themes being studied such as nutrition or animals. Each subject-specific center includes literacy materials as well: things to read, materials with which to write, things to listen to, and things to talk about. These materials create interest, new vocabulary and concepts, and a reason for participating in literacy activities. With each new theme studied, additional books, posters, artifacts, music, art projects, dramatic-play materials, and scientific objects can be added to create new interest. Chapter 4 describes general materials for each content-area center, and then discusses additions made for the study of a particular theme. The classroom floor plans in Figures 9.1 and 9.2 illustrate this type of learning environment from preschool through fifth grade.

Notice in Figure 9.1, in the preschool through first-grade floor plan, that the art center is placed by the sink for easy access to water. In this same area are children's cubbies for storing individual work. Because the working needs of early childhood classrooms are better met by table surfaces than by desks, children should be provided with these storage areas. The contents of the various centers diagrammed in the figure have been described in Chapter 4. In addition to all the materials available in them, it is important that each has books and writing materials. The music center, for example, can include picture storybooks adapted from songs, such as Ezra Jack Keats's *Over in the Meadow* (1971). In addition to looking at the book, children may choose to copy words from the story. Certainly social studies and science centers should hold informational books and children's literature that relate to topics being studied. The art center might have books with craft ideas, including directions and diagrams. Books are appropriate as well in the dramatic-play area. If the class is discussing space, the area should have books about space and space stories for pretend caregivers to read to their "children." The block center can contain books that help develop ideas for building. Books that contain maps or plans of communities might motivate children to create such communities in their block play.

In addition to generating a rich literacy atmosphere and an interdisciplinary approach, the room is designed to cater to different teaching methods, organizational strategies, and grouping procedures so that the differences among the children can be accommodated. The centers provide space for independent or social learning, exploration, and self-direction. The tables illustrated in the classroom floor plan (Figure 9.1) provide a place for whole-class instruction, as does the open area in the music center with the rug on which children can sit. The teacher's conference table is a place for individual learning or small-group

Figure 9.1

Classroom Floor Plan for Prekindergarten through First Grade

lessons. All furniture is, of course, movable so that any other needed teaching arrangement can be accommodated. The centers are located to create both quiet, relatively academic areas and places for more active play. The literacy center, for example, which houses the library corner and the writing and oral-language areas, is next to the math center. Because these areas generally house activities that require relative quiet, they are in close proximity. Alternatively, dramatic play, woodworking, and block play tend to be noisier activities, so they are placed at the opposite end of the room from the quiet areas. The art center can also be a noisy area and is set aside from the quieter sections of the room. The teacher's conference table is situated in a quiet area yet allows the teacher a view of the rest of the classroom. While the teacher is involved in small-group or individualized instruction at the conference table, the rest of the class is working independently. The table's location allows the teacher to see all the children even while working with just a few.

The plan for the physical environment is used in many nursery schools and kindergartens, and some first and second grades. The assumption is that it is for

Figure 9.2

Classroom Floor Plan for Second through Fifth Grade

younger children. Teachers in first and second grade should consider these designs because they encourage literacy learning. Figure 9.3 is a map for you to fill in the general materials for your centers and materials to add that are specific to a particular theme. Evaluate the richness of your literacy environment using the checklist on pages 299–300.

Thematic Units: Integrating Literacy Learning into Content Areas

Dewey (1966) was largely responsible for bringing the concept of an interdisciplinary approach to teaching to educators' attention. This interdisciplinary approach, or the integrated school day, teaches skills from all content areas, within the context of a topic or theme being studied. The themes that are studied

Figure 9.3

General Center Materials and Center Theme Materials

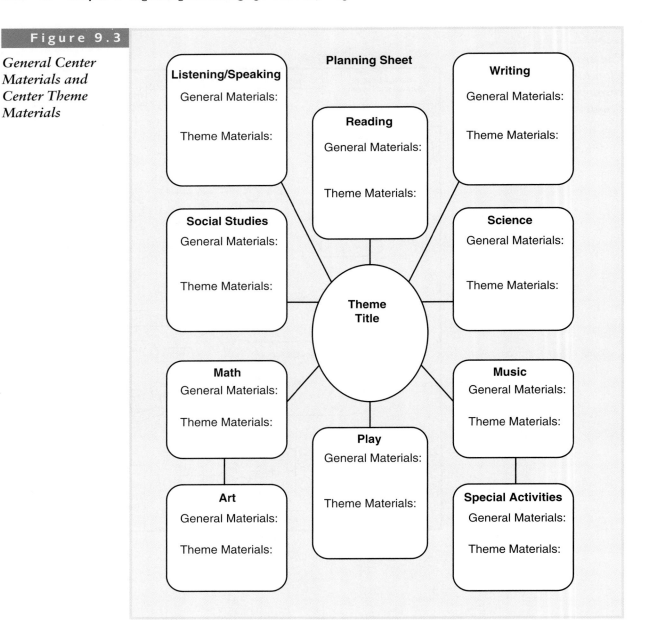

at school derive from children's real-life experiences and topics that they demonstrate an interest in. Learning experiences are socially interactive and process oriented, giving children time to explore and experiment with varied materials. If, for example, a class is studying dinosaurs, the students talk about them, read about them, write about them, do art projects related to dinosaurs, and sing songs related to the theme. In doing so, they learn about dinosaurs and develop skills in other content areas.

Literacy activities can be integrated into the study of themes and in all content areas throughout the school day. Several are described here to demonstrate how strategies to develop literacy that are discussed in previous chapters can be used in other areas of the curriculum (Pappas, Kiefer, & Levstik, 1995).

✓ **Checklist** *Evaluating and Improving the Literacy Environment*

The Literacy Center	Yes	No
Children participate in designing the center (e.g., develop rules, select a name for center, develop materials).		
Area is placed in a quiet section of the room.		
Area is visually and physically accessible, yet partitioned from the rest of the room.		
There are a rug, throw pillows, rocking chair, beanbag chair, and stuffed animals.		
There is a private spot in the corner such as a box to crawl into and read.		
The center uses about 10 percent of the classroom space and fits five to six children.		

The Library Corner

	Yes	No
Bookshelves for storing books with spines facing outward		
Organizational system for shelving books		
a. books shelved by genre	a.	
b. books shelved by reading level	b.	
Open-faced bookshelves for featured books		
Five to eight books per child		
Books represent three to four grade levels of the following types: (a) picture books, (b) picture story books, (c) traditional literature, (d) poetry, (e) realistic literature, (f) informational books, (g) biographies, (h) chapter books, (i) easy to read books, (j) riddle and joke books, (k) participation books, (l) series books, (m) textless books, (n) TV-related books, (o) brochures, (p) magazines, (q) newspapers.		
Twenty new books circulated every two weeks		
Check-out/check-in system for children to take books out daily		
Headsets and taped stories		
Felt-board and story characters with related books		
Materials for constructing felt stories		
Other story manipulatives (e.g., roll movie, puppets, with related books)		
System for recording books read		
Multiple copies of the same book		

(continued on next page)

The Writing Center (The Author's Spot)

	Yes	No
Tables and chairs		
Writing posters and bulletin board for children to display their writing themselves		
Writing utensils (e.g., pens, pencils, crayons, magic markers, colored pencils)		
Writing materials (many varieties of paper in all sizes, booklets, pads)		
Computers		
Materials for writing stories and making them into books		
A message board for children to post messages for the teacher and students		
A place to store Very Own Words		
Folders for children to place samples of their writing		
A place for children to send private messages to each other		

Literacy-Rich Environment for the Rest of the Classroom

The classroom should include literacy materials in all centers. Materials should be changed often to reflect the unit being studied—for example, in the science center there should be books on the unit topic, and in the music area posters of songs related to themes. Play areas should reflect units with themed play and literacy materials. All centers should contain the following:

	Yes	No
Environmental print, such as signs related to themes studied, directions, rules, functional messages		
A calendar		
A current events board		
Appropriate books, magazines, and newspapers		
Writing utensils		
Varied types of paper		
A place for children to display their literacy work		
A place for teachers and children to leave messages for each other		
A word wall		
Print representative of multicultural groups present in the classroom		

Content-area centers present are
- ☐ (circle centers)
- ☐ music ☐ art ☐ science ☐ social studies ☐ math ☐ dramatic play

Objectives for Art Experiences

In early childhood, art experience should offer children the opportunity to

1. be exposed to varied art materials.
2. explore and experiment with these materials.
3. express feelings through art.
4. represent experience through visual art forms.
5. gain an appreciation for varied art forms.
6. name and discuss content of art: line, color, texture, form, and shape.
7. experience literacy learning in art activities.

Art experiences allow children to explore and experiment with interesting materials such as finger paints, watercolors, printing, string painting, sponge painting, colored pencils, felt-tip markers, crayons, colored construction paper, tissue paper, foil, transparent wrap, paste, scissors, yarn, fabric scraps, pipe cleaners, clay, and play dough. If children are encouraged to discuss such materials as they use them, language development flourishes. Children immersed in finger painting, for instance, use such words as *mushy, smushy, gushy,* and *squiggle.* Playing with dough or clay elicits the words *pound, squeeze, roll, press,* and *fold.* Watercolors stimulate such comments as "Oooh, it's drippy," "The paint is running down the page like a stream of water," "Look how the colors all run together. The red is making the blue turn purple," and "My picture looks like a rainbow of colors across the sky." The teacher can take the opportunity to make word lists from the language generated in art activities and to encourage the children to share and talk about what they are doing. The words that individual children generate are a source of Very Own Words.

Children are often eager to exhibit their creations. This practice is likely to result in children's asking each other how they made their projects. The resulting description provides an excellent opportunity for literacy development. Children sometimes ask to dictate or write sentences and stories about their artwork, or write about it themselves. Individual works of art on similar subjects can be bound together in books that include captions, titles, or stories. Art activities also can highlight concepts such as the letter *p,* for example, through the use of purple and pink paint, paper, and play dough.

Objectives for Music Experiences

In early childhood, music experiences should include

1. having intense involvement in and responding to music.
2. exposure to different forms of music (instruments, singing, types of music) to be able to discriminate among them and develop an appreciation for varied forms.
3. music experiences that involve listening, singing, moving, playing, and creating.
4. expressing feelings through music experiences.
5. experiencing literacy learning in music activities.

Music provides ample means for literacy development. Children find new words in songs, thus increasing vocabulary. Songs emphasize word patterns and syllabic patterns, which should be brought to the children's attention. Songs can be written on charts and sung, the teacher pointing to the individual words as he or she tracks the print from left to right across the page. Picture storybooks adapted from songs, such as *Old MacDonald Had a Farm* (Quackenbush, 1972), provide predictable reading material for young children. Listening to classical music often creates images and is a rich source for descriptive language. Children can create stories about the music, describe their feelings, or describe the sounds of various instruments.

Objectives for Social Studies and Science Experiences

Social studies and science themes for the most part provide the meaning and function for learning, particularly for literacy learning. Themes provide a reason to read and write about topics of interest. Skills are learned within a context rather than in isolated lessons for skill development.

In early childhood, social studies experiences should include

1. fostering self-esteem.
2. learning social skills for functioning, such as sharing, cooperating, and communicating with others.
3. recognizing and respecting similarities and differences in others.
4. increasing knowledge of other cultures and ethnic and racial groups.
5. increasing understanding of the nature of our social world through the study of history, geography, and economics.
6. using the content of social studies to promote literacy development.

In early childhood, science experiences should include activities that involve

1. observing, hypothesizing, recording data, summarizing, analyzing, and drawing conclusions.
2. increasing understanding in
   a. biological science, the study of living things.
   b. physical science, including the study of
      (1) astronomy—heavenly bodies and their movements.
      (2) chemistry—materials found on the earth and the changes that occur in them.
      (3) meteorology—weather and air.
      (4) physics—the nature of matter and energy.
3. using the content of science to promote literacy development.

Science and social studies are probably the two content areas that provide the greatest opportunities for literacy development. Their contents typically generate enthusiasm, meaning, and a purpose for using literacy strategies. A unit about the farm can lead to oral language development through discussions about farm work, different types of farms, and farm animals. Word lists of farm animals, crops, and jobs on the farm can be made. Pictures of farm scenes, a trip to a farm, or a visit by a farmer generates discussion, reading, and writing. To

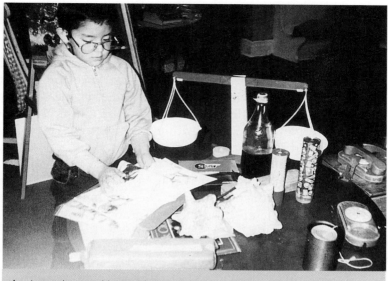

A science theme with experiments and interesting materials to investigate integrates literacy instruction into content-area instruction.

encourage positive attitudes toward books, the teacher can carefully select good pieces of children's literature about farms to read to the class. The *Petunia* series (Duvoisin, 1950) deals with a delightful goose who lives on a farm. *The Little Red Hen* (Galdone, 1973), *The Tale of Peter Rabbit* (Potter, 1902), *The Little Farm* (Lenski, 1965), and *Charlie Needs a Clock* (dePaola, 1973) are just a few examples of good children's literature that relate to the farm. The teacher should select some international trade books as well. These books will motivate youngsters to pick up the books on their own, retell them, role-play them, and share them with each other. A farm visit can be retold in stories or drawings bound into class books, recaptured in a language experience chart, or reflected in Very Own Words. The teacher can associate letters and sounds in farm words with those in children's names or in environmental print.

Science experiments and food preparation offer opportunities for discussion, and an exchange of interesting vocabulary. The block center, too, can stimulate literacy activities. For instance, when introducing a unit on transportation, the teacher can add toy trucks, trains, cars, boats, and airplanes to the block corner, along with travel tickets, luggage and freight tags, maps, travel guides, tour brochures, travel posters, and signs common to airports, train stations, and bus depots, such as gate numbers, names of carriers, and arrival and departure signs.

Objectives for Mathematics Experiences

Early childhood mathematics activities should involve

1. many opportunities to handle and deal with mathematical materials and ideas.
2. movement from dependence on the concrete to abstract ideas.
3. opportunities to classify, compare, seriate, measure, graph, count, identify, and write numbers and perform operations on numbers.

4. using mathematical vocabulary.

5. using mathematics to promote literacy development.

In all the other content areas, a teacher can feel confident that he or she is providing a fairly adequate program of study through the themed units used in social studies and science that incorporate music, art, play, and literacy development in early childhood. Math, however, is a specialized area that needs more attention than can be dealt with in a content-area unit. Still, there are many activities that bring meaning to mathematics through unit topics and that include literacy as well. Stories related to numbers can be read; children can count cookies for snack time to make sure there are enough for the class; and children can be in charge of collecting and counting milk money. When studying weather, a chart of daily temperatures can be graphed to observe the variability from day to day.

When literacy skills are developed in an integrated fashion, as in practices and approaches described here, children see purposes and reasons for becoming literate. When we teach literacy skills that do not reflect real-life experience and lack content, children are not likely to perceive their usefulness. When skills are taught in an integrated, interdisciplinary fashion, children ask for the skills they need in order to participate fully in experiences that interest them during their work and play at school and at home (Manning, Manning, & Long, 1994; Walmsley, 1994). During a unit on transportation in a kindergarten class of my own, children asked for even more materials than I had already made available in the several centers. Books on transportation led to requests for books on space travel and various maps of places not in the center. Many children added to their Very Own Words. Children asked for help preparing signs representing places they wanted to visit and highway signs indicating mileage to various destinations. Some dictated travel directions. The need for literacy information was created by preparing an environment that reflected interesting, real-life experiences. In such an environment, learning is to a great extent self-generated.

Objectives for Play Experiences

In early childhood, play experiences include providing opportunities for children to

1. problem solve.

2. acquire new understandings.

3. role-play real-life experiences.

4. cope with situations that require sharing and cooperating.

5. develop language and literacy through play.

Dramatic play provides endless possibilities for literacy development through the use of oral and written language and reading. The materials and activities typical of dramatic-play areas stimulate considerable language, and the addition of new props and materials provides the opportunity for continued growth. Dramatic play provides realistic settings and functional reasons for using print. New units in social studies and science trigger opportunities to add print materials that stimulate reading, writing, and oral language. A unit on community helpers—a topic familiar to early childhood teachers—invariably leads to a discussion of firefighters, police officers, supermarket clerks, doctors, nurses, mail carriers, and office workers. The mention of any of these community helpers is an opportunity to add literacy materials to the dramatic-play area.

Role-playing supermarket, for instance, is aided by the addition of food and detergent containers, a toy cash register, play money, note pads, a telephone and directory, store signs, a schedule of hours, advertisements, and posters for food and other products. Teachers or aides might visit a nearby supermarket to note for the classroom the print that is there, and to pick up outdated signs and posters. Store managers readily give away such materials when they no longer need them. Definitely include, among materials for dramatic play about super-markets, a bookshelf full of magazines and books "for sale." All these materials help children engage in conversation as they role-play a store manager, clerk, or shopper. They read posters, books, signs, and magazines and write shopping lists, orders, and new signs when they are needed.

Many topics lend themselves to dramatic play and incorporating literacy materials. A study of health-care personnel can lead to the creation of a doctor's office. A waiting room can be set up with magazines for the patients to read and pamphlets about good health. There can be a no-smoking sign, a notice containing the doctor's hours, and posters on the wall concerning good health habits. There should be an appointment book for the nurse, a pad for writing appointment reminders for patients to take with them, a pad for writing prescriptions, patient folders containing forms to be filled out, and a patient address and phone book.

When studying transportation, the class can create a travel agency. Here there would be maps, travel posters, pamphlets about places to visit, and tickets to be issued for planes and trains.

Children enjoy role-playing in these situations because the activity includes meaningful experiences. In dramatic play, children are voluntarily participating in reading and writing.

Dramatic play is considered appropriate in preschools and kindergartens; however, we seldom leave time for it in first and second grades or think of it as an area in which learning can take place. In classrooms that integrate content themes into dramatic play with six- to eight-year-olds, extremely sophisticated productions of reading, writing, and oral language result. It is suggested that first- and second-grade teachers incorporate play into their curriculum. As mentioned earlier in this book, technology has made it more acceptable to engage in dramatic play with second and third graders as they search the Internet for train and plane routes when role-play is about travel. Children also can use the Internet to find other information for any role-playing theme featured.

Preparing a Thematic Unit

Unit themes can be selected by the teacher and the children. Giving students choices concerning what they will learn is important. When a topic is selected, allow the children to brainstorm what they would like to know about. You might begin by suggesting categories to focus on and letting them fill in subheadings (Rand, 1993). In preparation for a unit on nutrition, I asked a class of kindergarten children to help decide what they might like to learn. I used a web to chart their ideas and started it for them with nutrition as the theme and four categories to focus on: Why is food important? What foods are good for you? Where do we get food from? and, How are different foods prepared to eat? The web in Figure 9.4 illustrates the children's responses and the content to be studied for the unit.

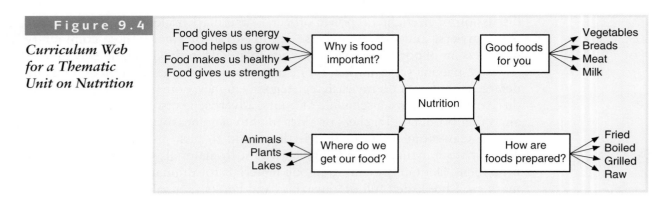

Figure 9.4

Curriculum Web for a Thematic Unit on Nutrition

In planning a unit, the teacher needs to include activities in all content areas. Create a plan and select activities related to the unit from different content areas to schedule throughout the school day. Following is a mini unit written by Ms. Ngai, a first-grade teacher. As you will see, she integrates content area activities throughout the day that focus on the theme.

Thematic Instruction: Good Food

An interesting theme can make learning come alive for children. With food as our theme, and popcorn as our weeklong focus, things were really "popping" in our first-grade classroom! Here are some exciting ways to make learning about popcorn fun, while tying in content-area instruction.

The Friday Before: *We planted popcorn kernels in baking tins lined with paper towels. We spread popcorn in the pans, watered the seeds, and covered the pans with plastic wrap. In a few days, the roots began to sprout (science).*

Monday: *Using a log, we recorded the growth of the seedlings over the weekend. We read* The Popcorn Book *by Tomie dePaola (1978). We discussed that the Native Americans introduced popcorn to the colonists. We used the compound word* popcorn *to trigger a list of other food compound words, such as* cupcake *and* milkshake, *which we wrote on a chart. Anytime a student thought of or came across a compound word, he or she would write it down on the chart. By the end of the week, the chart paper was full (science, language arts, social studies).*

Tuesday: *We set up an experiment chart for making popcorn. We asked ourselves, "What do I want to find out?" (How does a corn kernel change to popcorn?) "What do I think will happen?" "How will I find out?" "What actually happened?" and, "What did I learn?" We answered the first two questions. We used an air popper to pop the corn and then completed the experiment chart, answering the remaining questions. We also enjoyed the popcorn for our snack. We planted our seedlings in paper cups filled with soil (science).*

Wednesday: *We made more popcorn to create an estimation lesson for math. Each child grabbed a handful of popcorn from a large bowl and guessed how many kernels were in his or her hand. Then we used a simple record sheet to log estimations. We then counted to find the actual number. We tried it a second time to see if we arrived at a more accurate estimation (mathematics).*

Thursday: *One of the ways the Native Americans popped corn was to put an ear of corn on a stick and hold it over a fire until the kernels popped. Another way was to throw kernels into the fire until they popped out all over the place. Still another way was to use clay pots filled with hot sand, in which the kernels were mixed until they eventually popped to the top of the pot. We illustrated the method we thought was the best, and wrote a few sentences as to why we felt that way. We discussed how the Native Americans made necklaces out of popcorn. Using the popcorn from Wednesday, we gave it a try. We used large, blunt needles and heavy thread and created necklaces* (writing, art, social studies).

Friday: *As a culminating lesson, we had parent volunteers come into our classroom to make popcorn balls. We checked for any growth of our corn plants, and recorded the information in our science logs* (science, cooking).

See Appendix D for a complete integrated language arts unit entitled "Healthy Bodies, Healthy Minds" for use in the classroom.

Organizing Instruction to Meet Individual Needs: Guided Reading and Center Activities

There are a variety of strategies for organizing instruction. Children can be taught as a whole class, in small groups, and individually. Children can be in homogeneous or heterogeneous groups based on ability, needs, interests, or they can be divided into peer groups for cooperative learning. The use of a variety of organizational strategies is important because some children benefit more in one setting than in another. The use of several different grouping schemes within the same classroom also tends to eliminate the stigmas attached to a single grouping system. Variable grouping makes it likely that children will interact with all others in one group or another.

Whole-Group, Small-Group, and One-to-One Learning Settings

Whole-group instruction is not appropriate until children are almost three years old. Younger children lack the ability to concentrate or to sit in a large-group setting and listen for any period of time. Whole-group lessons, sometimes referred to as shared experiences, are appropriate when information needs to be introduced to all the children and the presentation can be understood by all. In early childhood literacy development, storybook readings by an adult, group singing, class discussions, and brainstorming sessions are appropriate whole-group activities.

Small groups are effective when close interaction with children is necessary for explicit instruction and assessment, as with guided reading and writing instruction. Small groups also are used for cooperative projects with children working independent of the teacher. Teachers should use many types of small-group formations, such as guided reading groups for explicit instruction of skills, groups based on friendships or interests, and independent reading and writing groups. In the description of the language arts block at the end of this chapter, many types of grouping configurations are included. Various group formations is for children to have experiences working with many others, and

Whole-group and small-group settings allow teachers to vary instructional presentation.

to avoid the stigma attached to being associated with only one group. When using grouping it is necessary to have children participating in many groups and for children's group placement to change from time to time.

Working with children on a one-to-one basis and allowing them to work independently are forms of *individualized instruction*. Although children need to work cooperatively with peers and adults, they also need to problem solve and accomplish tasks on their own. One-to-one instruction provides an opportunity for the teacher to offer personal attention to a child and to learn much about a child. When a teacher works with a child alone, he or she can take running records for assessment and do story retelling instruction and assessment. Children can get help with specific skills they are having difficulty with, and teachers can take story dictations or discuss a new piece of the child's writing.

I learned the value of meeting children one-to-one early in my teaching career. A mother of a child in my class told me that he liked to be absent from school. I was upset by the comment, assuming that her son was unhappy in my class. The mother said that her son liked being absent because when he returned to school he was given "private time with the teacher." I had made a practice of meeting with absentees on their return to school to share work we had accomplished when they were absent. I realized then that children enjoy time alone with their teacher. And, through private conferences, I learned a great deal about the instructional needs of my children, their emotional needs, and their interests.

Guided Reading and Writing: Explicit Instruction of Skills

Teachers need to provide direct instruction of skills for most youngsters. Direct instruction is designed for the needs of individuals and can take place in a whole group, in small groups, or on a one-to-one basis, although most often it occurs in small groups. Without the direct instruction component in literacy instruction, some children will miss learning many important skills. It is crucial that teachers be aware of the individual needs of their students and accommodate those needs with an appropriate balance of instructional strategies, both direct and open ended.

During one-to-one instruction, the teacher does frequent running records to determine a child's strengths, needs, and reading level.

Researchers have studied learning in small groups for the purpose of more direct instruction. In small-group instruction teachers are better able to obtain and retain students' attention. The small group offers the opportunity for more student participation (Lou, 1996; Slavin, 1987; Sorenson & Hallinan, 1986). In addition, teachers can change instructional methods and materials to meet the needs of each student in small groups. When groups are homogeneous it is possible for teachers to provide more individualized instruction at the appropriate level (Slavin, 1987). In small groups, instruction can be paced for students' rate of learning, teaching styles can be modified to meet different learning styles, and students are easier to control (Hallinan & Sorenson, 1983).

There are some disadvantages of grouping. For example, children from minority backgrounds are often disproportionately placed in low-ability groups. If groups are inflexible, once a student is tracked in a particular group, that placement may never change throughout his or her school career. This practice affects self-esteem and the type of instruction a student receives (Slavin, 1987). Another disadvantage of grouping is that frequently only one measure determines a child's group placement. Often there is a set number of groups, such as three, in which all children must fit. In addition, teachers sometimes have low expectations for students in the low groups, which can lead to continued low performance for these students (Hallinan & Sorenson, 1983).

Guided reading is a form of explicit instruction that typically takes place in small groups. Fountas and Pinnell (1996) define it as follows:

> In guided reading a teacher works with a small group. Children in the group are similar in their development of the reading process and are able to read about the same level of text. Teachers introduce the stories and assist children's reading in ways that help to develop independent reading strategies. Each child reads the entire text. The goal is for children to read independently and silently. The emphasis is on reading increasingly challenging books. Children are grouped and regrouped in a dynamic process that involves ongoing observation and assessment. (p. 4)

And, Spiegel (1992) writes,

> The overall purpose of guided reading is to enable children to read for meaning at all times. Guided reading instruction is systematic instruction with a scope of skills and objectives to accomplish. Activities are designed to meet the objectives. Skill instruction is not left to chance; it is assured. Although there is a systematic plan, guided reading instruction should allow for "teachable moments."

Teachers select the instructional materials for guided reading based on meeting the skill needs of the children. The texts can be any type, such as those from a reading program or children's literature; however, they must be at the instructional level of the child, neither too easy nor too hard. Leveled reading books, often called "little books," are the most common materials used for guided reading. These books have been leveled for difficulty, making it easy for teachers to select those needed for particular groups. The texts also must be at the child's instructional reading level. This means that the child can read the text with 90 to 95 percent accuracy (Clay, 1993b). If the text is too easy, there is no opportunity to teach new strategies; if the book is too difficult, children will not understand what they are reading, and the activity becomes an exercise in decoding words rather than trying to make meaning.

Selecting Children for Groups

With such a variety of group formations, many teachers ask, "How do I select children for each type of group?" Children can make decisions about participating in some groups such as those based on friendship and interest. Guided reading and writing groups are selected by the teacher because the instruction in these groups is based on need and instructional level, or ability.

Many pieces of information should be used to determine students' needs and abilities for guided reading and writing group selection. Throughout this book I have discussed several types of assessment that should form a composite picture of the child to help determine group placement. One of the most important pieces of information is teacher judgment. Other types of assessment that will help in group placement include the following:

Running records to determine text reading level, types of strengths and weaknesses in word analysis, fluency, and self-monitoring

Letter-recognition tests

High-frequency word tests

Comprehension evaluation

Standardized test scores

Alternate rank ordering is another way to assign children to groups. This method is mainly based on teacher judgment. List all the children in your class with the child you rank as having the highest literacy ability at the top and the others following to the last child whom you rank with the lowest ability. To assign groups, select the top and the bottom child to start two different groups. Place the next child from the top into the group with the top child, and place the next child from the bottom into the group with the child with the lowest ability. Continue this procedure, each time asking yourself if these children are alike enough to be in the same group. When the answer to that question is no, then start a new group. You should end up with four to six groups for your class with about five children per group. After several meetings, if the groups do not seem to be right for certain children, change their placement. As children are evaluated on a regular basis, their grouping placement could change.

Managing Small-Group Instruction during Guided Reading

In Chapter 8, I discussed organizing and managing independent periods for reading and writing, or literacy center time. The purpose of that small-group work is for children to learn to work independent of the teacher and in cooperative social settings with peers. It is a time for children to practice skills already learned. During center time children engage in self-selected reading and writing activities that they work on independent of the teacher. The teacher acts as a facilitator by answering questions and keeping children on task if necessary. During guided reading and writing, the teacher is occupied with small-group instruction and cannot be disturbed; therefore, the children not in the guided reading lesson need to know exactly what to do, when to do it, and where. The management plan in Chapter 8 for independent work is a good model for organizing and managing activity choices and rotation systems for working in independent centers to reinforce skills. However, it needs some modifications when children are being instructed in guided reading groups. A visit to Ms. Shea's second-grade classroom provides a look at the organization of independent work to suit the guided reading lesson format.

The activities that Ms. Shea models for her class for independent work are often skill and theme related. In the beginning of the school year, she spends time introducing children to the centers in the room and the types of activities they include. She has her class practice working on the different activities. At this time, Ms. Shea does not work with small groups during independent work; rather, she helps the children so that they eventually will be able to work independently.

The children are assigned some tasks and can select others to do. The tasks engage the children in reading and writing that will help with skill development. Ms. Shea assigns activities 1, 2, 3, and 4 (listed below) to all children. They can choose to do activities 5 or 6 (also below) after they finish the required tasks.

1. For *partner reading*, children pair off and read the same book together. They also may read separate books and then tell each other about the story they read. Because the class is studying animals, children are to select books from the open-faced bookshelves that include stories and expository texts about animals. Discussion about what is read is encouraged. Each child must fill out an index card with the name of the book read and one sentence about the story.

2. *The writing activity* requires the children to rewrite the story called *Ask Mr. Bear* that Ms. Shea read at the morning meeting. In their rewritings, children are to include story elements discussed, such as setting, theme, plot episodes, and the resolution. They may consult copies of the book in the classroom if necessary. Each day there is a different writing activity related to the story read.

3. For the *working with words* activity, the children are to find words around the room that have the *sh* and *ch* digraph in them. They classify these words by writing them on a sheet of paper under appropriate digraph headings. Children can look through books to find these digraphs.

4. *The listening center* has taped stories about animals. For each story, there is a sheet of paper with a question to answer about the story. Two titles on tape are *Is Your Mama a Llama?* (Kellogg, 1989) and *Arthur's Pet Business* (Brown, 1990).

5. *The art center* has magazines with many photos of animals that children can use to create animal collages.

6. *The computer center* has literacy software and writing activities.

Ms. Shea has an organizational chart that she uses for assigning children to centers. The rotations occur in coordination with the groups that she meets with for small-group instruction. If children finish before group rotations, they can start one of the optional activities or go on to the next task if there is space at the center. There is a basket for completed work, and every center has sign-in sheets and requires a finished product to be handed in.

Children work independently and in small groups in productive activities.

In the beginning of the school year, some teachers start center time in a structured fashion. They assign the groups and tasks. As children learn to function independently, they are given opportunities for decision making and select groups to work with or tasks to accomplish.

The management of center time is crucial for its success. Students must know their choices, the activities in which to participate, the rules that guide participation concerning the selection of materials, and what is to happen in groups or when working alone. Children can help generate the guidelines and rules for working independently. Figure 8.3 lists rules for children to follow when working independently. Some of the rules that are important for independent work during guided reading are as follows:

Rules for Using Materials and Completing Work

- Do all mandatory tasks before you do the optional tasks.
- Speak in soft voices; people are working.

- Put materials back in their place.
- Take care of the materials so they are in good condition for others.
- Put your completed work in a designated place.
- Record completed work on contract form or in a log.
- If you have questions, use the "Ask Three and Then Me," rule. Seek help from other students designated as helpers before asking the teacher when she is in a guided reading group.

Rules for Cooperating and Collaborating

- Share materials in collaborative activities.
- Take turns.
- Listen to your friends when they talk.
- Offer help to others you are working with if they need it.
- When you complete an activity, ask yourself if you were helpful to others, and if you shared materials.

Some teachers provide a list of activities to do during guided reading, as shown in Figure 9.5. This list may indicate that the first few activities are mandatory and the others are optional, if the children have time. Some teachers allow children to go from one activity to the next listed on the chart. With this system, children must sign in at a center on a form provided (see Figure 9.6). They can use the center only if there is an empty chair for them, a rule which avoids crowding. When a child finishes an activity, he or she places the product in a designated spot. Accountability for independent work is a necessity. In addition, the child reports the activities completed on his contract (see Figure 9.7 for a student contract agreement and Figure 8.7 for a student log for readers and non-readers).

Another way to designate independent work is through the use of a *center chart*. There are many variations on this type of system. The center chart in

---

Figure 9.5

Things to Do during Guided Reading

The mandatory activities are done first.

Mandatory Activities

- Read your guided reading book for review.
- Practice any skills your teacher indicated you need to work on.
- Write an informational piece about hibernating animals, based on the book read during the morning meeting. Include your new high-frequency words in your expository writing.
- Select the material modeled by the teacher from the word-study center that will enable you to practice making words by blending the initial consonants with ending phonograms.
- Listen to the winter story on the headsets, and answer the questions posed on a sheet of paper provided.

Optional Activities

- Tell a felt story with the story characters and felt-board.
- Create a roll story for a book related to the theme being studied.
- Make a winter collage at the art center.

Figure 9.6

Center Sign-in Sheet

Listening Center

Class List	Date: 11/18	Write Your Name Here:
1. Sarah Anders		
2. Barry Duke		
3. Kathleen Carin		
4. Narain Evat		
5. James Gala		
6. Megan Hand		
7. Jovaon Harris		
8. Christine Kim		
9. Dylan Kotter		
10. Kathryn Levin		
11. Irene Lopez		
12. John McNeal		
13. Andrea Penn		
14. Zachary Pierce		
15. Alyx Sax		
16. Gina-Marie Teal		
17. Micah Urani		
18. Max Valley		
19. Brandon Wimbush		

Figure 9.8 is an adaptation of the *Work Board* described by Fountas and Pinnell (1996). It designates several choices for three or four different heterogeneously grouped children. The chart is made of tagboard and has a row of figures representing center activities. At the top of each row is a place to attach names of children. The figures are movable, as are the name cards. They can be attached to the chart with Velcro, or the chart can have several pockets in it.

Some teachers prefer a more structured approach to assigning independent work, especially early in the school year. A teacher may assign children to the centers, then have them rotate from one to the next as the teacher rotates guided reading groups he or she works with. For example, Ms. Shea's second graders sit in groups of four desks pushed together, which she calls pods. These children are het-

Figure 9.7

Contract
Activities

Contract		
Name _____	**Date** _____	
Things to Do	Specific Activity	Done
	Reading	
	Writing	
	Oral Language	
	Language Arts Manipulatives	
	Listening Station	
	Math Manipulatives **1+4-2**	
	Other Activities:	

erogeneously grouped and move together from one center activity to another, or one activity to another as listed on the center chart. From time to time, Ms. Shea will change the pod groups so children have the opportunity to work with many different others. The groups of children often give themselves names. When Ms. Shea meets with her first guided reading group, the other children have designated center assignments. When the first guided reading lesson ends, all children move to the next center area with their group to work on a new project. Later in the school year, the children are allowed to select their activities and to do them in whatever order they wish. As they complete one activity, they immediately move to the next.

Putting a Guided Reading Lesson into Practice

Objectives for each guided reading lesson should focus on a systematic sequence of skills to be developed, on skills children are experiencing difficulty with, and on strategies they neglect to use. In the lesson many experiences are drawn upon to help children with phonograms, syntactic and semantic cues, and writing (Reutzel, 1997; Reutzel & Cooter, 2004). The objectives for the lessons, like the selection of the text, depend on the students' reading ability and needs.

There are marked differences between guided reading groups and reading groups of the past. Guided reading groups are characterized by the following:

1. Children are assessed regularly so that their group placement is changed when their reading ability changes and they are not fixed in one group forever.

Figure 9.8 *Center Chart*

Janine, Jen, Keith, Kelly, Rumon	Holly, Michael, Ben, Mat, Alexis	Darren, Tisha, Ivory, Sam, Matt	Sarah, Tim, Yassin, Josh, Kyle

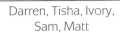

Buddy Reading	Listening Station	Oral Language	Journal Writing

Journal Writing	Computer Center	Word-Study Manipulatives	Buddy Reading

Oral Language	Word-Study Manipulatives	Buddy Reading	Listening Station

Word-Study Manipulatives	Buddy Reading	Journal Writing	Computer Center

Listening Station	Oral Language	Computer Center	Word-Study Manipulatives

Computer Center	Journal Writing	Listening Station	Oral Language

All figures and name cards are removable and can be changed around.

Source: Adapted by permission from *Guided Reading: Good First Teaching for All Children* by Irene C. Fountas and Gay Su Pinnell. Copyright © 1996 by Irene C. Fountas and Gay Su Pinnell. Published by Heinemann, a division of Reed Elsevier, Inc., Portsmouth, New Hampshire.

Teachers meet with guided reading groups three to five times a week for direct instruction of skills.

2. The teacher purposely uses other types of groups for instruction throughout the day so that students never associate themselves only with their guided reading group.
3. The number of groups formed is not set; it is determined by the number of different ability levels represented in a given classroom. Typically there are four to six groups.
4. Books selected for instruction meet the needs of the students regardless of their grade level.
5. Small-group instruction is designed to provide children with strategies for becoming independent fluent readers.
6. Activities provided for children who are not in guided reading groups are often in centers. Children are actively engaged in interesting, productive work practicing skills learned in guided reading lessons. (In the past the most commonly used method for occupying children was the use of workbook pages.)

A guided reading lesson can take almost any form. The major concern is that it be designed to meet the needs of the children in the group. Some particular

The teacher arranges her guided reading groups based on need and selects books for them to read based on their level of reading.

components are associated with the design of guided reading that follow a Reading Recovery lesson (Clay, 1991). The components are as follows:

1. The lesson begins with children reading something familiar that is easy. This creates fluent, smooth oral reading with good pronunciation, intonation, and flow.

2. The teacher introduces a new book to children by taking a "walk through the book" to build some background knowledge about it before it is read. This helps generate children's prior knowledge about the book's topic, which should help them comprehend what is read (Anderson & Pearson, 1984). Here are typical steps in the "walk through the book":
   a. Children are asked to make predictions about what they think might happen in the story.
   b. Children are asked to read the title, author's name, and illustrator's name.
   c. The teacher can give a short summary of the story.
   d. The teacher can introduce patterns in words.

3. With younger children the first reading of the book is done aloud. This is not round-robin reading with different children taking turns, nor is it choral reading. Each child reads his or her copy of the text at his or her own pace. Older children will read silently after the teacher provides a good reading model by reading a portion of the selection.

4. While the children read, the teacher listens to provide guidance or scaffolding when a child cannot figure out a word. The teacher also takes notes about the children's reading strengths and weaknesses. He or she may have a different child from each group sit next to him or her during the lesson. This is the student she will take most notes about, which makes record keeping easier. The next day a different focus child will sit next to the teacher during guided reading.

5. After the first reading, children reread for fluency and comprehension, which is easier during the second reading because children are not concentrating on decoding as much. Multiple readings of the same text help students become better readers (Clay, 1991).

6. After the readings, the teacher selects specific skills to concentrate on, based on the needs of the group. He or she might select a word chunk from the text that occurs frequently, such as /og/ in the word *frog*, and build other words that use that chunk. The teacher provides several activities for learning this skill, such as having children generate new words as a whole group that end with the /og/ chunk, such as *log, fog, jog*, and so on. The teacher also might give students magnetic letters with the /og/ chunk and ask them to create /og/ words on their own small magnetic board. To further reinforce the concept, the teacher may ask children to select an /og/ word and write it in a sentence, paying attention to punctuation and spelling. The teacher then cuts each sentence into separate words for students to sequence and read for practice.

7. The teacher often writes notes to parents during the guided reading lesson for children to take home. The note suggests homework for the child and how parents can help.

8. The last component of a guided reading lesson is a running record. This is usually done on an individual basis. A child is asked to stay after the lesson and read a passage to determine progress. The teacher evaluates the child's

reading needs and reading level, and determines whether the child should remain in his or her present group or move to a group where the work is easier or more difficult. A description of the administration and evaluation of a running record is in Chapter 2 with a sample evaluation form.

Be sure to refer to the guided reading lesson to understand the steps involved. It is important to note that during the guided reading lesson the teacher not only instructs but also determines children's strengths and needs. As mentioned, each time there is a guided reading lesson, one child sits next to the teacher for him or her to concentrate on. The teacher can take a running record as the child reads along with the group. Other types of assessment that should be collected and stored in a child's portfolio are frequent writing samples and observation notes about reading behaviors. Teachers should also use the checklists provided in each chapter in this book that deal with different aspects of literacy development. To help you further understand the use of guided reading groups, following is a discussion and description of guided reading in Mrs. Keefe's first-grade classroom.

Although grouping practices based on need and ability are controversial, Mrs. Keefe believes it is the only way she can learn what individual children know and what they need to learn in order to design her instruction. She has organized the class into five groups of four to five children who have similar reading needs, are capable of similar reading skills, and are reading at about the same level. Children frequently move from group to group based on Mrs. Keefe's ongoing assessment of their progress. She meets with each group four to five times a week for about 20 minutes. A typical lesson includes (1) reading something familiar for fluency and success, (2) working on a skill involving word analysis, (3) introducing a new book and the decoding or comprehension skills associated with it, (4) reading the new book with the support of the teacher and peers, (5) discussing the story, and (6) doing a writing activity. Mrs. Keefe assesses one or two children's reading development during each reading group by taking a running record of their oral reading and recording errors to determine skill needs and by listening to children's oral retellings of stories to check comprehension.

During a typical day, first Mrs. Keefe engages her children with independent work. When students are working well on their own, she calls on her first group for guided reading instruction. She begins her small-group reading lesson with a familiar text that each child has in his or her baggie. She calls this "a book in a bag," and every day the children bring it to reading group. She uses a familiar text for fluency, to create a feeling of success. The children enjoy the ease with which they can read this old friend.

Next, Mrs. Keefe engages the children in a minilesson, helping them with a skill they need to learn. She wants the children to use the text along with phonic clues to decode unknown words. She writes a sentence on a small white slate, leaving one word blank. She asks the children to predict what word might make sense in the blank. She then asks them to write the word onto their whiteboards. Mrs. Keefe has prepared a practice sheet with three more sentences that have words missing but that include the first letter of each missing word. She asks the children to work in pairs to figure out the missing words.

At this time, a new book about animals is introduced from a set of leveled books selected for the reading ability of the children with whom Mrs. Keefe is working. She introduces some new vocabulary words on 3-by-5 cards. As the children recite the words, she places them in a pocket chart. The children copy

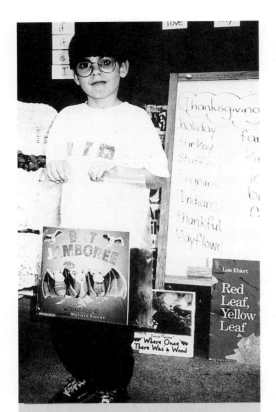

Children read from books at their reading level in guided reading groups. The books are stored in a plastic baggie that is often referred to as a "book in a bag."

the words on their white slates. Mrs. Keefe also has prepared sentence strips that come from the text of the new book, with the new vocabulary words left out. She places the sentence strips in the pocket chart, and the children fill in the blanks with the correct vocabulary word card.

For the first reading of the new book, Mrs. Keefe has the entire group chant the book with her. Following the first reading, she invites the children to read the book independently. Because these are beginning readers, they are to read aloud but in soft voices. She selects a focus child for the day for whom she takes a running record. Tomorrow when she meets with this group again, another child will sit by her side to be assessed.

After the second reading, the children and teacher discuss the story. Mrs. Keefe asks questions that relate to details in the text, as well as questions that require students to connect the story to circumstances in their own life.

As the lesson ends, Mrs. Keefe writes a short note to all the children's parents about their progress, what they were learning, what they needed help with, and what their homework is. Homework always requires the reading of the new book with a parent and the parent's signature. When the group finishes its work for the day, all members put their books in their plastic baggies with their homework note. They place their materials in their own box, which sits on the windowsill until it is time to go home.

Mrs. Keefe then meets with another group using books selected for their reading instructional level and carries out an appropriate lesson for them. She meets with three other groups until lunchtime.

The discussion concerning the instruction in these first and second grades includes practices suggested in two documents that have made an important impact on early literacy instruction. Both documents were edited by Burns, Griffin, and Snow. One is entitled *Preventing Reading Difficulties in Young Children* (1998) and the other *Starting Out Right: A Guide to Promoting Children's Reading Success* (1999).

Book boxes, one per child, are for storing guided reading materials such as children's "books in a bag."

Boxes of books leveled for difficulty are available for children to read and for use during guided reading lessons.

Organizing and Managing Literacy Instruction: Daily Schedules

Scheduling the daily routine in nursery school, kindergarten, and first, second, and third grade must take into account the social, emotional, physical, and intellectual levels of the children. It must also reflect the best from theorists' models of early childhood education, including those of Piaget, Froebel, Dewey, Montessori, the behaviorists, and Vygotsky. The environment should be prepared so that learning can take place naturally, but with the guidance and instruction that will help children achieve their fullest potential.

Young children cannot sit for long periods, so their schedule needs to vary. Whole-class lessons that require sitting and listening must be few and short. Children need large blocks of time for exploring environments. They need play situations, manipulative materials, learning centers, and outdoor areas. Activities that require sitting and listening need to be followed by ones that allow movement. Quiet times must be followed by noisier times. To nurture literacy, the teacher must allow for rich literacy experiences throughout the day, experiences in using and enjoying language in all its forms and functions.

In scheduling the school day, be sure to include *whole-class, small-group,* and *one-to-one* settings for learning. There need to be *teacher-directed* experiences and activities that children participate in *independently.* Children should have opportunities for *oral reading* and *silent reading* from books and from their own writing. They need to have time for *shared reading* experiences and *shared writing* experiences. Time should be set aside for periods of *guided reading* and *guided writing,* as well as *reading and writing independently.* Children should have the opportunity to *read and write collaboratively* with peers and to *perform* in formal and informal settings the products of their reading and writing. Figure 9.9 provides a self-analysis form concerning the organization of instruction. The form provides space for recording lessons taught. It also asks that lessons be identified as whole-group, small-group, or one-to-one settings, and

| Figure 9.9 | *Evaluation Strategies and Organization of Instruction* |

Planning Your School Day: Theme Topic _____

(TD-Teacher Directed, IN-Independent Activity, WG-Whole Group, SG-Small Group, 1 to 1)

CHANGE TIME SLOTS WHEN USING LONGER OR SHORTER PERIODS OF TIME

9:00 to 9:30 Activity and Content Area:	**9:30 to 10:30** Activity and Content Area:
Materials Used:	Materials:
Where Activity Takes Place:	Where:
TD or IN:	TD or IN:
WG, SG, 1–to–1:	WG, SG, 1–to–1:
10:30 to 11:30 Activity and Content Area:	**11:30 to 12:30** Activity and Content Area:
Materials:	Materials:
Where:	Where:
TD or IN:	TD or IN:
WG, SG, 1–to–1:	WG, SG, 1–to–1:

Lunch 12:30 to 1:30

1:30 to 2:30 Activity and Content Area:	**2:30 to 3:00** Activity and Content Area:
Materials:	Materials:
Where:	Where:
TD or IN:	TD or IN:
WG, SG, 1–to–1:	WG, SG, 1–to–1:

as teacher-directed or independent. There is a place to record the materials used in the lesson, and where the activity occurred in the classroom. If you record this information for a few days, it will help you analyze the teaching strategies you are using and identify those that you may need to incorporate.

The sample schedules that follow illustrate where and when specific opportunities to promote literacy can occur. The schedules provide a routine or structure for the day that seems to make children comfortable. Keep in mind that there is no one schedule for all classrooms. These are models with content, activities, and organization that should be included. The schedules and descriptions are found in the section *An Idea for the Classroom from the Classroom* and are presented in the following order:

1. Language program for kindergarten through third grade
2. Full-day preschool and kindergarten

3. Half-day preschool and kindergarten

4. Child-care centers for infants and toddlers

An Idea for the Classroom from the Classroom

■ Language Program for Kindergarten through Third Grade

The following is a description of a model for organizing and managing an early literacy language arts block, from a study of exemplary first-grade teachers from the Center for English Language Arts and Achievement at the State University of New York at Albany (Morrow & Asbury, 2003). The teachers in the study were identified by their supervisors as exemplary based on observation of their teaching. The exemplary nature of their teaching also was confirmed by other teachers, parents, students, and the children's scores on literacy tests. The teacher in the description (given the pseudonym Ms. Tracey) is a composite of many we observed when trying to discover a model for exemplary teaching. This description includes many theories and strategies discussed throughout the book.

8:30–9:00.   As soon as the children entered Ms. Tracey's class, they began to engage in literacy activities. They located their name and photograph on the attendance chart and turned the picture face up to indicate their attendance. Children who were buying lunch signed their names under their choices on the lunch chart. The children then focused their attention on the daily jobs chart, on which Ms. Tracey changed the children's names every day after school. Those with morning jobs quickly got busy. Damien watered the plants while Angel fed the rabbit. Patty and Ashley worked together to write the date on the calendar and complete the days of the week charts. Kelly was responsible for completing the weather graph and asked Dalton to help her. Stephanie and James were the reporters whose job it was to write one or two sentences of daily news, such as what was going to happen during the school day.

The children who were not assigned morning jobs were given a choice of three activities in which they could engage: journal writing, independent or buddy reading, or solving the daily word problem. Angelica chose to write about her upcoming sleepover. Darren finished his journal entry and began reading a book about winter, which was the content-area theme being studied. As they solved the day's theme-based word problem, David and Joel chorused, "Yes!" At 8:55, Ms. Tracey clapped a rhythm that indicated to the students they had five minutes to clean up and join her on the rug for their morning meeting.

9:00–9:40.   During the whole-group morning meeting, math and language concepts were integrated in a discussion around the calendar and the weather. The children counted how many days had passed and how many days remained in January. They wrote the date in tallies and represented it in popsicle sticks grouped in tens and ones. Discussion about the calendar was rich with new words learned in the winter thematic unit. The two daily reporters read their news aloud.

Ms. Tracey then began to write a theme-related morning message containing news about an upcoming trip to the ice-skating rink. She modeled conventions of print and good penmanship and punctuated her writing with explanations about how print works. Because she was working on punctuation with her students, she included a question and an exclamatory sentence in her message. As a result, the question mark and the exclamation point and their appropriate use were discussed and explained.

After the message was written and read, Ms. Tracey focused the children's attention to the print by asking them if there was anything in the message they noticed and wanted to point out to the class. The *sh* digraph was a "chunk" they had discussed. David said he noticed the *sh* in "shivers" and circled it in the message. Shanaya noticed the word "ink" in the word "rink." Ms. Tracey took the opportunity to reinforce looking for a little word you know inside of an unknown word as being an excellent strategy to use when reading. She asked the children to see if "rink" was written on their word wall under the "ink" chunk. Shanaya offered to write it on the chart along with an illustration.

Next, two children shared things brought from home with the class. In the biweekly newsletter, Ms. Tracey had explained to the parents that the children were learning about winter. She asked them to help the children choose something related to winter to bring to school and to write three clues about what they chose. The item and the clues were carried to school in a paper bag marked "secret" and "keep out." Each child removed the clues from the bag, being careful not to expose the item. As they read aloud each clue, they called on a classmate to guess the secret item.

Ms. Tracey then read a theme-related piece of children's literature, *The Wild Toboggan Ride* (Reid & Fernandes, 1992), about the last toboggan ride of the day, which becomes a zany adventure for a little boy, his grandpa, and some surprised toboggan riders. She chose this text because of its sequenced plot episodes and repeated language patterns. Before reading the story, she initiated a discussion about riding down a snow-covered hill. The children brainstormed ways to go down a snowy hill as Ms. Tracey listed their ideas. Using the cover illustration, she then explained a toboggan was a type of sled. The word *toboggan* was added to the posted winter words list.

Next, Ms. Tracey used a directed listening and thinking activity format. She set a purpose for reading by asking the children to listen while she read in order to learn who rides on the toboggan and why the ride is "wild." While reading aloud, she encouraged the children to join in by reading the repeated words and phrases.

After the story, the class talked about who rode on the toboggan and how they became involved in the ride down the hill. As the characters in the story were mentioned, Ms. Tracey wrote what the children said about their role in the story onto sentence strips. She then asked the children to read the strips and put them in the order in which they happened. Then she introduced the words *first*, *next*, and *last* as a means to express sequence in a story. She explained that the children would be writing about a time they went sledding or played in the snow. She showed the children a graphic organizer or story map they could use to help them sequence their own stories. The story map followed the model of the sentence strip activity. Copies of the map were placed in the writing center for the children's use when writing their own story response.

9:40–9:50. After engaging in shared reading and writing experiences, Ms. Tracey began what she called her Reading Workshop. She explained and modeled center activities for the children to participate in while she met with small groups for guided reading instruction. The following activities were available to the children during Reading Workshop:

Reading Alone or Buddy Reading. Children selected a book about the theme being studied. After reading alone or with a buddy, they made written recommendations about the book on 5-by-8 cards for others to read.

Writing Center. In the writing center, children wrote their responses to the shared book reading of *The Wild Toboggan Ride*. The graphic organizers that were previously modeled were in the center to help the children sequence their stories. The children collaborated with a partner while writing. They conferenced after completing the organizer to check if their stories were clearly sequenced and if their use of sequencing words was appropriate.

Listening Center. In the listening center, the children listened on headsets to tape-recorded stories. Ms. Tracey had placed several theme-based books of assorted genres in this area. Titles included *The Hat* (Brett, 1997), *Rabbit's Wish for Snow: A Native American Legend* (Tchin, 1997), *When Winter Comes* (Maass, 1993), and *Manatee Winter* (Zoehfeld, 1994). She also had made available two tape recorders for the students to record and listen to their own reading of favorite stories and poems. She found this to be a motivating way for the children to develop fluency and expression. After listening to this reading, they wrote evaluations of their reading.

Word Study. A copy of the winter words list was kept in the word-study area. Today, Ms. Tracey asked the children to choose a word from the list and, using letter tiles, see how many new words they could make from the letters of the selected word. They were to write their new words on a recording sheet. Completed recording sheets were placed in a marked folder. Recording sheets "still in progress" were placed in another folder for later use.

Computer Center. Two computers were used throughout the day. This morning, two children were copying winter poems, which had been learned earlier that week. Ms. Tracey frequently used poems along with children's books in her themed literacy instruction. She found poetry to be a rich context for teaching word chunks, high-frequency words, phonics, and rhyming. She also highly valued the joy of poetry. Many of the children had started their own books called "My Favorite Poems." They often used the computers to write and illustrate the poems they wanted to include in their collections.

Science Center. Ms. Tracey was planning to conduct an experiment with the class later in the day. The children would be timing how long it took different frozen items to melt. She wanted the children to think about, write, and explain their estimations before carrying out the experiment. A recording sheet was provided. Their predictions would be tallied and graphed prior to the experiment and confirmed and discussed after the experiment.

Art Center. Materials for making puppets were available to the children in this area. Ms. Tracey had chosen three winter stories with well-defined, sequenced plot episodes for use during shared reading: *The Wild Toboggan Ride* (Reid & Fernandes, 1992), *Do Like Kyla* (Johnson, 1990), and *The Mitten* (Brett, 1989). The children selected characters from the stories to make as puppets, which could be used in retellings of the stories. The class was going to work on the puppet shows and perform them for the kindergarten classes at the end of their winter unit.

The children were reminded they were required to do two of the activities—read alone or with a buddy and the writing response. They had to spend at least 20 minutes on each. They then could choose which center area they wanted to work in for the remainder of Reading Workshop. Because the science experiment was to be done that afternoon, Ms. Tracey reminded those who had not yet made their predictions to do so.

9:50–11:15.   While the children engaged in the self-directed activities, Ms. Tracey met with small groups of students for guided reading instruction. She had organized her class into five groups of four to five children who had similar reading behaviors, had control of like reading strategies, and were reading on the same level. It was common for the children to move frequently from group to group based on Ms. Tracey's ongoing assessment of the children's progress. She met with each group three or four times a week for 20–30 minutes. After each group, she selected one child to focus on and assessed reading development by taking a running record and listening to a story retelling.

This morning's first guided reading group began with a minilesson about attending to print. Ms. Tracey had observed that these children were attending only to the first letter of an unknown word, rather than gleaning all the information found in the print. She also wanted these children to learn to cross-check printed information by checking to see if the word they used made sense in the sentence. She wrote a sentence on a small whiteboard leaving one word blank. She asked the children to predict what word might make sense in the blank. She then asked them to predict what the word would look like by writing it onto their small writing boards. They then worked together to correctly fill in the missing word of the sentence. After doing three sentences this way, the children discussed with Ms. Tracey how this might help them when they are reading.

Then a new book was introduced to the group. Each child had his or her own copy of the story *The Crazy Quilt* (Avery & McPhail, 1993). Ms. Tracey used a set of leveled books for most of her guided reading instruction. She did, however, use a rubric to level some of her easier to read classroom books about winter. She used the books she leveled for guided reading instruction whenever appropriate. She did a page-by-page "book walk" with the children and discussed necessary background information and vocabulary so the children could read and comprehend the book independently. Following the book walk, she directed the children to begin reading. Because these were beginning readers, they read aloud in quiet voices. Ms. Tracey listened in as they read, guiding children when necessary.

After the children read the story twice, Ms. Tracey praised the use of good reading strategies she had observed in their reading. She particularly reinforced cross-checking behaviors and attending fully to print. The children then composed a sentence that modeled the repetitive pattern of the story. The sentence was cut apart and reassembled word by word. Ms. Tracey then selected two words from the sentence to be cut apart and reassembled, again emphasizing the need to attend to all the graphophonemic information in a word. As the group was dismissed, each child placed the book into his or her book basket to be read later during independent or buddy reading time. Ms. Tracey kept records regarding the children's performance during guided reading group on a clipboard. She wrote brief anecdotal notes during and after the group meeting. She also wrote a note to each parent letting them know what had been accomplished in the guided reading lesson, homework the child had to do, and how they could help. This all went in the child's baggie to take home. Reading Workshop ended at 11:20.

11:20–11:30.   Cleanup, bathroom.

11:30–12:20.   Lunch and recess followed Reading Workshop.

12:20–12:30.   When the children returned from recess, Ms. Tracey read aloud from *Little Polar Bear, Take Me Home!* (deBeer, 1996).

12:30–1:15.   This afternoon's instruction began with Writing Workshop. Ms. Tracey started the workshop with a 10-minute minilesson about the use of capital letters and punctuation. She noticed during her writing conferences with the students that they needed review about when to use capitals. Though most students were using periods and quotation marks regularly, she wanted them to use question marks and exclamation points consistently.

She had written a paragraph from *Little Polar Bear, Take Me Home!* onto an overhead transparency. She omitted capitals and punctuation from the paragraph. As a class, the children discussed where and why capitals and punctuation needed to be inserted as they edited the paragraph. The children were then dismissed to get their writing folder and worked for the remaining 35 minutes. Many chose to write books related to the winter theme.

Because the children worked independently, they were at different stages in their writing. Some were drafting new stories; others were editing or working on final drafts at the computer. Throughout the workshop, Ms. Tracey conferenced with students individually to discuss their progress and to help them plan the next step in their writing process. Because Ms. Tracey's minilessons often focused on how to peer tutor, the children productively and actively engaged with one another.

1:15–2:00.   After Writing Workshop, Ms. Tracey conducted the whole-group science lesson on melting.

2:00–2:45.   The science lesson was followed by a 45-minute Math Workshop.

2:45–3:00.   The day concluded with a 10-minute whole-class meeting in which two students' accomplishments were applauded: Paul and Linda had completed publishing their books that day and would share them with the class tomorrow. Ms. Tracey then gave last-minute reminders about homework and returning permission slips. Children packed their things for dismissal.

▨ Full-Day Program for Preschool (Three- and Four-Year-Olds)

Some preschool children cannot sit very long for whole-group lessons. During these times provisions need to be made for those unable to participate with the help of the aid in the classroom. As the year progresses there should be a greater expectation for participation in whole groups especially for four-year-olds.

8:00–8:30: Arrival at school and greeting, storage of outdoor clothing. Quiet activities and short circle time to explain new centers and activities for the day.

8:30–9:30: Exploration time with learning centers and special daily activities.

9:30–9:40: Cleanup and hand washing.

9:40–10:10: Whole-group music, movement, and dramatic play.

10:10–10:30: Morning snack.

10:30–11:00: Small-group guided literacy instruction. The rest of the class works at centers on special projects.

11:00–11:30: Center play or outdoor play if weather permits.

11:30–11:40: Cleanup and preparation for lunch.

11:30–12:15: Lunch and outdoor play or other activities to develop large-motor skills.

12:15–12:45: Shared storybook reading, creative storytelling, repeated story readings, role-playing, shared book readings, use of big books.

12:45–1:45: Rest time with music.

1:45–2:20: Play at centers.

2:20–2:45: Circle time. Summary of the day's activities, planning for the next day, sharing items brought from home that are related to a theme being studied, songs, story.

2:45–3:55: Cleanup and preparation for dismissal.

Full-Day Program for Kindergarten

(It should be noted that full-day schedules allow for larger blocks of time and more time for learning through exploration and manipulation of materials.)

8:30–9:00: Arrival at school, storage of outdoor clothing. Quiet activities.

9:00–9:30: Whole-group morning meeting, opening exercises, morning message, discussion of unit topic, songs and musical movement activity related to the unit topic, daily news, planning for the school day.

9:30–9:50: Whole-class lesson, either in language arts or mathematics, varying from day to day, with an assignment to complete that flows into the next period.

9:50–10:15: Small-group guided reading instruction. The rest of the class completes work from the whole-class lesson or works on individual contracts from small groups or at centers designated for use during this quiet period (literacy center, math, social studies, science).

10:15–10:45: Free play. All centers open, including dramatic play, blocks, and woodworking. Special art or food-preparation projects are set up in the art center once each week for small groups independent of the teacher.

10:45–11:00: Cleanup and snack.

11:00–11:30: Shared storybook reading, creative storytelling, repeated story readings, role-playing, shared book readings, use of big books.

11:30–12:15: Literacy center time. Children use materials in the literacy center (library corner, writing area, oral language area, language arts manipulatives), including Very Own Words.

12:15–1:15: Lunch and outdoor play, if time and weather permit. Otherwise, large-motor activities in the gymnasium.

1:15–1:45: Whole-group lesson in science or social studies incorporating language arts, music, or art.

1:45–2:15: Center time (literacy, mathematics, science, social studies). Special projects can be set up in any of these for small groups to rotate through in a given week. The teacher meets with small groups for instruction in math or literacy skills.

2:15–2:50: Whole-group circle time. Summary of the day's activities, planning for the next day, sharing of items brought from home that are related to study units, performance of work created by children, songs, and adult story reading.

2:50–3:00: Preparation for dismissal. Dismissal.

Half-Day Program for Preschool (Three- and Four-Year-Olds)

Some preschool children cannot sit very long for whole-group lessons. During these times provisions need to be made for those unable to participate with the help of the aid in the classroom. As the year progresses there should be a greater expectation for participation in whole groups, especially for four-year-olds.

8:00–8:30: Arrival at school and greeting, storage of outdoor clothing. Quiet activities and short circle time to explain new centers and activities for the day.

8:30–9:30: Exploration time with learning centers and special daily activities.

9:30–9:40: Cleanup and hand washing.

9:40–10:00: Whole-group music, movement, and dramatic play.

10:00–10:20: Snack.

10:20–10:50: Small-group guided literacy lessons. The rest of the class works at literacy centers or on special projects.

10:50–11:40: Free play or outdoor play.

11:40–12:00: Whole-group storybook reading using various strategies including shared book experiences, role-playing, creative storytelling. Summary of the day.

Half-Day Program for Kindergarten

8:30–8:50: Arrival at school, storage of outdoor clothing. Quiet activities.

8:50–9:20: Whole-group morning meeting, opening exercises, morning message, discussion of unit topic, songs or musical movement activities related to unit topic, daily news, planning for the school day.

9:20–9:40: Whole-class lesson in language arts, mathematics, social studies, or science, varying from day to day, with an assignment to complete that flows into the next period.

9:40–10:00: Small-group guided reading lessons. The rest of the class completes work from the whole-class lesson; children work on individual contracts in small groups or at designated centers (literacy, social studies, science, or mathematics).

10:00–10:35: Center time. All centers open, including art, music, blocks, dramatic play, literacy, science, and social studies. Special projects may be set up at different centers, such as art or science. Children work alone or in small groups independent of the teacher.

10:35–10:50: Cleanup and snack.

10:50–11:10: Literacy center time. Children use materials from the literacy center (library corner, oral language area, writing area).

11:10–11:30: Outdoor play, if weather permits, or large-motor games in the gymnasium.

11:30–12:00: Whole-group storybook reading with various strategies, including shared book experiences, role-playing, creative storytelling. Summary of the school day. Dismissal.

■ Child-Care Centers

FULL-DAY PROGRAM FOR INFANTS AND TODDLERS

6:45–7:45: Arrival, caring for infants' needs (diapering, feeding). When involved in these routine activities, caregivers talk to babies, sing nursery rhymes, recite poems, reinforce babies' responses.

Activity period consisting of play (in small groups or one-to-one) with blocks, manipulative toys, books, or paper and crayons. Teacher and aides provide language models by identifying materials and talking about their use and provide positive reinforcement for such literacy activities as attempting oral language, looking at books, and using crayons on sheets of paper.

7:45–8:30: Breakfast for toddlers, accompanied by song or poetry. (Infants are fed whenever necessary.)

8:30–9:00: Free play.

9:00–9:15: Cleanup. Washing, diapering, caring for babies' needs. Adults interact with children verbally through conversation, song, or rhymes.

9:15–9:30: Morning snack.

9:30–10:30: Exploration time at learning centers. This time may include a brief whole-group lesson.

10:30–11:00: Outside play.

11:00–11:45: Lunch. Conversation involves the taste, smell, and texture of the food.

11:45–12:00: Bathroom, wash up. Babies are readied for nap time with washing and diapering.

12:00–12:15: Storybook reading.

12:15–2:15: Nap time/quiet time. Naps are begun with a song and carried through with quiet background music.

2:15–2:30: As children wake, their needs are taken care of again, and a small snack is provided.

2:30–3:40: Indoor and outdoor play. In either setting, adults work with small groups, reading stories, encouraging responses from children, pointing out print.

3:40–4:00: Teacher attempts a group session involving singing a song or reading a book aloud. The last 10 minutes of the day are spent preparing the children to leave—toileting, diapering, and general care.

As noted in the introduction to this chapter, child-care centers need to emulate as much as possible homes with rich literacy environments if they are to ensure the natural development of literacy in infants and toddlers.

Activities and Questions

1. Answer the focus questions at the beginning of the chapter.

2. Plan a school day with a balanced perspective in literacy instruction. Select a grade level of your choice from pre-K to third grade.
   a. Prepare the environment to provide rich literacy materials and to accommodate the thematic unit studied.
   b. Prepare a letter to send home to parents concerning the activities happening in class and inviting them to participate. Chapter 10 dealing with the family has a sample letter.
   c. Include guided reading instruction and independent center activities during guided reading.

3. Observe an early childhood classroom to evaluate the literacy environment. Use the "Checklist: Evaluating and Improving the Literacy Environment" provided in this chapter.

4. Review the sample materials you have collected in the assessment portfolio you began for a child at the beginning of the year. Write a summary concerning the child's literacy development at this time and the progress he or she has made in the months you have been collecting the materials; include suggestions you have for his or her program of instruction.

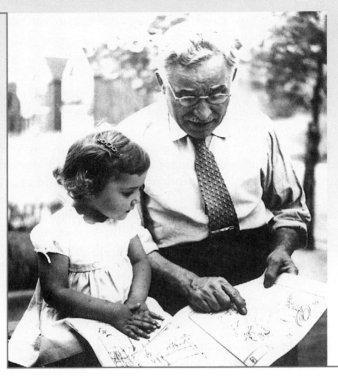

Family Literacy Partnerships

Home and School Working Together

You may have tangible wealth untold:
Caskets of jewels and coffers of gold.
Richer than I you can never be—
I had a Mother who read to me.

—Strickland Gillian "The Reading Mother"
from *Best Loved Poems of the American People*

Focus Questions

- Write descriptions of family involvement and intergenerational family literacy programs.
- List and discuss factors described throughout the chapter that help promote quality family literacy environments in the home.
- What reading and writing materials should be present in a home, and where should they be placed to help promote children's literacy development?
- What reading and writing activities can families involve their children in to help promote literacy development?
- Define the term "family literacy."
- What are some concerns surrounding family literacy intervention programs with diverse, multicultural populations?
- What elements make for a successful family literacy program?
- What activities are successful in getting families involved in literacy activities with their child at home and in school?

Mrs. Feller spread the newspaper on the floor as her two grandchildren (Adasha, 6, and Jonnelle, 4), started to put down the paint jars, water can, brushes, and paper to paint. She always used newspaper to protect the floor when the girls did something messy. As she spread the paper, she said, "Now let's see what section of the newspaper we have out on the floor today." "Oh look," said Adasha, "It's the sports section. Some team won that baseball game 7 points to 0." "That's right," said Mrs. Feller, "the Mets beat the Dodgers 7 to 0." Mrs. Feller always had the girls look at the contents of the newspaper on the floor. The children often would continue to investigate the newspaper and almost forget their clay or paint. Sometimes they would paint about what they had just read. Mrs. Feller was taking advantage of the print in her environment that was a familiar part of the children's lives and was making it a pleasurable experience that would enrich their literacy knowledge.

Roxana, a student in one of my graduate courses, said:

When I was young I don't remember being read to. What I do remember is storytelling. I remember listening to personal stories told over and over by my parents, grandparents, and relatives that had to do with funny, sad, but all real-life happenings about the family. Everyone took a part in telling the stories, adding parts they felt were missing. This was a special and favorite family tradition that took place every Sunday after church as we sat around the table having lunch in my grandmother's kitchen. I remember looking forward to it. The stories were often the same, but I wanted to hear them again and again.

Theory and Research on Family Literacy

The term "family literacy" is a complex concept. Here are some descriptions of family literacy based on several sources (Morrow, Paratore, & Tracey, 1994; Bus, van Ijzendoorn, & Pellegrini, 1995; Melzi, Paratore, & Krol-Sinclair, 2000; Donahue et al., 2001):

1. Family literacy encompasses the ways families, children, and extended family members use literacy at home and in their community.

2. Family literacy occurs naturally during the routines of daily living and helps adults and children "get things done."

3. Examples of family literacy might include using drawings or writing to share ideas, composing notes or letters to communicate messages, keeping records, making lists, following written directions, or sharing stories and ideas through conversation, reading, and writing.

4. Family literacy may be initiated purposefully by a family member, or it may occur spontaneously as families and children go about the business of their daily lives.

5. Family literacy activities also may reflect the ethnic, racial, or cultural heritage of the families involved.

6. Family literacy activities may be initiated outside the home in institutions such as school or the public library. These activities are often intended to support the acquisition and development of schoollike literacy behaviors of children and families.

7. Family literacy activities by outside institutions may include family storybook reading, completing homework assignments, or writing essays and reports.

Family Literacy: Why Is It Important?

Family members who care for children are children's first teachers. They are also children's teachers for the longest time. Beginning at birth, children's experiences affect their success in becoming literate. The success of the school literacy program frequently depends on the literacy environment at home. Studies carried out in homes have been a major catalyst for new early literacy strategies. Because some children come to school already reading and writing, apparently without formal instruction, investigators began to study the characteristics of those children and of their homes.

This line of investigation has been extremely helpful from two points of view. First, the findings reveal home practices that could be successful in school settings. Second, they provide information on the crucial role a family plays in the development of children's literacy and on how they can help. The school can disseminate this information to their parents. Additionally, the school must involve families as an integral part of their literacy programs.

I can attest to the vital role of the home in the development of early literacy. From the day of our daughter Stephanie's birth, my husband and I read to her. I read to her daily while she sat on my lap, always in the same chair. We looked at books. I talked about the pictures and read the stories. By five months, Stephanie would listen as we read to her. We chose mostly cardboard picture storybooks with only a few words on each page. From time to time, her eyes focused intently on the brightly colored pictures. First she would be serious; next she would smile broadly. Sometimes she reached out to touch the book. Occasionally she made pleasant sounds that seemed attempts to imitate my reading voice. Because the experience was daily and positive, she became familiar with story readings and welcomed them.

As Stephanie grew older, her responses to the readings increased. Before she could talk, she pointed to pictures and made sounds as if naming objects or characters. As she acquired oral vocabulary, she labeled things in the book as I read. Naturally I responded with pleasure, reinforcing her attention and understanding of the concepts. Often I explained things beyond the words in the book. Both of us looked forward to these times we shared. They were relaxing, warm, and pleasurable.

By the time she was 14 months old, Stephanie often could be found sitting on the floor reading a book—that is, reading as a 14-month-old child can. She knew how to hold the book right side up, she knew which was the beginning of the book and which was the end, and she knew how to turn the pages. She looked at the pictures and chanted in tones similar to the sound of my reading. Except for a few words, little of her language was understandable, but from a distance one might think that she was reading. Actually she was—not in the conventional manner, but by demonstrating early literacy behavior.

Books were all around the house. Stephanie had an accessible shelf of books in her room. We kept a crate of books with her toys on the floor of a closet, and she was free to use them at all times. There were books in the kitchen, the bathroom, and play areas. My husband and I had many books of our own, and we read a lot, both professional literature and recreational materials such as novels, magazines, and newspapers. Stephanie saw her parents reading frequently, and at times she joined us with her own books.

In addition to books, Stephanie had access to pencils, crayons, markers, and large supplies of different kinds of paper. At the age of two and a half, it was natural for her to pick up a pencil and a sheet of paper, sit down and draw a picture, and even write about it. I could not identify what Stephanie had drawn, but she would talk about it. She was well aware of the difference between drawing and writing, and the squiggles of "print" looked different from the scribbles of her drawing. Although not yet capable of either drawing or writing in the conventional sense, she attempted to do both and differentiated between them.

In the house and on trips to the supermarket or post office, environmental print surrounded her as it does other children. Cognizant of its importance in early literacy development, I pointed out STOP signs at street corners and asked her to read as many signs as she could as we drove along. At home we read cereal boxes, directions for assembling new toys, letters that came in the mail, and e-mail. As a result, her awareness of the print around her and of its functions was heightened. She naturally learned to ask what labels said and looked to print for information.

When she was three and four, our story readings became more interactive. Stephanie asked questions and commented about pictures and episodes. I responded with answers and comments that expanded the discussion. She began to narrate familiar stories with me as I read. Occasionally she asked what certain words were as her attention focused more and more on print as well as on pictures.

One day, Stephanie was sitting in the back seat of the car on the way home from our weekly trip to the library. She was looking through one of the books she had selected and began reading it out loud. It was a humorous story called *Ten Apples Up on Top* (LeSieg, 1961). The book used a limited number of words, repetitive vocabulary, and rhyme. The attractive illustrations reflected the text. As she read, I first assumed that the book was one we had read together. Suddenly I realized it was not. I pulled to the side of the road and with great excitement confirmed what I thought was true. Stephanie was reading, actually reading on her own! She had made the transition from part-reading, part-narrating stories to reading each word.

Stephanie had reached this point in her literacy development gradually. I had offered some informal instruction, but not a great deal. Because of her constant exposure to books and print from birth, she had developed a large sight vocabulary and a number of reading skills. Her ability to read did not just happen. Rather, it developed within an environment that fostered literacy through the guidance, modeling, and encouragement of supportive adults.

Strategies That Promote Literacy Development in the Home

The information that follows on the next few pages comes from the parent involvement framework, suggesting an American mainstream approach to family literacy. The constructs are appropriate in homes in which schoollike literacy activities are a comfortable and natural part of the environment. It assumes that the family members have the literacy and language ability to share the experiences discussed; however, they would be appropriate if used in the native language of any family. After this initial presentation, which sets the groundwork for some basic ideas and strategies, a broader perspective will be discussed to take into consideration families who have limited literacy ability, speak a different language, and may not be comfortable with typical schoollike literacy activities.

Various researchers have studied homes in which children read and write early without direct instruction (Morrow, 1983; Neuman, 1997; Teale, 1984). The results have consistently established that certain characteristics are common to these homes. Early readers have family members who read to them and readily help them with writing and reading. These family members read a variety of material, including novels, magazines, newspapers, and work-related information. They own or borrow books, both for themselves and for their children. Reading and writing materials can be found throughout their homes. Family members in these homes often take their children to libraries and bookstores (Morrow, 1983; Morrow, 1997; Neuman, 1997). The homes hold ample supplies of books and writing materials, and reading and writing are generally valued as important activities. Books are associated with pleasure, and literary activities are rewarded. The homes are well organized, with scheduled daily activities, rules, and designated responsibilities for family members. They provide a setting where interactions between adults and children are socially, emotionally, and intellectually conducive to literacy interest and growth (Anderson et al., 1985).

The families of early readers and writers tend to be small. Many of the family members have college educations, but it is argued that it is a literacy-rich environment, not the parents' education, occupation, or socioeconomic level, that correlates most highly with children's early literacy ability. Children with an early interest in reading and writing tend to spend playtime at home writing and drawing with paper and crayons or looking at books. Family members in these homes enforce rules for selecting and limiting television viewing. These children are rated by their teachers as higher than average in social and emotional maturity, work habits, and general school achievement (Applebee, Langer, & Mullis, 1988; Morrow, 1983).

Family members frequently ask teachers what they can do at home to help their children learn to read and write. When families provide a rich literacy environment at home, teaching reading and writing becomes easier for both the teacher and the child at school. Because most children do not enter public school before age five and formal preschool before age three, if at all, teachers need to take responsibility for disseminating information in the community that families can implement at home. From this discussion it appears that three elements affect the quality of the literacy environment in the home: (1) interpersonal interactions or the literacy experiences shared by children, family members, and other individuals in the home; (2) the physical environment or literacy materials in the home; (3) the emotional and motivational climate or the attitudes of literacy and family aspirations for literacy achievement (Leichter, 1984). The information that follows includes mainstream strategies and

The interactive behavior between parent and child during storybook reading involves negotiating, mediating, and constructing meaning related to the print.

Books should be available for babies in their cribs and playpens; waterproof books are available for bathtubs.

assumes that families have the literacy ability and language ability to implement the suggestions offered.

Materials to Read in the Home

Researchers have found that books were readily accessible to children who read early (Applebee, Langer, & Mullis, 1988; Hannon, 1995). Family members can provide library corners for their children, preferably in their bedrooms. Books can be placed in a cardboard box or plastic crate to serve as a bookshelf. In addition, books can be made available all around the house. Kitchens and bathrooms are important, because children spend considerable time in both places. If there is a playroom or a place for toy storage, it should contain books. Every room can hold books that are visible and accessible. Before babies are crawling or walking, books can be brought to them in cribs and playpens; waterproof books are available for bathtubs.

A variety of books should be selected for the home. For babies up to 18 months, brightly colored concept books with cardboard, plastic, or cloth pages are appropriate. They must be safe, with rounded edges, and sturdy enough to withstand chewing and other rough treatment. As the child becomes a toddler, preschooler, and kindergartener, nursery rhymes, fairy tales, folktales, realistic literature, informational books, picture books, alphabet books, number books, poetry, books related to favorite television programs, and easy-to-read books (those with limited vocabularies, large print, and pictures closely associated with the text) should be made available. Children's magazines offer attractive print material for children and are a special treat if they come in the mail. In addition to children's literature, print material for adults, including books, magazines, newspapers, and work-related material, should be obvious in the home.

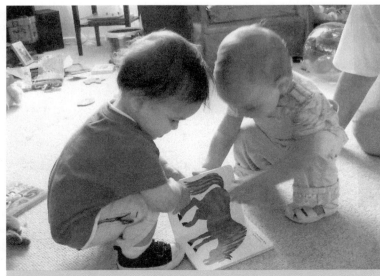

For babies up to 18 months, brightly colored books with cardboard, plastic, or cloth pages are appropriate.

Reading as a Home Activity

Research indicates that children who are read to regularly by parents, siblings, or other individuals in the home, and who have family members who are habitual readers themselves, become early readers and show a natural interest in books (Teale, 1984; Bus, van Ijzendoorn, & Pellegrini, 1995). That is not surprising. Through frequent story readings, children become familiar with book language and realize the function of written language. Story readings are almost always pleasurable, and the pleasure that is experienced builds a desire for and interest in reading (Cullinan, 1992; Huck, 1992). Continued exposure to books develops children's vocabularies and sense of story structure, both of which help them learn to read.

It is clear that verbal interaction between adult and child during story readings has a major influence on literacy development (Cochran-Smith, 1984; Ninio, 1980). Such interaction offers a direct channel of information for the child and thus enhances literacy development (Heath, 1982; Morrow, 1987a). It leads children to respond to story readings with questions and comments. These responses become more complex over time and demonstrate more sophisticated thinking about printed material. Research on home storybook readings has identified a number of interactive behaviors that affect the quality of read-aloud activities. Those behaviors include questioning, scaffolding (modeling dialogue and responses), praising, offering information, directing discussion, sharing personal reactions, and relating concepts to life experiences (Edwards,1995; Roser & Martinez, 1985; Taylor & Strickland, 1986).

The following transcription from the beginning of a story reading between a mother and her four-year-old son Ian illustrates how the adult invites and scaffolds responses, answers questions, offers positive reinforcement, and responds supportively to the child's questions and comments. As a result of the prompts, information, and support, Ian pursues his questions and receives additional information.

Mother: Are you ready for our story today, Ian? This is a new book. I've never read it to you before. It's about a mother and her baby bird.

Ian: (points to the title on the front cover) Hey, what's this for?

Mother: That's called a title. It says *"Are You My Mother?"* That's the name of the book. See, it's right here, too: *"Are You My Mother?"*

Ian: (long pause, then points to the words) *"Are You My Mother?"*

Mother: Right, you read it. See, you know how to read.

Ian: It says, *"Are You My Mother?"* (points again with finger)

Mother: You read it again. Wow, you really know how to read!

Ian: Um, now read the book and I'll read it, too. (Morrow, 1986)

Ian's mother read the story. Each time they came to the words *Are You My Mother?*, she paused and looked at Ian, pointed to the words, and exaggerated her reading of the sentence. After two such episodes, Ian no longer needed prompting and simply read along each time they came to the phrase.

Research findings suggest that teachers should encourage family members to read to their children daily. Reading can begin the day a child is born. However, an infant's ability to listen attentively is generally limited and varies from one reading to the next. An infant may prefer to chew on the book or pound it

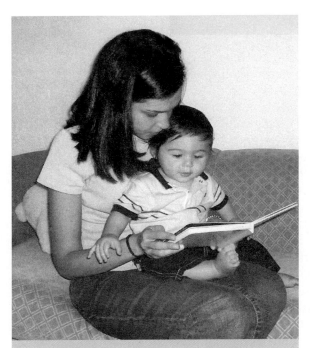

Babies who are read to often take a leadership role in turning pages, babble in tones that sound like reading, and show strong involvement in shared reading experiences.

rather than listen to it. However, babies read to from birth begin to be attentive in story-reading situations sooner than others not read to.

One of my graduate students shared this story in his class journal about his first literacy experience with his new baby. She was born during the semester he was taking a course with me.

Our First Literacy Experience by John T. Shea

When my wife and I packed for the trip to the hospital on the night before her scheduled caesarean procedure, one of the items that I included in my travel bag was my childhood copy of The Real Mother Goose, *a book my mother had given back to me when she learned that she was going to be a grandmother. My first literacy experience with Casey came much sooner than I had expected.*

After she was born, Casey was taken to the nursery and placed under a heat device designed to help her body adjust to the change in temperature she experienced at birth. There were some chairs set up next to the heat devices for new fathers. As I sat beside my daughter and marvelled at her beauty, it suddenly occurred to me that I wanted to read to her at that very moment. I asked the nurse if I could take a book into the nursery to read to my child. The nurse smiled and said, "You're the first father in my 20 years as a maternity nurse to make such a request. I guess it's okay."

I was with Casey for the first hours of her life in the nursery, sitting by her side, listening to her breathe, and reading selections from The Real Mother Goose *to her. Prior to my reading she had been moving and crying, on and off. When I started reading she became very quiet and hardly stirred.*

Reading to Children at Home from Birth to Eight

From *birth to three months*, a child's attention to book reading is erratic. The baby who stares at the pictures and seems content and quiet can be considered receptive. If the baby wiggles, shows discomfort, or cries, the adult might just as well stop reading until the next time.

From *three to six months*, babies become more obviously involved in book readings. They begin to focus on pictures and to listen. Often, they will grab for a book, pound it, and try to put it in their mouths. As long as they seem content, they are probably involved with the reading.

Six- to nine-month-olds can be purposefully involved in story readings. They might try to turn pages. They might respond to changes in the reader's intonation or make sounds and movements to demonstrate involvement and pleasure. They sometimes begin to show preferences for books that have been read to them before.

Fathers, mothers, siblings, grandparents, and great-grandparents should read together with young children.

One-year-old babies will show strong involvement in being read to. They might take a leadership role in turning pages, or babble along in tones that sound like reading. They actively look in the book for familiar things that they remember from other readings.

By *15 months*, babies who have been read to can tell which is the front and which is the back of a book, and if the book is right side up. They begin to identify and name characters in the book. They read along with the adult, verbalizing a great deal (Burns, Griffin & Snow, 1999).

Fathers, mothers, grandparents, babysitters, and older siblings should all read to younger children. Let reading become a ritual, done at the same time and in the same place each day. Bedtime is a favorite time, and bedtime stories are a good reading habit to establish. Both child and family members look forward to it as a time to share at the end of the day. Reading before children go to sleep has a calming effect; it establishes a routine for the children, who will eventually read by themselves before going to bed.

Spontaneous readings are encouraged as well, and if a family member finds it easier to read at different times of the day, it is certainly more desirable to do this than not to read at all. Reading to babies requires that the infant be held in the family member's arms. When the youngster is able to sit up alone, family members and child should be close to each other, preferably with the child on the adult's lap. The book with its pictures and print must be visible to the child. Children should be considered active participants in the story reading. Their comments and questions should be encouraged and acknowledged. Family members should relate comments about the story to life experiences whenever possible and question children about familiar things in a relaxed manner to encourage their involvement.

Reading to children does not end when they begin to read themselves. This is a crucial time to continue to support and guide them in this activity. When children are able to read, the bedtime story tradition can change to the child's reading to the family member. Or it can continue with the families reading books above the reading level of the child. *Six- to eight-year-olds* are often interested in books with chapters but are not yet ready to read them themselves.

Family members can take this opportunity to share more grown-up pieces of literature with these youngsters to encourage their interest. Another important parent motivation is making sure that children have new material to read that is always accessible and of interest to them. Keep track of what your youngster has read. Sometimes we must continually put new books right in their hands even as they grow older and seem to have the reading habit established. As soon as we stop our interest in their reading, their reading interest could wane.

In addition to reading to their children and reading themselves, families should make a point of providing time for the family to read together. Sitting together around the kitchen table or in the living room, each member of the family reading his or her own book, makes for a pleasant, rich literacy activity. Talking about what family members are reading is an important experience as well.

Materials for Writing in the Home

Some researchers have suggested that writing develops before reading. Many children invent writing systems of their own that seem to have meaning for them. Whether reading comes before writing or writing before reading is an unsettled issue. What is known, however, is that learning to read is enhanced by concurrent experiences with writing and that the development of writing is facilitated by experiences with reading (McGee & Richgels, 2000).

One implication of these findings is that writing materials should be made available for children at home. A variety of sizes of unlined white paper is preferable, especially for babies. As children become preschoolers, smaller sheets can be added to the household supply. A child approaching kindergarten might like lined paper as well. Pencils, crayons, colored pencils, a chalkboard and chalk, and white slates and markers are appropriate home writing tools. Manipulatives such as magnetic, felt, or wooden letters are also useful. Children should be exposed to them early and have free access to them. In addition, home computers encourage writing and are appropriate for preschoolers. (A list of computer software for young children can be found in Appendix C.)

As with book reading, youngsters need to see their families involved in writing activities. Family members should communicate with their children through writing as often as possible. When children begin preschool, notes can be placed in lunch boxes that say simply, "Hi! Love, Mommy and Daddy." Notes on pillows can say "Good night" or "Good morning."

Make writing a family event whenever possible. Families can write thank-you notes and letters together. They can fill out school forms with children or make up the family grocery list together. Children will emulate family members who take opportunities to communicate through writing.

Responsive Adults Encourage Literacy

The family members of early readers answer their children's questions about books and print, offer information, provide experiences that enhance literacy development, and praise children for participating in literacy behaviors. Such channels of information and support systems in the home naturally encourage the development of reading. Durkin (1966) found that families who attempted to teach children more formally were not as successful as family members who simply responded to children's requests for information about reading.

Responsiveness between family members and child needs to begin early and be cultivated. Language provides a primary opportunity for developing this behavior. Responsive adults not only answer questions; they also initiate activities that promote literacy. While dressing, diapering, or feeding an infant, for instance, a family member should talk to the child, sing, recite nursery rhymes, and tell stories. The baby responds by smiling, cooing, and moving, thus encouraging the family member to continue, and a cycle of mutual responsiveness develops.

Environmental print surrounds children and holds meaning for them. This natural source of reading material provides literacy experiences with items familiar to children (Neuman & Roskos, 1993, 1997). Children begin to read and ask about environmental print probably before they are interested in the print found in books. Families that are aware of the importance of environmental print can point out familiar labels and other information on cereal boxes, vitamin bottles, detergent containers, and food packages. Children are naturally interested in telephone books, cookbooks, television guides, advertisements, and mail. They are particularly interested in personal letters, fliers, greeting cards, bills, catalogs, and magazines. The outside world presents a wealth of environmental print: road signs, street signs, and the names of fast-food restaurants, gas stations, and other well-known chains. Families note the environmental print that is meaningful to children and encourage children to do the same, pointing out specific letters in these familiar words and even sounding the letters. This game-like involvement in skills has been found to promote early literacy.

In addition to responding to requests about books and print, family members of early readers generally respond to the need to provide varied experiences for their children. They take them to libraries and bookstores. They talk to them a great deal, a habit which builds the children's vocabulary. Trips to zoos, fire stations, airports, and parks all foster literacy growth if they are accompanied by oral language and positive social interactions. It should be emphasized that a trip not only broadens a child's experience but also allows verbal interactions between a family member and child before, during, and after. Those interactions include providing the child with background information about the place to be visited and the things to be seen, answering questions about the experience, offering information, reading stories related to the experience, and discussing the trip afterward so that new ideas are absorbed. Suggesting that the child record the experience by drawing a picture about it and dictating a story for the family member to write will further expand literacy growth.

Television is part of our lives. To make the most of TV viewing, family members should watch some programs with their youngsters, posing questions, raising critical issues, and changing passive viewing into responsive interaction. They should also choose programs for

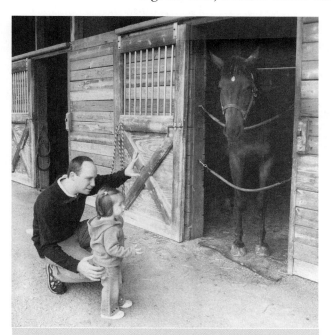

Trips to the zoos, fire stations, airports, and parks foster literacy growth if accompanied by oral language and positive social interaction.

which parallel books are available, such as "Sesame Street" and "Reading Rainbow." When specific stories are scheduled on television, such as *How the Grinch Stole Christmas* (Seuss, 1957a), family members can borrow the book from the library or purchase it.

In a series of informal interviews with family members whose children were early readers, it became apparent that literacy was embedded in daily activities that were meaningful, functional, and part of the mainstream of their lives. Various print materials were visible in the homes. Language was used interactively and frequently, in all its forms and in a positive emotional climate. There was praise for literacy activity and pleasure and joy in reading and writing. When asked what they believed helped their children become literate so early, the parents found it difficult to answer because they had not viewed the experiences they offered their children as attempts to promote reading and writing. Most of these activities had other functions, such as keeping the house running smoothly. Many of the experiences had social objectives—to promote positive interpersonal relationships and to teach responsibility and manners, for example. Here are some ideas related by these parents:

> *I started a baby book for each of my children from the day they were born, with information about their weight and height, and I included pictures. I reported major events, such as first words, first steps, and events of interest to me. I looked at the book frequently, and my toddler would snuggle beside me showing great interest. I've continued the books, and as the children are getting older they add to them and read them over and over. They are without a doubt among their favorite books.*
>
> —*Stephanie Bushell*

> *As a grandfather I don't get to see my grandchildren as frequently as I would like. In order to keep close contact, I often send them things through the mail. I'll enclose games cut from the children's section of the newspaper, which I'll ask them to complete. I send them pictures of famous people and ask them to call and tell me who they think they are, as well as questions to respond to me about.*
>
> —*Milton Mandel*

> *From the time they were very young, my children were required to write thank-you notes for gifts received. At first they dictated them and I wrote down what they said. Later they were able to write simply "thank you." One good incentive for the task was to allow them to choose their own stationery for note writing.*
>
> —*Lynn Cohen*

> *The public library has provided many fine experiences for my children. One in particular is to help prepare them for experiences to come and allow them to relive experiences they have. Before we went to the circus, we took a circus story out of the library in preparation for our trip. After seeing the circus we enjoyed another circus story from the library. Going to the public library for books is such a good habit to get into.*
>
> —*Bonnie Hayes*

> *I started leaving notes for my children in surprise places before they could read. Somehow they managed to find out what the notes said, even at the pre-reading stage. Now I put messages in their lunch boxes. The notes often*

just say "hello." Sometimes I'll write a riddle or a joke, and sometimes the note may require an answer. This has become a family tradition, and lately I find surprise notes addressed to me left in the most unusual places.

—Diane Tracey

The amount of TV viewing by our three- and four-year-old children was a source of aggravation to us. To make the experience more meaningful, we read the television program guide to decide on what programs to watch and to limit the number of selections in one day. We try to watch some programs with them and ask who, what, when, *and* where *questions to elicit recall of facts. We also ask* why *questions to encourage more interpretive responses.*

—Darren Clark

I've always kept a journal recording my daily experiences. My four-year-old found me writing in it one day and asked about what I was doing. She wanted to do the same thing, so we started a joint journal. I'd write things that happened to me during the day, and she'd tell me what to write for her. Soon she was able to do her own writing. Sometimes I'd ask her questions about what she'd written. I did this by writing in the journal.

—Michael Friedland

Researchers have found that home environments possessing the characteristics described here will generally instill in children an interest in reading and writing, a desire to read and write, and the ability to read and write early. However, there are children from homes that display all characteristics described who are not early readers and writers and have difficulty learning to read and write. There are also early readers and writers from environments lacking the characteristics described. Obviously there are factors other than the environment that affect successful literacy development. But it has been demonstrated that environmental factors play a strong role in fostering literacy. A rich literacy environment at home gives children a better chance to learn to read and write easily and to enjoy reading and writing as well.

Family Involvement in Your Literacy Program: What Teachers Can Do

When I speak about parents in this section I am referring to any adult or older sibling who can be involved with the child at home. Teachers need to view parents as partners in the development of literacy. Every teacher has the responsibility to inform families about what is happening in school on a regular basis and how they can help their child. Teachers need to involve family members in school activities during the day, and provide activities for family members to do at home. Family members need to feel that they are welcome in school. Families should be partners with the school in the education of their child. They should be given the opportunity to offer input about what they would like their child to learn, to express how they feel about what happens in school, and to offer suggestions for change. Following are some suggestions about ways to make families an integral part of the school. Be concerned about sending home materials in the languages represented in the classroom.

1. At the beginning of the school year, send home the goals to be achieved for the grade level you teach for literacy development, in a format that can be understood by all.

2. With each new unit of instruction or concept being taught in literacy, send a newsletter to let family members know what you are studying and what they can do to help.

3. Invite family members to school for informational workshops, family meetings about curriculum decisions, conferences, and school programs.

4. Invite families to help with literacy activities in the classroom such as reading to children, helping with bookbinding, taking written dictation of stories, and supervising independent activities while teachers work with small groups and individual children.

5. Send home activities for parents and children to do together and require feedback about working together. Include activities such as writing in journals together, reading together, visiting the library, recording print in the environment they see, writing notes to each other, cooking together and following recipes, putting toys or household items together that require following directions, and watching and talking about programs on television. Participating in homework assignments is extremely important.

6. Invite families to school to share special skills they have, to talk about their cultural heritage, and so on.

7. Send home notes when a child is doing well. Don't wait to send notes just for problems.

8. Provide lists of literature for family members to share with their children. Appendix A provides suggested books.

9. Family members should be invited to school to participate with their children in literacy activities. During center time, for example, parents can read and write with their children, see what the literacy environment is like at school, and become a more integral part of the child's literacy development.

10. Have family member and child meetings when they come to school to work together on projects.

11. Include family members in helping to assess their child's progress. Provide forms for them to fill out about their child's literacy activities and things they do with their child at home. Have them contribute information about their child's progress at parent conferences. Two forms that can be used for this process are "Guidelines: Promoting Early Literacy at Home" and "Checklist: Observing My Child's Literacy Growth."

The school needs to get information to homes about the need for rich literacy environments even before children enter school. Information can be disseminated at a special meeting for expectant parents, in hospital maternity wards, in obstetricians' and pediatricians' offices, and through churches, synagogues, and community agencies. A succinct handout such as "Guidelines: Promoting Early Literacy at Home" will be a helpful start and should be printed in languages found in the community in which you live. It is provided here in Spanish and English. (Booklets and pamphlets on the development of literacy at home can be found on page 357.)

Guidelines *Promoting Early Literacy at Home*

Your child's ability to read and write depends a lot on the things you do at home from the time he or she is born. The following list suggests materials, activities, and attitudes that are important in helping your child learn to read and write. Check off the things you already do. Try to do something on the list that you have not done before.

Materials

☐ 1. Have a space at home for books and magazines for your child.

☐ 2. If you can, subscribe to a magazine for your child.

☐ 3. Place some of your child's and some of your books, magazines, and newspapers in different parts of your home.

☐ 4. Provide materials that will encourage children to tell or create their own stories, such as puppets, dolls, and story tapes.

☐ 5. Provide materials for writing, such as crayons, markers, pencils, and paper in different sizes.

Activities

☐ 1. Read or look at books, magazines, or the newspaper with your child. Talk about what you looked at or read.

☐ 2. Visit the library and take out books and magazines to read at home.

☐ 3. Tell stories together about books, about your family, and about things that you do.

☐ 4. Look at and talk about written material you have such as catalogs, advertisements, work-related materials, and mail.

☐ 5. Provide a model for your child by reading and writing at a time when your child can see you.

☐ 6. Point to print outside, such as road signs and names of stores.

☐ 7. Write with your child and talk about what you write.

☐ 8. Point out print in your home such as words on food boxes or recipes, directions on medicine, or instructions on things that require assembly.

☐ 9. Visit the post office, supermarket, and zoo. Talk about what you saw and read. When you get home, draw and write about it.

☐ 10. Use print to talk to your child. Leave notes for each other. Make lists to do things, such as food lists, lists of errands, and lists for holiday shopping.

Foster Positive Attitudes toward Reading and Writing

☐ 1. Reward your child's attempts at reading and writing, even if they are not perfect, by offering praise. Say kind words like:

  "What nice work you do." "I'm happy to see you are reading." "I'm happy to see you are writing. Can I help you?"

☐ 2. Answer your child's questions about reading and writing.

☐ 3. Be sure that reading and writing are enjoyable experiences.

☐ 4. Display your child's work in your home.

☐ 5. Visit school when your child asks. Volunteer to help at school, attend programs in which your child is participating, attend parent conferences, and attend parent meetings. This lets your child know you care about him or her and school.

(continued on next page)

Guidelines *(continued from previous page)*

Visit School and Speak to Your Child's Teacher
☐ 1. if you want to volunteer help in any way.
☐ 2. if you want to visit your child's class during school hours.
☐ 3. if you have concerns about your child's reading and writing.
☐ 4. if you feel your child has problems with vision, hearing, or other things.
☐ 5. if you need help because the language you speak at home is not English.
☐ 6. if you need help with reading and writing yourself.
☐ 7. if you would like to know more about how you can help your child at home.
☐ 8. if you want to know more about what your child is learning at school.

Guía *Fomentar en el hogar el desarrollo temprano de la capacidad de leer y de escribir*

La capacidad de su jovencito de leer y de escribir depende mucho de las cosas que hacen en casa desde el momento de su nacimiento. Usted puede hacer muchas cosas que no ocuparán mucho de su tiempo. La lista siguiente sugiere materiales, actividades, y actitudes que son importantes en ayudar a su hijo(a) a aprender, a leer y a escribir. Ponga una marca al lado de la sugerencia que usted ya practica en su casa. Procure hacer algo de la lista que no ha hecho antes.

Materiales
☐ 1. Prepare un lugar en su casa para poner libros y revistas para su hijo(a).
☐ 2. Si es posible, subscríbase a una revista para su hijo(a).
☐ 3. Coloque algunos de los libros de su hijo(a) y algunos de los suyos, incluyendo revistas y periódicos, en diferentes lugares en su casa.
☐ 4. Provea materiales, tales como títeres, muñecos, y cuentos grabados, que animarán a los niños a contar o a crear sus propios cuentos.
☐ 5. Provea materiales para escribir, tales como creyones, marcadores, lápices, y papel de various tamaños.

Actividades
☐ 1. Junto con su hijo(a), lean u hojeen libros, revistas o el periódico. Hablen sobre lo que hayan hojeado o leído.
☐ 2. Visiten la biblioteca y saquen algunos libros y algunas revistas para leer en casa.
☐ 3. Juntos, cuenten cuentos sobre libros, sobre su familia, y sobre las cosas que hacen.
☐ 4. Hojeen y hablen sobre el material escrito que tengan en su casa, tal como catálogos, anuncios, material relacionado con su trabajo, correo.

☐ 5. Sea un modelo para su hijo(a) leyendo y escribiendo en los momentos cuando él o ella le pueda observar.

☐ 6. Llame a la atención de su hijo(a) cosas impresas afuera, tales como letreros en la carretera y nombres de tiendas.

☐ 7. Escriba con su hijo(a) y hablen sobre lo que hayan escrito.

☐ 8. Indique palabras impresas en su casa, tales como las que están en cajas de comida, en recetas, en las instrucciones para medicinas, o en objetos que hay que armar.

☐ 9. Visiten la oficina de correos, el supermercado, el jardín zoológico. Hablen sobre lo que hayan visto y leído. Cuando regresen a su casa, hagan dibujos y escriban sobre estas experiencias.

☐ 10. Use la escritura para hablar con su hijo(a). Déjense notas el uno para el otro, hagan listas de cosas que hacer, tales como listas de comida para la compra, listas de tareas que hacer, listas de cosas que comprar para los días de fiesta.

Fomente actitudes positivas hacia la lectura y la escritura

☐ 1. Recompense con elogios los intentos de su hijo(a) por leer o escribir, aun cuando sus esfuerzos no sean perfectos. Use palabras bondadosas, tales como:

> "¡Qué trabajo más bueno haces! Estoy muy contento(a) de ver que estás leyendo. Estoy muy contento(a) de ver que estás escribiendo. ¿Te puedo ayudar en algo?"

☐ 2. Responda a las preguntas de su hijo(a) sobre la lectura y la escritura.

☐ 3. Procure que el leer y el escribir sean experiencias agradables.

☐ 4. Exhiban el trabajo de sus hijos en la casa.

☐ 5. Visite la escuela cuando su hijo(a) se lo pida. Ofrezca su ayuda en la escuela, asista a los programas en los cuales su hijo(a) esté participando, asista a las conferencias y reuniones de padres. Esto permite que su hijo(a) se dé cuenta de que usted se interesa por él o por ella y por la escuela.

Visite la escuela y hable con el maestro o la maestra de su hijo(a)

☐ 1. . . . si usted quiere ayudar de alguna manera.

☐ 2. . . . si usted quiere visitar la clase de su hijo(a) durante las horas cuando la escuela está en sesión.

☐ 3. . . . si usted tiene dudas acerca del desarrollo do la lectura y la escritura en su hijo(a).

☐ 4. . . . si usted cree que su hijo(a) tiene problemas especiales con su visión, con su oído, o con cualquier otra cosa.

☐ 5. . . . si usted necesita ayuda porque el idioma que habla en casa no es el inglés.

☐ 6. . . . si usted necesita ayuda con sus propias habilidades de lectura y de escritura.

☐ 7. . . . si a usted le gustaría saber más sobre cómo puede ayudar a su hijo(a) en el hogar.

☐ 8. . . . si a usted le gustaría saber más y comprender mejor lo que su hijo(a) está aprendiendo en la escuela.

✓ Checklist *Observing My Child's Literacy Growth*

Child's name _____ Date _____

	Always	Sometimes	Never	Comments
1. My child asks to be read to.				
2. My child will read or look at a book alone.				
3. My child understands what is read to him/her, or what he/she reads to himself/herself.				
4. My child handles a book properly, knows how to turn pages, and knows that print is read from left to right.				
5. My child will pretend to read or read to me.				
6. My child participates in the reading of a story, with rhymes and repeated phrases.				
7. My child will write with me.				
8. My child will write alone.				
9. My child will talk about what he/she has written.				
10. My child reads print in the environment such as signs, and labels.				
11. My child likes school.				

Comments about Your Child:

Multicultural Perspectives Concerning Family Involvement and Family Literacy

In this chapter, family literacy has been approached from the perspective of family members helping children to support their reading and writing development on their own or as a result of involvement in literacy activities at school. In the United States, many families do not speak English and therefore are not able to help their children in the ways that schools may suggest. In addition, there are many families who have limited literacy ability and although eager to help cannot do so in the mainstream approach. In some cases the parent is a teenager who has dropped out of school. Therefore, when we speak of family literacy, in many situations we need to recognize that it must be an intergenerational matter in which environments are created to enable adult learners to enhance their own literacy, and at the same time promote the literacy of their children. However, there is evidence that many low-income, minority, and immigrant families cultivate rich contexts for literacy development. Their efforts are different from the school model we are accustomed to. We must learn

Teachers should invite parents to school to share their cultural heritage. A father reads the Spanish version of *The Three Little Pigs* to his son's kindergarten class.

from and respect families and children from cultures in which books are not readily available although evidence of literacy activity, such as storytelling, exists (Morrow, 1995).

Research shows that the types and forms of literacy practiced in some homes are different from those that children encounter in school (Auerbach, 1989; Heath, 1993; Paratore, Melzi, & Krol-Sinclair, 2003; Taylor & Dorsey-Gaines, 1988). Although literacy activity is present in one form or another in most families, the particular kinds of events that some family members or caregivers share with children may have a great deal of influence on school success. Conversely, the kinds of literacy practiced in classrooms may not be meaningful for some children outside school. As mentioned, low-income, minority, and immigrant families cultivate rich contexts for literacy development and support family literacy with exceptional effort and imagination (Auerbach, 1989). Family literacy must be approached to avoid cultural bias, and intervention must be supportive rather than intrusive.

Family Literacy: What Has Been Done?

Studying the Ways Literacy Is Used by Families

Researchers are interested in advancing understanding of the ways in which literacy is used within families. In these studies, emphasis is placed on the richness of one's heritage and experiences rather than on perceived educational deficits. In some cases, researchers are exploring literacy events that occur naturally

Family literacy must avoid cultural bias, and intervention must be supportive rather than intrusive.

within diverse families. In other cases, researchers are describing the effects family literacy has on children's developing concepts about literacy. With the knowledge gained from such studies, educators can better understand the literacies that exist in diverse families and can help make literacy instruction in school more meaningful for both family members and children.

Delgado-Gaitan (1992) carried out a study to determine the attitudes of Mexican American families toward the education of their children and the roles played by these families. A major goal was to observe and describe the physical surroundings, emotional and motivational climates, and interpersonal interactions between parent and child.

Results of the study demonstrated that the Mexican American parents provided special areas for study for their children, in spite of space limitations. The parents wanted their children to succeed in school. Parents sought the help of friends, relatives, and others to assist them or their children with school-related matters. Parents punished their children for poor grades and rewarded them for doing well. Parents' attempts to help children with homework sometimes were fruitless, because they could not understand the directions and often misled their children. All parents believed that a person cannot be considered well educated through "book learning" alone but also must learn to be respectful, well mannered, and helpful to others. Family stories about life in Mexico guided the children's moral learning.

From the findings about these families, it seems that schools need to respond to Latinos' concerns that children learn good manners and respect in the curriculum. The schools need to be aware of and help with language problems that families encounter when they want to help their children. They also need to incorporate oral history and storytelling into the curriculum because it is an important aspect of the Latino culture familiar to both parents and children (Paratore et al., 1995).

Family Involvement Initiatives

Family involvement initiatives include programs that are designed to involve and inform families about activities that will promote their children's literacy learning in school. Such programs involve families as agents in supporting their child's literacy development and may originate from school, the library, or other community agencies. Often they are collaborative efforts among these agencies. A basic premise of parent involvement programs is to enlist the help of families to increase reading achievement of their children.

Running Start (RS) is an example of a family involvement initiative. This school-based project created by Reading Is Fundamental (RIF) is designed to get books into the hands of first-grade children and to encourage and support family literacy. The goals of RS are (1) to increase first graders' motivation to read so they eagerly turn to books for both pleasure and information, (2) to involve families in their children's literacy development, and (3) to support schools and teachers in their efforts to help children become successful readers. Participating classroom teachers are provided with funds to select and purchase high-quality fiction and informational books for their classroom libraries. Children are challenged to read (or have someone read to them) 21 books during the 10-week program. A Reading Rally is held to involve the community in supporting literacy development, and families are encouraged to support their child in meeting the 21-book challenge by sharing books and stories with their children in a variety of ways. When a child meets the 21-book goal, he or she gets to select a book for his or her own personal library. Studies have demonstrated that first graders' reading motivation as well as family members' literacy activities in the home significantly increased in families that participated in the program (Gambrell et al., 1995).

A family involvement program can be teacher initiatiated, such as having family members read to the class regularly, help supervise independent center time, or keep family and child journals at home.

Intergenerational Literacy Initiatives

Intergenerational literacy initiatives are specifically designed to improve the literacy development of both adults and children. These programs view family members and children as colearners, and are generally characterized by planned and systematic instruction for both adults and children. Instruction may occur when family members and children work in either collaborative or parallel settings. The instruction for adults is intended to improve their literacy skills while teaching them how to work with their children to aid their development.

Parents and Children Together is a nationwide intergenerational family literacy program established by the National Center for Family Literacy (NCFL) in Louisville, Kentucky. Parents who lack a high school diploma and their three- and four-year-old children attend school together three to five days a week. An early childhood program is provided for the children, while the parents attend an adult education program to learn reading, math, and parenting skills.

In the adult education portion of the program, parents work on improving their reading and math skills, and are taught to set goals and collaborate with other parents in the program. "Parent Time" is a component of the program during which the adults discuss a variety of topics ranging from discipline to self-esteem. The last component of the program is "Parent and Child Together" time. During this hour, families play together. The activities are led by the children. Parents find they can learn both with and from their children (National Center for Family Literacy, 1993).

What Makes a Family Involvement Literacy Program Successful?

 Because no two communities are the same, family literacy programs need to be tailored to the needs of the individuals they serve. Here are some tested guidelines to follow that will help programs be successful.

Objectives for Family Literacy Programs

- Respect and understand the diversity of the families you serve.
- Build on literacy behaviors already present in families. Although they may be different from conventional schoollike literacy, most families use literacy in the routine of their daily lives. These behaviors should be identified, acknowledged, respected, preserved, and used in family literacy programs.
- Be aware of the home languages used within the community so that materials can be translated and understood.
- Family literacy programs should not take a "fix the family" attitude. Rather, they should view intervention as a supplement to the interactions that already exist.
- Hold meetings at varied times of the day and days of the week to accommodate all schedules (see Figures 10.1 and 10.2).
- Hold meetings in accessible locations that are friendly and nonthreatening. Transportation needs to be provided if no public transportation is available, or if family members do not have a way of getting to meetings. Provide child care at meetings.
- Provide food and refreshments at meetings.
- Follow sound educational practices appropriate for literacy development of children and adults. Use varied strategies for literacy learning. Include writing together, reading together, and sharing materials that are fun and interesting for all.
- You may work with family members alone and with parents and children together. There should be sharing times when parents and children work together.
- Programs can provide support groups for family members to talk about helping their children and to find out what they want to know.
- Family literacy programs seek not only to help with literacy development but to improve interactions between parents and children.
- Programs should provide family members with ideas and materials to use at home.
- Good programs provide easy-to-carry-out functional literacy activities that families consider useful such as talking and reading about child-rearing concerns, community life problems, housing, and applying for jobs and keeping them.
- Programs should include the opportunity for family members' participation in school activities during school hours.
- Portions of school and home programs should parallel each other. Activities done in school should be the same as those sent home for family members to do with children. When this occurs family members can participate in their children's learning.

Models for family literacy programs must be developed in which family literacy activities are intended to promote parent/child interaction in a wide range of

Figure 10.1

Invitation for Family Participation in English

FAMILY MEMBERS WANTED
To Visit Your Child's Class

Dear Family Members,

Please come to school and be a part of our reading and writing time. On the form below list the types of things you can do when you visit. There is a space for you to let us know the time of day and dates that you can attend. We are flexible and will arrange our time when it is convenient for you. All family members are welcome—brothers and sisters, babies, grandparents, and of course parents. Please come and get involved in your child's education, and help us form a true home and school partnership.

Sincerely,

Mrs. Abere's second-grade class

- -

Please fill out the following form and send it back to school with your child:

Your name _____

Your child's name _____

The days I can come during the week are _____

The time of day I can come to school is _____

When I come to school I would like to do the following:

☐ 1. Watch what the children are doing.

☐ 2. Participate with the children.

☐ 3. Read to a small group of children.

☐ 4. Read to the whole class.

☐ 5. I am from another country and I would like to tell the children about my country and show them clothing, pictures, and books from there.

☐ 6. I have a hobby and would like to share it with the class.
My hobby is: _____

☐ 7. I have a talent and would like to share it with the class.
My talent is: _____

☐ 8. I'd like to tell the children about my job.
My job is: _____

☐ 9. Other ideas you would like to do: _____

☐ 10. Give children who need it some extra help.

☐ 11. I'd like some help in deciding what to do.

☐ 12. I would like to come on a regular basis to help.
I can come at the following times: _____

Figure 10.2

*Invitation for
Family
Participation in
Spanish*

SE BUSCAN MIEMBROS DE FAMILIA
Para Visitar la Clase de su Niño

Ayudenos Aprender–

Comparta sus Talentos y Envuélvase con Nuestra Clase:

Observe la clase y su niño

Cuente historias

Hable de su cultura

Lea libros

Comparta su pasatiempo favorito

Traiga su bebé o animal mimado

Explique su trabajo

Cocine o traiga dulces para la clase

Venga a cantarle a los niños

Comparta con nuestras actividades de "Highlights"

Por favor ponga los días, o día, que pueda venir a la clase:

Mes: _____ Dia(s): _____ Horas: _____

_____

- -

Devuelva este papel a la maestra de su niño.

Nombre: _____.

Visitaré la clase en esta fecha _____ y a esta hora _____.

Me gustaría compartir: _____.

literacy events. Programs must view participating families from the perspective of the richness of their experiences and heritage, rather than from the perspective of their deficits and dilemmas. Home school programs need to be easy to use. Materials sent home should be introduced to children in school first. The content should be nonthreatening and culturally diverse, and the activities need to be fun. For example, a school district I worked with used *Highlights for Children* magazine (Honesdale, PA) as the home–school connection material. Teachers featured articles in the magazine at school, and each child had a school copy. Another copy was sent home with activities for family members and children to do together that were similar to what was being done in school. The program was successful because children knew what to do with the materials. In addition, the magazine provided the following features that should be present in any home–school connection material: (1) multiple options for families to select activities from, (2) a nonthreatening format that is not schoollike, (3) activities appropriate for many age levels and abilities, (4) culturally diverse content, (5) some activities that do not require the ability to read, and (6) activities that are fun and therefore engage families and children in literacy together (Morrow, Scoblionko, & Shafer, 1995; Morrow & Young, 1997).

Educators are recognizing that the family is the key to successful literacy development for both children and their families. Policymakers from a wide range of agencies need to collaborate and form partnerships in their efforts to create and support effective family literacy programs. Literacy programs in school will be more successful if they have home support; therefore, family literacy programs are crucial.

Appendix A provides a bibliography of children's literature about families for teachers and families to share with children. The books are representative of diverse cultural backgrounds. Each book illustrates some special relationship between family and extended family members. It could be parents, grandparents, an aunt or uncle, sisters or brothers, or a person who becomes like family although he or she is not actually related.

Learning More about Family Literacy

Agencies, associations, and organizations that deal with family literacy can be contacted for further information on ways to establish, administer, and evaluate family literacy programs. A few are listed here as a starting place.

The Barbara Bush Foundation for Family Literacy, 1112 16th Street, NW, Suite 340, Washington, DC 20036, www.barbarabushfoundation.com

Even Start Compensatory Education Programs, U.S. Department of Education, 400 Maryland Avenue, SW, Washington, DC 20202, www.evenstart.org

International Reading Association, 800 Barksdale Road, PO Box 8139, Newark, DE 19714-8139, www.reading.org

National Center for Family Literacy, Waterfront Plaza, Suite 200, 325 West Main Street, Louisville, KY 40202-4251, www.famlit.org

Reading Is Fundamental (RIF), 600 Maryland Avenue, SW, Suite 600, Washington, DC 20024, www.rif.org

Resources for Families

Beginning Literacy and Your Child: A Guide to Helping Your Baby or Preschooler Become a Reader

I Can Read and Write! How to Encourage Your School-Aged Child's Literacy Development

Explore the Playground of Books: Tips for Parents of Beginning Readers *

Get Ready to Read! Tips for Parents of Young Children *

Summer Reading Adventure! Tips for Parents of Young Readers *

Library Safari: Tips for Parents of Young Readers and Explorers *

Making the Most of Television: Tips for Parents of Young Viewers *

See the World on the Internet: Tips for Parents of Young Readers—and Surfers *
   (Booklets and brochures available from the International Reading Association, 800 Barksdale Road, PO Box 8139, Newark, DE 19714.)

---

*Also available in Spanish.

Raising a Reader, Raising a Writer: How Parents Can Help
(Brochure available from the National Association for the Education of Young Children, 1509 16th Street, NW, Washington, DC 20036.)

Choosing a Children's Book
(Brochure available from the Children's Book Council, Inc., 568 Broadway, Suite 404, New York, NY 10012.)

Lipson, E. R. (2000). *New York Times Parent's Guide to the Best Books for Children*. New York: Crown Publishing Group.

Stillman, P. R. (1989). *Families Writing* (2nd ed.). Portland, ME: Calendar Islands Publishers.

Thomas, A., Fazio, L., & Steifelmeyer, B. L. (1999). *Families at School: A Handbook for Parents*. Newark, DE: International Reading Association.

Trealease, J. (2001). *The Read-Aloud Handbook*. New York: Penguin Books.

An idea for the Classroom from the Classroom

■ Thematic Backpacks

For this first-grade activity, you'll need to assemble a theme-based backpack with the following materials: a class journal; 5–7 books that represent a variety of genres and reading levels; a folder with games, poems, songs, and/or experiments related to the theme under study; and other related items such as videos, cassettes, and stuffed animals. The children take the backpack home weekly on a rotating basis. Instruct the children to share the activities and books with their family members. It may be helpful to show a backpack and model some of the activities for families at Back-to-School Night. They may also be put on display at parent-teacher conferences so family members may become acquainted with the materials and procedures.

Under family members' guidance, the children respond to what is asked of them in the class journal that is in the backpack. The questions may include "Which was your favorite book, and why was it your favorite?" Or, to go along with a food theme for example, the children may be asked to share a family recipe. A music theme may include a tape recorder and blank tape to record a favorite song. When the backpack is returned to school, the child shares the journal response with the class. The kids and family members can hardly wait until it is their turn for the next backpack!

Shannon Corcoran, Graduate Student,
Graduate School of Education, Rutgers University

An Idea for the Classroom Suited for Diverse Learners

■ Highlighting Family Involvement at School

Every month in our school several family involvement activities occur. These activities provide opportunities for children to bond with their own families and other families, and to share their diverse cultural backgrounds with their classmates. To emphasize the importance of these activities and others, teachers in all grades began a showcase called "Highlighting Family Involvement." They keep cameras in school so when families participate, the teachers take their pictures for the showcase. The following are the activities at school that help fill the showcase and bring families to the building:

- **Theme Nights:** These are evenings devoted to different topics such as other countries where children and families can learn together. Families share artifacts and then read, write, and do art projects about the theme.
- **Cooking Nights:** Families bring easy favorite recipes to share and make together. The best part is eating the goodies when the cooking is done.
- **Book-Sharing Evenings:** Everyone brings a favorite book and reads or tells about their favorite part. The book can be in another language, and if necessary, a translator is used so everyone can participate.
- **Sharing Family Photos:** On this night we ask everyone to bring family pictures they want to share. We talk and write about them. Each family makes an album with the photos, and we encourage them to continue to fill the album they started at school.

Margaret Youssef, Teacher

Activities and Questions

1. Answer the focus questions posed at the beginning of the chapter.

2. Interview members of your family or friends who are parents. Ask them to relate specific activities they have done with their children to promote literacy with natural events that arose from daily living. Collect ideas from all members of the class and put them together in a newsletter or pamphlet format to distribute to family members of early childhood youngsters.

3. Using the memories of your own home when you were a young child or the home of a friend or family member who is a parent of a young child, observe the physical characteristics and record activities done with children that promote literacy development. Determine elements that could improve the richness of the literacy environment you analyzed.

4. Select a child and his or her family to begin a portfolio of assessment materials to collect throughout the semester. Start a portfolio in a folder for the child that you will keep, and provide a folder for the family. Make a copy of the "Guidelines: Promoting Early Literacy at Home" on pages 347–348 (and pages 348–349 for the Spanish version) for yourself and one for the family you will be working with. Ask a family member to fill out the form for themselves, and a copy for you. Provide the family member with two copies of the form entitled "Checklist: Observing My Child's Literacy Growth" on page 350. Have them fill it out at the beginning of the semester and at the end. Be sure to get a copy for your folder as well.

5. Create a family literacy program for a familiar community. If it is a community in which families have literacy and English skills, you will probably want to develop a family involvement program; if it is in a community where families speak other languages, or have limited literacy ability, you may need to engage in an intergenerational program that involves development of literacy skills for families as well as training them to help their children. Be sure that, whichever program you design, a portion of the home and school activities are similar to each other.

Afterword

We must reignite our romance with the written word.

—Steven Spielberg, 1987

This volume has presented a theory- and research-based program for developing literacy in early childhood. It has emphasized the importance of literacy-rich environments; social interaction; peer collaboration; and whole-class, small-group, and individual learning with explicit instruction and problem-solving experiences. The activities suggested underscore the concurrent, integrated nature of learning how to use oral language, reading, and writing. The volume has outlined education that is functional and related to real-life experiences and is thus meaningful and interesting to the child. It has provided for the integration of literacy activities into content areas through units of study that are based on themes that add enthusiasm, motivation, and meaning. It has suggested careful monitoring of individual growth through direct instruction and frequent assessment using multiple measures and allowing ample space for children to learn through play, manipulation, and exploration. Attending to children with special needs has been a concern throughout the volume.

New information about learning is constantly being generated and subsequently changes the strategies we use to help children learn. Teachers must stay abreast of the constant stream of literature that is available after they complete their formal education. Teachers need to be researchers and reflect upon their own teaching to discover their strengths and weaknesses. When teachers are researchers, they will increase their knowledge and skill. To be a teacher–researcher means to formulate questions about teaching strategies, child development, classroom environment, curriculum develop-

ment, or other relevant topics that will clarify issues or help generate new information. Questions should generate from your daily experiences in the classroom and be of interest to you personally.

When an area of inquiry is decided upon, the teacher should focus on collecting data that will help answer questions posed or clarify issues. Data can be collected in the following ways: Observe and record anecdotes of classroom experiences that are relevant to the question being asked; videotape classroom segments; collect samples of children's daily work over a period of time; interview children, teachers, and parents; administer formal and informal tests; and try new techniques.

As a teacher–researcher, you will always be on the cutting edge of what is current and appropriate. You will always find your teaching interesting because you will be learning about new things on a daily basis. You will enjoy your work more because you have extended your role to include additional professional activities. As a teacher–researcher, you are practicing both the art and science of teaching. The science involves inquiry, reading, observing, and collecting data. The art involves reflecting on findings and making appropriate changes. Teacher–researchers empower themselves to be decision makers and catalysts for making change in their schools. As they study questions for which they have tangible data, they are more likely to be heard when they propose new ideas and change. Rather than having change mandated based on the research by individuals outside your school district or by administrative personnel, take the responsibility for the changes that will occur by researching issues yourself. Each year that you teach, select another area of inquiry to study. When appropriate, collaborate with your colleagues on research projects. Collaboration with adults, as with children, results in projects that you might not have been able to do alone.

What we have learned over the years concerning learning theory and early literacy development is due to research by college professors and classroom teachers. Professional associations hold conferences and publish journals to inform and move the field forward. Appendix E provides a list of such groups and journals, along with other publications dealing with early literacy, for future study and reference. A total professional will be involved in teacher research projects and professional development organizations.

The program described in this volume is meant to be motivating for teachers and children. Motivation allows the teacher to work with vigor and enthusiasm. Motivation allows the child to associate literacy with a school environment that is pleasurable, positive, and designed to help children succeed. One of the most important elements in learning to read and write is a teacher who can encourage children to want to read and write. Wanting to read and write motivates a desire to learn the skills necessary to become proficient in literacy. With the skills develops a lifelong interest in refining and using literacy skills. The program is designed to help us "reignite our romance with the written word" (Spielberg, 1987).

Children's Literature

Revised by Julie Anastasi

BOOKS FOR BABIES

Cardboard Concept Books

Brown, M. (1997). *Say the magic word.* New York: Random House.

DK Board Books. (2002). *Things that go.* New York: DK.

Elgar, R. (1998). *Jack, it's playtime/bathtime/bedtime/Happy Birthday.* New York: Kingfisher.

Lamut, S. (1997). *1 2 Peek a boo.* New York: Grosset & Dunlap.

Tracy, T. (1999). *Show me!* New York: HarperCollins.

What's the weather? (2002). New York: Backpack Books.

Cloth Books

McPartland, S. (2002). *Peekaboo, I love you.* Chicago: Learning Curve International.

Pienkowski, J. (1995). *Friends.* New York: Little Simon.

Tong, W. (1996). *Zoo faces/Farm faces.* Santa Monica, CA: Piggy Toes Press.

Tucker, S. (1994). *Toot toot/Quack quack.* New York: Little Simon.

Tucker, S. (1997). *Yum yum.* New York: Little Simon.

Plastic Books

Aigner-Clark, J. (2003). *Baby Einstein: Water, water everywhere.* New York: Hyperion Books.

Barkan, J. (1998). *Splish! Splash!* New York: Random House.

Crossley, D. (2003). *Bunnies on the farm.* New York: Backpack Books.

London, J. (2001). *Froggy takes a bath.* New York: Grosset & Dunlap.

Man-Kong, M. (1999). *Theodore's splash.* New York: Random House.

Touch and Feel

Boynton, S. (1998). *Dinosaur's binkit.* New York: Little Simon.

Kunhardt, D. (1984). *Pat the Bunny/Cat/Puppy.* New York: Golden Books.

Milne, A. A., & Shepard, E. H. (1998). *Pooh's touch and feel visit.* New York: Dutton Children's Books.

Pledger, M. (2000). *In the ocean.* San Diego: Silver Dolphin Books.

Saltzberg, B. (2000). *Animal kisses.* San Diego: Harcourt.

Watt, F., & Wells, R. (2002). *That's not my dinosaur . . .* Tulsa, OK: EDC Publishing.

CONCEPT BOOKS

Davis, K. (2001). *Soft shapes: On and off.* Norwalk, CT: Innovative KIDS.

DK Board Books. (2002). *Things that go.* New York: DK.

Hoban, T. (1998). *More, fewer, less.* New York: Greenwillow Books.

It's about time. (2002). New York: Backpack Books.

Miller, M. (1998). *Big and little.* New York: Greenwillow Books.

Murphy, C. (1998). *Black cat white cat: A book of opposites.* New York: Little Simon.

ALPHABET BOOKS

Andrae, G. (2003). *K is for kissing a cool kangaroo.* New York: Scholastic.

Diaz, J., & Gerth, M. (2003). *My first jumbo book of letters.* New York: Scholastic.

Fujikawa, G. (2002). *A to Z picture book.* New York: Backpack Books.

Golding, K. (1998). *Alphababies.* New York: DK Publishing.

Kirk, D. (1998). *Miss Spider's ABC.* New York: Scholastic.

Mazollo, J. (2000). *I spy little letters.* New York: Scholastic.

NUMBER BOOKS

Beaton, C. (2000). *One moose, twenty mice.* Cambridge, MA: Barefoot Books.

Ehlert, L. (2001). *Fish eyes: A book you can count on.* San Diego: Harcourt Brace.

Falconer, I. (2002). *Olivia counts.* New York: Atheneum.

Gerth, M. (2000). *Ten little ladybugs.* Santa Monica, CA: Piggy Toes Press.

Strickland, P. (1997). *Ten terrible dinosaurs.* New York: Dutton Children's Books.

NURSERY RHYMES

Douglas, V. (2002). *Mother Goose rhymes*. Boston: McGraw-Hill.

Fujikawa, G. (2002). *Mother Goose*. New York: Backpack Books.

Opie, I. (Ed.) (2002). *The very best of Mother Goose*. Cambridge, MA: Candlewick Press.

Rader, L. (1993). *Mother Hubbard's cupboard: A Mother Goose surprise book*. New York: Tambourine Books.

Scarry, R. (1992). *Richard Scarry's Mother Goose and Rhymes and nursery tales*. New York: Golden Books.

WORDLESS STORYBOOKS

Aliki. (1995). *Tabby: A story in pictures*. New York: HarperCollins.

Banyai, I. (1995). *Zoom*. New York: Viking.

Crossley, D. (2003). *Bunnies on the farm*. New York: Backpack Books.

Jenkins, S. (1995). *Looking down*. Boston, MA: Houghton Mifflin.

Pienkowski, J. (1995). *Animals*. New York: Little Simon.

POETRY BOOKS

Bierhorst, J. (Ed.) (1994). *On the road of stars: Native American night poems and sleep charms*. New York: Macmillan.

Feldman, T. (2003). *First foil haikus: Love*. Los Angeles: Piggy Toes Press.

Florian, D. (2000). *Mammalabilia*. San Diego: Harcourt.

Hoberman, M. (2001). *You read to me, I'll read to you*. New York: Little, Brown.

Kuskin, K. (2003). *Moon, have you met my mother? The collected poems of Karla Kuskin*. New York: HarperCollins.

Prelutsky, J. (Selector). *The 20th century children's poetry treasury*. New York: Random House.

TRADITIONAL LITERATURE (FAIRY TALES, FABLES, MYTHS, AND FOLKTALES)

Charles, V. M. (1993). *The crane girl*. New York: Orchard.

French, V. (1995). *Red hen and sly fox*. New York: Simon & Schuster.

Grimm Brothers. (1995). *The sleeping beauty: A fairy tale. Little Red-cap. Iron Hans, The golden goose*. New York: North-South.

Harrison, M., & Stuart-Clark, C. (Selectors). (1994). *The Oxford treasury of children's stories*. Andover, MA: Oxford.

Pilling, A. (1993). *Realms of gold: Myths and legends from around the world*. New York: Kingfisher.

EASY-TO-READ BOOKS WITH LIMITED VOCABULARY

Capucilli, A. S. (2003). *Biscuit loves school*. New York: HarperFestival.

Demuth, P. (1996). *Johnny Appleseed*. New York: Grosset.

Eastman, P. D. (1960). *Are you my mother?* New York: Random House.

Raschka, C. (1993). *Yo! Yes?* New York: Greenwillow.

St. Pierre, S. (1998). *It's not easy being big!* New York: CTW/Random House.

Yolen, J., & Teague, M. (2003). *How do dinosaurs get well soon?* New York: the Blue Sky Press.

BOOKS ABOUT REALISTIC ISSUES

Buehner, C., & Buehner, M. (1997). *I did it, I'm sorry*. New York: Dial.

Davies, S. (1997). *Why did we have to move here?* Minneapolis: Carolrhoda Books.

Hess, D. (1994). *Wilson sat alone*. New York: Simon & Schuster.

Newman, L. (1998). *Too far away to touch*. New York: Clarion.

Padoan, G. (1987). *Remembering Grandad: Facing up to death*. New York: Child's Play.

Vigna, J. (1995). *My two uncles*. Morton Grove, IL: Albert Whitman.

INFORMATIONAL BOOKS (EXPOSITORY TEXTS LISTED BY GRADE LEVEL)

Pre-K

Cobb, A. (1996). *Wheels*. New York: Random House.

Collard, S. B. (1997). *Animal dads*. New York: Scholastic.

Ellwand, D. (1996). *Emma's elephant and other favorite animal friends*. New York: Dutton.

Hewitt, S. (1999). *The five senses*. Danbury, CT: Children's Press.

Klingel, C., & Noyed, R. B. (2001). *Pumpkins*. Chanhassen, MI: Child's World.

Miller, M. (1991). *Whose shoe?* New York: Greenwillow.

Morris, A. (1998). *Work*. New York: Lothrop, Lee & Shepard.

Parnall, P. (1988). *Feet!* New York: Simon & Schuster.

Siddals, M. M. (1997). *Tell me a season*. Boston: Houghton Mifflin.

Grades K–1

Barton, B. (1989). *Dinosaurs, dinosaurs*. New York: HarperCollins.

Cuyler, M. (2001). *Stop, drop, and roll*. New York: Simon & Schuster.

Dussling, J. (1996). *Stars*. New York: Grosset & Dunlap.

Fowler, A. (1998). *Let's visit some islands*. New York: Scholastic Library.

Glaser, L. (1992). *Wonderful worms*. Riverside, NJ: Millbrook Press.

Hewitt, S. (2000). *Nature for fun projects*. Riverside, NJ: Millbrook Press.

Hoban, T. (1983). *I read signs*. New York: Morrow, William.

Hurd, E. T. (1990). *Starfish*. New York: HarperCollins.

Johnson, S. (1995). *Alphabet city*. New York: Penguin Group.

Katzen, M., & Henderson, A. (1994). *Pretend soup and other real recipes: A cookbook for preschoolers and up.* Berkeley, CA: Ten Speed Press.

Klingel, C., & Noyed, R. B. (2001). *Pigs.* Chanhassen, MI: Child's World.

Lewin, T., & Lewin, B. (2000). *Elephant quest.* New York: HarperCollins.

Lundell, M. (1995). *A girl named Helen Keller.* New York: Scholastic.

Montanari, D. (2001). *Children around the world.* Tonawanda, NY: Kids Can Press.

Morris, A. (1990). *On the go.* New York: William Morrow.

Parks, R., & Haskins, J. (1997). *I am Rosa Parks.* New York: Penguin Putnam Books.

Reid, M. (1996). *Let's find out about ice cream.* New York: Scholastic.

Rockwell, A. (2001). *Bugs are insects.* New York: HarperCollins.

Royston, A. (1991). *Diggers and dump trucks.* New York: Simon & Schuster.

Selsam, M. E. (1995). *How to be a nature detective.* New York: HarperCollins.

Taylor, B. (1998). *A day at the farm.* New York: DK.

Walsh, M. (1997). *Do monkey's tweet?* Boston: Houghton Mifflin.

Grades 1–2

Armentrout, P. (1997). *The wedge.* Vero Beach, FL: Rourke Press.

Bancroft, H., & Van Gelder, R. G. (1997). *Animals in winter.* New York: HarperCollins.

Brown, C. (1995). *Tractor.* New York: Greenwillow.

Cherry, L. (1992). *A river ran wild.* Orlando, FL: Harcourt, Brace.

Demuth, P. (1996). *Johnny Appleseed.* New York: Grosset & Dunlap.

Gibbons, G. (1995). *Sea turtles.* New York: Scholastic.

London, J. (2001). *Crocodile: Disappearing dragon.* Cambridge, MA: Candlewick Press.

Maestro, B., & Maestron, G. (2000). *Struggle for a continent: The French and Indian wars.* New York: HarperCollins.

Robinson, F. (1995). *Recycle that!* Danbury, CT: Children's Press.

Schaefer, L. (2001). *Who works here? Fast-food restaurant.* Chicago: Heinemann.

Showers, P. (1992). *Look at your eyes.* New York: HarperCollins.

Simon, S. (1997). *The brain: Our nervous system.* New York: Scholastic.

Yolen, J., & Stemple, H. (2001). *The wolf girls.* New York: Simon & Schuster.

Grades 2–3

Angelou, M. (1996). *Kofi and his magic.* New York: Clarkson Potter.

Atwell, D. (1999). *River.* Boston: Houghton Mifflin.

Branley, F. M. (1998). *Day light, night light.* New York: HarperCollins.

Darling, K. (1996). *Rain forest babies.* New York: Walker.

Demuth, P. (1997). *Achoo!* New York: Grosset & Dunlap.

Gibbons, G. (1998). *Marshes and swamps.* New York: Holiday House.

Hickman, P. (2001). *Animals eating: How animals chomp, chew, slurp, and swallow.* Tonawanda, NY: Kids Can Press.

Hodge, D. (1997). *Whales, killer whales, blue whales and more.* Tonawanda, NY: Kids Can Press.

Kramer, S. (1997). *Wagon train.* New York: Grosset & Dunlap.

Markle, S. (2001). *Rats and mice.* New York: Atheneum Books for Young Readers.

Penner, L. R. (1995). *Sitting Bull.* New York: Grosset & Dunlap.

Rabe, T. (1999). *On beyond bugs! All about insects.* New York: Random House.

Ripley, C. (1997). *Why does popcorn pop? And other kitchen questions.* Toronto: Firefly Books.

Senisi, E. (2001). *Berry smudges and leaf prints.* New York: Dutton Children's Books.

Wallace, K. (1999). *Duckling days.* New York: DK Publishing.

Woelfein, L. (1995). *Metamorphosis.* New York: Penguin Books.

Informational Text Series

All Aboard Books. New York: Grosset & Dunlap.
Eyewitness Junior Series. New York: Alfred A. Knopf.
Let's-Read-and-Find-Out Books. New York: HarperCollins.

BIOGRAPHY

Anderson, W. (2003). *River boy: The story of Mark Twain.* New York: HarperCollins.

Demi. (2001). *Gandhi.* New York: Simon & Schuster.

Heslewood, J. (1993). *Introducing Picasso.* New York: Little, Brown.

Greenfield, E. (1995). *Rosa Parks.* New York: Harper Trophy.

Schanzer, R. (2003). *How Ben Franklin stole the lightning.* New York: HarperCollins.

Walker, A. (2002). *Langston Hughes: American poet.* New York: HarperCollins.

Biography Series Books

Creative Minds. Minneapolis: Carolrhoda.
Meet the Author Series. Katonah, NY: Richard C. Owen.
Picture Book Biographies. New York: Holiday House.
Step-Up Biographies. New York: Random House.

MAGAZINES FOR CHILDREN

Chickadee. Young Naturalist Foundation, 17th and M Streets, NW, Washington, DC 20036 (ages 4–8).

Cricket. Open Court Publishing Co., Box 100, La Salle, IL 61301 (ages 6–12).

The Dinosaur Times. CSK Publications/B&W Publications, 500 S. Buena Vista Street, Suite 101, Burbank, CA 91521-6018 (all ages).

Highlights for Children. 803 Church Street, Honesdale, PA 18431 (ages 2–12).

Your Big Backyard. National Wildlife Federation, 1412 16th Street, NW, Washington, DC 20036 (ages 1–4).

PREDICTABLE BOOKS

Repetitive Phrases

Cameron, A. (1994). *The cat sat on the mat.* Boston: Houghton Mifflin.

Chapman, C. (1994). *Snow on snow on snow.* New York: Dial.

Fox, M. (1993). *Time for bed.* New York: Harcourt Brace.

Sendak, M. (1962). *Chicken soup with rice.* New York: Harper & Row.

Wilson, K., & Rankin, J. (2003). *A frog in the bog.* New York: Margaret K. McElderry Books.

Rhyme

Ashman, L. (2002). *Can you make a piggy giggle?* New York: Dutton Children's Books.

Fleming, D. (2001). *Pumpkin eye.* New York: Scholastic.

Kuskin, K. (1995). *James and the rain.* New York: Simon & Schuster.

McMillan, B. (1995). *Puffins climb, penguins rhyme.* New York: Harcourt Brace.

Newcome, Z. (2002). *Head, shoulders, knees and toes and other action rhymes.* Cambridge, MA: Candlewick Press.

Familiar Sequences (days of the week, numbers, letters, months of the year, etc.)

Carle, E. (1969). *The very hungry caterpillar.* New York: Philomel.

Carlstrom, N. W. (1996). *Jesse Bear, what will you wear?* New York: Aladdin.

Carlstrom, N. W. (1999). *How do you say it today, Jesse Bear?* New York: Macmillan.

Updike, J. (1999). *A child's calendar.* New York: Holiday House.

Van Allsburg, C. (1987). *The Z was zapped.* Boston: Houghton Mifflin.

Cumulative Patterns (as the story progresses, the previous line is repeated)

Carle, E. (1994). *The very lonely firefly.* New York: Philomel.

Kharms, D. (translated by J. Gambrell). (1993). *The story of a boy named Will, who went sledding down the hill.* New York: North-South.

Tompert, A. (1993). *Just a little bit.* Boston: Houghton Mifflin.

Wilson, K., & Rankin, J. (2003). *A frog in the bog.* New York: Margaret K. McElderry Books.

Wood, A. (1994). *The napping house wakes up.* New York: Harcourt Brace.

Stories with Conversation

Cooper, H. (1997). *The boy who wouldn't go to bed.* New York: Dial.

Johnson, P. B. (1999). *The pig who ran a red light.* New York: Orchard.

Modarressi, M. (1998). *Monster stew.* New York: Dorling Kindersley.

Polacco, P. (1998). *Thank you, Mr. Falker.* New York: Philomel.

Woodson, J. (2001). *The other side.* New York: G. P. Putnam's Sons.

Books That Foster Critical Discussions

Cannon, J. (1993). *Stellaluna.* Orlando, FL: Harcourt Brace.

Curtis, J. L. (1996). *Tell me again about the night I was born.* New York: HarperCollins.

Martin, J. B. (1998). *Snowflake butterfly.* Boston: Houghton Mifflin.

Pumphrey, J., & Pumphrey, J. (2003). *Creepy things are scaring me.* New York: HarperCollins.

Winn, C. M., with D. Walsh. (1996). *Clover's secret.* Minneapolis: Fairview Press.

BOOKS FOR ENHANCING LISTENING AND DISCRIMINATION OF SOUNDS

Clements, A. (1997). *Double trouble in Walla Walla.* New York: Scholastic.

Conrad, P. (1995). *Animal lingo.* New York: HarperCollins.

Krull, K. (2003). *M is for music.* San Diego: Harcourt.

Kushkin, K. (1994). *City noise.* New York: HarperCollins.

Wojtowycz, D. (2001). *Can you moo?* New York: Scholastic.

FAVORITE WELL-KNOWN PICTURE STORYBOOKS

The following books represent a careful selection of some distinguished authors and excellent children's literature not to be missed.

Barrett, J. (1970). *Animals should definitely not wear clothing.* New York: Atheneum.

Bemelmans, L. (1939). *Madeline.* New York: Viking.

Berenstain, S., & Berenstain, J. (1966). *The bear's picnic.* New York: Random House.

Brown, M. W. (1957). *Goodnight moon.* New York: Harper & Row.

Carle, E. (1969). *The very hungry caterpillar.* New York: Philomel.

dePaola, T. (1975). *Stregna Nona: An old tale.* Englewood Cliffs, NJ: Prentice Hall.

Eastman, P. D. (1960). *Are you my mother?* New York: Random House.

Flack, M. (1932). *Ask Mr. Bear.* New York: Macmillan.

Galdone, P. (1975). *The little red hen.* New York: Scholastic.

Hoban, R. (1969). *Best friends for Frances.* New York: Harper & Row.

Hughes, S. (1979). *Up and up.* New York: Lothrop, Lee & Shepard.

Hutchins, P. (1978). *Don't forget the bacon.* New York: Puffin Books.

Johnson, C. (1955). *Harold and the purple crayon*. New York: Harper.

Keats, E. J. (1962). *The snowy day*. New York: Viking.

Kellogg, S. (1971). *Can I keep him?* New York: Dial.

Kraus, R. (1971). *Leo the late bloomer*. New York: Windmill.

Lionni, L. (1973). *Swimmy*. New York: Random House.

Lobel, A. (1972). *Frog and toad together*. New York: Harper & Row.

Mayer, M. (1974). *One monster after another*. Racine, WI: Western.

McCloskey, R. (1948). *Blueberries for Sal*. New York: Penguin.

Piper, W. (1954). *The little engine that could*. New York: Platt & Munk.

Potter, B. (1902). *The tale of Peter Rabbit*. New York: Scholastic.

Rey, H. A. (1952). *Curious George rides a bike*. Boston: Houghton Mifflin.

Sendak, M. (1963). *Where the wild things are*. New York: Harper & Row.

Seuss, Dr. (1940). *Horton hatches the egg*. New York: Random House.

Shaw, C. (1947). *It looked like spilled milk*. New York: HarperCollins.

Slobodkina, E. (1947). *Caps for sale*. Reading, MA: Addison-Wesley.

Steig, W. (1969). *Sylvester and the magic pebble*. New York: Simon & Schuster.

Viorst, J. (1972). *Alexander and the terrible, horrible, no good, very bad day*. New York: Atheneum.

Waber, B. (1975). *Ira sleeps over*. Boston: Houghton Mifflin.

Wiesner, D. (1988). *FreeFall*. New York: Lothrop, Lee, & Shepard.

Wiesner, D. (1992). *Tuesday*. New York: Clarion Books.

▪ BOOKS FOR BUILDING SOUND–SYMBOL RELATIONSHIPS

Consonants

B

Blackstone, S. (2000). *Bear's busy family*. Cambridge, MA: Barefoot Books.

Klinting, L. (1997). *Bruno the baker*. New York: Henry Holt.

McPhail, D. (2003). *Big brown bear's up and down day*. San Diego: Harcourt.

Walker, R. (Reteller). (1998). *The barefoot book of pirates*. Cambridge, MA: Barefoot Books.

Yep, L. (1995). *The butterfly boy*. New York: Farrar, Strauss, & Giroux.

C (hard)

Albee, S. (2000). *Brought to you by the letter C*. New York: Random House.

Gibbons, G. (1993). *Caves and caverns*. New York: Harcourt Brace.

Klingel, C., & Noyed, R. B. (2003). *Amazing letter C*. Chanhassen, MI: Child's World.

Owens, M. B. (1993). *Counting cranes*. Boston: Little, Brown.

Sabuda, R. (1997). *Cookie count*. New York: Little Simon.

C (soft)

Duqennoy, J. (1996). *The ghosts in the cellar*. New York: Harcourt Brace.

Falconer, I. (2001). *Olivia saves the circus*. New York: Simon & Schuster.

Fowler, S. G., & Catalanotto, P. (1998). *Circle of thanks*. New York: Scholastic.

Kuskin, Karla. (1994). *City noise*. New York: HarperCollins.

Swain, G. (1999). *Celebrating*. New York: First Avenue Editions.

D

Bunting, E. (1995). *Dandelions*. New York: Harcourt Brace.

Carmine, M. (1997). *Daniel's dinosaurs*. New York: Scholastic.

Cole, B. (1994). *Dr. Dog*. New York: Knopf.

Numeroff, L. J. (1996). *Dogs don't wear sneakers*. New York: Simon & Schuster.

Pfister, M. (2000). *Dazzle the dinosaur*. New York: North-South.

F

Bourgeois, P. (2000). *Franklin's baby sister*. New York: Scholastic.

Carlstrom, N. W. (1993). *Fish and flamingo*. Boston: Little, Brown.

London, J. (1997). *Froggy learns to swim*. New York: Puffin.

San Souci, R. D. (1995). *The faithful friend*. New York: Simon & Schuster.

Silverman, E. (1994). *Don't fidget a feather*. New York: Macmillan.

G (hard)

Berger, B. (1996). *Grandfather twilight*. New York: Philomel.

Grejniec, M. (1993). *Good morning, good night*. New York: North-South.

Grimm, J., & Grimm, W. (1995). *The golden goose*. New York: Farrar, Straus, & Giroux.

Kimmel, E. (Reteller). (1995). *The goose girl: A story from the Brothers Grimm*. New York: Holiday House.

Rathmann, P. (1996). *Good night, gorilla*. New York: Putnam.

G (soft)

Bornstein, R. (1999). *Gingerbread baby*. New York: Putnam.

Galdone, P. (1975). *The gingerbread boy*. New York: Clarion.

Lionni, L. (1979). *Geraldine, the music mouse*. New York: Random House.

Peck, J. (1998). *The giant carrot*. New York: Dial.

Silverstein, S. (1964). *A giraffe and a half*. New York: HarperCollins.

H

Hadithi, M. (1994). *Hungry hyena*. Boston: Little, Brown.

High, L. O. (1995). *Hound heaven*. New York: Holiday House.

Hooks, B. (2001). *Happy to be nappy*. New York: Hyperion.

Wormell, M. (1995). *Hilda hen's happy birthday*. New York: Harcourt Brace.

Yolen, J., & Greenberg, M. H. (1995). *The haunted house*. New York: HarperCollins.

J

Grossman, B. (1997). *The bear whose bones were Jezebel Jones*. New York: Dial.

Hoban, T. (1996). *Just look*. New York: Greenwillow Books.

Mayer, M., & Mayer, G. (2003). *Just a baseball game*. New York: Golden Books.

Ogburn, J. K. (1998). *The jukebox man*. New York: Dial.

Saltzman, D. (1995). *The jester has lost his jingle*. Palos Verdes, CA: Jester Company.

K

Demi. (1999). *Kites*. New York: Crown Publishing.

Ford, J. G. (1996). *A Kente dress for Kenya*. New York: Scholastic.

O'Connor, J. (1995). *Kate skates*. New York: Grosset.

Polacco, P. (1988). *The keeping quilt*. New York: Simon & Schuster.

Senisi, E. (1994). *Kindergarten kids*. New York: Scholastic.

L

Bornstein, R. (2000). *Little gorilla*. New York: Clarion.

Bunting, E. (2003). *Little bear's little boat*. New York: Clarion Books.

London, J. (1996). *Let's go, Froggy*. New York: Puffin.

Raimondo, L. (1994). *Little Lama of Tibet*. New York: Scholastic.

Yerxa, L. (1994). *Last leaf first snowflake to fall*. New York: Orchard.

M

Brennan, H. (1995). *The mystery machine*. New York: Margaret K. McElderry.

Cousins, L. (1999). *Maisy makes gingerbread*. Cambridge, MA: Candlewick Press.

Lyon, G. E. (1994). *Mama is a miner*. New York: Orchard.

McPhail, D. (2001). *Mole music*. New York: Henry Holt.

Raschka, C. (2000). *Moosy moose*. New York: Disney Press.

N

Bartoletti, S. C. (2003). *Nobody's nosier than a cat*. New York: Hyperion.

Fehlner, P. (1996). *No way!* New York: Cartwheel.

Masner, J. (1989). *Nicholas Cricket*. New York: Harper & Row.

O'Connor (1997). *Nina, Nina, ballerina*. New York: Grosset.

Wells, R. (1997). *Noisy Nora*. New York: Scholastic.

P

Bynum, J. (2003). *Pig enough*. San Diego: Harcourt.

Dale, P. (2003). *Princess, princess*. Cambridge, MA: Candlewick Press.

Palatini, M. (1995). *Piggie pie!* New York: Clarion.

Papademetriou, L. (1998). *My pen pal, Pat*. Brookfield, CT: Millbrook Press.

Pledger, M. (2001). *Ping-Ping panda*. San Diego: Silver Dolphin Books.

Q

Arnold, M. (1996). *Quick, quack, quick!* New York: Random House.

Good, M. (1999). *Reuben and the quilt*. New York: Good Books.

Holtzman, C. (1995). *A quarter from the tooth fairy*. New York: Scholastic.

Johnston, T., & dePaola, T. (1996). *The quilt story*. New York: Penguin Putnam.

Wood, A. (1997). *Quick as a cricket*. New York: Scholastic.

R

Gantos, J. (1994). *Not so rotten Ralph*. Boston: Houghton Mifflin.

Pinkwater, D. (1998). *Rainy morning*. New York: Atheneum.

Weeks, S. (1995). *Red ribbon*. New York: HarperCollins.

Wells, R. (2002). *Ruby's beauty shop*. New York: Penguin Putnam.

Willis, R. (2002). *Raccoon moon*. Middletown, DE: Birdsong Books.

S

Garland, S. (1995). *The summer sands*. New York: Harcourt Brace.

Raschka, C. (2000). *Sluggy slug*. New York: Disney Press.

Robb, L. (Selector). (1995). *Snuffles and snouts*. New York: Dial.

Schreiber, A. (1995). *Slower than a snail*. New York: Cartwheel.

Teague, M. (1999). *The secret shortcut*. New York: Scholastic.

T

Bunting, E. (1997). *Twinnies*. San Diego: Harcourt Brace.

Cocca-Leffler, M. (1999). *Mr. Tannen's ties*. Morton Grove, IL: Albert Whitman.

Gershator, P. (Reteller). (1994). *Tukama tootles the flute: A tale from the Antilles*. New York: Orchard.

Griffing, A. (1999). *Trashy town*. New York: HarperCollins.

Rader, L. (2003). *Tea for me, tea for you*. New York: HarperCollins.

V

Bovetz, M. (1993). *Machines*. Bothell, WA: Wright Group.

Cannon, J. (1997). *Verdi*. New York: Harcourt Brace.

Schweninger, A. (1990). *Valentine friends.* New York: Scholastic.

Williams, M. (1981). *The velveteen rabbit.* New York: Scholastic.

Williams, S. (1998). *Let's go visiting.* New York: Harcourt Brace.

W

Brenner, B. (1995). *Wagon wheels.* New York: Scholastic.

Milord, S. (2003). *Willa the wonderful.* Boston: Houghton Mifflin.

Raschka, C. (2000). *Wormy worm.* New York: Disney Press.

Williams, S. (1996). *I went walking.* New York: Gulliver.

Zolotow, C. (1997). *When the wind stops.* New York: HarperTrophy.

X

Langen, A., & Droop, C. (1996). *Felix explores planet earth.* New York: Abbeville Kids Press.

Thomas, P. (1979). *There are rocks in my socks said the ox to the fox.* New York: Lee, Lothrop, & Shepard.

Wells, R. (1998). *Max and Ruby in Pandora's box.* New York: Penguin Putnam.

Wells, R. (2002). *Max cleans up.* New York: Penguin Putnam.

Y

Kellogg, S. (1996). *Yankee doodle.* New York: Aladdin Paperbacks.

Marshall, J. (1973). *Yummers.* Boston: Houghton Mifflin.

Oram, H. (Reteller). (1997). *Baba Yaga and the wise doll.* New York: Dutton.

Seuss, Dr. (1958). *Yertle the turtle and other stories.* New York: Random House.

Wells, R. (1998). *Yoko.* New York: Hyperion.

Z

McDermontt, G. (1996). *Zomo the rabbit: A trickster tale from West Africa.* New York: Scholastic.

Moss, L. (1995). *Zin! Zin! Zin! A violin.* New York: Simon & Schuster.

Most, B. (1999). *Z—Z—Zoink!* New York: Harcourt Brace.

Steig, W. (1994). *Zeke Pippin.* New York: HarperCollins.

Wynne-Jones, T. (1993). *Zoom at sea.* New York: HarperCollins.

Vowels (long and short)

A

Berenstein, M. (1998). *That cat!* Brookfield, CT: Millbrook Press.

Holabird, K. (2002). *Angelina ballerina.* Middleton, WI: Pleasant Company.

Hooks, B. (2001). *Happy to be nappy.* New York: Hyperion.

Karlin, N. (1996). *The fat cat sat on the mat.* New York: Harper Trophy.

Lachner, D. (1995). *Andrew's angry words.* New York: North-South.

E

Grace, E. S. (1993). *Elephants.* San Francisco: Sierra.

Johnson, S. A. (1994). *A beekeeper's year.* Boston: Little, Brown.

Rothstein, G. (2003). *Sheep asleep.* New York: HarperCollins.

Shaw, N. (1997). *Sheep in a jeep.* Boston: Houghton Mifflin.

Wood, A. J. (1993). *Egg! A dozen eggs. What will they be?* Boston: Little, Brown.

I

Bornstein, R. (2000). *Little gorilla.* New York: Clarion.

Fleming, D. (1998). *In the small, small pond.* New York: Henry Holt.

Kinerk, R. (1998). *Slim and Miss Prim.* Flagstaff, AZ: Rising Moon.

Marston, H. I. (1993). *Big rigs.* New York: Dutton.

Numeroff, L. (1998). *If you give a pig a pancake.* New York: HarperCollins.

O

Falconer, I. (2000). *Olivia.* New York: Simon & Schuster.

Leonard, M. (1998). *Spots.* Brookfield, CT: Millbrook Press.

Parr, T. (1999). *The okay book.* New York: Little, Brown.

Willis, R. (2002). *Raccoon moon.* Middletown, DE: Birdsong Books.

Wilson, K., & Rankin, J. (2003). *A frog in the bog.* New York: Margaret K. McElderry Books.

U

Alborough, J. (1995). *Cuddly Dudly.* Cambridge, MA: Candlewick Press.

Allen, S. (1995). *The bug and the slug in the rug.* Bridgeport, CT: Green Bark Press.

Anderson, H. C. (1994). *The ugly duckling.* New York: Dorling Kindersley.

Raschka, C. (2000). *Sluggy slug.* New York: Disney Press.

Digraphs

CH

Archambault, J., & Martin, B., Jr. (1989). *Chicka chicka boom boom.* New York: Scholastic.

Denchfield, N. (1997). *Charlie the chicken.* New York: Little Simon.

Henkes, K. (1996). *Chrysanthemum.* New York: Mulberry.

Onyefulu, O. (1994). *Chinye: A West African folk tale.* New York: Viking.

Updike, J. (1999). *A child's calendar.* New York: Holiday House.

PH

Govan, C. (1968). *Phinny's fine summer.* New York: World.

SH

Brown, M. (1995). *Shadow.* New York: Aladdin Paperbacks.

Rothstein, G. (2003). *Sheep asleep.* New York: HarperCollins.

Shaw, N. (1996). *Sheep in a shop.* Boston: Houghton Mifflin.
Shaw, N. (1997). *Sheep in a jeep.* Boston: Houghton Mifflin.
Simon, S. (1995). *Sharks.* New York: HarperCollins.
Wells, R. (2001). *Shy Charles.* New York: Penguin Putnam.

TH
Cowley, J. (1987). *One thousand currant buns.* Bothell, WA: Wright Group.
Loedhas, S. (1962). *Thistle and thyme.* Toronto: Alger.
Munsinger, L. (1996). *Three cheers for Tacky.* Boston: Houghton Mifflin.
Simms, L. (1998). *Rotten teeth.* Boston: Houghton Mifflin.

Word Families
Butler, A., & Neville, P. (1987). *May I stay home today?* Crystal Lake, IL: Rigby.
O'Connor, J. (1995). *Kate skates.* New York: Grosset.
Seuss, Dr. (1957). *The cat in the hat.* New York: Random House.
Willis, R. (2002). *Raccoon moon.* Middletown, DE: Birdsong Books.
Wilson, K., & Rankin, J. (2003). *A frog in the bog.* New York: Margaret K. McElderry Books.

■ BOOKS FOR FOLLOWING DIRECTIONS
Carle, E. (1993). *Draw me a star.* New York: Scholastic.
Cousins, L. (1999). *Dress Maisy.* Cambridge, MA: Candlewick Press.
Gibbons, G. (1990). *How a house is built.* New York: Scholastic.
Scarry, R. (1995). *Pig will and pig won't: A book of manners.* New York: Random House.
Yolen, J., & Teague, M. (2003). *How do dinosaurs get well soon?* New York: Blue Sky Press.

■ SERIES BOOKS
Bemelmans, L. (1977). *Madeline.* New York: Puffin Books.
Bourgeois, P. (2000). *Franklin.* New York: Scholastic.
Danziger, P. (2003). *Amber Brown.* New York: G. P. Putnam's Sons.
Parish, P. (1970). *Amelia Bedelia.* New York: Scholastic.
Park, B. (2002). *Junie B. Jones.* New York: Random House.

■ EXPOSITORY AND NARRATIVE BOOKS RELATED TO THEMES

All about Me Books
Cain, J. (2000). *The way I feel.* Seattle: Parenting Press.
Carlson, N. L. (1998). *I like me.* New York: Viking Children's Books.
Numuoff, L. J. (1996). *Why a disguise?* New York: Simon & Schuster.
Williams, S. (1996). *Mommy doesn't know my name.* (pet names) Boston: Houghton Mifflin.
Ziefert, H. (1997). *Waiting for baby.* New York: Puffin Books.

Animal Books
Bancroft, H., & Van Gelder, R. G. (1997). *Animals in winter.* New York: HarperCollins.

Conrad, P. (1995). *Animal lingo.* New York: HarperCollins.
Driscoll, L. (1997). *The bravest cat! The true story of Scarlett.* New York: Grosset & Dunlap.
Ellwand, D. (1996). *Emma's elephant and other favorite animal friends.* New York: Dutton.
Ganeri, A. (1995). *Animals in disguise.* New York: Simon & Schuster.
Hawes, J. (2000). *Why frogs are wet.* New York: HarperCollins.
Hickman, P. (2001). *Animals eating: How animals chomp, chew, slurp, and swallow.* Tonawanda, NY: Kids Can Press.
Lewin, T., & Lewin, B. (2000). *Elephant quest.* New York: HarperCollins.
Markle, S. (2001). *Rats and mice.* New York: Atheneum Books for Young Readers.
Riley, L. C. (1995). *Elephants swim.* New York: Houghton Mifflin.

Dinosaurs
Carter, D. (2001). *Flapdoodle dinosaurs.* New York: Little Simon.
Lewis, J. (2001). *Dinosaur 123 ABC.* London: Tucker Slingsby.
Maynard, C. (1998). *The best book of dinosaurs.* New York: Kingfisher.
Mitton, T. (2002). *Dinosaurumpus!* New York: Scholastic.
Wood, A. J. (1998). *Countdown to extinction.* New York: Disney Press.
Zoehfeld, K. W. (2001). *Terrible tyrannosaurus.* New York: HarperCollins.

Ecology
Cherry, L., & Plotkin, M. J. (1998). *The Shaman's apprentice: A tale of the Amazon rain forest.* New York: Scholastic.
Dunphy, M. (1994). *Here is the tropical rain forest.* New York: Hyperion.
Fleming, D. (2000). *Where once there was a wood.* New York: Henry Holt.
Garland, S. (1995). *The summer sands.* San Diego: Harcourt.
Rauzon, M. J., & Bix, C. O. (1994). *Water water everywhere.* San Francisco: Sierra.

Families

Multicultural Books and General Books about Families
Anholt, C., et al. (1998). *Catherine and Laurence Anholt's big book of families.* Cambridge, MA: Candlewick Press.
Hausheir, R. (1997). *Celebrating families.* New York: Scholastic.
Kuklin, S. (1998). *How my family lives in America.* New York: Simon & Schuster.
Yem, S. S. (1997). *All kinds of families.* Birmingham, AL: New Hope.

Books about African American Families
Kroll, V. (1997). *Masai and I.* New York: Aladdin Paperbacks.

Kroll, V. (1998). *Africa brothers and sisters*. New York: Aladdin Paperbacks.

Strickland, D. S., & Strickland, M. R. (1996). *Families. Poems celebrating the African-American experience*. Honesdale, PA: Boyds Mills Press.

Books about Asian Families

Pomeranc, M. H. (1998). *The American Wei*. New York: Albert Whitman.

Say, A. (1993). *Grandfather's journey*. Boston: Houghton Mifflin.

Young, A. (1989). *Lon Po Po: A Red Riding Hood story from China*. New York: Philomel.

Books about Latino Families

Garza, C. L. (1996). *In my family*. Danbury, CT: Children's Press.

Morta, P. (1992). *A birthday basket for Tia*. New York: Macmillan.

Pampa, C. M. (1991). *On the Pompas*. New York: Holt.

American Eskimo

Joosse, B. (1991). *Mama, do you love me?* New York: Scholastic.

Irish

Bailan, L. (1980). *Leprechauns never lie*. Nashville: Abingdon.

Yezerski, T. (1998). *Together in pinecone patch*. New York: Farrar, Straus, & Giroux.

Italian

dePaola, T. (1989). *Tony's bread*. New York: Putnam.

Jamaican

Hoffman, M. (1991). *Amazing Grace*. New York: Scholastic.

Jewish Folktale

Gilman. P. (1994). *Something for nothing*. New York: Scholastic.

Native American

Goble, P. (1980). *The gift of the sacred dog*. New York: Macmillan.

Miller, J. (1997). *American Indian families* (True book). Danbury, CT: Children's Press.

Russian Family Folktale

Polacco, P. (1990). *Babushka's doll*. New York: Simon & Shuster.

Five Senses

Adolph, A. (1989). *Chocolate dreams*. New York: Lothrop, Lee, & Shepard.

Hewitt, S. (1999). *It's science! The five senses*. Danbury, CT: Children's Press.

Miller, M. (1994). *My five senses*. New York: Simon & Shuster.

McMillan, B. (1994). *Sense suspense: A guessing game for the five senses*. New York: Scholastic.

Moncure, J. B. (1997). *Clang, boom, bang: My five senses series*. Elgin, IL: Child's World.

How Things Work

Cobb, A. (1996). *Wheels*. New York: Random House.

Lafferty, P. (1995). *Why do balls bounce? First questions and answers about how things work*. Richmond, VA: Time Life.

Ripley, C. (1997). *Why does popcorn pop? And other kitchen questions*. Toronto: Firefly Books.

Schaefer, L. (2001). *Who works here? Fast-food restaurant*. Chicago: Heinemann.

Showers, P. (2001). *What happens to a hamburger?* New York: HarperCollins.

Insects and Reptiles

Baher, K. (1995). *Hide and snake*. New York: Voyager Picture Books.

Nickle, J. (1999). *The ant bully*. New York: Scholastic.

Petie, H. (1975). *Billions of bugs*. Englewood Cliffs, NJ: Prentice Hall.

Saunders-Smith, G. (1998). *Butterflies*. Danbury, CT: Children's Press.

Simon, S. (1999). *Crocodiles and alligators*. New York: HarperCollins.

Ocean Life

Andreae, G. (1998). *Commotion in the ocean*. Waukesha, WI: Little Tiger Press.

Gibbons, G. (1999). *Exploring the deep dark sea*. Boston: Little, Brown.

Lionni, L. (1973). *Swimmy*. New York: Random House.

Savage, S. (1997). *Animals of the ocean*. Chatham, NJ: Raintree/Steck Vaughn.

Seelig, T. L. (1999). *Ocean*. San Francisco: Chronicle Books.

Seasons and Holidays

Autumn

Hunter, A. (1996). *Possum's harvest moon*. New York: Houghton Mifflin.

Robbins, K. (1998). *Autumn leaves*. New York: Scholastic.

Russel, C. Y. (1997). *Moon festival*. Honesdale, PA: Boyds Mills Press.

Saunders, G. (1998). *Autumn*. Danbury, CT: Children's Press.

Schecter, B. (1993). *When will the snow trees grow?* New York: HarperCollins.

Winter

Blake, R. J. (1997). *Akiak: A tale from the Iditarod*. New York: Philomel.

Brown, M. W. (1994). *The winter noisy book*. New York: HarperCollins.

Ehlert, L. (1995). *Snowballs* (Picture book). New York: Harcourt Brace.

Frank, J. (2003). *A chill in the air: Nature poems for fall and winter*. New York: Hyperion.

Schotter, R., & Schotter, R. (1994). *There's a dragon about: A winter's revel*. New York: Orchard.

Spring

Adoff, A. (1997). *In for winter, out for spring.* New York: Harcourt Brace.

Daigneault, S. (1998). *Bruno springs up.* New York: HarperCollins.

Preller, J. (1994). *Wake me in spring.* New York: Scholastic.

Rylant, C. (1996). *Henry and Mudge in puddle trouble.* New York: Aladdin Paperbacks.

Spelter, J. (1999). *Lily and Trooper's spring.* Asheville, NC: Front Street Press.

Summer

Brown, M. W. (1993). *The summer noisy book.* New York: HarperCollins.

Hesse, K. (1999). *Come on, rain!* New York: Scholastic.

Lerner, C. (1996). *Backyard birds of summer.* New York: William Morrow.

Maass, R. (1993). *When summer comes.* New York: Holt.

Sturges, P. (1995). *Rainsong snowsong* (Predictable rhyming text). New York: North-South.

Space

Gaffney, T. R. (1996). *Grandpa takes me to the moon.* New York: William Morrow.

Graham, I. (1998). *The best book of spaceships.* New York: Kingfisher Books.

Hansen, R. (1998). *Astronauts today.* New York: Random House.

Simon, S. (1988). *Galaxies.* New York: Morrow Junior Books.

Sims, L. (1996). *Exploring space.* Chatham, NJ: Raintree/Steck-Vaughn.

■ CULTURAL DIVERSITY

African American Books

Hopkinson, D. (1999). *A band of angels: A story inspired by the Jubilee Singers.* New York: Simon & Schuster.

Kroll, V. (1998). *Faraway drums.* New York: Little, Brown.

London, J. (2000). *Who bop?* New York: HarperCollins.

San Souci, R. D. (1997). *The hired hand: An African-American folktale.* New York: Dial.

Woodson, J. (2001). *The other side.* New York: G. P. Putnam's Sons.

Asian Books

Bunting, E. (1998). *So far from the sea.* New York: Clarion Books.

Chang, M., et al. (1997). *The beggar's magic: A Chinese tale.* New York: Margaret K. McElderry.

Ho, M. (1997). *Brother rabbit: A Cambodian tale.* Lothrop, Lee, & Shephard.

Lin, G. (2002). *Kite flying.* New York: Random House.

Martin, R., et al. (1998). *The brave little parrot.* New York: Putnam.

Peacock, C. A. (2000). *Mommy far, mommy near: An adoption story.* Morton Grove, IL: Albert Whitman.

Yolen, J., & Young, E. (1998). *Emperor and the kite.* New York: Putnam.

Latino Books

Bunting, E. (1998). *Going home.* New York: Harper Trophy.

Colon-Villa, L. (1998). *Salsa.* Houston: Arte Publico Press.

Dorros, A. (1997). *Abuela* (English with Spanish phrases). New York: Puffin.

Johnston, T. (1997). *Day of the dead.* New York: Harcourt Brace.

Mora, P. (1997). *A birthday basket for Tia.* New York: Aladdin Picture Books.

Native American Books

Bruchac, J. (1998). *The earth under Sky Bear's feet: Native American poems of the land.* New York: Paper Star.

Fisher, L. E. (1997). *Anasazi.* New York: Atheneum.

Goble, P. (1998). *Adopted by the eagles: A Plains Indians story of friendship.* New York: Aladdin Paperbacks.

Lind, M. (2003). *Bluebonnet girl.* New York: Henry Holt.

McAuliffe, B. (1998). *Chief Joseph of the Nez Perce.* Mankato, MN: Capstone Press.

■ CHILDREN'S SPECIAL NEEDS

Communication Problems (speech and language differences)

Butler, D. (1995). *What happens when people talk.* Chatham, NJ: Raintree/Steck-Vaughn.

Dedieu, T., et al. (1997). *The boy who ate words.* New York: Harry N. Abrams.

Hamilton, V. (1985). *The people could fly.* New York: Knopf.

Hulme, J. N. (2000). *Through the open door.* New York: HarperCollins.

Lester, H. (1999). *Hooway for Wodney Wat.* New York: Walter Loraine Publisher.

Physical Disabilities (visual, hearing, physical)

Brighton, C. (1984). *My hands, my world.* New York: Macmillan.

Carter, A. R. (1999). *I'm tougher than asthma.* Morton Grove, IL: Albert Whitman.

Millman, I. (2002). *Moses goes to a concert.* New York: Farrar, Straus, & Giroux.

Mulder, L. (2001). *Sarah and Puffle: A story for children about diabetes.* Washington, DC: American Psychological Association.

Senisi, E. (1998). *Just kids: Visiting a class for children with special needs.* New York: Dutton.

Thomas, P. (2002). *Don't call me special: A first look at disability.* New York: Barron's Educational Series.

Learning Disabilities

Janover, C. (1997). *Josh: A boy with dyslexia.* San Francisco: Waterfront Books.

Lears, L. (1998). *Ian's walk: A story about autism.* Morton Grove, IL: Albert Whitman.

Lears, L. (1999). *Waiting for Mr. Goose.* Morton Grove, IL: Albert Whitman.

Shriver, M. (2001). *What's wrong with Timmy?* New York: Little, Brown.

Smith, M. (1997). *Pay attention, Slosh!* New York: Albert Whitman.

Quality Television Programs with Associated Children's Books

ARTHUR

Brown, M. (2000). *Arthur's fire drill*. New York: Random House.

Brown, M. (1999). *Arthur's new baby book*. New York: Random House.

Brown, M. (1998). *Arthur tricks the tooth fairy*. New York: Random House.

Brown, M. (1996). *Glasses for D. W.* New York: Random House.

Brown, M. (1996). *Arthur's reading race*. New York: Random House.

CLIFFORD

Bridwell, N. (1984). *Clifford family*. New York: Scholastic.

Bridwell, N. (1975). *Clifford's good deeds*. New York: Scholastic.

Bridwell, N. (1963). *Clifford: The big red dog*. New York: Scholastic.

DORA THE EXPLORER

Beinstein, P. (2002). *Count with Dora!: A counting book in English and Spanish*. New York: Simon & Schuster Children's.

Ricci, C. (2002). *Dora the Explorer: Good night Dora!* New York: Simon & Schuster Children's.

Willson, S. (2002). *Dora the Explorer: Little star*. New York: Simon & Schuster Children's.

FRANKLIN

Bourgeois, P. (1999). *Franklin's class trip*. New York: Scholastic.

Bourgeois, P. (1997). *Franklin's bad day*. New York: Scholastic.

Bourgeois, P. (1997). *Franklin rides a bike*. New York: Scholastic.

Bourgeois, P. (1986). *Franklin in the dark*. New York: Scholastic.

MAURICE SENDAK'S LITTLE BEAR

Minarik, E. H. (1984). *Little Bear's friend* (I Can Read Book Series). New York: HarperCollins Children's Books.

Minarik, E. H. (1984). *A kiss for Little Bear* (I Can Read Book Series). New York: HarperCollins Children's Books.

Minarik, E. H. (1979). *Little Bear's visit* (I Can Read Book Series). New York: HarperCollins Children's Books.

Minarik, E. H. (1978). *Father Bear comes home* (I Can Read Book Series). New York: HarperCollins Children's Books.

Minarik, E. H. (1978). *Little Bear* (I Can Read Book Series). New York: HarperCollins Children's Books.

MAISY

Cousins, L. (2001). *Doctor Maisy*. Cambridge, MA: Candlewick Press.

Cousins, L. (2001). *Maisy's morning on the farm*. Cambridge, MA: Candlewick Press.

Cousins, L. (2001). *Maisy at the fair*. Cambridge, MA: Candlewick Press.

Cousins, L. (1999). *Where is Maisy?* Cambridge, MA: Candlewick Press.

MAX & RUBY

Wells, R. (2002). *Max and Ruby's busy week*. New York: Penguin Putnam.

Wells, R. (2000). *Max's dragon shirt*. New York: Penguin Putnam.

Wells, R. (2000). *Max's chocolate chicken*. New York: Penguin Putnam.

Wells, R. (1998). *Max and Ruby in Pandora's box*. New York: Penguin Putnam.

appendix C

Literacy-Related Computer Software and Web Sites

COMPUTER SOFTWARE

Preschool Parade Grade: Pre-K–1

Description: Children work with clowns and animals to learn the alphabet, counting, shapes, and more.

Hardware: MacPlus or higher; 1 MB RAM; System 7.0 or later; hard drive; sound card recommended; Win 95/98/Me/2000

Availability: Nordic Software

Elmo's Reading Preschool and Kindergarten Grade: Pre-K–1

Description: Children play with Sesame Street characters while building comprehension, phonics, and vocabulary.

Hardware: Win 486-66, 8MB RA, 2 X CD-ROM; Mac System 7.1, 8MB RAM, 2 X CD-ROM; color monitor

Availability: Creative Wonders

I SPY Junior Puppet Playhouse Grade: Pre-K–2

Description: These riddles based on the I SPY books emphasize listening and reading skills as well as creativity.

Hardware: Win 95/98/Me/2000/XP, 16 MB RAM, Pentium 90 or faster; Mac version available; sound card

Availability: Scholastic

Stickybear's Reading Room Grade: Pre-K–3

Description: This bilingual program in Spanish and English includes activities in sentence building, word matching, and word finding.

Hardware: Mac DOS System 6.07 with 2MB RAM or System 7.0 with 4MB RAM; Win 95/98; color monitor

Availability: Optimum Resource

Arthur's Reading Grade: Pre-K–3

Description: Children can join one of their favorite characters to play games that develop literacy skills. Focus on reading comprehension, phonics, word recognition, and vocabulary building.

Hardware: Win 95/98/Me or NT 4.0, 8MB RAM, 2 X CD-ROM; Mac, 6MB RAM, CD-ROM; sound card

Availability: Creative Wonders

WEB SITES

The Reading Zone

Address: http://ipl.si.umich.edu/div/kidspace/browse/rzn0000

Description: Students can read a variety of stories and poems and research their favorite authors through links to the authors' web sites. This site also provides interviews with some well-known children's authors.

LiteracyCenter.Net—The Early Childhood Education Network

Address: http://www.literacycenter.net

Description: This site offers games that allow children to work with letter identification, shapes, writing, word building, numbers, colors, and typing, each at the appropriate developmental level. These games are available in English, Spanish, German, and French.

Sesame Workshop

Address: http://www.sesameworkshop.org

Description: This Sesame Street site provides games, stories, art, music, and the opportunity for children to e-mail their favorite characters, as well as helpful information for parents and teachers.

Between the Lions: Get Wild about Reading

Address: http://pbskids.org/lions

Description: Tied to the popular PBS show, this site offers fun stories, games, and songs that all focus on literacy development. This site is also a great resource for teachers who might want to use these literacy-based games and songs in their classroom.

Intercultural E-mail Classroom Connections

Address: http://www.iecc.org

Description: Students can sign up for keypals anywhere in the world. Great way to promote leisure writing.

HarperChildrens.com

Address: http://www.harperchildrens.com

Description: This site explains the process of how a book is made to children. It has links to the web sites of favorite authors, contains games, features books, and contains book-related activity pages.

Suggestions for Instructors

Literacy Development in the Early Years: Helping Children Read and Write was written for students in graduate and undergraduate classes in courses such as Early Literacy Development and Reading in the Elementary School, or in an Early Childhood Curriculum course that includes literacy development as a major component. The book can also be used for staff development courses for classroom teachers. The book suggests several activities to do with students. I'd like to highlight a few that I have used successfully in class sessions or as assignments. I have also added a complete integrated language arts thematic unit, which teachers can use as a model for beginning literacy programs in their preschool through third-grade classrooms.

◼ ASSIGNMENTS AND IN-CLASS ACTIVITIES

At the beginning of each chapter are focus questions that students should read prior to reading the chapter. At the end of every chapter are activities contributed by classroom teachers that relate to the chapter. In addition, there are activities to engage in. Read the activities; you might find that some of them are appropriate for class interaction in small groups and for discussion. Be sure in all planning that a discussion about English language learners and issues of diversity are included.

Activities to participate in as you work your way through the book are as follows:

1. Chapter 2 suggests that each student start his or her own portfolio of class work. Included in the portfolio should be the instructor's assignments. As students do assignments, they collect the work in the portfolio and record grades. Teachers should meet with each student once a semester to confer about his or her progress and review the portfolios.

2. In Chapter 2 it is suggested that students select a child that they can study as they read the book. The child should be between the ages of 2 and 8 years. The student is to begin a portfolio for the child and meet with him or her from time to time, to try strategies and assess and describe certain behaviors.

Specifically, the students should obtain a sample of writing, drawing, oral language, and a story retelling from the child. In addition, several of the measures provided in the book can be used to accumulate data about the child. For example:

a. When reading Chapter 4 on language development, collect a language sample and analyze it for sentence length and number of different words. To elicit language from children, ask them to tell you about family, pets, TV shows they like, or games they play. Tape-record the discussion and transcribe it for analysis.

b. In Chapter 5, evaluate the child's knowledge about print with the checklist included.

c. When reading Chapter 6, have the child retell a story that was read to him or her. Tape-record the retelling and transcribe it. Analyze it with the retelling instrument in the chapter. Children can also be asked to rewrite the story. The rewriting can be analyzed with the same tool.

d. In Chapter 7, collect a writing sample from the child to determine the stage of writing, and analyze it for sense of story structure, the mechanics of writing, and so on. To elicit a writing sample you might have the child draw a picture and write about it. Talk about ideas to write before writing. For emergent writers, assure them that any way they can write is fine. Show them samples of children's writing from the text for them to see that one letter or scribble writing is fine.

e. When reading Chapter 8, interview the child using the form in that chapter that evaluates motivation for reading and writing (Figure 8.9).

f. When studying the family, interview the child's parents with the checklist concerning the home literacy environment found in Chapter 10.

3. At least three or four times during the semester, have the class break up into groups to deal special issues presented in the text—for example, in Chapter 6 the activity about Teachers 1, 2, and 3 is a good small-group activity. Have the students respond to the questions posed about the teachers, and discuss which teacher each would wish to be. The students must select one. Discuss the pros and cons of each of the teachers presented.

4. Have students keep dialogue journals about readings that have made an impression on them. They can also include incidents in class that were particularly interesting, fun, or of concern. Respond to their journals with comments of your own.

5. Have your students take a vocabulary test, using words from the glossary. Teachers need to be aware of the technical language associated with early literacy when talking with peers, interviewing for a job, and explaining issues to parents.

6. Have students bring six genres of children's literature to class to share in groups. Three books should be nonfiction or informational text and three fiction or narrative text. This assignment gives them the opportunity to browse through lots of books and see the variety of genres available. Set the books up as if they were going into a classroom. They will gain a sense of the numbers and types of books that should be in a literacy center.

7. Ask students to draw a floor plan for their ideal classroom using the philosophy and strategies learned. Pay particular attention to the literacy center. Be sure they create plans to support literacy instruction for whole groups, small groups, and one-to-one settings.

8. Ask each student to be involved in a storytelling project. Give students a list of early literacy skills from those outlined on the checklists provided in the book. Have them select a skill they would like to teach. Ask them to find a picture story book that will enable that skill to be taught. For example, if their skill is to teach sequencing, a story such as *I Know an Old Lady* provides a sequence of events that are easily followed. The student then selects a technique for storytelling from those described in Chapter 8, such as a chalk talk, roll story, felt story, or other techniques they create themselves. A lesson plan is developed in which the teacher will present the story and teach the skill through the use of the material created. The material is designed for children to use to practice the skill taught. In Chapter 8 the "Idea from the Classroom for the Classroom" concerning the story *A Bunny Called Nat* illustrates this type of assignment. Students present the storytelling in class.

9. Have the students select a group to work with. Have the group select a topic for a thematic unit. Using the guide for the unit in Chapter 9, divide the sections and prepare a thematic unit for a classroom of children from ages 2 through 8 years.

10. Have students participate in a teacher–researcher project. Each student will select a topic dealing with early literacy and carry out a ministudy. The study should include a statement of purpose, a short literature review related to the topic, a description of methods and procedures to follow during the study, a discussion of how the data will be analyzed, a report of the results of the data collection, and a discussion concerning the results. This is a large project that is introduced to students early in the semester in order for them to have ample time to carry it out. When writing the literature review, the students should be required to consult a few articles from professional journals. Some topics for study are literacy and play, computers and early literacy, family literacy, multicultural concerns in early literacy, and early intervention programs.

11. Have students bind their own books based on the directions given in Chapter 7. Have them use the book for their dialogue journal or for writing their storytelling lesson plan.

12. Encourage students to join a professional organization such as the International Reading Association or the National Association for the Education of Young Children.

13. Encourage your students to subscribe to a professional journal and a commercial teacher magazine.

14. One important activity to offer your students is to let them experience what it would be like to be a child learning to read. For this demonstration, I am providing you with materials and a plan for a class experience. This activity should take about 45 minutes of class time and should be done early in the semester when you are teaching theory. The lesson involves learning how to read with an alphabet called the *Confusabet*. Following is a plan for carrying out the Confusabet. Materials needed are provided in this appendix. You can photocopy them for use in your lesson plan before beginning the lesson or use the pages in the book.

▨ THE CONFUSABET LESSON

Objective: To experience how it feels to learn to read and write for a better understanding of the process and how children feel when they are learning.

Materials

Confusabet alphabet and translation
Confusabet sight words and their translation
Confusabet worksheets
Confusabet reading book and translation (books must be assembled)

Procedures

1. Before the lesson, ask students to think about and write the following during the experience:

a. What methods were used to teach reading? Which were good and which were not particularly good?

b. What emotions did you experience while learning to read and write the Confusabet?

c. What strategies did you use to teach yourself how to read and write?

2. Hand out or turn to the Confusabet alphabet and pictures that have the names of the Confusabet characters on them.

3. Name the characters and have the students repeat their names.

4. Hand out or turn to worksheet 1. Ask students to find the character's name among other Confusabet words.

5. Hand out or turn to the list of Confusabet words. Provide students with context clues for each word to help them figure out what it says. For example: The color of the traffic light that means you should stop is _____. Have the students fill in the word and point to the Confusabet word that is *red*. Context clues are provided in the translations at the end of Appendix D.

6. Do this step for all words, and provide your own context clues.

7. Repeat the words with the students. You may repeat them all together, call on those who raise their hands, and call on students who do not raise their hands.

8. Turn to or hand out worksheet 2 with the Confusabet words just introduced and ask students to underline and name the word in each list that is the same as the first word at the top of the list.

9. Turn to or distribute the Confusabet primer. Call on students to read a line or a page at a time. Try round-robin reading as well.

During the Confusabet lesson, role-play as if you are a teacher of six-year-olds. Praise students for doing well. Do some positive reinforcing, and use some positive teaching techniques. Try techniques that are often used and words that are often said to students that are punitive, such as "If you don't get this work correct you won't get to take the book home to your parents" or "You weren't listening; that's why you don't know the words" or "If you don't stop talking, you'll be sent to the principal's office."

During the Confusabet exercise, students will talk to each other naturally to try and work things out. When they do, say, "Please do your own work and keep your eyes on your own paper" or " Don't help each other; you have to learn to do it yourself" or "It's too noisy in here" and "We can't wait

for you even though you haven't finished your work." When students have answers and are very anxious to give them say: "You've already had your turn; give someone else a chance" or "Please settle down; you are disrupting the rest of the class." When students look ahead to preview materials handed out, say, "Please wait for me to tell you when to turn the page" or "Don't go ahead of me, we aren't up to that yet." This type of role-playing allows students to experience even more how children feel in the classroom, where these types of comments often occur.

10. After reading the Confusabet materials, ask students to write their names and then the sentence: "I like to read and write," with Confusabet symbols.

11. At the end of the lesson ask the questions posed at the beginning:

a. What methods did I use that were good? What methods did I use that were not very good?

b. What emotions did you experience?

c. How did you teach yourself to learn to read?

d. How did you go about learning to write?

Students will express that they experienced fear, anger, and frustration when they were having trouble. They will suggest that they wanted to tune out and not participate. Those who were succeeding will suggest that they were excited, they wanted to continue, and they wanted to share their excitement. Frequently students who are succeeding will be greeted with remarks such as "You've already had a turn, settle down and let me give someone else a chance." When asked how they felt about this response, they will say that their excitement was drained.

When students discuss the strategies they used to learn to read, they will often make comments similar to the following:

1. I used my past experience with knowledge from our real alphabet to help. For example, the Confusabet words have the same number of symbols as our alphabet. They also resemble some of the letters of our alphabet, and I was able to make associations.

2. I used the picture clues.

3. I used surrounding words or the context to figure out the word (contextual and syntactic clues).

4. I memorized symbols from one page to the next to try and remember.

5. Some words were long or had an unusual shape, which helped me to get a word (configuration).

6. I looked at the first letter of a word to give me help in figuring it out.

When students are asked some of the things they did to help them read they may say:

1. I pointed to the print to help me find my place.
2. I moved my eyes around the page to try and find clues.
3. I called out words one at a time, the way young children do.

What the students realize as a result of participating in the Confusabet experience is that they look to meaning, past experience, associative strategies, and visual clues to figure out the words, more than they do individual skills such as phonics.

The Confusabet lesson presented here is adapted from materials created by Mildred Letton Wittock from the University of Chicago.

▥ CONFUSABET ALPHABET LETTERS

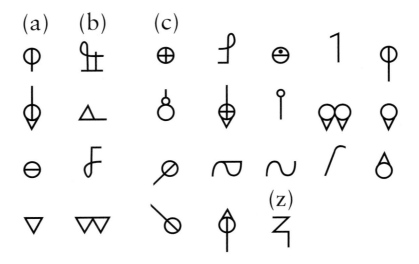

▥ CONFUSABET STORY CHARACTERS

Directions: Instructor names the characters for the students. Students repeat the names.

■ CONFUSABET VOCABULARY WORDS

Directions: Instructor gives a context clue for each word to help student to read it. Students repeat the words. Clues are on page 381.

■ CONFUSABET WORKSHEET 1

Directions: Circle the name of the character in the list of words under his or her name. Say the name as you circle it.

▧ CONFUSABET WORKSHEET 2

Directions: Circle the underlined word in each column. Say the word as you circle it.

▧ CONFUSABET PRIMER

■ **CONFUSABET STORY 1**

■ **CONFUSABET STORY 2**

■ **CONFUSABET STORY 3**

1ᐃ⌂F ɸƍʇ ໐ᕐᕐᚼᚼ

ᚼⴹᗯⴻ 1ᐃ⌂F. ᚼⴹᗯⴻ ໐ᕐᚼᚼᚼ.
ᚼⴹᗯⴻ ɸƍʇ ◡ⴹⴹ.
ᚼⴹᗯⴻ ɸƍʇ ◡ⴹⴹ ∫ɸⴻ ɸ໐∫ⴹᗯⴻ☩ᐃ໐.
ᚼⴹᗯⴻ ɸƍʇ ◡ⴹⴹ ∫ɸⴻ ◠ⴹʇ ɸ໐∫ⴹᗯⴻ☩ᐃ໐.
ᚼⴹᗯⴻ 1ᐃ⌂F. ᚼⴹᗯⴻ ໐ᕐᚼᚼᚼ.
໐ⴹⴹᚼ ɸƍʇ ◡ⴹⴹ.

■ **CONFUSABET STORY 4**

∫ɸⴻ ◠ⴹʇ ɸ໐∫ⴹᗯⴻ☩ᐃ໐

໐ⴹⴹᚼ ɸ∫ ∫ɸⴻ ◠ⴹʇ ɸ໐∫ⴹᗯⴻ☩ᐃ໐.
ᚼⴹᗯⴻ ɸƍʇ ໐ⴹⴹᚼ ɸ∫ ᐃ∫.
ᐃ∫ ᐃ◡ 1໐ƍ. ໐ⴹⴹᚼ ɸ∫ ᐃ∫.

■ **CONFUSABET STORY 5**

ᚼᚼᗯF ᚼF ɸƍʇ ◠ᚼƍ 1ᐃ⌂F.
ᚼᚼᗯF ᚼF ɸƍʇ ◠ᚼƍ ☩ᐃ໐໐.
໐ⴹⴹᚼ ᗯɸ◠ᚼ. ⴹɸƍ ɸⴹᚼ ◡ⴹⴹ ∫ɸⴻᗯ

CONFUSABET TRANSLATIONS

Story Character Names

1. Mary 2. Bill 3. Nancy 4. Flip 5. Lucky

Vocabulary Translations with Context Clue Sentences

6. see— With my eyes I _____.
7. come— Please _____ over here.
8. , (comma) . (period) ? (question mark)
9. red— The top color on a traffic signal is _____.
10. automobile— Another name for a car is an _____.
11. run— When I go fast on my feet I _____.
12. funny— A clown is _____.
13. up— When we take off in a airplane we go _____.
14. jump— When I play with a rope I _____ up.
15. go— The green traffic light means for us to _____.
16. look— A word that rhymes with book and means to see is _____.
17. you— Not me but _____.
18. at— Come and look _____ it.
19. the— _____ red automobile
20. it— Let's get into _____.
21. is— It _____ fun to ride in.
22. them— I'm going over there to be with _____.
23. can— Yes I _____.
24. and— Come _____ play with me.
25. oh— When I am surprised I say _____.
26. fun— When I play with my friend I have _____.

Story Translations for Primer

Primer Title — *Look and See*

Story 1 — *Bill*
Look at Bill.
Look at Bill jump.
Look at Bill jump up.
Jump up, jump up.

Story 2 — *Nancy and Bill and Mary*
Look Bill. Look Mary.
See Nancy.
Look and see Nancy.
Funny funny Nancy.

Story 3 — *Flip and Lucky*
Come Flip, come Lucky.
Come and see.
Come and see the automobile.
Come and see the red automobile.
Come Flip, come Lucky.
Look and see.

Story 4 — *The Red Automobile*
Look at the red automobile.
Come and look at it.
It is fun. Look at it.

Story 5 — *(Without pictures)*
Jump up and run Flip.
Jump up and run Bill.
Look Mary. Can you see them?

■ INTEGRATED LANGUAGE ARTS THEMATIC UNIT: "HEALTHY BODIES, HEALTHY MINDS"

On the following pages, you will find a thematic unit dealing with "Healthy Bodies, Healthy Minds," written for children in preschool through third grade. This unit includes all content areas and weaves literacy instruction throughout. When using the unit, adapt and select the ideas for the children you teach, making sure to repeat activities to reinforce the concepts being taught. When carrying out the unit, samples from each student's work should be gathered through formal and informal assessment measures. This is an excellent way to track the student's progress, and it can be used in portfolio assessment. Using this unit as a guide, try your hand at creating another thematic unit for the youngsters in your classroom.

Factual Information

What Does It Mean To Be Healthy in Body and Mind?
Eating nutritious food, exercising regularly, getting enough sleep, keeping ourselves clean, and feeling good about ourselves, are all very important to keeping fit and healthy in body and mind.

Why Should We Eat Healthy Foods?
Good foods are needed to supply your body and mind with the energy it needs to function and grow every day. All people need food to eat and water to drink to live. Food and water are also necessary for animals and most plants to live. Nutrients are the substances in food that give us the energy and strength we need to grow, work, and play.

What Are the Five Food Groups?
Eating properly, along with plenty of sleep and exercise, will keep a person's body healthy and strong. There are many types of food. Foods are separated into five major groups, and eating a proper amount of each daily will help ensure good health. Foods are categorized in the following manner:

1. *Vegetable:* Most vitamins and roughage are obtained from vegetables. A good diet should contain dark green and yellow vegetables, like broccoli, lettuce, carrots, spinach, and squash. It is recommended that three to four servings be eaten daily from this group.

2. *Fruit:* Fruit is a healthy sweet treat, with plenty of vitamins and nutrients. Some examples include apples, oranges, pears, bananas, and strawberries. It is recommended that two to three servings be eaten daily from this group.

3. *Bread-Cereal Group:* This group includes breads; rolls; bagels; crackers; cereals, such as oats and rice; and pastas. Carbohydrates, necessary for the energy to work and play, and fiber are the primary benefits of this group. Four daily servings are suggested.

4. *Meat-Poultry Group:* Also included in this group are fish, beans, nuts, and eggs. This group provides minerals and much of the protein in one's diet. Protein is essential for building and maintaining muscles. It is also important for overall growth. Two servings are suggested daily.

5. *Milk-Cheese Group:* This group includes all dairy products, such as milk, cheese, yogurt, and cottage cheese. These products are also high in protein and contain nutrients that build strong bones and teeth. Many products in this group tend to have a high fat content. Two to three servings are the recommended daily intake.

A proper diet, including ample portions from the five food groups, is essential for a healthy, growing child. However, there are also foods known as "fats, sweets and oils" or "junk foods." These items provide no vitamins, minerals, or protein and are not necessary for good heath. Foods in this group include soda, candies, potato chips, and some seasonings and spices. On occasion these foods are fine in moderate amounts; however, a well-rounded diet containing items from the five major food groups is best.

People from different cultures eat different food. Because the United States is home to people from many cultures, numerous American dishes have been influenced by Mexican, Asian, French, Italian, and Jamaican cooking, among others. It is fun to try ethnic foods and learn about different multicultural backgrounds.

Why Are Exercise, Rest, and Cleanliness Important?
Exercising by ourselves or with others can be fun. It gives us stronger muscles and healthier hearts, and it makes our bodies and minds feel good. It helps circulate our blood and makes us feel refreshed and relaxed.

People around the world exercise regularly to keep healthy. Many of the sports or exercises here in the United States have been influenced by other cultures. For example, baseball was influenced by a British game called cricket, and American football was developed from rugby, a similar contact sport. Regular exercise helps in relieving stress and in getting a good night's sleep.

We spend a third of our lives sleeping. When we sleep, we give our bodies and minds time to rest, during which our heart rate and blood pressure decrease and breathing slows down. This is so our bodies and minds can work hard when we are awake. Getting too little sleep can affect your body's and mind's ability to function and grow.

How Does Self-Esteem Affect Your Body and Mind?
People who feel good about themselves have self-esteem. They take care of their bodies and minds, and stay away from junk food, drugs, and alcohol. They look healthy and share their energy and good feelings with others around them.

Good mental health is important for coping with the demands of everyday life. Sometimes when you do not feel very good about yourself, it might help to make a list of all the things you can do, for example,

ride a bike, read a book, draw a picture, or cook a dish. People can also help us solve our problems and make us feel better. These people include parents, siblings, friends, and teachers. However, it is important to realize that we all have strengths and weaknesses.

It is healthy to express our feelings in appropriate ways. When someone does not take the time to think about his or her feelings and speak calmly in words, feelings may come out in other ways. Getting plenty of sleep, eating nutritious meals, exercising outdoors, and keeping up personal hygiene will help you feel better about yourself.

Newsletter to Parents about Healthy Bodies, Healthy Minds

Dear Parents:

Your child will be participating in a unit that explores what it means to be healthy in body and mind. This unit will include study of why we should eat healthy foods, the five food groups, exercise, rest, cleanliness, and the importance of self-esteem.

The good health unit will cover all subject areas—play, art, music, social studies, science, math, and literacy (reading, writing, listening, and oral language) which will be incorporated in the theme. Some of the exciting activities we do here at school may also be carried out at home with your child.

At School and at Home
Art: Your child will refine eye-hand coordination and visual discrimination skills and explore and experiment with different art materials. At school we will be creating food collages and abstract bean mosaics. At home you can encourage your child to use his or her imagination by providing these and other food-related materials for art activities. Remember that art is for exploring what can be done with different materials, rather than copying an adult model.

Science: We will be making applesauce, which will give the children an opportunity to listen, follow directions, and learn where apples come from and how they are grown, as well as how food changes as it is cooked. Making healthy snacks at home, such as a fruit or lettuce salad, and involving your child in the preparation by using simple recipes will help to extend listening skills.

Literacy: Please assist at home by labeling healthy food items with the letters *h*, *f*, and *b* (associated with *health, food,* and *body*) or pointing out words that have these and other beginning sounds. Read signs and point out these letters when you are outside the home as well.

Please read stories, poems, informational books, cookbooks, exercise magazines, and other literature related to our theme of good health to your child. Some books that will be featured in the unit include:

Achoo! by P. Demuth, 1997
Children around the World by D. Montanari, D, 2001
Gregory, the Terrible Eater by M. Sharmat, 1984
No More Baths by B. Cole, 1989
Mooncake by F. Asch, 1983

(continued on next page)

(continued from previous page)

We Need Your Help

We would like your assistance with our multicultural food of the week or your favorite food at home. If you are able to prepare a snack one day and discuss it, please sign your name and tell what type of snack you would like to prepare on the attached sheet.

If you can come in and read your child's favorite bedtime story to the class, please sign your name and tell what date you are available on the attached sheet.

If you have any other materials at home related to our theme, such as empty food containers, seeds, nuts, beans, or exercise or yoga magazines that we may use in our dramatic-play area, please send them in with your child.

Other Activities to Do with Your Child

Go to the supermarket with your child. Prepare a list beforehand of the food you need to purchase. Have your child check the things off as you put them in the cart. Try to purchase food from each food group.

Plant watermelon, avocado, carrot seeds at home. Keep a diary or record of their growth, making comparisons between them.

Make simple, nutritious recipes at home, such as fruit salad, mixed green salad, butter, or peanut butter, to help our lessons carry over from class to home.

Take the time to engage in some exercise with your child each day. A brisk walk or bike ride will help your child learn that exercise is fun and should be done often. It is an activity your family will enjoy together.

Remind your child at bedtime that rest is important for our bodies. Share a special bedtime story each night with your child.

Child's Corner

Ask your child to write or draw something he or she did in school related to our theme.

Help your child keep a journal of what foods he or she eats each day. Keep track of any exercises your child does. Keep track of how many hours of sleep your child gets, writing the number in the journal. Graph the numbers. The journal can be written in a notebook, on a pad, or on pieces of paper stapled together like a book.

If you have any questions about the unit or have any additional ideas, please contact me. If you are in a profession that is related to our theme, such as a nutritionist or any fitness-related career, please consider coming into class and talking to us.

Sincerely,

Lisa Lozak

- -

I would like to prepare the following snack for your healthy bodies, healthy minds unit:

Snack:_____   Parent's Name: _____

I am able to come in on the following date for a storyreading: Date: _____

Book: _____   Parent's Name: _____

Preparing Classroom Environment

To begin the unit on healthy bodies, healthy minds, prepare the room so that the theme is evident to those who enter. Begin with some of the following suggestions, and continue to add others as the unit progresses. Display environmental signs and labels about nutrition, personal hygiene, exercise, rest, and self-esteem wherever possible.

1. *Dramatic Play:* The dramatic-play center can be turned into either a restaurant or a fitness center. As a restaurant, the center should include menus, receipts, order-taking slips, recipe cards, cookbooks, baking utensils, prop foods, signs commonly seen in restaurants, a cash register, play money, food posters, and waiter and waitress clothing. As a health club, the center could include light weights or dumbbells, jump ropes, balls, a balance beam, mats, gym membership cards, stop watches, heart-rate posters, sign-up sheets for aerobic classes, and towels.

2. *Block Area:* To create places that food comes from such as farms and supermarkets, the following items can be added: farm props (animals and plants), supermarket props (play foods, receipts, money, and bags), environmental print signs and posters displaying food information, and cards for making signs.

3. *Outdoor Play:* A health club/fitness center can be created outside by providing the following items: tables for stands or desks; exercise equipment including jump ropes, balls, and a balance beam; play money; cash register; receipts; signs displaying the hours of business; and paper and pencils, so children learn that this is a place to go to keep our bodies healthy.

4. *Music:* Various songs on nutrition, exercise, personal hygiene, and good self-esteem can be added to the music center. All tapes should be accompanied by the written lyrics posted on the wall. Props to act out the songs may also be motivating. Students should also be encouraged to write and sing their own songs about good health.

5. *Art:* Include play dough and a poster with play dough recipes to make play foods. Include cooking and health magazines, dry foods to make collages, and fruit- and vegetable-shaped sponges for printing with paint.

6. *Science:* Materials for various health and nutrition projects may be added: a stethoscope, a heart-rate chart, blood pressure device, foods to be classified into the five food groups, seed packages, and planting equipment. All these items should be accompanied with charts and journals to record ongoing progress. Posters of the human body showing the muscles and skeleton and informational books should also be added.

7. *Social Studies:* Pictures of foods and the five food groups, and maps that depict where certain food comes from, as well as where the children's families are from should be included. In addition, posters displaying various athletic events from around the world may appear in the center. Recipe books representing different cultures may also be added.

8. *Math:* Various foods can be used as counters, such as macaroni or dried beans. Charts and graphs to record various activities, such as eating favorite fruit, laps around the school yard, or number of hours slept per night, should be included. Blank books for children to create their own number books are also needed.

9. *Literacy Center*
   a. *Writing Center:* Materials needed include a recipe box to share favorite recipes, food-shaped blank books, and a message board on which to share the morning message.
   b. *Library Corner:* Include health and fitness magazines, cooking magazines, pamphlets about good nutrition and general health, and a collection of books pertaining to the unit from all genres. (See the following list and the bibliography at the end of the unit.)

Library Corner Booklist with Suggested Activities

Asch, F. (1983). *Mooncake.* Englewood Cliffs, NJ: Prentice Hall.

Brandenberg, F. (1976). *I wish I was sick, too.* NY: Greenwillow.

Carle, E. (1969). *The very hungry caterpillar.* New York: Philomel.

Chambers, W. (1974). *The lip-smackin', joke-crackin' cookbook for kids.* New York: Golden Press.

Cole, J. (1988). *The magic school bus inside the human body.* New York: Scholastic.

Curtis, J. L. (2002). *I'm gonna like me: Letting off a little self-esteem.* New York: HarperCollins.

de Brunhoff, L., & Weiss, E. (2002). *Babar's yoga for elephants.* New York: Harry N. Abrams.

Demuth, P. (1996). *Johnny Appleseed.* New York: Grosset & Dunlap.

Demuth, P. (1997). *Achoo!* New York: Grosset & Dunlap.

dePaola, T. (1975). *Strega Nona: An old tale.* Englewood Cliffs, NJ: Prentice Hall.

dePaola, T. (1978). *The popcorn book.* New York: Holiday House.

Eberts, M. (1984). *Pancakes, crackers, and pizza.* Chicago: Children's Press.

Faulkner, M. (1986). *Jack and the beanstalk.* New York: Scholastic.

Hoban, R. (1976). *Bread and jam for Frances.* New York: Harper & Row.

Hopkins, L. B. (1985). *Munching: Poems about eating.* Boston: Little, Brown.

Irving, W. (1987). *Rip Van Winkle*. New York: Puffin Books.

Izawa, T. (1968). *The little red hen*. New York: Grosset & Dunlap.

Katzen, M., & Henderson, A. (1994). *Pretend soup and other real recipes: A cookbook for preschoolers and up*. Berkeley, CA: Ten Speed Press.

Kellogg, S. (1988). *Johnny Appleseed: A tall tale*. New York: Morrow Jr. Books.

Krauss, R. (1945). *The carrot seed*. New York: Scholastic.

Mayer, M. (1968). *There's a nightmare in my closet*. New York: Penguin.

McCloskey, R. (1948). *Blueberries for Sal*. New York: Penguin.

Montanari, D. (2001). *Children around the world*. Tonawanda, NY: Kids Can Press.

Numeroff-Joffe, L. (1985). *If you give a mouse a cookie*. New York: Scholastic.

Raffi. (1987). *Shake my sillies out*. New York: Random House.

Reid, M. (1996). *Let's find out about ice cream*. New York: Scholastic.

Ripley, C. (1997). *Why does popcorn pop? And other kitchen questions*. Toronto: Firefly Books.

Rockwell, L. (1999). *Good enough to eat: A kid's guide to food and nutrition*. New York: HarperCollins.

Sharmat, M. (1984). *Gregory, the terrible eater*. New York: Macmillan.

Shaw, C. (1947). *It looked like spilled milk*. New York: HarperCollins.

Showers, P. (1997). *Sleep is for everyone* (Let's read-and-find-out science book). New York: HarperCollins.

Silverstein, A., Silverstein, V. B., & Silverstein Nunn, L. (2000). *Eat your vegetables! Drink your milk!* New York: Scholastic.

Simon, S. (1997). *The brain: Our nervous system*. New York: Scholastic.

Suess, Dr. (1960). *Green eggs and ham*. New York: Random House.

Taylor, B. (1998). *A day at the farm*. New York: DK Publishing.

Thomas, P. (2002) *My amazing body: A first look at health and fitness*. Hauppauge, NY: Barron's Educational Series, Inc.

Westcott, N. B. (1980). *I know an old lady*. Boston: Little, Brown.

Zolotow, C. (1962). *Mr. Rabbit and the lovely present*. New York: Harper & Row.

Introductory Lesson

Objective
A written message will provide for vocabulary development and sound–symbol associations. Print will be recognized as functional because it relays a message.

Activity: Morning Message—Introduce the students to the good health unit by writing a message on the board. The message could look something like this:

"*Today, we are going to begin learning about how to keep our bodies and our minds healthy. To take care of ourselves we need to eat good food, sleep, exercise, keep our bodies clean, and feel good about ourselves.*" Read the message to the class using a pointer to track the print. Afterward discuss the content of the message as well as the special words, letters, and sounds. Allow the children to add to the message. Do a morning message daily to inform students of new health facts, as well as any special events or questions that are related to the unit.

Concepts about Print
Objective 1
Increase oral and sight vocabulary through a discussion involving the seeing and writing of Very Own Words. Knowledge of nutrition will be gained.

Activity: Very Own Words—Before reading the story *I Know an Old Lady Who Swallowed a Fly* (Westcott, 1980), discuss with the children why it is dangerous to eat inappropriate food. After reading the story, the children will discuss food they should not eat. Then ask them to name foods they like that are also good for them and *The Old Lady*. Write each child's favorite food on a 3-by-5 index card to be stored in their Very Own Word container.

Objective 2
Increase sight vocabulary and the ability to follow directions by using a chart with functional environmental print.

Activity: Environmental Print—A helper chart will be made that lists jobs for students to perform. The chart should be located in a visible area and relate directly to the unit. Jobs may include cafeteria monitor, reading the lunch menu, and helping with the daily snack.

Objective 3
An alphabet book that reviews many nutrition words learned in the unit will be created. Knowledge of letters, both vowels and consonants, and words that are identified with specific letters and sounds will be demonstrated.

Activity: Nutrition Alphabet Book—An alphabet book will be made and photocopied for each child in the class. Each letter will relate to nutrition (i.e., *A—apple, B—bread, C—carrot, D—dairy, E—eggs, F—fish*.), and a complete sentence will be written with each letter (i.e., I like ___). The students will read the letters, words, and sentences with the teacher and with each other.

Oral Language

Objective 1

Speaking skills will be improved by speaking in complete sentences.

Activity: Show and Tell—Have students bring in their favorite foods from home representing different cultural backgrounds. Display and discuss with the class. Another activity would be to have children share a healthy habit they practice at home or at school.

Objective 2

Appropriate vocabulary for the level of maturity will be used when retelling a story.

Activity: Story Retelling—Read a story related to nutrition, such as *The Very Hungry Caterpillar* (Carle, 1969), and allow the class to retell the story using food props that are in the book.

Objective 3

Language complexity will be increased through the use of adjectives.

Activity: Webbing and Creating Poetry—Brainstorm characteristics of nutritious food, such as milk, and provide a graphic presentation with a web (see below). List the characteristics of the food by writing adjectives to describe it. Create a web on the chalkboard. Encourage children to assist in putting together a poem by using the information on the web. Write the poem on the chalkboard. Encourage children to read it with you, tracking print from left to right as you read. Rewrite the poem on chart paper to display.

Motivating Reading and Writing

Objective 1

A story is read by a class parent to increase family literacy. Using the context of the story, outcomes will be predicted.

Activity: Prop Story—A child's family member will read *If You Give a Mouse a Cookie* (Numeroff-Joffe, 1985) to the class. Use props such as a mouse doll, a plastic cup, an empty box of cookies, and so on to tell the story again to the class. Encourage participation by having the children use their knowledge of rhyme and context. Place the props in the library corner for the children to use.

Objective 2

A graphic organizer will be created to motivate interest and help comprehend an informational text.

Activity: The Food Pyramid—Read *Good Enough to Eat: A Kid's Guide to Food and Nutrition* (Rockwell, 1999) and discuss the food in the book. Next, have the children work together to create a food pyramid on the board, based on the information in the book. After they have drawn the pyramid, they can add the name of their favorite food to the appropriate food group. Discuss the nutritional value of these foods.

Concepts about Books

Objective 1

Learn to differentiate print from pictures and know what books are for.

Activity: Big Book—Create a class big book that contains pictures and sentences of each child's favorite exercise or sport. When it is completed, read the book together. Place the big book in the library corner for repeated readings.

Objective 2

See and understand that print is read from left to right.

Activity: Poetry Reading—Display a poem (such as "Shake My Sillies Out", Raffi, 1987) about movement

Our Poem about Milk

Milk tastes cold and delicious,
Milk is healthy and refreshing,
Milk is a white liquid that is good for you.

or exercise on a large chart and read with the class. Use a pointer to show that print is read from left to right. Act out the poem and then create a class poem. Display and read it in the same manner.

Comprehension

Objective 1

Learn about story structure by identifying story elements (setting, theme, characters, plot episodes, resolution).

Activity: Story Structure—The story *There's a Nightmare in My Closet* (Mayer, 1968) has been read to the children in the past. Before reading the story a second time, ask the children to try and remember the time that the story takes place, where the story takes place, and who the characters are. After reading the story the second time, have the children identify the three setting elements: *time, place,* and *characters.* Do the same thing with other story elements such as the *theme, plot episodes,* and *resolution.* Have the children prepare a roll movie with five headings: Setting, Theme, Characters, Plot Episodes, and Resolution. Do one section of the roll movie at a time. Encourage them to draw pictures and include narrative for each of the sections. Repeat with other stories.

Objective 2

Create a **K-W-L** chart (what they **K**now, what they **W**ant to know, and what they have **L**earned).

Activity: K-W-L Activity—Begin a discussion about exercise and how it affects the body. Ask what the children know about the importance of exercise. List their responses on chart paper under the heading "What We Know." Ask the students what they might want to learn about the subject, and list those responses on chart paper as well under the heading "What We Want To Know." Introduce and read

several informational books, posters, pamphlets, and magazines about exercise and a healthy body, such as *My Amazing Body: A First Look at Health and Fitness* (Thomas, 2002). After several days of discussion and activities in conjunction with these books, refer back to the lists you made at the beginning of the lesson. Create a new heading titled, "What We Learned" and ask the students to share things they learned about exercise over the past several days. Compare this list to the list of what they wanted to know about exercise. Ask questions like, How are they different? What could you do if you didn't learn something you wanted to know? Have the students complete similar charts before and after other lessons.

Writing

Objective 1

Emerging authors and illustrators: Learn that books are written by authors, and that pictures are drawn by illustrators. Children will participate in brainstorming, drafting, conferencing, editing, and revising and engage in an experience chart as a prewriting activity.

Activity: Bed-Shaped Book—Read the books *Mooncake* (Asch, 1983) and *Sleep Is for Everyone* (Showers, 1997). Create a story web on experience chart paper as students talk about characteristics of sleep (why it is important, what happens when you sleep). Each child will be writing a story about sleep while teacher conferences take place. Finished products will be written in books shaped like a bed. This activity can be extended to other topics related to the theme. For example, books may also be shaped like a bathtub or bar of soap if the story is about personal hygiene.

Objective 2

Communicate through writing about exercise and nutrition. See and use functional writing.

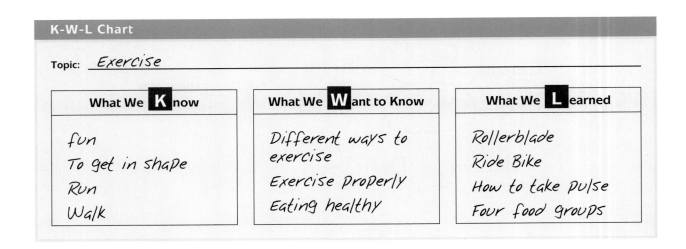

K-W-L Chart

Topic: _Exercise_

What We **K**now	What We **W**ant to Know	What We **L**earned
fun To get in shape Run Walk	Different ways to exercise Exercise properly Eating healthy	Rollerblade Ride Bike How to take pulse Four food groups

Activity: Notice Bulletin Board—A notice bulletin board with student and teacher sections will be prepared in the classroom. Children may display their work on the board, as well as leave and receive messages in their spaces. Students can share messages, such as what they had for lunch and what food group each item belonged to or what exercise or sport they played in gym or at home. They may also decorate their personal space by drawing pictures related to these topics.

Play

Objective 1
Follow written directions and use print in a functional manner in an outdoor play activity.

Activity: Outdoor Play. Health Club—Set up a health club outside with different exercise stations. Have a sign-in sheet at each numbered station. Have children choose roles such as directing an exercise class, pouring water, filling in membership cards, or writing receipts. Encourage the children to name their club and hang posters as advertisements.

Objective 2
Engage in dramatic play while building self-esteem and respect for each other.

Activity: Dramatic Play. "I'm Glad I'm Me" Kingdom—Watch *Sesame Street*'s "I'm Glad I'm Me" with Prince Charming Bird. Create an "I'm Glad I'm Me" Kingdom in the dramatic-play area. Hang flags the children have made to represent the things each child is proud of and likes about him- or herself. Supply crowns, robes, scepters, and so on. Place a basket of fairytale books in the center.

Art

Objective 1
Self-esteem and self-assessment will be fostered over the course of the unit.

Activity: I'm "Thumb Print" Body Books—Children will be given blank books to illustrate. On the cover, they will put their thumb print and write the words "I'm (thumb print) Body." Each week, they will draw a picture of something they have accomplished or are proud of. Encourage them to write beginning sounds or engage in invented spelling to accompany their pictures or take dictations in the books. After each entry, collect books and make motivational comments to the children. At the end of the unit, ask children to make a final comment on what they think their biggest accomplishment was.

Objective 2
Gain an appreciation for creativity and ingenuity by designing pictures and jewelry based on different cultures. Increase visual discrimination and enrich vocabulary through observation and discussion.

Activity: Macaroni Art—Pictures using macaroni, beans, dried fruits, seeds, and so on can be made. Jewelry can also be made by using macaroni and string. Macaroni can be dyed by placing it in food coloring and water for three minutes. Provide students with pictures, books, or authentic examples of multicultural jewelry, such as Mexican or Native American necklaces, bracelets, or rings. Encourage children to design such types of jewelry. Students will observe and model each other's work and describe their own to the class.

Music

Objective 1
Recall skills will be enhanced, as children relate their own bedtime experiences to the group.

Activity: Bedtime Round—Listen to "Bedtime Round" by Tom Chapin. Post the lyrics and track from left to right as the children listen. Talk about bedtime and list other things children say in order to delay going to sleep. After practicing, try to sing the song in rounds as in the recording.

Objective 2
Increase sight word vocabulary. Talk about feelings and emotions in a supportive environment.

Activity: If You're Happy and You Know It—Sing the song "If You're Happy and You Know It." For each emotion, draw the corresponding face on a paper plate with the emotion written on it. Make a variety of plates—for example, if you're sad and you know it, if you're angry and you know it. Practice the song with the picture cards until the children can recognize the words without the drawings. Talk about each feeling. Make a list of things that make you feel each type of emotion.

Social Studies

Objective 1
The children should gain an appreciation for other cultures' influence on popular sports for exercise and should increase their knowledge of geography and other cultures.

Activity: Sports Study—Students work in small groups to research the popular sports from other counties. Each group's contributions are added to a class Big Book about the topic. Play the different sports on the playground.

Objective 2
By introducing foods and customs of different countries, an appreciation for the differences and contributions of

other people and cultures will be developed. Oral and written communication skills will be increased.

Activity: Country of the Week—Read *Children around the World* (Montanari, 2001). A "Country of the Week" will be focused on. Customs, foods, and major contributions of each will be highlighted. Children will discuss the differences and similarities among the countries, with an emphasis on foods and the healthfulness of each. The students may also write about their favorite food from each country. Different foods will be featured at snack time.

Science
Objective 1
The connection between oral and written language will be made through a discussion about how you catch a cold.

Activity: I Wish I Was Sick, Too—Read *I Wish I Was Sick, Too* (Brandenberg, 1976). Use an experience chart to record what the children know about catching a cold. Discuss the importance of cleanliness and the prevalence of germs in our lives. Allow each child to collect a sample of germs from objects and place on an agar petri dish. Students can then predict which samples will grow faster than others. Children can then record their observations of any significant growth. Provide microscopes and/or magnifying glasses for more detailed observations.

Objective 2
Observe changes that occur in the form of food while following directions in preparing a recipe.

Activity: Making Applesauce—Read *Johnny Appleseed* (Demuth, 1996) to the class. Discuss the nutritional value of apple products. Make applesauce with the class. Post the recipe and use it as a reference to point out all the steps involved in making applesauce.

Math
Objective 1
The connection between oral and written communication will be made by observing and recording the sleep patterns of animals.

Activity: Sleep Patterns—Students will observe and record the sleep patterns of the class pet and graph daily results. Compare any differences on the graphs, and discuss how animals need different amounts of sleep at different times of the day.

Objective 2
Relate pictures to text, and see that pictures and print go together. Classify objects according to shape (triangles, circles, squares).

Activity: Sort a Food—Read *Pancakes, Crackers, and Pizza* (Eberts, 1984) to the class. Emphasize the different shapes of food as you read: round pancakes, square crackers, and triangular shaped pieces of pizza. Create a chart with three columns (triangles, circles, squares). Encourage children to classify cut-out pictures of food from magazines or newspapers in the appropriate columns on the chart. Provide three shoe boxes labeled with each shape so that children can continue to classify different foods on their own.

Culminating Activity
Objective 1
Share the products of the unit with children's family, friends, or other classes in the school.

Activity: Prepare a nutritious food, such as fruit salad and applesauce, for a snack to share with guests.

Activity: Sing a song related to the importance of rest from the unit, such as "Bedtime Round," or related to the importance of personal hygiene, such as "Brush Your Teeth."

Activity: Display art projects related to the unit, and describe how they were made.

Activity: Show plants from the science portion of the unit and discuss how they grew.

*Written by Lesley Morrow
with Rutgers Graduate Students
Julie Anastasi, Kathleen Cunningham,
Patty DeWitt, Erica Erlanger, Pam Kelliher,
Lisa Lozak, Donna Ngai, and Melody Olsen*

appendix E

Professional Associations and Related Journals Dealing with Early Literacy

What we have learned over the years concerning learning theory and early literacy development is due to research by college professors and classroom teachers. Professional associations hold conferences and publish journals to inform and move the field forward. This appendix provides a list of such groups and journals, along with other publications dealing with early literacy, for future study and reference.

American Library Association (ALA), 50 East Huron Street, Chicago, IL 60611, www.ala.org

American Montessori Society, Inc. (AMS), 281 Park Avenue South, 6th Floor, New York, NY 10010, www.amshq.org

Association for Childhood Education International (ACEI), 17904 Georgia Avenue, Suite 215, Olney, MD 20832, www.acei.org
Journals: *Childhood Education; Journal of Research in Childhood Education*

Child Welfare League of America, Inc. (CWLA), 440 First Street NW, 3rd Floor, Washington, DC 20001, www.cwla.org
Journal: *Child Welfare*

Children's Bureau, Office of Child Development, U.S. Department of Health, Education and Welfare, Washington, DC 20201
Journal: *Children Today*

Gordon and Breach Science Publishers, Inc., PO Box 32160, Newark, NJ 07102
Journal: *Early Child Development and Care*

Highlights for Children, PO Box 269, Columbus, OH 43215-0269
Publication: *Teaching PreK–8* (www.teachingk-8.com)

High/Scope Educational Research Foundation, 600 North River Street, Ypsilanti MI 48198-2898, www.highscope.org
Publications, videos, research, professional development

International Reading Association (IRA), 800 Barksdale Road, PO Box 8139, Newark, DE 19711, www.reading.org
Journals: *The Reading Teacher; Reading Research Quarterly;* brochures, pamphlets, and monographs

National Association for the Education of Young Children (NAEYC), 1509 16th Street NW, Washington, DC 20036, www.naeyc.org
Journals: *Young Children; Early Childhood Research Quarterly;* pamphlets and monographs

National Center for Family Literacy, 325 West Main Street, Suite 300, Louisville, KY 40202-4237, www.famlit.org
Newsletter: *Momentum*

National Child Care Information Center, 243 Church Street NW, 2nd Floor, Vienna, VA 22180, www.nccic.org

National Council of Teachers of English (NCTE), 1111 Kenyon Road, Urbana, IL 61801, www.ncte.org
Journal: Language Arts

National Education Association, 1201 16th Street NW, Washington, DC 20036, www.nea.org
Journal: *NEA Today*
Magazine: *Tomorrow's Teachers*

National Even Start Association, 2225 Camino del Rio South, Suite A, San Diego, CA 92108, www.evenstart.org
Journal: *Family Literacy Forum*

National Head Start Association, 1651 Prince Street, Alexandria, VA 22314, www.nhsa.org
Publication: *Children and Families Magazine*

National Reading Conference (NRC), 11 East Hubbard St., Chicago, IL 60603
Journal: *Journal of Literacy Research*

Office of Early Childhood Development, 717 14th Street NW, Suite 450, Washington, DC 20005

Reach Out and Read National Center, 29 Mystic Avenue, Somerville, MA 02145, www.reachoutandread.org

Reading Is Fundamental, 1825 Connecticut Avenue NW, Washington, DC 20009, www.rif.org
Newsletter: *Read All about It*

Scholastic, Inc., 555 Broadway, New York, NY 10012, www.scholastic.com
Publications: *Early Childhood Today; Instructor*

Society for Research in Child Development (SRCD), 5750 Ellis Avenue, Chicago, IL 60637, www.srcd.org
Journal: *Child Development*

Glossary

aesthetic talk   A form of conversation revolving around narrative literature in which children interpret and discuss what has been heard or read in relation to themselves.

aliterate   An individual who can read but chooses not to.

alphabetic principle   Knowing that words are composed of letters and that there is a systematic relationship between the letters and the sounds they hear.

antiphonal reading   A choral reading in which parts are taken by groups.

auditory discrimination   The ability to hear, identify, and differentiate among familiar sounds, similar sounds, rhyming words, and letter sounds.

authentic assessment   Assessment based on activities that represent and reflect the actual learning and instruction in the classroom.

balanced approach to literacy instruction   The selection of theory and strategies to match learning styles of children. Constructivist and explicit strategies are both used.

behaviorist approach   A learning theory in which adults provide a model and children learn through imitation encouraged by positive reinforcement.

big books   Oversized books designed to allow children to see the print as it is being read.

blend   A reader's ability to hear a series of isolated speech sounds then recognize and pronounce them as a complete word.

buddy reading   The pairing of a child from an upper grade with a younger child for storybook reading.

choral reading   A small group or the entire class reads along with the teacher, who provides pacing and expression.

chunk   Any group of letters within a word that is taught as a whole pattern; a chunk could be a phonogram, digraph, blend, etc.

comprehension   An active process whereby a reader interprets and constructs meaning about the text based on prior knowledge and experience.

conference   Meeting with the teacher or a peer to discuss work in progress.

consonant blends   Two or three letters that, when placed together, merge into one sound while retaining representations of each letter sound (e.g., *bl* or *str*).

constructivist theory   A theory that views learning as an active process where children construct knowledge to learn by problem solving, guessing, and approximating.

context clues   The use of syntax and semantic meaning of text to aid in word identification.

contracts   Assignment sheets designating specific activities to be carried out by individual learners based on their needs, interests, and ability levels.

cooperative learning   An instructional strategy in which children come together to learn through debate and discussion.

cultural diversity   Reference to the wide variety of backgrounds, languages, customs, and environments represented within the larger society or a given classroom.

descriptive writing   Writing with language that describes precisely.

decoding   Identifying words by using letter-sound and structural analysis.

digraph   Consonant digraphs are two consonants that, when placed together, make one new sound unlike the sound of either individual letter (e.g., *th* or *ch*). Vowel digraphs are two vowels together that make one sound which could be the sound of either vowel or a new sound (e.g., *ie, ai, oo, ou*).

directed listening and thinking activity (DLTA) and **directed reading and thinking activity (DRTA)**   A framework which offers directions and strategies for organizing and retrieving information from a text that is read by or to a child. The steps in DLTA or DRTA include preparation for listening/reading with prequestions and discussion, setting a purpose for reading, reading the story, and a follow-up postreading discussion based on the purpose set prior to reading.

Drop Everything and Read (DEAR) time   Quiet time for children to engage in silent reading.

early intervention   Programs, for children with special needs or those who are "at risk," in early childhood education intended to prevent potential problems in literacy development. The focus of the programs is on developmentally appropriate instruction using authentic reading and writing experiences. The program can be a pullout or inclusion setting.

echo reading   The teacher reads a line of text and then the child reads the same line. The number of lines read is increased as the child's reading improves.

efferent talk   A formal mode of conversation about expository text used to inform and persuade.

emergent literacy   As coined by Marie Clay, refers to a child's early unconventional attempts at reading, writing, and listening.

English language learners   Children whose first language is not English. These children can have varying levels of English ability from no English to some.

environmental print   Familiar print found in the surroundings such as logos, food labels, and road signs.

explicit instruction   A teacher-directed strategy with emphasis on teaching a task and the specific steps needed to master it.

expository text   Text in any form that is informational and nonfiction.

expository writing   Writing that includes many types of experiences and is usually about information that comes from content-area subjects such as social studies or science. This involves collecting information and summarizing it.

family literacy   Refers to the different ways in which family members initiate and use literacy in their daily living.

fluency   Level of reading ease and ability; a fluent reader is able to read on- or above-level books independently with high comprehension and accuracy.

functional print   Print for a purpose such as informational signs, directions, greeting cards, lists, letters to pen pals, and messages for the notice board.

functional writing   Writing that serves clear, real-life purposes, including greeting cards and thank-you notes.

genre   A specific type of literature such as picture storybook, informational book, or poetry.

gifted   Demonstrating exceptional ability.

graphemes   Letters that make up individual sounds.

guided reading   Explicit reading instruction usually in small groups based on literacy needs.

high-frequency words   Words that are frequently found in reading materials for children.

high-stakes assessment   Standardized measures whose scores might determine major decisions about school districts, such as ratings of districts and promotion or retention decisions.

inclusion   Special help and enrichment are offered in the regular classroom with the help of resource teachers and regular teachers planning together and teaching all children. This is in place of or in addition to pull-out programs for special help.

independent reading and writing periods (IRWP)   A socially interactive time wherein children select among books and other literacy-related materials.

informal reading inventory   Informal tests to determine a child's independent, instructional, and frustration level of reading.

integrated language arts   An approach to literacy instruction that links reading, writing, listening, and language skills.

interdisciplinary literacy instruction   Integration of content-area learning with literacy.

intergenerational literacy initiatives   Planned, systematic programs specifically designed to improve the literacy development of both adults and children.

invented spelling   Improvised spelling for words unknown in conventional spelling wherein one letter often represents an entire syllable.

journal writing   Written entries in notebooks by children including: *dialogue*, which is shared with teachers or peers who respond to what they read; *personal*, involving private thoughts related to children's lives or topics of special interest; *reading response*, writing in response to text reading; and *learning log*, a record of information usually involving other content areas.

K-W-L   A cognitive strategy that enhances comprehension by assessing with students what they *Know*, what they *Want* to know, and what they *Learned* before and after reading.

language experience approach (LEA)   A reading instruction method aimed at linking oral with written language on the premise that what is thought can be said, what is said can be written, and what is written can be read.

learning centers   Spaces in the classroom filled with materials for independent student activity focusing on current topics of study within content areas and including literacy materials as well.

learning disabled   Demonstrating significant difficulty in the acquisition and use of reading, writing, listening, speaking, and/or mathematical skills.

literacy center   A classroom area composed of a library corner and writing area.

literature-based instruction   An approach to teaching reading in which varied genres of children's literature are used as the main source of reading material.

literature circles   Discussion groups used to encourage critical discussions about literature among children.

mapping and webbing   Strategies for understanding text through the use of graphic representations for categorizing and structuring information. Maps deal with more detailed representations.

mental imagery   Visualization of readings used to increase comprehension and clarify thought.

metacognition   Awareness of one's own mental processes concerning how learning takes place.

morning message   A daily message about items of interest to children written by the teacher who points out concepts about print.

narrative writing   Writing stories.

nativist theory   The theory that language develops innately.

neural shearing   Loss of brain cells.

nonstandard English   A dialectal form of English that differs from the standard form in words, syntax, and language patterns.

onset   Initial letter or letters before the first vowel in a word.

paired reading   A more able reader from the same class or another class acts as a tutor while reading with a less fluent student.

parent-involvement programs   Programs designed to involve and inform parents about activities that will promote their children's literacy development in school.

partner reading   Peers reading together either simultaneously side by side or taking turns reading to each other.

persuasive writing   Writing that involves trying to get someone to have your point of view.

phonemes   Sounds made by individual letters and combinations of letters that make a single sound.

phonemic awareness   Knowing that words are composed of a sequence of spoken sounds and being able to hear and identify those sounds. Phonemic awareness includes the ability to segment and blend individual sounds. Phonemic awareness is strictly an oral activity without association to symbols.

phonics   A strategy that involves learning the alphabetic principles of language and knowledge of letter-sound relationships. Children learn to associate letters with the phonemes or basic speech sounds of English, to help them break the alphabetic code and become independent readers in the pronunciation of words.

phonogram   A series of letters that begin with a vowel and are often found together (for example, *ack, ed, ight, ock, ush,* etc.).

phonological awareness   The ability to identify and manipulate individual speech sounds as well as syllables and whole words. Children can segment and blend single phonemes, syllables, and words.

poetry writing   Poems can be rhymes or can follow other formulas such as haiku or acrostics.

portfolio assessment   A strategy for measuring student progress by collecting samples of their work that is placed into a folder called a portfolio. Materials include samples of student's written work or drawings, anecdotal records, audiotapes, videotapes, checklists, and teacher-made and standardized test results, among others.

process approach to writing   Steps involved in the production of text including prewriting, drafting, conferencing, revising, editing, and performing.

pull-out programs   Programs in which students are taken out of their classrooms for special help in literacy instruction or enrichment.

reader's theater   The oral reading of a short play, in which children have parts and practice them for presentation.

reading readiness   Various skills considered prerequisite in learning to read such as auditory discrimination, visual discrimination, and motor skills.

Reading Recovery   An early intervention program devised by Marie Clay in which first graders experiencing difficulties with reading receive intensive, one-on-one instruction using developmentally appropriate integrated language arts techniques.

reading workshop   A period of time set aside for children to work on reading skills, reading books, and conferencing with the teacher.

repeated reading   Reading the same book or story over and over until it is repeated or known. This familiarity offers the opportunity for fluent reading.

response groups   A strategy for enhancing comprehension where students exchange or refine ideas and think critically about issues related to what they have listened to or read.

rich literacy environments   Environments rich with materials that encourage reading and writing and support instruction.

rime   Ending part of a word that contains the vowel and the remainder of the word. Onsets and rimes make up words.

running record   An assessment strategy that involves the close observation and recording of a child's oral reading behavior. Running records may be used for planning instruction.

scaffolding   A strategy in which teachers provide children with modeling and support to help them acquire a skill.

segment   To divide words into segments based in their sound components; cat is "c-a-t."

self-monitoring   A student's ability to read and self-correct words as they are read.

semantics   Meaning that language communicates.

shared book experiences   Whole- or small-group reading instruction through literature selections, in which big books are often used so that children can see the print and pictures. Big books enable children to listen and participate in actual book readings.

sight words   The words that are known immediately by a reader. Once a word becomes a sight word, the reader does not need to use word-attack skills to read it.

standards   Achievement goals that are defined at a state or national level and identify what students should know at the end of each grade level.

standardized tests   An assessment measure, commercially prepared and norm-referenced, that reports results in terms of grade level scores and percentile ranks.

story retellings   The recital of familiar stories, in children's own words, in written or oral form to develop and assess comprehension of story.

story structure   The elements of a well-constructed story including setting, theme, plot episodes, and resolution.

sustained silent reading (SSR)   A time allocated for children to read silently.

synaptogenesis   Connecting of brain cells, or rapid development of neural connections.

syntax   The structure of language or rules that govern how words work together in phrases, clauses, and sentences.

tape-assisted reading   Listening to fluent reading samples on audiotapes while following the written text.

telegraphic speech   A form of speech used by children at about twelve months of age in which content words, such as nouns and verbs, are used, for example "Mommy cookie," but function words, such as conjunctions and articles, are omitted.

thematic unit   A topic of study is learned through explorations across all areas of the curriculum.

think-aloud   A comprehension strategy in which children talk about what they have read or other ideas they have about a story.

think, pair, share   A discussion strategy that combines think time with cooperative learning. Following teacher-posed questions, the teacher first has children *think* about their answers; then children *pair* with a partner to discuss their responses; and finally, during *share,* the students share responses with the group.

t-chart   A graphic organizer that helps to comprehend expository and narrative text by classifying similarities and differences in characters, facts, and ideas.

t-unit   An independent clause with all its dependent clauses attached that is helpful in measuring a child's language complexity.

Very Own Words   Favorite words generated by children, written on index cards, and kept in a container for them to read and write.

visual discrimination   The ability to note similarities and differences visually between objects, including the ability to recognize colors, shapes, and letters.

whole language   A philosophy from which strategies are drawn for literacy development. Strategies include the use of real literature, with the concurrent instruction of reading, writing, and oral language in meaningful, functional, and cooperative contexts, to help students become motivated to read and write.

word-study skills   Knowledge about print including the use of phonics context and syntax to decipher unknown words; the development of sight vocabulary; and the use of word configuration and structural analysis.

word wall   A type of bulletin board or classroom display that features challenging and/or high-frequency words organized alphabetically.

writing mechanics   Skills related to writing such as spelling, handwriting, punctuation, and spacing.

writing workshop   A period of time set aside for children to practice writing skills, work on writing projects, and confer with the teacher.

zone of proximal development   Based on Vygotsky's theory, this term refers to the period of time when a child has been guided by an adult and no longer needs the help. The adult retreats and allows the child to work on his or her own.

Aliki. (1974). *Go tell Aunt Rhody.* New York: Macmillan.

Archambault, I., & Martin, B., Jr. *Chicka-Chicka-Boom-Boom.* (1989). New York: Scholastic.

Avery, K., & McPhail, D. (1993). *The crazy quilt.* Glenview, IL: Scott Foresman.

Base, G. (1987). *Animalia.* New York: Harry N. Abrams.

Bemelmans, L. (1939). *Madeline.* New York: Viking.

Bemelmans, L. (1953). *Madeline's rescue.* New York: Viking.

Berenstain, S., & Berenstain, J. (1987). *The Berenstain bears and too much birthday.* New York: Random House.

Branley, F. M. (1985) *Volcanoes.* New York: Harper & Row Junior Books

Brenner, B. (1972). *The three little pigs.* New York: Random House.

Brett, J. (1989). *The mitten.* New York: Putnam & Grosset.

Brett, J. (1997). *The hat.* New York: Putnam & Grosset.

Brown, M. (1939). *The noisy book.* New York: Harper.

Brown, M. (1947). *Goodnight moon.* New York: HarperCollins.

Brown, M. (1957). *The three billy goats gruff.* New York: Harcourt Brace.

Brown, M. (1990). *Arthur's pet business.* New York: Little Brown.

Burton, V. L. (1943). *Katy and the big snow.* Boston: Houghton Mifflin.

Carle, E. (1969). *The very hungry caterpillar.* New York: Philomel.

Cole, J. (1987). *The magic school bus inside the earth.* New York: Scholastic.

deBeer, H. (1996). *Little polar bear, take me home!* New York: North-South Books.

dePaola, T. (1973). *Charlie needs a clock.* Englewood Cliffs, NJ: Prentice Hall.

dePaola, T. (1978). *The popcorn book.* New York: Holiday House.

Duvoisin, R. (1950). *Petunia.* New York: Alfred A. Knopf.

Eastman, P. D. (1960). *Are you my mother?* New York: Random House.

Emberley, B. (1967). *Drummer Hoff.* Englewood Cliffs, NJ: Prentice Hall.

Fowler, A. (1992). *Frogs and toads and tadpoles, too!* Chicago, Children's Press.

Fujikawa, A. (1980). *Jenny learns a lesson.* New York: Grosset & Dunlap.

Galdone, P. (1973). *The little red hen.* Boston: Houghton Mifflin.

Hazen, B. S. (1983). *Tight times.* New York: Picture Puffins.

Hennessy, B. G. (1991). *The missing tarts.* New York: Puffin Books.

Hennessy, B. G., & Pearson, T. C. (1989). *The queen of hearts.* New York: Picture Puffins.

Hoban, R. (1964). *Bread and jam for Frances.* New York: Harper & Row.

Hoberman, M. A. (2001). *You read to me, I'll read to you.* New York: Little Brown

Holdsworth, W. (1968). *The gingerbread boy.* New York: Farrar, Straus & Giroux.

Hurd, E. (1980). *Under the lemon tree.* Boston: Little, Brown.

Hutchins, P. (1968). *Rosie's walk.* New York: Collier Books.

Izawa, T. (1968a). *Goldilocks and the three bears.* New York: Grosset & Dunlap.

Izawa, T. (1968b). *The little red hen.* New York: Grosset & Dunlap.

Johnson, A. (1990). *Do like Kyla.* New York: Scholastic.

Johnson, C. (1955). *Harold and the purple crayon.* New York: Harper & Row.

Kasza, K. (1988). *The pig's picnic.* New York: Putnam.

Keats, E. (1962). *The snowy day.* New York: Viking.

Keats, E. (1966). *Jenny's hat.* New York: Harper & Row.

Keats, E. J. (1967). *Peter's chair.* New York: Harper & Row.

Keats, E. J. (1968). *A letter to Amy.* New York: Puffin.

Keats, E. J. (1971). *Over in the meadow.* New York: Scholastic.

Keats, E. J. (1974). *Pet show.* New York: Aladdin Books.

Kellogg, S. (1989). *Is your mama a llama?* New York: Scholastic.

Lenski, L. (1965). *The little farm.* New York: Henry Z. Walek.

LeSieg, T. (1961). *Ten apples up on top.* New York: Random House.

Lillegard, D., & McPhail, D. (1993). *Potatoes on Tuesday.* Glenview, IL: Scott Foresman.

Lionni, L. (1963). *Swimmy.* New York: Pantheon.

Livingston, M. C. (1993). *Abraham Lincoln: A man for all people.* New York: Holiday House.

Lobel, A. L. (1979). *Frog and toad are friends.* New York: HarperCollins.

Maass, R. (1993). *When winter comes.* New York: Scholastic.

Magee, D., & Newman, R. (1999) *All Aboard ABC.* New York: Penguin Books

Merriam, E. (1989). *Where is everybody?* New York: Simon and Schuster.

McCloskey, R. (1948). *Blueberries for Sal.* New York: Viking.

McGovern, A. (1967). *Too much noise.* Boston: Houghton Mifflin.

McNulty, F. (1979). *How to dig a hole to the other side of the world.* New York: Harper & Row.

Neitzel, S. (1991). *The jacket I wear in the snow.* New York: Greenwillow Books.

Parrish, P. (1970). *Amelia Bedelia.* New York: Avon Books.

Piper, W. (1954). *The little engine that could.* New York: Platt and Munk.

Potter, B. (1902). *The tale of Peter Rabbit.* New York: Scholastic.

Quackenbush, R. (1972). *Old MacDonald had a farm.* New York: Lippincott.

Quackenbush, R. (1973). *Go tell Aunt Rhody.* New York: Lippincott.

Rankin, L. (1991). *The handmade alphabet.* New York: Dial Books

Reid, S., & Fernandes, E. (1992). *The wild toboggan ride.* New York: Scholastic.

Rey, H. A. (1941). *Curious George.* Boston: Houghton Mifflin.

Sendak, M. (1962). *Chicken soup with rice.* New York: Harper & Row.

Sendak, M. (1962). *Pierre.* New York: HarperCollins.

Sendak, M. (1963). *Where the wild things are.* New York: Harper & Row.

Seuss, Dr. (1940). *Horton hatches the egg.* New York: Random House.

Seuss, Dr. (1957a). *How the Grinch stole Christmas.* New York: Random House.

Seuss, Dr. (1957b). *The cat in the hat.* New York: Random House.

Seuss, Dr. (1960). *Green eggs and ham.* New York: Random House.

Seuss, Dr. (1970). *Mr. Brown can moo! Can you?* New York: Random House.

Shelby, A., & Travis, I. (1991) *Potluck.* New York: Orchard Books

Slobodkina, E. (1947). *Caps for sale.* Reading, MA: Addison-Wesley.

Tchin (1997). *Rabbits wish for snow: A Native American legend.* New York: Scholastic.

Viorst, J. (1972). *Alexander and the terrible, horrible, no good, very bad day.* New York: Atheneum.

Westcott, N. B. (1980). *I know an old lady.* Boston: Little, Brown.

White, E. B. (1952). *Charlotte's web.* New York: Scholastic.

Zoehfeld, K. W. (1994). *Manatee winter.* Hartford, CT: Trudy Corporation.

Zolotow, C. (1962). *Mr. Rabbit and the lovely present.* New York: Harper & Row.

Bibliography

Adams, M. J. (1990). *Beginning to read: Thinking and learning about print*. Urbana: University of Illinois Center for the Study of Reading.

Adams, M. J. (2001). Alphabetic anxiety and explicit, systematic phonics instruction: A cognitive science perspective. In S. B. Neuman & D. K. Dickinson (Eds.), *Handbook of early literacy research* (pp. 66–80). New York: Guilford Press.

Adams, M. J., Bereiter, C., Brown, A., et al. (2002). *Open court reading*. DeSoto, TX: SRA McGraw Hill.

Allen, R. V. (1976). *Language experience in communication*. Boston: Houghton Mifflin.

Allington, R. L., & Cunningham, P. M. (1996). *Schools that work: Where all children read and write*. New York: HarperCollins.

Altwerger, A., Diehl-Faxon, J., & Dockstader-Anderson, K. (1985). Reading aloud events as meaning construction. *Language Arts, 62,* 476–484.

Anderson, R. C., Hiebert, E. H., Scott, J. A., & Wilkinson, I. A. G. (1985). *Becoming a nation of readers*. Washington, DC: National Institute of Education.

Anderson, R. C., & Pearson, P. D. (1984). A schema-theoretic view of basic processing in reading. In P. D. Pearson (Ed.), *Handbook of reading research*. New York: Longman.

Anderson, R. C., Fielding, L. G., & Wilson, P. T. (1988). Growth in reading and how children spend their time outside of school. *Reading Research Quarterly, 23,* 285–303.

Applebee, A. N., & Langer, J. A. (1983). Instructional scaffolding: Reading and writing as natural language activities. *Language Arts, 60,* 168–175.

Applebee, A. N., Langer, J. A., & Mullis, M. (1988). *Who reads best? Factors related to reading achievement in grades 3, 7, and 11*. Princeton, NJ: Educational Testing Service.

Armstrong, T. (1994). Multiple intelligences in the classroom. Alexandria, VA: Association for Supervision and Curriculum Development.

Ashton-Warner, S. (1959). *Spinster*. New York: Simon & Schuster.

Ashton-Warner, S. (1963). *Teacher*. New York: Bantam.

Au, K. H. (1998). Constructivist approaches, phonics, and the literacy learning of students of diverse backgrounds. In T. Shanahan & F. V. Rodriguez-Brown (Eds.), *Forty-seventh yearbook of the National Reading Conference* (pp. 1–21). Chicago: National Reading Conference.

Auerbach, E. (1989). Toward a social-contextual approach to family literacy. *Harvard Educational Review, 56.* 165–181.

Banks, J., & Banks, C. (1993). Multicultural education: Issues and perspectives (2nd ed.). Boston: Allyn & Bacon.

Barone, D. (1998). How do we teach literacy to children who are learning English as a second language. In S. Neuman & K. Roskos (Eds.) Children achieving: Best practices in Early literacy. Newark, DE: International Reading Association.

Baumann, J. F. (1992). Effect of think aloud instruction on elementary students' comprehension monitoring abilities. *Journal of Reading Behavior, 24(2),* 143–172.

Bear, D. R., Invernizzi, M., Templeton, S., & Johnston, D. (1996). *Words their way*. Englewood Cliffs, NJ: Prentice Hall.

Beck, I. L., & McKeown, M. G. (2001). Text talk: Capturing the benefits of read-aloud experiences for young children. *The Reading Teacher, 55,* 10–20.

Bergeron, B. (1990). What does the term whole language mean? A definition from the literature. *Journal of Reading Behavior, 23,* 301–329.

Berk, L. (1997). *Child development*. Boston: Allyn & Bacon.

Blachowicz, C. L. Z., & Fisher, P. J. (2002). Best practices in vocabulary instruction: What effective teachers do. In L. M. Morrow, L. Gambrell, & M. Pressley (Eds.), *Best practices in literacy instruction* (2nd ed., pp. 87–110). New York: Guilford Press.

Bloom, L. (1990). Development in express: Affect and speech. In N. Stein & T. Trabasso (Eds.), *Psychological and biological approaches to emotion* (pp. 215–245). Hillsdale, NJ: Erlbaum.

Bond, G. L., & Dykstra, R. (1967a). The Cooperative Research Program in First-Grade Reading Instruction. *Reading Research Quarterly, 2,* 5–142.

Bond, G. L., & Dykstra, R. (1967b). Coordinating Center for First Grade Reading Instruction Programs. (Final Report of Project No. x-001, Contact No. OES10–264) Minneapolis: University of Minnesota.

Bromley, K. (2003). Building a sound writing program. In L. M. Morrow, L. B. Gambrell, & M. Pressley (Eds.), *Best practices in literacy instruction* (2nd ed.). New York: Guilford Press.

Brown, R., Cazden, C., & Bellugi-Klima, U. (1968). The child's grammar from one to three. In J. P. Hill (Ed.), *Minnesota symposium on child development*. Minneapolis: University of Minnesota Press.

Burns, M. S., Snow, C. E., Griffin, P. (1998). *Preventing reading difficulties in young children*. Washington, DC: National Academy Press.

Burns, M. S., Snow, C. E., & Griffin, P. (Eds.), (1999). *Starting out right: A guide to promoting children's reading success*. Washington, DC: National Academy Press.

Bus, A. G., van Ijzendoorn, M. H., & Pellegrini, A. D. (1995). Joint book reading makes for success in learning to read: A meta-analysis in intergenerational transmission of literacy. *Review of Educational Research, 65,* 1–21.

Byrne, B., & Fielding-Barnsley, R. (1993). Evaluation of a program to teach phonemic awareness to young children: A one-year follow-up. *Journal of Educational Psychology, 85,* 104–111.

Byrne, B., & Fielding-Barnsley, R. (1995). Evaluation of a program to teach phonemic awareness to young children: A Two- and Three-year follow-up and a new preschool trial. *Journal of Educational Psychology, 87,* 488–503.

Calkins, L. M. (1986). *The art of teaching writing.* Exeter, NH: Heinemann.

Center for the Improvement of Early Reading Achievement (CIERA). (2001). *Put Reading First; The Research Building Blocks for Teaching Children to Read.* Washington, DC: National Institute for Literacy.

Chomsky, C. (1965). *Aspects of a theory of syntax.* Cambridge, MA: MIT Press.

Clay, M. M. (1966). *Emergent reading behavior.* Doctoral dissertation, University of Auckland, New Zealand.

Clay, M. M. (1979). *The early detection of reading difficulties: A diagnostic survey with recovery procedures.* Auckland, New Zealand: Heinemann Educational Books.

Clay, M. M. (1987). Implementing reading recovery: Systematic adaptations to an educational innovation. *New Zealand Journal of Educational Studies, 22,* 35–38.

Clay, M. M. (1991). *Becoming literate: The construction of inner control.* Portsmouth, NH: Heinemann.

Clay, M. M. (1993a). *An observation survey of early literacy achievement.* Portsmouth, NH: Heinemann.

Clay, M. M. (1993b). *Reading Recovery: A guidebook for teachers in training.* Portsmouth, NH: Heinemann.

Cochran-Smith, M. (1984). *The making of a reader.* Norwood, NJ: Ablex.

Cohen, M. (1980). *First grade takes a test.* New York: Dell.

Connell, R. W. (1994). Poverty and education. *Harvard Educational Review, 64,* 125–149.

Cox, C. (2002). *Teaching language arts: A student- and response-centered classroom* (4th ed.). Boston: Allyn & Bacon.

Cullinan, B. E. (1992). *Invitation to read: More children's literature in the reading program.* Newark, DE: International Reading Association.

Cunningham, P. (1995). *Phonics they use.* New York: HarperCollins.

Cunningham, P. M., and Cunningham, J. W. (1992). Making words: Enhancing the invented spelling–decoding connection. *The Reading Teacher, 46.* 106–115.

Daniels, H. (1994). *Literature circles: Voice and choice in the student centered classroom.* Portland, ME: Stenhouse Publications.

Delgado-Gaitan, C. (1992). School matters in the Mexican-American home: Socializing children to educa-

tion. *American Educational Research Journal, 29,* 459.

Delpit, L. (1995, December). Other People's Children. Presentation at the National Reading Conference, New Orleans, Louisiana.

Dewey, J. (1966). *Democracy and education.* New York: First Press.

Dickinson, D. K., & Tabors, P. O. (Eds.). (2001). *Beginning literacy with language.* Baltimore: Brookes.

Donahue, P., Daane, M., & Grigg, W. Educational Testing Service. (2003). Nation's Report Card. National Assessment of Educational Progress. http://nces.ed.gov/nationsreportcard/

Donahue, P. L., Finnegan, R. J., Lutkus, A. D., Allen, N. L., & Campbell, J. R. (2001). *The nation's report card: Reading 2000.* Washington, DC: U.S. Department of Education, Office of Educational Research and Improvement.

Duke, N. (2000). 3.6 minutes per day: The scarcity of information texts in first grade. *Reading Research Quarterly, 35,* 202–224.

Duke, N. K., & Kays, J. (1998). Can I say "Once upon a time?" Kindergarten children developing knowledge of information book language. *Early Childhood Research Quarterly, 13*(2), 295–318.

Durkin, D. (1966). *Children who read early.* New York: Teachers College Press.

Durkin, D. (1978–79). What classroom observations reveal about reading instruction. *Reading Research Quarterly, 14,* 481–533.

Dyson, A. H. (1985). Individual differences in emerging writing. In M. Farr (Ed.), *Advances in writing research.* Vol. 1: *Children's early writing development.* Norwood, NJ: Ablex.

Dyson, A. H. (1986). Children's early interpretations of writing: Expanding research perspectives. In D. Yoden & S. Templeton (Eds.), *Metalinguistic awareness and beginning literacy.* Exeter, NH: Heinemann.

Dyson, A. H. (1993). *Social worlds of children learning to write in an urban primary school.* New York: Teachers College Press.

Edwards, P. A. (1995). Combining parents' and teachers' thoughts about storybook reading at home and school. In L. M. Morrow (Ed.), *Family literacy connections in schools and communities* (pp. 54–69). Newark, DE: International Reading Association.

Edwards, S. A., Maloy, R. W., & Verock-O'Loughlin, R. (2003). *Ways of writing with young kids: Teaching creativity and conventions unconventionally.* Boston: Allyn & Bacon.

Englemann, S., & Bruner, E. (1968). *DISTAR: Direct Instruction System for Teaching Arithmetic and Reading.* Chicago: Science Research Associates.

Erickson, K. A., & Koppenhaver, D. A. (1995). Developing a literacy program for children with severe disabilities. *The Reading Teacher, 48,* 676–684.

Espinosa, L. M., & Burns, M. S. (2003). Early literacy for young children and English-language learners. In C. Howes (Ed.), *Teaching 4 to 8-year-olds:*

Literacy, math, multiculturalism, and classroom community. Baltimore: Paul H. Brooks.

Fitzpatrick, J. (1997). *Phonemic awareness.* Cypress, CA: Creative Teaching Press.

Fletcher, R., & Portalupi, J. (2001). *Writing workshop: The essential guide.* Portsmouth, NH: Heinemann.

Foster, C. R. (1982). Diffusing the issues in bilingualism and bilingual education. *Phi Delta Kappan, 63,* 338–345.

Fountas, I. C., & Pinnell, G. S. (1996). *Guided reading: Good first teaching for all children.* Portsmouth, NH: Heinemann.

Freeman, D., & Freeman, Y. (1993) Strategies for promoting the primary languages of all students. *The Reading Teacher, 46,* 18–25.

Froebel, F. (1974). *The education of man.* Clifton, NJ: Augustus M. Kelly.

Gambrell, L. B., & Almasi, J. (1994). Fostering comprehension development through discussion. In L. M. Morrow, J. K. Smith, & L. C. Wilkinson (Eds.), *Integrated language arts: Controversy to consensus* (pp. 71–90). Boston: Allyn & Bacon.

Gambrell, L. B., Almasi, J. F., Xie, Q., & Heland, V. (1995). Helping first graders get off to a running start in reading: A home-school-community program that enhances family literacy. In L. Morrow (Ed.), *Family literacy connections at school and home.* Newark, DE: International Reading Association.

Gambrell, L. B., & Koskinen, P. S. (2002). Imagery: A strategy for enhancing comprehension. In C. C. Block & M. Pressley (Eds.), *Comprehension instruction: Research-based best practices* (pp. 305–319). New York: Guilford Press.

Gambrell, L., Pfeiffer, W., & Wilson, R. (1985). The effect of retelling upon comprehension and recall of text information. *Journal of Educational Research, 78,* 216–220.

Garcia, E., & McLaughlin, B. (Eds.), with Spodek, B., & Soracho, O. (1995). *Meeting the challenge of linguistic and cultural diversity in early childhood education.* New York: Teachers College Press.

Gardner, H. (Ed.). (1993). *Multiple intelligences: The theory in practice.* New York: Basic Books.

Gaskins, I. W. (2003). A multidimensional approach to beginning literacy. In D. M. Barone & L. M. Morrow (Eds.), *Literacy and young children: Research-based practices* (pp. 45–60). New York: Guilford Press.

Genishi, C., & Dyson, A. (1984). *Language assessment in the early years.* Norwood, NJ: Ablex.

Gesell, A. (1925). *The mental growth of the preschool child.* New York: Macmillan.

Gollnick, D. M. and Chinn, P. C. (2002). *Multicultural education in a pluralistic society.* Upper Saddle River, NJ: Merrill Prentice Hall.

Goodman, K. S. (1967). Reading: A psycholinguistic guessing game. *Journal of the Reading Specialist, 4,* 126–135.

Goodman, Y. (1980). The root of literacy. In M. Douglas (Ed.), *Claremont Reading Conference forty-fourth yearbook.* Claremont, CA: Claremont Reading Conference.

Goodman, Y. (1984). The development of initial literacy. In H. Goelman, A. Oberg, & F. Smith (Eds.), *Awakening to literacy.* Exeter, NH: Heinemann.

Graves, D. (1994). *A fresh look at writing.* Portsmouth, NH: Heinemann.

Graves, D., & Hansen, J. (1983). The author's chair. *Language Arts, 60,* 176–183.

Graves, D. H. (1983). *Writing: Teachers and children at work.* Exeter, NH: Heinemann.

Graves, M. F., Juel, C., & Graves, B. B. (1998). *Teaching reading in the 21st century.* Boston: Allyn & Bacon.

Gundlach, R., McLane, J., Scott, F., & McNamee, G. (1985). The social foundations of early writing development. In M. Farr (Ed.), *Advances in writing research.* Vol. 1: *Children's early writing development.* Norwood, NJ: Ablex.

Gunning, T. G. (2003). *Creating literacy instruction for all children* (4th ed.). Boston: Allyn & Bacon.

Guthrie, J. T. (2002). Engagement and motivation in reading instruction. In M. L. Kamil, J. B. Manning, & H. J. Walberg (Eds.), *Successful reading instruction* (pp. 137–154). Greenwich, CT: Information Age.

Hall, M. A. (1976). *Teaching reading as a language experience.* Columbus, OH: Merrill.

Halliday, M. A. K. (1975). *Learning how to mean: Exploration in the development of language.* London: Edward Arnold.

Hallinan, M. T., & Sorenson, A. B. (1983). The formation and stability of instructional groups. *American Sociological Review, 48,* 838–851.

Hannon, P. (1995). *Literacy, home and school: Research and practice in teaching literacy with parents.* London: Falmer.

Hansen, J. (1987). *When writers read.* Portsmouth, NH: Heinemann.

Harp, W. (2000). Assessing reading and writing in the early years. In S. Strickland & L. M. Morrow (Eds.), *Beginning reading and writing, kindergarten to grade 2.* New York: Teachers College Press.

Harste, J., Woodward, V., & Burke, C. (1984). *Language stories and literacy lessons.* Exeter, NH: Heinemann.

Hart, B., & Risley, T. R. (1999). *The social world of children learning to talk.* Baltimore, MD: Brookes.

Heath, S. B. (1982). What no bedtime story means. *Language in Society, 11,* 49–76.

Heath, S. B. (1993). *Ways with words.* Cambridge, England: Cambridge University Press.

Hiebert, E. H. (1981). Developmental patterns and interrelationships of preschool children's print awareness. *Reading Research Quarterly, 16,* 236–260.

Hiebert, E. H. (1986). Using environmental print in beginning reading instruction. In M. R. Sampson (Ed.), *The pursuit of literacy: Early reading and writing.* Dubuque, IA: Kendall/Hunt.

Hiebert, E. H., & Taylor, B. (1994). *Getting reading right from the start.* Newark, DE: International Reading Association.

Hill, S. (1997). *Reading manipulatives.* Cypress, CA: Creative Teaching Press.

Holdaway, D. (1979). *The foundations of literacy.* Sydney: Ashton Scholastic.

Huck, C. S. (1992). Books for emergent readers. In B. E. Cullinan (Ed.), *Invitation to read: More children's literature in the reading program.* Newark, DE: International Reading Association.

Hunt, K. W. (1970). *Syntactic maturity in children and adults.* Monograph of the Society for Research in Child Development (vol. 25). Chicago: University of Chicago Press.

International Reading Association. (1998). *Phonemic awareness and the teaching of reading: A position statement of the Board of directors of the International Reading Association.* Newark, DE: Author.

International Reading Association. (1999). *Position statement: Using multiple methods of beginning reading instruction.* Newark, DE: Author.

International Reading Association (2001). Association issues position statement on second-language literacy instruction. *Reading Today.* Retrieved on May 14, 2003 from http://www.findarticles.com

International Reading Association & National Association for the Education of Young Children. (1998). *Learning to read and write: Developmentally appropriate practices for young children.* Newark, DE: International Reading Association.

International Reading Association & National Council of Teachers of English. (1996). *Standards for the English language arts.* Newark, DE: International Reading Association.

Invernizzi, M. (2003). Concepts, sounds, and the ABCs: A diet for a very young reader. In D. M. Barone & L. M. Morrow (Eds.), *Literacy and young children: Research-based practices* (pp. 140–157). New York: Guilford Press.

Irving, A. (1980). *Promoting voluntary reading for children and young people.* Paris: UNESCO.

Ivey, G. (2002). Building comprehension when they're still learning to read the words. In C. C. Block & M. Pressley (Eds.), *Comprehension instruction: Research-based best practices* (pp. 234–247). New York: Guilford Press.

Jewell, M., & Zintz, M. (1986). *Learning to read naturally.* Dubuque, IA: Kendall/Hunt.

Johns, J., & Berglund, R. L. (2002). *Fluency: evidence-based strategies.* Dubuque, IA: Kendall/ Hunt.

Johns, J., Lenski, S. D., & Elish-Piper, L. (1999). *Early literacy assessments and teaching strategies.* Dubuque, IA: Kendall/Hunt.

Johnson, D., & Pearson, P. D. (1984). *Teaching reading vocabulary* (2nd ed.). New York: Holt, Rinehart, & Winston.

Juel, C. (1989). The role of decoding in early literacy instruction and assessment. In L. Morrow & J. Smith (Eds.), *Assessment for instruction in early literacy* (pp. 135–154). Englewood Cliffs, NJ: Prentice Hall.

Juel, C. (1994). Teaching phonics in the context of the integrated language arts. In L. Morrow, J. K. Smith, & L. C. Wilkinson (Eds.), *Integrated language arts: Controversy for consensus* (pp. 133–154). Boston: Allyn & Bacon.

Kinzer, C. K., & McKenna, M. C. (1999, May). *Using technology in your classroom literacy program: Current and future possibilities.* Paper presented at the Annual Convention of the International Reading Association, San Diego, CA.

Kuhl, P. (1994). Learning and representation in speech and language. *Current Opinion in Neurobiology, 4,* 812–822.

Kuhn, M. R., & Stahl, S. A. (2003). Fluency: A review of developmental and remedial strategies. *Journal of Educational Psychology, 95,* 3–21.

Labbo, L. D., & Ash, G. E. (1998). What is the role of computer related technology in early literacy? In S. B. Neuman & K. A. Roskos (Eds.), *Children achieving: Best practices in early literacy* (pp. 180–197). Newark, DE: International Reading Association.

Labbo, L. D., Reinking, D., & McKenna, M. (1998). The use of technology in literacy programs. In L. Gambrell, L. M. Morrow, S. B. Neuman, & M. Pressley (Eds.), *Best practices in literacy instruction.* New York: Guilford Press.

Leichter, H. P. (1984). Families as environments for literacy. In H. Goelman, A. Oberg, & F. Smith (Eds.), *Awakening to literacy.* Exeter, NH: Heinemann.

Lennenberg, E. (1967). *Biological foundations of language.* New York: John Wiley.

Lennenberg, E., & Kaplan, E. (1970). Grammatical structures and reading. In H. Levin & J. Williams (Eds.), *Basic studies in reading.* New York: Basic Books.

Leu, D. J., & Kinzer, C. (1991). *Effective reading instruction K–8* (2nd ed.). New York: Merrill.

Lindfors, J. (1989) The classroom: A food environment for language learning. In P. Rigg & V. Allen (Eds.), *When they don't all speak English: Integrating the ESL student into the regular classroom* (pp. 39–54). Urbana, IL: National Council of Teachers of English.

Lou, Y., Abrami, P. C., Spence, J. C., Poulsen, C., Chambers, B., & d'Apollonia, S. (1996). Within-class grouping. A meta-analysis. *Review of Educational Research, 66*(4), 423–458.

Loughlin, C. E., & Martin, M. D. (1987). *Supporting literacy: Developing effective learning environments.* New York: Teachers College Press.

Manning, M., Manning, G., & Long, R. (1994). *Theme immersion: Inquiring-based curriculum in elementary and middle schools.* Portsmouth, NH: Heinemann.

Marriott, D. (1997). *What are the other kids doing?* Cypress, CA: Creative Teaching Press.

Martinez, M., & Teale, W. (1987). The ins and outs of a kindergarten writing program. *The Reading Teacher, 40,* 444–451.

Martinez, M., & Teale, W. (1988). Reading in a kindergarten classroom library. *The Reading Teacher, 41*(6), 568–572.

Mason, J. (1980). When do children begin to read? An exploration of four-year-old children's letter and word reading competencies. *Reading Research Quarterly, 15,* 203–227.

Mason, J., & McCormick, C. (1981). *An investigation of pre-reading instruction: A developmental perspective*

(Technical Report 224). Urbana: University of Illinois, Center for the Study of Reading.

McCarrier, A., Pinnell, G. S. & Fountas, I. C. (2000). *Interactive writing: How language & literacy come together, K–2.* Portsmouth, NH: Heinemann.

McCormick, C., & Mason, J. (1981). What happens to kindergarten children's knowledge about reading after summer vacation? *The Reading Teacher, 35,* 164–172.

McGee, L. M., & Richgels, D. J. (2000). *Literacy's beginnings: Supporting young readers and writers.* Boston: Allyn & Bacon.

McKenna, M. C. (2001). Development of reading attitudes. In L. Verhoeven & C. Snow (Eds.), *Literacy and motivation: Reading engagement in individuals and groups* (pp. 135–158). Mahwah, NJ: Lawrence Erlbaum Associates.

McLaughlin, M. (2003). *Guided comprehension in the primary grades.* Newark, DE: International Reading Association.

McNeil, D. (1970). *The acquisition of language: The study of developmental psycholinguistics.* New York: Harper & Row.

Meers, T. B. (1999). *101 best web sites for kids.* Lincolnwood, IL: Publications International.

Melzi, G., Paratore, J. R., & Krol-Sinclair, B. (2000). Reading and writing in the daily lives of Latino mothers participating in an intergenerational literacy project. *National Reading Conference Yearbook, 49,* 178–193.

Miramontes, O. B., Nadeau, A., & Commins, N. L. (1997). *Restructuring schools for linguistic diversity: Linking decision making to effective programs.* New York: Teachers College Press.

Montessori, M. (1965). *Spontaneous activity in education.* New York: Schocken Books.

Moore, G. (1986). Effects of the spatial definition of behavior settings on children's behavior: A quasi-experimental field study. *Journal of Environmental Psychology, 6*(3), 205–231.

Morphett, M. V., & Washburne, C. (1931). When should children begin to read? *Elementary School Journal, 31,* 496–508.

Morrison, G. S. (2003). *Fundamentals of early childhood education* (3rd ed.). Upper Saddle River, NJ: Prentice Hall.

Morrison, G. S. (2004). *Early childhood education today* (9th ed.). Upper Saddle River, NJ: Pearson.

Morrow, L. M. (1978). Analysis of syntax in the language of six-, seven-, and eight-year-olds. *Research in the Teaching of English, 12,* 143–148.

Morrow, L. M. (1982). Relationships between literature programs, library corner designs, and children's use of literature. *Journal of Educational Research, 75,* 339–344.

Morrow, L. M. (1983). Home and school correlates of early interest in literature. *Journal of Educational Researach, 76,* 221–230.

Morrow, L. M. (1984). Reading stories to young children: Effects of story structure and traditional questioning strategies on comprehension. *Journal of Reading Behavior, 16,* 273–288.

Morrow, L. M. (1985). Retelling stories: A strategy for improving children's comprehension, concept of story structure, and oral language complexity. *Elementary School Journal, 85,* 647–661.

Morrow, L. M. (1986). *Promoting responses to literature: Children's sense of story structure.* Paper presented at the National Reading Conference, Austin, TX.

Morrow, L. M. (1987a). The effects of one-to-one story readings on children's questions and comments. In S. Baldwin & J. Readance (Eds.), *36th yearbook of the National Reading Conference.* Rochester, NY: National Reading Conference.

Morrow, L. M. (1987b). Promoting voluntary reading: The effects of an inner city program in summer day care centers. *The Reading Teacher, 41,* 266–274.

Morrow, L. M. (1988). Young children's responses to one-to-one story readings in school settings. *Reading Research Quarterly, 23*(1), 89–107.

Morrow, L. M. (1990). Preparing the classroom environment to promote literacy during play. *Early Childhood Research Quarterly, 5,* 537–554.

Morrow, L. M. (1992). The impact of a literature-based program on literacy achievement, use of literature, and attitudes of children from minority backgrounds. *Reading Research Quarterly, 27,* 250–275.

Morrow, L. M. (1995). *Family literacy connections at school and home.* Newark, DE: International Reading Association.

Morrow, L. M. (1996). Story retelling: A discussion strategy to develop and assess comprehension. In L. B. Gambrel & J. F. Almasi (Eds.), *Lively discussions: Fostering engaged reading* (pp. 265–285). Newark, DE: International Reading Association.

Morrow, L. M. (2002). *The literacy center: Contexts for reading and writing* (2nd ed.). York, ME: Stenhouse.

Morrow, L. M. (2003). *Organizing and managing the language arts block.* New York: Guilford Press.

Morrow, L. M., & Asbury, E. (2003). Best practices for a balanced early literacy program. In L. M. Morrow, L. Gambrell, & M. Pressley (Eds.), *Best practices in literacy instruction* (2nd ed., pp. 49–67). New York: Guilford Press.

Morrow, L. M., & O'Connor, E. (1995). Literacy partnerships for change with "at risk" kindergartners. In R. Allington & S. Walmsley (Eds.), *No quick fix: Rethinking literacy programs in America's elementary schools* (pp. 97–115). New York: Teachers College Press.

Morrow, L. M., O'Connor, E. M., & Smith, J. (1990). Effects of a story reading program on the literacy development of at-risk kindergarten children. *Journal of Reading Behavior, 20*(2), 104–141.

Morrow, L. M., Paratore, J. R., & Tracey, D. H. (1994). *Family literacy: New perspectives, new opportunities.* Newark, DE: International Reading Association.

Morrow, L. M., Pressley, M., Smith, J., & Smith, M. (1997). The effects of integrating literature- based instruction into literacy and science programs. *Reading Research Quarterly, 32,* 54–77.

Morrow, L. M., & Rand, M. (1991). Promoting literacy during play by designing early childhood classroom environments. *The Reading Teacher, 44,* 396–405.

Morrow, L. M., Scoblionko, J., & Shafer, D. (1995). The family reading and writing appreciation program. In L. M. Morrow (Ed.), *Family literacy connections in schools and communities* (pp. 70–86). Newark, DE: International Reading Association.

Morrow, L. M., Sharkey, E., & Firestone, W. (1994). Collaborative strategies in the integrated language arts. In L. M. Morrow, J. K. Smith, & L. C. Wilkinson (Eds.), *Integrated language arts: Controversy to consensus* (pp. 155–176). Boston: Allyn & Bacon.

Morrow, L. M., & Smith, J. K. (1990). The effect of group setting on interactive storybook reading. *Reading Research Quarterly, 25,* 213–231.

Morrow, L. M., Strickland, D. S., & Woo, D. G. (1998). *Literacy instruction in half- and whole-day kindergarten: Research to practice.* Newark, DE: International Reading Association.

Morrow, L. M., & Tracey, D. (1997). Strategies for phonics instruction in early childhood classrooms. *The Reading Teacher, 50*(8), 2–9.

Morrow, L. M., & Tracey, D. H. (1996). Instructional environments for language and learning. Considerations for young children. In J. Flood, S. B. Heath, & D. Lapp (Eds.), *Handbook for literacy educators: Research on teaching the communicative and visual arts.* New York: Macmillan.

Morrow, L. M., & Weinstein, C. S. (1986). Encouraging voluntary reading: The impact of a literature program on children's use of library centers. *Reading Reasearch Quarterly, 21,* 330–346.

Morrow, L. M., & Young, J. (1997). A family literacy program connecting school and home: Effects on attitude, motivation, and literacy achievement. *Journal of Educational Psychology, 89,* 736–742.

Moss, B., Leone, S. & Dipillo, M. L. (1997). Exploring the literature of fact: Linking reading and writing through information trade books. *Language Arts, 74*(6), 418–29.

Moustafa, M. (1997). *Beyond traditional phonics: Research discoveries and reading instruction.* Portsmouth, NH: Heinemann.

Nagy, W. (1988). *Teaching vocabulary to improve reading comprehension.* Newark, DE: International Reading Association.

National Center for Family Literacy. (1993). Parents and children together. In *Creating an upward spiral of success* (pp. 6–8). Louisville, KY: Author.

National Center for Family Literacy. (2004). Report of the National Early Literacy Panel. Washington DC: National Institute for Literacy.

National Center on Education and the Economy & Learning Research and Development Center at the University of Pittsburgh. (1999). *Reading and writing grade by grade: Primary literacy standards for kindergarten through third grade.* Washington, DC: National Center on Education and the Economy.

National Reading Panel Report. (2000). *Teaching children to read.* Washington, DC: National Institute of Child Health and Human Development.

Neuman, S. B. (1997). Guiding your children's participation in early literacy development: A family program for adolescent mothers. *Early Childhood Development and Care.* 119–129.

Neuman, S. B., & Roskos, K. (1992). Literary objects as cultural tools: Effects on children's literacy behaviors in play. *Reading Research Quarterly, 27*(3), 203–225.

Neuman, S., & Roskos, K. (1993). *Language and literacy learning in the early years: An integrated approach.* Orlando, FL: Harcourt, Brace.

Neuman, S., & Roskos, K. (1994). Building home and school with a culturally responsive approach. *Childhood Education, 70,* 210–214.

Neuman, S. B., & Roskos, K. (1997). Knowledge in practice: Contexts of participation for young writers and readers. *Reading Research Quarterly, 32,* 10–32.

Newberger, J. J. (1997). New brain development research: A wonderful window of opportunity to build public support for early childhood education. *Young Children, 52*(4), 4–9.

Newman, J. (1984). *The craft of children's writing.* Exeter, NH: Heinemann.

Ninio, A. (1980). Picture book reading in mother-infant dyads belonging to two subgroups in Israel. *Child Development, 51,* 587.

O'Flahavan, J., Gambrell, L. B., Guthrie, J., Stahl, S., & Alverman, D. (1992, April). Poll results guide activities of research center. *Reading Today,* p. 12.

Ogle, D. (1986). K-W-L: A teaching model that develops active reading of expository text. *The Reading Teacher, 39,* 564–570.

Pappas, C., Kiefer, B., & Levstik, L. (1995). *An integrated language perspective in the elementary school: Theory into action.* New York: Longman.

Paratore, J. R., Homza, A., Krol-Sinclair, B., Lewis-Barrow, T., Melzi, G., Stergis, R., & Haynes, H. (1995). Shifting boundaries in home and school responsibilities: Involving immigrant parents in the construction of literacy portfolios. *Research in the Teaching of English, 29,* 367–389.

Paratore, J. R., Melzi, G., & Krol-Sinclair, B. (2003). Learning about the literate lives of Latino families. In D. M. Barone & L. M. Morrow (Eds.), *Literacy and young children: Research-based practices,* 101–120.

Parker, R. (1983). Language development and learning to write. In R. Parker & F. Davis (Eds.), *Developing literacy: Young children's use of language.* Newark, DE: International Reading Association.

Pearson, P. D., Roehler, L. R., Dole, J. A., & Duffy, G. G. (1992). Developing expertise in reading comprehension. In S. J. Samuels & A. E. Farsturp (Eds.), *What research has to say about reading instruction* (2nd ed., pp. 145–199), Newark, DE: International Reading Association.

Pellegrini, A., & Galda, L. (1982). The effects of thematic fantasy play training on the development of children's story comprehension. *American Educational Research Journal, 19,* 443–452.

Pflaum, S. (1986). *The development of language and literacy in young children* (3rd ed.). Columbus, OH: Merrill.

Piaget, J., & Inhelder, B. (1969). *The psychology of the child.* New York: Basic Books.

Pinker, S. (1994). *The language instinct: How the mind creates language.* New York: William Morrow.

Pinnell, G. S., Freid, M. D., & Estice, R. M. (1990). Reading recovery: Learning how to make a difference. *The Reading Teacher, 43*(4), 282–295.

Pittelman, S. D., Heimlich, J. E., Berglund, R. L., & French, M. P. (1991). *Semantic feature analysis: Classroom applications.* Newark, DE: International Reading Association.

Pittelman, S. D., Levin, K. M., & Johnson, D. P. (1985). *An investigation of two instructional settings in the use of semantic mapping with poor readers* (Program Report 85-4). Madison: Wisconsin Center for Educational Research, University of Wisconsin.

Prescott, O. (1965). *A father reads to his child: An anthology of prose and poetry.* New York: Dutton.

Pressley, M. (1998). *Reading instruction that works: The case for balanced teaching.* New York: Guilford Press.

Pressley, M., & Afflerbach, P. (1995). *Verbal protocols of reading: The nature of constructively responsive reading.* Hillsdale, NJ: Erlbaum.

Pressley, M., & Hilden, K. (2002). How can children be taught to comprehend text better? In M. L. Kamil, J. B. Manning, & H. J. Walberg (Eds.), *Successful reading instruction* (pp. 33–53). Greenwich, CT: Information Age.

Rand, M. (1993). Using thematic instruction to organize an integrated language arts classroom. In L. M. Morrow, J. K. Smith, & L. C. Wilkinson (Eds.), *Integrated language arts: Controversy to consensus* (pp. 177–192). Boston: Allyn & Bacon.

Rand Reading Study Group. (2002). *Reading for understanding: Toward a research and development program in reading comprehension.* Washington, DC: Author/OERI/Department of Education.

Rasinski, T. (1990). Effects of repeated reading and listening while reading on reading fluency. *Journal of Educational Research, 83,* 147–150.

Report of the National Early Reading Panel (2004), Washington, DC: National Institute for Literacy.

Reutzel, D. R. (1997, March). Maintaining balance as a teacher of children: Reading instruction for all. In L. M. Morrow (Director), Rutgers 29th Annual Conference on Reading and Writing, Rutgers University, New Brunswick, NJ.

Reutzel, D. R., & Cooter, R. B. (2004). *Teaching children to read: Putting the pieces together* (4th ed.). Upper Saddle River, NJ: Pearson/Merrill Prentice Hall.

Ritchie, S., James-Szanton, J., & Howes, C. (2003). Emergent literacy practices in early childhood classrooms. In C. Howes (Ed.), *Teaching 4- to 8-year-olds* (pp. 71–92). Baltimore: Brookes.

Rosenblatt, L. M. (1988). *Writing and reading: Transactional theory* (Report No. 13). University of California, Berkeley: Center for the Study of Writing.

Rosencrans, G. (1998). *The spelling book: Teaching children how to spell, not what to spell.* Newark, DE: International Reading Association.

Roser, N., & Martinez, M. (1985). Roles adults play in preschool responses to literature. *Language Arts, 62,* 485–490.

Roskos, K. A., & Christie, J. F. (Eds.). (2000). *Play and literacy in early childhood: Research from multiple perspectives.* Mahwah, NJ: Erlbaum.

Rossi, R., & Stringfield, S. (1995). What we must do for students placed at risk. *Phi Delta Kappan, 77,* 73–76.

Rousseau, J. (1962). *Emile* (ed. and trans. William Boyd). New York: Columbia University Teachers College. (Original work published 1762)

Ruddell, R., & Ruddell, M. R. (1995). *Teaching children to read and write: Becoming an influential teacher.* Boston: Allyn & Bacon.

Rusk, R., & Scotland, J. (1979). *Doctrines of the great educators.* New York: St. Martin's Press.

Sampson, M. B. (2002). *Confirming K-W-L: Considering the source. The Reading Teacher, 55*(6), 528–532.

Schickedanz, J. A. (1993). Designing the early childhood classroom environment to facilitate literacy development. In B. Spodek & O. N. Saracho (Eds.), *Language and literacy in early childhood education: Yearbook in early childhood education* (vol. 4). New York: Teachers College Press.

Schickedanz, J. A., York, M. E., Stewart, I. S., & White, A. (1990). *Strategies for teaching young children.* Englewood Cliffs, NJ: Prentice Hall.

Seefeldt, C., & Barbour, N. (1986). *Early childhood education: An introduction.* Columbus, OH: Merrill.

Shaywitz, S. (2003). *Overcoming dyslexia.* New York: Alfred A. Knopf.

Shore, K. (2001). Success for ESL students: 12 practical tips to help second-language learners. *Instructor, 1,* 110, 30–32, 106.

Skinner, B. F. (1954). The science of learning and the art of teaching. *Harvard Educational Review, 24,* 86–97.

Skinner, B. F. (1957). *Verbal behavior.* Boston: Appleton-Century-Crofts.

Slavin, R. (1998). *Success for all.* Baltimore: Success for All Foundation.

Slavin, R. E. (1987). Ability grouping and student achievement in elementary schools: A best-evidence synthesis. *Review of Educational Research, 57,* 292–336.

Slavin, R. E. (1997). *Educational psychology: Theory and practice* (5th ed.). Needham Heights, MA: Allyn & Bacon.

Slavin, R. E., & Madden, N. A. (1989). What works for students at risk: A research synthesis. *Educational Leadership, 46,* 4–13.

Smith, F. (1971). *Understanding reading.* New York: Holt, Rinehart, & Winston.

Snow, C. E., Burns, M. S. & Griffin, P. (1998). *Preventing reading difficulties in young children.* Washington, DC: National Academy Press.

Sorenson, A. B., & Hallinan, M. T. (1986). Effects of ability grouping on growth in academic achievement. *American Educational Research Journal, 23,* 519–542.

Spandel, V. (2001). *Creating writers through six-trait writing assessment and instruction.* New York: Longman.

Spiegel, D. L. (1992). Blending whole language and systematic direct instruction. *The Reading Teacher, 46,* 38–44.

Spielberg, S. (1987). Acceptance speech at the Academy Award Ceremonies, Los Angeles.

Spodek, B. (1988). Conceptualizing today's kindergarten curriculum. *The Elementary School Journal, 89,* 203–212.

Stahl, S. A. (2003). No more "madfaces": Motivation and fluency development with struggling readers. In D. M. Barone & L. M. Morrow (Eds.), *Literacy and young children: Research-based practices* (pp. 195–209). New York: Guilford Press.

Stanovich, K. E. (1986). Mathew effects in reading: Some consequences of individual differences in the acquisition of literacy. *Reading Research Quarterly, 21,* 360–407.

Stauffer, R. G. (1980). *The language-experience approach to the teaching of reading* (2nd ed.). New York: Harper & Row.

Stine, H. A. (1993). *The effects of CD-ROM interactive software in reading skills instructions with second grade Chapter 1 students.* Doctoral dissertation, The George Washington University. Ann Arbor, MI: University Microfilms International.

Strickland, D., & Snow, C. (2002). *Preparing our teachers: Opportunities for better reading instruction.* Washington, D.C.: Joseph Henry Press.

Sullivan, N. W., & Buchanan, C. D. (1963). Programmed Reading Series. New York: McGraw-Hill.

Sulzby, E. (1985). Children's emergent reading of favorite storybooks. *Reading Research Quarterly, 20,* 458–481.

Sulzby, E. (1986a). Kindergarteners as writers and readers. In M. Farr (Ed.), *Advances in writing research.* Vol. 1: *Children's early writing.* Norwood, NJ: Ablex.

Sulzby, E. (1986b). Children's elicitation and use of metalinguistic knowledge about "word" during literacy interactions. In P. Yaden & S. Templeton (Eds.), *Metalinguistic awareness and beginning literacy.* Exeter, NH: Heinemann.

Tabors, P. (1998) What early childhood educators need to know: Developing effective programs for linguistically and culturally diverse children and families. *Young Children, 53*(6), 20–26.

Tafa, E. (1998). *Inclusive education for children with learning and behavioral problems.* Athens, Greece: Ellinika Grammata.

Tafa, E. (2001). *Reading and writing in preschool education.* Athens, Greece: Ellinika Grammata.

Taylor, B. M., Frye, B. J., & Maruyama, M. (1990). Time spent reading and reading growth. *American Educational Research Journal, 27,* 351–362.

Taylor, B. M., Strait, J., & Medo, M. A. (1994). Early intervention in reading: Supplemental instruction for groups of low-achieving students provided by first-grade teachers. In E. H. Hiebert & B. Taylor (Eds.), *Getting reading right from the start* (pp. 107–123). Newark, DE: International Reading Association.

Taylor, D. (1983). *Family literacy.* Exeter, NH: Heinemann.

Taylor, D., & Dorsey-Gaines, C. (1988). *Growing up literate.* Portsmouth, NH: Heinemann.

Taylor, D., & Strickland, D. (1986). *Family storybook reading.* Exeter, NH: Heinemann.

Teale, W. (1984). Reading to young children: Its significance for literacy development. In H. Goelman, A. Oberg, & F. Smith (Eds.), *Awakening to literacy.* Exeter, NH: Heinemann.

Teale, W. (1986). The beginning of reading and writing: Written language development during the preschool and kindergarten years. In M. Sampson (Ed.), *The pursuit of literacy: Early reading and writing.* Dubuque, IA: Kendall/Hunt.

Teale, W. (2003). Questions about early literacy learning and teaching that need asking—and some that don't. In D. M. Barone & L. M. Morrow (Eds.), *Literacy and young children: Research-based practices* (pp. 140–157). New York: Guilford Press.

Temple, C., Nathan, R., Burris, N., & Temple, F. (1988). *The beginnings of writing.* Boston: Allyn & Bacon.

Templeton, S. (1991). Teaching the integrated language arts. Boston: Houghton Mifflin.

Tompkins, G. E. (2000). *Teaching writing: Balancing process and product* (3rd ed.). Upper Saddle River, NJ: Prentice Hall.

Tompkins, G. E. (2003). *Literacy for the 21st century: Teaching reading and writing in prekindergarten through grade 4.* Upper Saddle River, NJ: Pearson/Merrill Prentice Hall.

Tompkins, G. E., & Koskisson, I. K. (1995). *Language arts content and teaching strategies.* Englewood Cliffs, NJ: Prentice Hall.

U.S. Department of Education. (2001). *No child left behind legislation.* http://www.nochildleftbehind.gov

Veatch, J., Sawicki, F., Elliot, G., Barnett, E., & Blackey, J. (1973). *Key words to reading: The language experience approach begins.* Columbus, OH: Merrill.

Vukelich, C., Evans, C., & Alberson, B. (2003). Organizing expository texts: A look at the possibilities. In D. M. Barone & L. M. Morrow (Eds.), *Literacy and young children: Research-based practices* (pp. 261–290). New York: Guilford Press.

Vygotsky, L. S. (1978). *Mind in society: The development of psychological processes.* Cambridge, MA: Harvard University Press.

Vygotsky, L. S. (1981). The genesis of higher mental functions. In J. J. Wertsch (Ed.), *The concept of activity.* White Plains, NY: M. E. Sharpe.

Walmsley, S. A. (1994). *Children exploring their world: Theme teaching in elementary school.* Portsmouth, NH: Heinemanan.

Ward, M., & McCormick, S. (1981). Reading instruction for blind and low vision children in the regular classroom. *The Reading Teacher, 34,* 434, 444.

Weinstein, C. S., & Mignano, A. J., Jr. (2003). *Elementary classroom management* (3rd ed.). Boston: McGraw Hill.

Wepner, S., & Ray, L. (2000). Sign of the times: Technology and early literacy learning. In D. S. Strickland & L. M. Morrow (Eds.), *Beginning reading and writing* (pp. 168–182). New York: Teachers College Press.

Wittrock, M. C. (1986). Students' thought processes. In M. C. Wittrock (Ed.), *Handbook of research on teaching* (pp. 297–314). New York: Macmillan.

Wylie, R., & Durrell, D. D. (1970). Teaching vowels through phonograms. *Elementary English, 47,* 787–791.

Xu, H. (2003). The learner, the teacher, the text, and the context: Sociocultural approaches to early literacy instruction for English language learners. In D. M. Barone & L. M. Morrow (Eds.), *Literacy and young children: Research-based practices* (pp. 61–80). New York: Guilford Press.

Yaden, D. (1985). *Preschoolers' spontaneous inquiries about print and books.* Paper presented at the Annual Meeting of the National Reading Conference, San Diego.

Yopp, H. K. (1992). Developing phonemic awareness in young children. *The Reading Teacher, 45,* 696–703.

Yopp, H. K. & Yopp, R. H. (2001). Supporting phonemic awareness development in the classroom. *The Reading Teacher, 54,* 130–143.

Yopp, R. H. & Yopp, H. K. (2000). Sharing informational text with young children. *The Reading Teacher, 53*(5), 410–423.